VATICAN DIPLOMACY AND THE JEWS DURING THE HOLOCAUST 1939-1943

VATICAN DIPLOMACY AND THE JEWS DURING THE HOLOCAUST 1939-1943

By

JOHN F. MORLEY

WITHDRAWI

KTAV PUBLISHING HOUSE, INC.

NEW YORK

1980

Library of Congress Cataloging in Publication Data

Morley, John F., 1936-
   Vatican diplomacy and the Jews during the Holocaust, 1939–1943.

   Bibliography: p.
   Includes index.
   1. Holocaust, Jewish (1939-1945)   2. Catholic
Church—Relations (Diplomatic)   3. World War, 1939-1945
—Catholic Church.   I. Title.
D810.J4M588   943.086   80-198 √
ISBN 0-87068-701-8

In memory of my parents,
John and Hannah Morley

CONTENTS

ACKNOWLEDGMENTS

At the end of a project which has occupied so much of my time and interest for several years, I feel it both a duty and a pleasure to acknowledge my gratitude toward all those who have assisted me in some way.

As a member of the Seton Hall University priest faculty, I am grateful to my priest colleagues for their consistent encouragement. In particular, I single out our late President, Monsignor Thomas Fahy, and the present Dean of the Priest Community, the Reverend Charles Stengel, who have both shown great kindness to me. I thank also the Reverend Donald Smith for his translation assistance and the Reverend James Sharp for the many services which he rendered to me in the university library. The Reverend John Radano, Chairman of the Department of Religious Studies, has been most supportive of me in this long venture. To him and all my colleagues in the department I express many thanks. I appreciate also the ongoing concern manifested for me by Monsignor John Oesterreicher.

I wish to acknowledge my appreciation to the staff of the Yad Vashem Library and Archives, and especially to Miss Ora Alcalay, Chief Librarian. Professor Meir Michaelis, whom I met at Yad Vashem, was most gracious in sharing with me not only his scholarship but also the hospitality of his home. I appreciate also the hospitality and aid of the Fathers and Sisters of Zion with whom I stayed at Ratisbonne Monastery during my research in Jerusalem.

My research at the Centre de Documentation Juive Contemporaine in Paris was rewarding, and for that I am grateful to M. Hessel of the Centre's staff. The files of the British Section of the World Jewish Congress were of great benefit to my research. I am deeply grateful to Dr. Elizabeth Eppler of the Institute of Jewish Affairs in London for allowing me access to these records and for her other assistance. I appreciate also the cooperation given to me by the staff of the World Jewish Congress in New York City, and, in particular, Mrs. Elisabeth Maier.

The Reverend Robert A. Graham, S.J., the English-speaking editor of the Vatican documents, has been most kind and helpful to me in many ways. To him, I owe great thanks.

I gratefully acknowledge also the interest and support given to me over many years by Professors David Rudavsky and Nathan Winter of the Institute of Hebrew Culture and Education of New York University. Moreover, I thank both of them for their assistance in the writing of this book. Professor Janice Gorn has aided me in a myriad of ways, both professional and personal, and has given me incalculable support and encouragement. I particularly appreciate the interest of Professor Gabriel Carras, who kindly rendered me great assistance. I use this occasion to remember with gratitude Professor Jonah Blustain, who aided me in the early stages of my work.

In concluding these acknowledgments, I cannot forget my deceased parents, who would have greatly rejoiced to see this project completed. Uneducated themselves in the formal sense, they possessed a wisdom from which I have learned much. My sisters and brother are always most kind to me and their support has helped much in the past years. I thank finally all my friends for their words and deeds of encouragement, and for their understanding, over so many years.

I thank also the Lord God Almighty, who gave me the grace and strength to bring this task to conclusion.

ABBREVIATIONS

ADSS: *Actes et Documents du Saint Siège relatifs a la Seconde Guerre Mondiale*
    I. SSGE: *Le Saint Siège et la Guerre en Europe, 1939–1940,* 2d ed., 1970.
    II. LPEA: *Lettres de Pie XII aux Evêques Allemands, 1939–1944,* 2d ed., 1967.
    III. SSSRP: *Le Saint Siège et la Situation Religeuse en Pologne et dans les Pays Baltes, 1939–1945,* 2 vols., 1967.
    IV. SSGE: *Le Saint Siège et la Guerre en Europe, Juin 1940–Juin 1941,* 1967.
    V. SSGM: *Le Saint Siège et la Guerre Mondiale, Juillet 1941–Octobre 1942,* 1969.
    VI. SSVG: *Le Saint Siège et les Victimes de la Guerre, Mars, 1939–Décembre 1940,* 1972.
    VII. SSGM: *Le Saint Siège et la Guerre Mondiale, Novembre 1942–Décembre 1943,* 1973.
    VIII. SSVG: *Le Saint Siège et les Victimes de la Guerre, Janvier 1941–Décembre 1942,* 1974.
    IX. SSVG: *Le Saint Siège et les Victimes de la Guerre, Janvier–Décembre 1943,* 1975.

CDJC: Centre de Documentation Juive Contemporaine, Paris.
FO: British Foreign Office, Public Record Office, London.
IJA: Institute for Jewish Affairs, World Jewish Congress, London.
NG: Documents from the Nuremberg Trials.
WJC: World Jewish Congress archives, New York City.
YV: Yad Vashem Martyrs' and Heroes' Remembrance Authority, Jerusalem.

CHAPTER ONE

Introduction

More than three decades have passed since the end of the Holocaust. Historians have attempted to research all facets of it, ranging from studies of the causes and the motivations of those responsible, to the reactions and fate of those so brutally victimized. All of these endeavors contribute not only to the historiography of the Holocaust itself but also to that of World War II.

This campaign of mass execution was unique and unparalleled in human history. It differed from all other previous massacres of the Jews

in its conscious and explicit planning, in its systematic execution, in the absence of any emotional element in the remorselessly applied decision to execute *everyone*, but *everyone*; in the exclusion of any possibility that someone, when his turn came to be liquidated, might escape his fate by surrendering, by joining the victors and collaborating with them, by converting to the victors' faith, or by selling himself into slavery to save his life.[1]

Research on such an event necessarily leads to the question of how this slaughter could have occurred at this advanced stage of history and on a continent so civilized and ostensibly "Christian." The Holocaust historian, perhaps like no other, must confront the real issue of how the various military and political powers, whether under the sway of the Nazis or not, reacted to it. *A fortiori,* the reaction of the Holy See, unique in its moral power and its claim on the religious allegiance of millions of Roman Catholics, must be examined.

The problem, as one author wrote a few years ago, is that "There are few issues in the historiography of the Holocaust that are colored by more emotion and based on less knowledge than the Vatican's response to 'the final solution to the Jewish question.' "[2] The emotions aroused by the killing of six million Jews will not, and should not, diminish in the years ahead. The memory of these victims should be

1

preserved both to honor them and the Jewish people, of whom they were members, as well as to ensure that such an act of genocide will never again occur.

That these emotions should simultaneously impugn the Vatican would indicate a lack of appreciation of the historical circumstances of the time, and, worse, would betray an ignorance of the Vatican's awareness of its responsibility to historical research. For the past ten years the Vatican has been publishing the records of its activities during the Second World War. Among these, of course, are those dealing with the Holocaust.[3]

These documents are diplomatic exchanges between the Secretariat of State of the Vatican and its emissaries in the various European capitals. Diplomatic records, as a source of research for the historian, have been described as "the most reliable of reports."[4] These dispatches contain both instructions and orders from the Vatican to its representatives, as well as accounts from them of what they heard, saw, and did. In addition, the volumes contain notes and memoranda composed by members of the Secretariat of State or sent to it by outside parties.

The Vatican has dispensed with its general rule of a seventy-five-year delay and has made available to the editors of the series all of the documents in the archives. Over four thousand of these records have been published, covering the years from the election of Pius XII in March 1939 to the end of 1943. Some of these had been published previously, but most have been released for the first time in these volumes.

It has been the purpose of the researcher to survey and study these diplomatic records and other pertinent sources, especially those in Jewish archives, to discover how the Vatican and its representatives reacted to the various phases of the Nazi persecution of the Jews from 1939 to 1943. The first date chosen, 1939, marked the beginning of the papacy of Pius XII, as well as the outbreak of the war; the study ceases at the end of 1943 because the Vatican records published to the present extend only to that date, and also because the majority of the Jews of Europe had already been killed by then.

The writer has also attempted to ascertain whether there was any pattern or common policy underlying the reaction of the Vatican and its representatives. Allied to this was an effort to judge the effectiveness of Vatican diplomacy vis-à-vis the Holocaust and to consider what other alternatives the Holy See might have had.

When Pius XII became Pope, there were papal nuncios in, among other capitals, Belgrade, Berlin, Berne, Brussels, Bucharest, Budapest, the Hague, Paris, Prague, Rome, and Warsaw.[5] The circumstances of war reduced this number and changed the location and level of some of the diplomatic representations. The end-result of these modifications was that during the years 1939–1943, the Secretariat of State was in diplomatic contact with its emissaries in Berlin, Rome, Vichy, Berne, Bratislava, Zagreb, Bucharest, and Budapest. In addition, active communications were maintained with the apostolic delegates in London, Washington, and Ankara.

In an interview with the Reverend Robert A. Graham, S.J.,[6] the English-speaking editor of the Vatican documentary series, the researcher was assured that Graham and his co-editors had total access to all the records. The editors attempted to publish those items which they judged important and illustrative, omitting those things which they considered repetitive. Father Graham stated strongly that the published documents are an accurate reflection of the total collection for the period. Furthermore, the editors have supplied the researcher, on request, with any documents that the text refers to but does not contain.

The documents are reproduced in the language in which composed. Most of them were written in Italian, although there are some in French, German, Latin, and English.[7]

These documents constituted the primary sources for this historical research. Corroborating and elaborating data were sought and discovered by the researcher in the archives of the Yad Vashem Martyrs' and Heroes' Memorial Authority in Jerusalem, the Centre de Documentation Juive Contemporaine in Paris, the British Section of the World Jewish Congress at the Institute for Jewish Affairs in London, the World Jewish Congress in New York City, and the Public Record Office in London. Research was also done in the Myron Taylor archives at the Roosevelt Library in Hyde Park, New York. Secondary sources were consulted at the library of *La Civiltà Cattolica* in Rome, the New York Public Library, and the libraries of the YIVO Institute for Jewish Research in New York City, New York University, and Seton Hall University.

The countries studied, with two exceptions, were those in which the Vatican had some diplomatic representation during the years 1939–1943. One exception was the case of Croatia, where the Vatican's emissary did not have diplomatic status, but was accorded it unilaterally by the government of the state. The Secretariat of State had no diplomatic contacts in Poland after the explusion of the nuncio in September 1939 at the time of the German invasion, although it did maintain diplomatic relations with the Polish government-in-exile.

Nevertheless, an attempt was made to study the situation in that country because of its unique place in Hitler's designs against the Jews.

Belgium, the Netherlands, and Luxembourg were not directly researched because their nuncios were forced to leave their posts when these nations were overrun by German troops. The nuncio in Berlin was theoretically responsible for these areas, while the original officials retained their titles *de jure,* although in residence in Rome. The nuncios in the Baltic countries were likewise expelled by German or Soviet troops and thus these nations could not be part of this study.

Hungary was not included because the tragic events directed against the Jews in that land did not occur until 1944. Bulgaria, likewise, was not treated. It did not have diplomatic relations with the Vatican and the dispatches from the apostolic delegate there were too few to provide sufficient data for the study. The Scandinavian countries were excluded because they were not in diplomatic contact with the Vatican.

The neutral states—Portugal, Spain, and Switzerland—were not studied directly, but the reports from their nuncios were often considered germane to the research. The nuncio in Switzerland was a particularly valuable source of information for the Secretariat of State. This was also true of the reports received from the apostolic delegates in Ankara, London, and Washington, who had access to information that only those nations could supply.

Thus, the Vatican had an extensive network of representatives throughout Europe from 1939 to 1943, the majority of whom were diplomats in the formal sense. The Holy See was very conscious and proud of its diplomatic status and maintained that it benefited not only the Catholic Church and its members, but also all other men because of its commitment to the ideals of justice and brotherhood.[8]

It was the purpose of the researcher to investigate whether Vatican diplomatic effort, in fact, was directed toward the rights of the Church and its members, as well as being oriented toward the needs of non-Catholics, specifically Jews. This twofold standard, developed and proclaimed by the Vatican, and imposed on its diplomacy, can be the only criterion with which to judge the success or failure of its diplomatic efforts vis-à-vis the Jews during the Holocaust. If it were found that the interests and activity of the papal diplomats were devoted primarily to defending Church interests and only peripherally or minimally to more humanitarian concerns, then Vatican diplomacy would have to be judged to have failed. This would have been a most unfortunate failure, not only because the lives of so many Jews were at stake, but also because Vatican diplomacy would be seen as failing itself because it had not practiced the ideals it claimed to espouse.

No institution can make claims to a unique status, particularly that of a religious and moral nature, if, in practice, it acts and reacts like other self-interested institutions. The Holy See has loudly and repeatedly proclaimed its uniqueness as a religious and moral power. If the records demonstrated that its diplomatic activity during the Holocaust was parochial and self-serving, it would, of necessity, stand condemned by its own criterion.

To discover this, the first task for the researcher was to establish chronologically the various phases of the Holocaust in each country. The general procedure was the racial legislation which isolated and pauperized the Jews, followed later by deportations to ghettos and camps. The reactions of each Vatican diplomat to these events had to be studied. Had he protested the legislation and the deportations? In what forum? To whom? What, if any, instructions did he receive from the Secretariat of State? What appeals were made to him? How much information did he have about the eventual true fate of the Jews? How did he describe the situation in his reports to his superiors in Rome?

To respond to these questions and to place the actions of the various ecclesiastics involved within the context of the Holocaust was the weightiest task and required the examination of all sources, Catholic, Jewish, and secular.

Once this task was completed, a corollary problem emerged. It was necessary to analyze the diplomatic activity of the various individuals to search for causal factors. Was there an attitude of the Vatican toward the Jews, the Nazis, ecclesiastical prerogatives, or something else, that contributed to the way in which it did or, perhaps, did not act?

In a structured institution like the Vatican, actions by its personnel are not performed haphazardly or unilaterally. Diplomats in general, and the Vatican's representatives in particular, were not men to act spontaneously or without recourse to directives from the Secretariat of State. It had to be presumed, therefore, that their action, or lack of action, was decided according to the needs and interests of the Secretariat of State. To ascertain this motivation was the second and, possibly, the most difficult task of the researcher.

At first glance, the killing of six million Jews would seem to preclude any discussion of the success of efforts on their behalf by the Vatican or any other body. In the face of such a loss, all efforts might be considered as having been futile. Success and failure, however, cannot be measured in such simple terms. It is evident that the Vatican's diplomatic activity during the Holocaust saved few, if any, Jews from their Nazi-ordained fate. From that point of view, its effectiveness was nil. If, on the other hand, it can be shown that the Vatican's diplomats raised their voices in protest against the treatment of the Jews, or if they in some way or another attempted to show their solidarity with the suffering Jews, then it cannot be said unconditionally that the Vatican diplomatic effort was without any effect.

The third task of the researcher, therefore, was to evaluate the success or failure of Vatican diplomacy not only by the amount of lives it saved or did not save, but also by the application of its own criterion that it should be a moral voice defending the rights of all men. This, then, became a question with a twofold ramification, involving, as it did, the unparalleled plight of the Jews, which, if ignored or minimized by the Vatican diplomats, cast doubt on the very *raison d'être* of the Church's diplomatic activities.

This question was part of the larger issue of whether any effort could have saved the Jews from the death decreed from them by Nazi officials. The wider issue was beyond the purview of the research, which concentrated only on the success of Vatican diplomacy in helping some Jews, or saving some lives, while at the same time being the moral voice that it purported to be.

Vatican diplomacy was the principal instrument used by the Catholic Church in attempting to exert its moral authority during the Second World War. It is true that individual churchmen here and there spoke out against the atrocities against the Jews and did all they could to prevent them. The Church, as Church, with the full certitude that it is the people of God and the mystical body of Christ in the world, could have echoed some of the words of its Founder as He preached and personified the ideals of justice and brotherhood.

The Pope—the Vicar of Christ as he is considered by Church members—relied on diplomacy to achieve the moral and Christian ideals of the Church. What other alternatives he might have had was the subject of the last task of this researcher. The Pope chose diplomacy as the method to confront the evils of war. Could he have made other, or additional, choices? Diplomacy is an acceptable and even valuable way for the Pope and the Vatican state he heads to make religious and humanitarian concerns known throughout the world. However, the question at issue was whether it was the best way to make these concerns known during the height of war, and in the face of such atrocities committed against one group of people.

The year 1978 witnessed a great surge of interest in the Holocaust. The commemoration of the thirtieth anniversary of the establishment of the State of Israel, as well as a television series, "The Holocaust," contributed to this. The publicity given to the American Nazi Party demonstrations has also focused attention on the Holocaust as the culmination of all anti-Semitic movements. That this trend is more than a popular fad is evidenced by the increasing scholarly interest in the Holocaust, manifested in conferences, bibliographies, articles, and the recent publication of a journal devoted exclusively to Holocaust themes.

It is the hope of the writer that this research will contribute to a deeper understanding of the Holocaust. The particular point of departure was concentration on the reaction not of the perpetrators or the victims, but of the bystanders. The bystanders referred to were not nameless individuals present in the circumstances by accident, but prelates of the Catholic Church and representatives of its religious and diplomatic status. They were, therefore, witnesses, whose very presence on the scene was not by chance but part of a carefully planned ecclesiastical mission. A study of how and why they reacted to the Holocaust will answer questions about the past and will become part of the historiography of the Holocaust.

Moreover, this research has revealed attitudes prevalent among Vatican officials at the time. Finally, it should lead to conclusions that have ramifications for the present and future as to how the Vatican Secretariat of State and the diplomats representing it reacted to the Nazi persecution against the Jews.

This is a justifiable historical quest, which, however, had to avoid two possible pitfalls. The emotions aroused in mourning the death of six million Jews had to be kept in check, lest they affect the historical process. Likewise, the veneration and faith of Church members could not be allowed to cloud historical judgment.

The researcher believes that he has avoided these two dangers in this study of Vatican diplomacy and the Jews. The conclusions reached should not only shed light on the actions of men of thirty-five years ago, but should also provide insight into the ever-continuing relations between the Catholic Church and the Jews.

CHAPTER TWO

Vatican Diplomacy

At the beginning of Pope Pius XII's reign in March 1939, thirty-eight nations maintained diplomatic missions of some sort at the Vatican. Thirteen of these were at the ambassadorial level while most of the rest were at the ministerial level. Likewise, there were papal representatives in thirty-eight countries. In several cases, the diplomatic relations were not entirely mutual and, thus, the lists of nations sending and receiving representatives do not completely correspond. In addition, twenty-three other envoys without diplomatic status were assigned by the Vatican to various states.[1]

Historical Aspects

The question of Vatican diplomacy, its definition, purposes, justification, and relationship to the Roman Catholic Church, is fairly complex. Historically, the origins of such diplomacy may be seen in the emissaries sent by the different Popes to the court of the emperor of Constantinople, and then later to other European sovereigns. By the eleventh century, these papal envoys were called nuncios ("messengers"). In the sixteenth century, the word "nuncio" came to refer exclusively to a papal representative with permanent diplomatic status.[2]

Until the Papal States became part of a united Italy, the role of the nuncio resembled quite closely that of any ambassador representing his country's interests in another nation. That the nuncio might also have had ecclesiastical or religious concerns did not visibly alter this role.

Lateran Treaty

After the forced dissolution of the papal territories by King Victor Emmanuel II in 1870, the Popes isolated themselves in protest in the

8

Vatican Palace. The so-called Roman Question was not settled until February 11, 1929, when the Lateran Treaty between Pope Pius XI and the Fascist government of Benito Mussolini was signed. Nevertheless, during the intervening six decades many nations continued their diplomatic relations with the papacy, even though it was totally deprived of any territorial jurisdiction. For example, in 1890, there were eighteen nations accredited to the papal court, in 1914, fourteen, and in 1921, twenty-four.[3]

Status of Pope in International Law

Diplomatic relations with the Pope during these decades might be interpreted as a sign of sympathy or recognition by these nations of the papal claims to the expropriated territory. That this was not the case may be seen in the fact that many of the same states sent ambassadors to the newly united Kingdom of Italy. It is unlikely that they would have done this if they explicitly continued to recognize any such papal claims. In fact, there soon developed a dual diplomatic corps in Rome, with various nations sending two envoys, one to the Pope and the other to the Italian king.

In addition, during the years 1870 to 1929, concordats between the papacy and various states were concluded, in the same form as treaties between sovereign nations. Moreover, during this period the Popes acted as arbitrators in a number of territorial disputes. It appears, therefore, that these nations wanted representation at the papal court, not because the Pope was a territorial sovereign, but because of his role as head of the Roman Catholic Church. In other words, even after the abolition of the Pope's temporal power through the loss of the papal territories, the papacy was recognized as a subject of international right in many nations.[4] These states, therefore, wanted to preserve diplomatic relations with the Pope, whether or not he was a territorial sovereign.

By the Lateran Treaty the Pope gained sovereignty over 108 acres centered around the Basilica of St. Peter and the Vatican Palace, as well as several other pieces of property throughout Rome. This new state, Vatican City, contained a minimum of territory but was sufficient for the external recognition of the Pope's temporal power. He, in turn, acknowledged the Kingdom of Italy with Rome as its capital.

The international aspects of Vatican City were described in Article 24 of the treaty.

With regard to the sovereignty belonging to it in international matters, the Holy See declares that it remains and shall remain outside all temporal rivalries between other States and shall take no part in international congresses summoned to settle such matters, unless the parties in dispute make jointly appeal to its mission of peace; in any case, however, the Holy See reserves the right of exercising its moral and spiritual power.

Consequently, the Vatican City shall always and in any event be considered as neutral and inviolable territory.[5]

As head of a sovereign state, the Pope may send and receive accredited diplomatic representatives. Catholic theologians and canon lawyers deny that the Pope's temporal power is the only source of his status in international law. The decades from 1870 to 1929 indicate that the Pope's primary position as head of the Catholic Church and not his territorial sovereignty was the foundation of his recognition as an international power.

According to this view, the Church is both a supranational organism, inasmuch as it is a spiritual union of believers all over the world, and also a juridic organism, inasmuch as it is a social, external, and regulated institution. In this latter case, it is by right equal to other international groups.[6]

The assertion of the international juridic personality of the Church is important because of the protection inherent in such a status. On the one hand, the Church is defended from any notions of regalism or ultranationalism that might interfere with the free exercise of its spiritual power; on the other hand, it is an affirmation that the Church is not just a simple association without any juridic foundation.[7]

The Pope, as head of the Church and bishop of Rome, exercises spiritual sovereignty, but he is not entirely distinct from the Church itself. He not only represents authority but is actually the authority. This is the reason why the Pope cannot be considered as distinct from the "Holy See," a term which is not only the name of the diocese of Rome but also includes the sovereign pontiff, as well as the Roman congregations, tribunals, and offices through which he ordinarily handles the affairs of the universal Church.[8]

The Holy See may be considered the juridic personification of the Church, and Vatican City may be viewed as a state created to assure the absolute and visible independence of the Holy See. Both the Holy See and the Vatican state are distinct subjects of international law. This is historically verified because the Holy See preexisted Vatican City, and it is also evident in various provisions of the Lateran Treaty which speak about both entities.[9]

Both the Holy See and the Vatican state are subject to the supreme authority of the Pope, who exercises temporal authority as head of Vatican City and spiritual authority as head of the Holy See. The same chief authority is thus engaged in separate and autonomous activities, religious and political.[10]

According to this view, it would appear that the best term to be used for diplomatic exchanges would be "papal," since the Pope combines in himself a unique amalgam of spiritual and temporal authority. In practice the terms "papal," "Vatican," and "Holy See" will be used synonymously, even though the existence of distinctions among them is admitted.

Definitions of Vatican Diplomacy

Vatican diplomacy may be defined as a

system by which, through accredited public agents, the Holy See carries on stable, formal and reciprocal intercourse with the states. It is the instrumentality by which the supreme authority of the Catholic Church communicates within the framework of standard international practice, with the supreme authority of the states, in the transaction of current or special problems which arise on the part of either Church or State, for the resolution of which the common accord of the ultimate authority of both parties is required. This consensus may take the shape of treaties (concordats) or less formal understandings. . . . In short, by papal diplomacy is here meant the system of reciprocal permanent representation . . .[11]

The nuncio to Vichy France during the war years, Archbishop Valerio Valeri, publicly discussed the meaning and purposes of Vatican diplomacy in a speech given several years after the end of the war. He stated:

. . . It is clear that the activity of the Holy See is not limited, and cannot be limited, to purely diplomatic efforts, in the strict sense of that word, inasmuch as it indicates certain juridic relations between States. The Roman Pontiff is identified with the Church . . . [which] has a universal mission that distinguishes it from every other earthly society and it basically tends to continue through the centuries the salvific work of its Divine Founder. With such a mission the Church has entered into history and it has the highest awareness of this.

The development in time and according to circumstances of this mission can also be called diplomacy, if one wishes, but only in an elevated sense, above the purely natural and political order. From this point of view, the supreme law of the Church, and indeed, of the Holy See, is the salvation of souls. All of its activity is always directed to this end . . . even when the Church, because of historical circumstances, had to concern itself with its temporal interests.[12]

It is true that according to the Church's own concept of itself and its mission, it is imbued with the divine Presence to the extent that it has no essential need of diplomacy. Nevertheless, the universal character of the Church, and the fact that its members live in various states, makes the Church's use of diplomacy not only legitimate but also an effective means of fulfilling its role.[13]

Objections to Vatican Diplomacy

There are, however, objections to papal diplomacy. For example, it is claimed that the Church may compromise itself in the practice of diplomacy both by using earthly means to obtain spiritual goals and by possible intrigue or interference in the internal affairs of a country. To this objection it is pointed out that papal diplomacy is exclusively concerned with religious matters submitted to the authority of the Pope. As a spiritual sovereign, his actions cannot be viewed as interference. To protect the rights of religion and the Church, wherever they are not recognized or where they are violated, he must use representatives, and to do so hardly compromises the dignity and uniqueness of the Church.[14]

Another objection to Vatican diplomacy is that papal representatives from outside the country are not necessary and local ecclesiastical officials could perform the same functions. This, of course, remains theoretically possible, but there is the real problem of the preparation and background of the local clergy to perform such tasks. Moreover, many of the problems between Church and state involve international law and thus are beyond the competence of the local hierarchy.[15]

Ideals of Vatican Diplomacy

Far from being merely tolerated, Vatican diplomacy, on the contrary, is proposed as a model for civil diplomacy. The ideal of ecclesiastical diplomacy is the brotherhood of men, and, whether or not it succeeds in achieving this goal, it serves as a guide for civil diplomacy which attempts to make reason prevail over force and to contribute to the growth of individual states in harmony with all others. In fact, according to this view, it would be a positive loss for civil diplomacy if Vatican diplomacy ceased to be practiced.[16]

Thus, the envoys of the Holy See are sent to the various countries, not just to defend the rights of the Church, but also to defend the rights and to serve the needs of the people there. For the Church diplomacy is a form of love and service because "The ecclesiastical diplomat brings words of understanding; he is the advocate of the just causes of the population; he collaborates with the government and with the nation in which he is a guest."[17]

The ordinary diplomatic emissary of the Holy See is the nuncio, who has the rank of ambassador and represents the Pope before the government and the Church of the country to which he is posted. According to canon law, the nuncios are charged with the twofold task of fostering relations between the Vatican and the civil governments to which they are accredited and reporting on the condition of the Church in the same nation.[18] Ordinarily, diplomatic relations involving the Vatican are mutual, but the papacy claims the right, independent of any civil authority, to send its representatives into every part of the world.[19]

The Vatican considers the twofold responsibility described in canon law to be only a minimum for its diplomats. For example, the goal of Vatican diplomatic service has been described as a dedication to the principles of justice and charity.[20] Moreover, the Vatican diplomat has been depicted as representing Christ and the Church, indeed of bearing Christ in his heart.[21]

The current nuncio to Belgium, Luxembourg, and the European Economic Community, Archbishop Hyginus Cardinale, admits that the first concern of a Vatican diplomat must be for the Church in the country to which he is assigned. In addition, Cardinale states:

His mission . . . includes the moral, cultural and social problems which belong to the major interests of mankind such as the respect for human rights, the promotion of international order, the development of friendly ties among all nations through peaceful co-existence, through respect for justice and the promotion of human progress.[22]

These descriptions, admittedly, were all stated after the war, but there is nothing in them to indicate that they constituted a new approach to, or new appreciation of, the role of the Vatican diplomat. The criteria, therefore, developed by the Holy See itself for the nuncio's activities go beyond the narrow juridic confines of canon law to embrace a humanitarian and Christ-like concern for the needs of all those residing in the nuncio's host country.[23] The recently deceased Pope Paul VI summarized this in averring that the nuncio "must concern himself zealously with the problem of peace, of progress and of the collaboration of peoples in view of the spiritual, moral and material good of the entire human family."[24]

The nuncio's unique role among diplomats has traditionally been acknowledged by his recognition as dean of the diplomatic corps in the various states. As recently as 1961, at a United Nations Conference on Diplomatic Relations and Immunities, the precedence of the nuncio was specifically mentioned.[25] This precedence has always been granted to the Papal nuncio in homage to the Holy See which he represents. For among the members of the international community, the Holy See alone is distinguished by its special nature and by the peculiar characteristics of its methods and aims. These are directly inspired by spiritual and moral values and ideals, and constitute all that is most sublime, most precious and most worthy of respect in the eyes of all nations.[26]

Other Vatican diplomatic functionaries are the internuncio and the chargé d'affaires. The internuncio is appointed to those countries where, for certain reasons, a nuncio cannot be sent. He has a lower diplomatic rank although his responsibilities parallel those of the nuncio. The chargé d'affaires is the third class of papal diplomat and functions as head of a diplomatic mission in the absence of the nuncio or internuncio. He is accredited to the foreign minister rather than to the head of state of the host country.[27]

Another category of papal emissary is the apostolic delegate, who represents the Pope before the hierarchy, clergy, and faithful of the state. He has no official relations with the government and possesses no diplomatic character. His main responsibility is to oversee the condition of the Church in the country to which he is assigned and make periodic reports concerning it to Rome.[28]

Vatican Representation During the War

During the years of World War II, nuncios were assigned to the following European countries: France, Germany, Hungary, Italy, Portugal, Romania, Spain, and Switzerland. The nuncios in Belgium, the Netherlands (actually, an internuncio), and Poland were expelled by the Nazis, although they retained their status *de jure*. Those in Estonia, Latvia, and Lithuania were forced out by the Soviet occupation of their countries. A chargé d'affaires represented the Vatican in the newly created state of Slovakia. In addition, there were apostolic delegates in Albania, Bulgaria, and Great Britain, as well as Turkey and the United States, among other countries.[29] An apostolic visitor was sent to Croatia.[30]

Secretary of State

All of these representatives worked under the jurisdiction of the cardinal secretary of state, whose main responsibility was the relationship of the Holy See to foreign governments. It was he who set the policy which the envoys followed, who sent them their instructions, and to whom they directed their reports. After the Pope, the secretary of state is the most important and recognized figure in the Vatican.[31]

The newly elected Pius XII appointed Cardinal Luigi Maglione as his secretary of state on March 11, 1939. Their friendship dated back to their seminary days and each had had long experience in the Vatican Secretariat of State.

Maglione was born in 1877 in Casoria, near Naples, and was ordained a priest in 1901. He later acquired degrees in philosophy, theology, and canon law, and studied at the papal academy for diplomats. From 1908 to 1918 he was a professor in this same academy.

He was named apostolic delegate to Switzerland in 1918. At Berne he was active in transmitting the first accounts of the prisoners-of-war to their families and also explained the Church's position on certain religious questions to the fledgling League of Nations. In 1920 full diplomatic relations with Switzerland were resumed, and Maglione became the nuncio there.

Pope Pius XI appointed him nuncio to France in 1926, and he remained in that post until 1935, when he was named a cardinal and brought back to Rome. He was later appointed prefect of the Congregation of the Council. He died before the war was over on August 22, 1944.[32]

The choice of Maglione seemed a logical one for Pius XII. He gave the impression of being someone with whom the new Pope could collaborate and whose experience in France apparently balanced the Pope's own in Germany. The appointment of Maglione was interpreted to indicate "that the principles and policies which the new Pope would adopt in dealing with the already critical European situation would not be molded to fit Axis models."[33]

To a certain extent, the mind and personality of Maglione will be revealed in the texts to be studied. There is always the caveat of uncertainty, however, because it is almost impossible to know what controls were exercised upon him by the Pope. His decisions and instructions might have been his exclusively, or the Pope's, or some amalgam of the two. It is noteworthy that when Maglione died, Pius did not appoint a successor and acted as his own secretary of state. This would appear to indicate that he was merely continuing what he was doing when Maglione held the office.

Maglione was respected by his diplomatic colleagues. He inspired confidence in them, and his reticence was viewed as an effort to maintain the Vatican's freedom of action.[34] He was considered shrewd, broad-minded, and cultured,[35] as well as foresighted and perspicacious.[36] His southern Italian origins gave him an "exuberant temperament" that as a diplomat he had to moderate.[37] He succeeded so well in this that his patience became legendary.[38]

Maglione's two principal assistants were Monsignor Domenico Tardini, head of the Section for Extraordinary Ecclesiastical Affairs, and Monsignor Giovanni Battista Montini (later Pope Paul VI), chief of the Section for Ordinary Ecclesiastical Affairs. Tardini's department handled all questions brought to the attention of the Holy See, through the nuncios or the diplomats accredited to the Vatican, which related to civil laws. In addition, certain papal documents were prepared and dispatched by this office. Montini's section received all the reports from the various nunciatures, analyzed them, and prepared instructions in return. Other purely ecclesiastical duties, such as the awarding of papal honors, were also under his purview.[39]

Analysis

It is evident that some authors might not be willing to accept what they would consider an exalted and unrealistic version of Vatican diplomacy. They would attribute to the decisions and actions of the Secretariat of State far more mundane and self-interested attitudes than those presented here. For example, one author has described the situation under Pius XII as "a kind of precise Byzantinism, formality for formality's sake, and generously touched with intrigue and decay."[40]

No attempt is being made here to prove that Vatican diplomacy achieves or exemplifies the goals that it claims guide all its activity. Vatican diplomacy has defined itself and has expressed in various ways its evaluation of itself. This, of necessity, must be the point of departure for a study that attempts to investigate how the diplomats involved fulfilled their functions.

If the Vatican did not allege that it was unique in being a combination of religious, moral, and temporal interests, then it should not be expected to have reacted any differently to the Holocaust than other governments. If this uniqueness is denied a priori, then the presumption must logically be that the Vatican, like all institutions and governments, acted always in what it considered its best interests. If this be so, its activity and decisions can hardly be challenged on any other grounds.

Vatican diplomacy purported to be a model and ideal for all states. The officials involved appeared to sincerely believe this, and certainly many adherents of the Catholic Church, and possibly of other churches as well, accepted it also. Moreover, those governments that automatically considered the nuncio as dean of the diplomatic corps attributed to him some intrinsic quality that the other diplomats accredited to them did not possess.

It is in this context that the actions of Vatican diplomacy toward the Jews will be studied. By its own avowal, the injustices committed against the Jews, to say nothing of the atrocities, should have been a major source of effort for it during the years from 1939 to 1943.

CHAPTER THREE

The Brazilian Visa Project

One of the principal concerns of the Vatican, especially in the early days of the war, was those Jews who had converted to Catholicism, the so-called Catholic or Christian non-Aryans. The Vatican considered these Jews full-fledged members of the Church and attempted to save them from the Nazis' anti-Jewish measures. Moreover, the Vatican justified its interest in these baptized Jews because they were cut off from support or assistance by the Jewish relief organizations, which viewed them as apostates.[1]

Concession of Visas by Brazil

At the end of March 1939, representatives of the German Catholic hierarchy wrote the newly elected Pius XII asking him to petition the Brazilian government to grant 3,000 immigration visas for German Catholic Jews to settle in Brazil.[2]

For the next two years, this project occupied the attention of the Vatican diplomats. It began with the instructions of Luigi Cardinal Maglione, the Vatican secretary of state, to the nuncio in Rio de Janeiro, Archbishop Aloisi Masella, to request the visas from Brazilian President Getulio Dornellas Vargas,[3] and their subsequent concession by the president on June 20, 1939.[4]

Problems

From the beginning the proposal, which was in reality a matter of life and death to some, was beset with questions and problems, some

18

necessary, others obstructionist. First of all, it was decided that not only the baptized Jews of Germany but also those in other countries would be eligible.[5] Later the applicants were required to submit a recommendation from the nunciature in their respective countries.[6] Another condition imposed afterwards was the stipulation that the applicants have financial resources and be interested in working in agriculture or industry.[7]

Most devastating of all for those attempting to flee the Nazis was the requirement that they possess proof of having been baptized before 1933.[8] A question about the use of the visas by Protestant Jews was answered negatively,[9] and later clarified with the statement that Brazil's interest was religious, i.e., Catholic, not racial.[10] Brazil, as a Catholic country, was willing to aid Catholics of Jewish origin but did not care to welcome Protestants of Jewish origin. In the midst of all of this, appeals came from various places and groups begging for allotments of visas.

More complications arose. It was alleged that a private agency was not only selling the visas, but selling them to non-baptized Jews.[11] This was denied by the Brazilian authorities.[12] A different type of problem was the complaint by the Brazilian ambassador that some of the Jews who had emigrated to Brazil earlier had made a bad impression upon his countrymen. This was compounded by the fact that many of them appeared to have been baptized after 1933—in fact, as recently as the current year, 1939.[13] The Vatican Secretariat of State felt obliged to assure the ambassador that those recommended had been vouched for by their respective bishops as sincere Catholics.[14] So full of difficulties had the whole project become that there was even some consideration of ignoring the needs of the Catholic Jewish refugees and obtaining the visas for Catholic refugees not of Jewish origin.[15]

Requests from Innitzer

On February 4, 1941, the archbishop of Vienna, Theodore Cardinal Innitzer, wrote to Pius XII asking his immediate aid for the granting of the visas because the deportation of 60,000 Viennese Jews had already begun, and among them were 11,000 who had been baptized.[16] Maglione replied explaining the various difficulties which the Vatican faced in trying to obtain the visas and added that the Vatican's efforts, even if not always successful, did result in the amelioration of conditions for certain Catholic Jews.[17]

Innitzer was not satisfied with this diplomatic response, and he complained again at the end of February that the baptized Jews were being ignored by the very Church which they had adopted, and that for them it was a particular injustice because all aid from their former co-religionists had been shut off. [18]

The visa program was suspended on September 3, 1940, [19] and finally officially ended on November 20, 1941, just prior to American entry into the war. [20] Reinforcing the Brazilian government's decision were the parallel refusals of the Spanish and Portuguese governments to issue transit visas for the refugees to embark from their countries. [21]

Several months later, on May 20, 1942, Innitzer seemed to be admitting defeat when he informed the secretary of state that the Jewish deportations were in full swing and not much more could be done. [22] The Vatican made one last effort in July 1942 but was rebuffed by the Brazilian embassy's reply that it did not judge it opportune, in the light of the international situation, to make any exceptions to the laws on the entry of foreigners into Brazilian territory. [23]

Maglione's Comments

Shortly after the cancellation of the project, in December 1941, Maglione wrote to the bishop whose original request had initiated the whole affair. He indicated to him not only that all available money had been spent, but also his own disappointment.

As you have certainly been informed . . . many emigrants have departed and—I regret to say—from what I have been told, a good many of them, both by their improper conduct and alleged demands, have not corresponded to the concern which the Holy See has shown in their behalf. [24]

The cardinal's chagrin was not caused by the failure of the Vatican diplomatic effort and the ensuing problems that it caused the converted Jews, but he was piqued at the conduct and lack of gratitude of those who obtained the visas.

Results

The final results of the whole venture are difficult to verify. Maglione spoke of the departure of a number of emigrants and must have been referring to those able to procure visas from the 1,000 allotted to the Brazilian embassy at the Vatican. Most of these were apparently used. The remaining 2,000, in the control of Brazilian officials in Germany itself, were never granted, not even during the first year or so before the military positions became definitive. [25]

At the cessation of a project that had so occupied it, the Vatican was remarkably acquiescent. Maglione's feelings undoubtedly had a role to play. When the Brazilian ambassador announced the cancellation of the entire venture, he added his personal hope that, in the not too distant future, world conditions would permit his government to reinstate the whole program.[26] The Vatican's response was agonizingly impersonal and diplomatic: "The Holy See has learned with sorrow the news of this measure [the ending of the visa program] which will hinder its efforts in helping those suffering, and it hopes that the wish expressed by Your Excellency regarding the revocation of this measure will be realized as soon as possible . . ."[27]

Importance of the Brazilian Visa Project

The Brazilian visa project may appear as a very limited action involving only a handful of Europe's Jews, but it is uniquely important in its contribution toward understanding the Vatican's attitudes and practices during the Holocaust.

First of all, it indicates that during the early years of the war, the Vatican was primarily, almost exclusively, concerned about baptized Jews. This solicitude was readily justified for two reasons. By virtue of their baptisms these Jews were members of the Church and were, therefore, legitimate subjects for its efforts or protests. This was a question of the rights of the Church and its members and was continually on the minds of Vatican officials. It will be seen in country after country that the Vatican would intervene whenever it felt that Church privileges were being restricted or violated. In addition, the baptized Jews were often ignored by Jewish aid groups.

Secondly, the visa project demonstrates how much the Vatican relied on diplomatic means to achieve its goals. Cables and reports were exchanged; diplomatic procedures were observed; the language was always courteous. Throughout it all the very real sufferings and needs of those involved were ignored. Diplomacy almost appears to have become an end in itself, rather than the means to attain the end.

Thirdly, the study of this project demonstrates how reluctant the Vatican was to disturb the status quo. Even when a staunchly Catholic country reneged on its promise to the Pope, no strong words of protest were issued. The matter of 2,000 visas not granted was admittedly small in the context of the time, but in accepting one government's failure to live up to its agreement, the Vatican may have been preparing itself to accept other similar refusals. Perhaps it also feared that any protest might result in restrictions on the Church in the country involved.

Finally, the efforts expended on behalf of the Brazilian visa project appear never to have been forgotten by the Vatican officials. They frequently reiterated how much the Vatican had done for the Jews. In the absence of many other efforts on behalf of Jews, baptized or not, it must be presumed that this project is being referred to. It became then, in some ways, the apologia for the Vatican's attitude toward the Jews during the early part of the war.

CHAPTER FOUR

Romania

In prewar Romania the ethnic minorities constituted almost 30 percent of the population. Many of them had been in the country since medieval times, but were generally considered foreigners by the Romanians.

Introduction

Among these minorities, of course, were the Jews, who numbered between 700,000 and 800,000, just over 4 percent of the country's total population.[1] Antipathy toward them was particularly pronounced for several reasons. Jewish commercial interests exercised control in a large number of industries. In the professions, Jews were represented far more highly than their proportion in the population. In addition, the Jews were a highly urbanized group and in a number of cities made up one-quarter to one-half of the residents.[2] As anti-Semitism spread across Europe, such factors as these were misinterpreted to generate fear and hatred of the Jews.

Romanian anti-Semitism was basically xenophobic. The Jews appeared or were portrayed as foreigners who remained unassimilated and who exploited the Romanians financially. The appeals by Jewish leaders to outside powers when they felt the Romanian government had violated their rights under the Minorities Protection Treaty of 1919 served to heighten this impression. In addition, the commercial and capitalistic values of the Jewish community were seen as alien influences in contrast to the peasants' traditional life-style.[3]

POLITICAL SITUATION

When war broke out in September 1939, King Carol sought neutrality for his country and hoped to balance it between alliances with England

23

and France and economic cooperation with Germany. In the following months, however, the growing strength of Germany could not be ignored, especially after the fall of France.

For all practical purposes, Romania was to have little choice about its eventual alignment with Germany. At the end of June 1940 the Soviet government presented an ultimatum demanding the return of Bessarabia and the northern half of Bukovina to the Soviet Union. The king could not turn to defeated France or beleaguered England for any assistance and so appealed to Germany. Hitler's government was interested in preserving the Soviet Union as its ally and so advised the Romanians to acquiesce to the Soviet demand. This was to be a particularly momentous decision for the Jews of these provinces. Their evident joy at the departure of the anti-Semitic Romanian leaders and their active welcome of the Soviets would be the excuse a year later for vicious persecution by the newly returned Romanians.

A second and more serious loss of Romanian territory occurred on August 30, 1940, when, again following Germany's advice, Romania ceded to Hungary almost half of Transylvania. Bulgaria, at the same time, put in a claim for southern Dobruja and shortly afterward received it.

This loss of one-third of Romania's territory and population was so unpopular that King Carol was forced to abdicate on September 6, 1940, in favor of his son, Michael. Effective power, however, was in the hands of General Ion Antonescu, who had only recently been appointed to head the government by Carol. For a few months Antonescu had to share his power with Horia Sima, the leader of the Iron Guard and vice-premier. The Iron Guard legionaries, however, were not content with dual sources of authority and openly revolted against Antonescu in January 1941. Germany, it would have been thought, would have supported the heavily fascist Iron Guard but chose to favor Antonescu. With the help of the army the revolt was crushed, and for the next four years Antonescu became the sole ruler of Romania.[4]

RELATIONSHIP TO VATICAN

According to the 1930 census, the number of Roman Catholics in Romania was just over 1,000,000, or 6.6 percent of the population. Another 1,300,000 Romanians were Eastern Rite Catholics in union with Rome.[5] The legal status of the Roman Catholic Church in Romania had been formalized in a concordat between the Vatican and the government approved on July 7, 1929. Article I of the concordat allowed the free and public exercise of the Catholic faith in the entire kingdom; Article XIX acknowledged the right of the Church to conduct its own sectarian schools at its own expense, while Article XX permitted the Church to give religious instruction to students in the state schools.[6]

The papal nuncio in Bucharest, appointed on June 14, 1936, was Archbishop Andrea Cassulo. He succeeded Valerio Valeri, who had been assigned to Paris. From 1921 to 1927 Cassulo had served as apostolic delegate to Egypt and Arabia, and from 1927 to 1936 he held the same position in Canada. By the time he began his duties in Romania, Cassulo was already sixty-seven years of age. He was destined to remain in the country until 1947, when he was forced out by the Communists. He then became apostolic delegate to Turkey, where he died in 1952.[7]

1939–1941

BAPTIZED JEWS

Cassulo's early efforts on behalf of the Jews concerned almost exclusively those who had been baptized Catholic. For example, in February 1939 he passed on to the Secretariat of State of the Vatican the proposal of a Romanian group that 50,000 converted Jewish families, numbering approximately 150,000 persons, be permitted to emigrate from Romania and settle in Spain. The project was never pursued, not only because the notion of so many conversions was totally unrealistic, but also because, quite expectedly, the response of the Spanish government was strongly negative.[8]

During 1940 and 1941, therefore, Cassulo's principal concern was for the rights of the Jews who had been baptized. Legislation passed by the government in August 1940 stated that Jews converted to Christianity would continue to be considered Jews, and that marriages between Jews and ethnic Christians were forbidden.[9] The startling feature of these regulations was that for the first time Romania was defining Jews by criteria not based on religion.[10] It was the first step, and a large one at that, to further racial legislation.

The concordat remained for Cassulo the legal justification for all his protests. Legislation had been enacted allowing only 6 percent of the Jewish students to attend the public schools[11] and requiring the remainder to attend Jewish schools, even those who had been baptized.[12] In a letter to the minister of foreign affairs on October 22, 1940, the nuncio maintained that Catholic parents, whether formerly Jewish or not, had the right to give their children a Catholic education, a right that was formally guaranteed by the concordat.[13]

Cassulo later protested to Antonescu, the head of government, on three separate occasions. The first letter, on November 20, 1940, merely pointed out the difficulties of such legislation.[14] His letter of December 2, 1940 reminded Antonescu that the concordat clearly allowed Catholic parents the right to educate their children in their faith. In addition, while acknowledging the right of the state to establish professional and civil standards, Cassulo emphasized the right of Catholic students to attend their own schools.[15]

The Vatican diplomat's third letter, on February 16, 1941, brought some results. He repeated his previous arguments but also pointed out the complaints he had received from the parents of children in this situation. These children were rejected by the Jewish schools because of their baptism and were prevented from attending Catholic schools because of their parents' Jewish origin.[16] Five days later, Antonescu informed the nuncio that he had just signed a decree allowing Christian students of any ethnic origin to attend their own religious schools.[17] Cassulo viewed this decision as a significant sign that even during wartime the Romanian government was willing to respect the liberty of the Church and family.[18]

FIRST CONTACT WITH THE JEWISH PROBLEM

The archbishop's first contact with the Jewish problem, as such, appears to have occurred during his meeting with Antonescu on March 18, 1941. It is evident that the recent Iron Guard uprising was on the general's mind and also, perhaps, the new anti-Jewish legislation that would soon be enacted. He wanted the nuncio to know how concerned he was for the moral and material welfare of his countrymen both in the past and at the present time. Evidence of this was the aid he claimed to have given to the Jews who had suffered so much during the recent troubles.

The general's humanitarian interest in the Jews was superficial and short-lived. He had at hand to show the nuncio a whole set of statistics purportedly proving the preponderance of Jewish capital and control of the country's commerce. Cassulo realized that such statistics were not pertinent to their conversation or their relationship but were meant to provide an explanation or justification for the forthcoming anti-Semitic legislation.[19] His suspicion was soon substantiated. On March 27 the government decreed the expropriation of all Jewish real estate.[20]

CONVERSION OF THE JEWS

Much more worrisome to the Vatican, however, as a telegram from Maglione to Cassulo indicated, was a report that the Romanian government had forbidden the conversion of Jews to Christianity, ostensibly for reasons of racial purity. According to this decree of March 18, 1941, Jews who attempted conversion or priests who cooperated were threatened with severe penalties.[21]

Cassulo was informed by the foreign minister that the source of this decree was not his ministry but the minister of cults. The nuncio wanted to impress upon the foreign minister, and through him upon the government, the Vatican's conviction that any such law would be a direct violation of the concordat and an infringement of the Church's liberty. The Church alone had the right to decide whether to accept or reject a person seeking baptism.[22]

The government's reply was issued by the minister of foreign affairs on May 9. He denied, first of all, that the decree of March 18 affected the rights of the Catholic Church in Romania. Moreover he maintained that there was no obstacle to the conversion of Jews to Christianity but that this change of religion would have no effect upon their civil status according to the laws of the country.[23]

The blatant racism of this reply was ignored or not recognized by the Vatican diplomats. The sole interest of Luigi Cardinal Maglione, the Vatican's secretary of state, was that the converted Jews be given the same rights as those guaranteed to Catholics by the concordat. He himself listed them: free profession of the Catholic faith, admission to Catholic schools, religious instruction, and spiritual assistance in various areas of society, such as the army and hospitals.[24]

For the Vatican, at least, the matter seemed settled with the note from the minister of foreign affairs of July 21, 1941.

. . . Christian students are admitted, no matter what their ethnic origin, to the confessional schools on the primary and secondary levels, of the Christian denominations. Christian students, with one Jewish parent, are even admitted to certain non-confessional schools. Consequently, Jews who have converted to the Catholic religion enjoy, in religious matters, all the rights recognized by the Concordat, and especially, the right to religious instruction, the right to the spiritual assistance of Catholic priests as well as the right of admission to all Catholic primary and secondary schools.[25]

JEWS IN TRANSNISTRIA

Romania joined Germany in the attack on the Soviet Union in June 1941 and quickly recaptured Bessarabia and Bukovina. Antonescu was not content to stop at the Dniester River, the boundary of Bessarabia, but also occupied the territory between that river and the Bug River, naming it Transnistria. As a result of these conquests, the general was promoted to marshal. Transnistria itself would soon become one of the worst areas of Jewish suffering under Romanian control.[26]

Cassulo's report to Maglione early in August referred to the problems of the Jews in these territories. He informed the secretary of state that the government suspected the Jews of being Communists and of supporting the Soviets. As a result, it had been very severe on them. On many sides, the nuncio stated, he had been asked to intervene to mitigate some of the suffering. He described himself, however, as reluctant to say much because he considered the situation quite delicate. Nevertheless, he informed his superior, he had achieved, on the basis of charity, what he considered the most important effect: in educational and religious matters the baptized Jews enjoyed all the liberty granted them by the concordat as Catholics.[27]

Appeals from baptized and unbaptized Jews still were sent to the nuncio. On October 20, 1941, he met with the minister of foreign affairs and vice-premier, Mihai Antonescu. The minister admitted that in the liberated territories some members of the Iron Guard had been excessively cruel to Jews whom they considered Bolshevik sympathizers, but the government was developing a plan to regulate the Jewish question and had no desire to be harsh toward the Jews. The nuncio, on his part, was wary of being accused of interfering in the internal affairs of the country and attempted to emphasize the religious aspects of his mission.[28]

Deportations from Bukovina and Bessarabia to Transnistria began in full earnest in October 1941.[29] Toward the end of the year, the chief rabbi of Bucharest, Alexandre Safran, made a secret visit to the queen mother, Helena, and described to her the sufferings of the deported Jews, especially the children. According to Safran's own account, the queen discussed the matter with Cassulo, who advised her to see Mihai Antonescu. This she did and received his assurance that aid could be sent to the Jews deported to Transnistria. The general commissar for Jewish affairs, Raul Lecca, received instructions that relief materials, especially medical supplies, could be sent to Transnistria.[30]

In a report to Maglione on December 5, 1941, Cassulo appears to have information similar to that which Safran related to the queen mother. Because some Jews had been sympathetic to the Bolsheviks, the government had decided to punish all Jews. Many Jewish families, among whom were some who had been baptized, were subject to deportation or to what he described as "odious" measures. The nuncio admitted that in spite of all the appeals that were coming to him, he had been torn between the desire to become involved in aiding those who were suffering and the fear of meddling in the internal affairs of the government.[31]

INTERVENTION ON BEHALF OF BAPTIZED JEWS

The nuncio did decide, however, to intervene on behalf of the baptized Jews. On December 4 he wrote to Mihai Antonescu:

To involve without distinction these Catholic families in the obligations, restrictions, and conditions of life of their former co-religionists, would be to make it impossible for them to live their religious life, or to give their children the religious education to which they are obliged and have the right. Neither special privilege nor protection is being sought, but only that conditions favorable to the moral and spiritual life of Christians be permitted.[32]

Moreover, Cassulo informed the secretary of state that in addition to this letter he had also intervened on behalf of non-baptized Jews. At the government's invitation, he had presented it with a list of names of Jews who were not involved in any action hostile to the government. The nuncio felt certain that those on the list would not be molested or subjected to restrictions.[33]

1942

PROBLEM OF THE INCREASING NUMBER OF CONVERSIONS

The ability of the papal diplomat to bring his protests to the attention of the government and his interest in the welfare of converted Jews led to a whole series of new problems between the Vatican and the Romanian government. In a report to Maglione on December 22, 1941, Cassulo described a dilemma that had long been on his mind. It was the ever-increasing number of Jews, threatened with laws that endangered their lives and their property, who were seeking to be baptized as Catholics.

Several months previously, Cassulo had received instructions from the Holy Office about the conversion of Jews. These directives made no allowance for the country's racial laws and permitted all Jews who were sincere in their motivation to be baptized. There had been no doubt in the mind of the Vatican officials that the desire for baptism could have been caused by other than religious reasons, and so the clergy were directed to be diligent in their judgment of prospective converts. It was not enough to simply accept their word, but all during the six-month period of their instruction and preparation, their conduct, interest, and desire to reform their lives according to Catholic principles were to be observed. If, after all this, there were any doubts about their motivation, the baptism was to be postponed.[34]

Cassulo was perplexed by the developing situation. By the end of December 1941, circumstances had changed to the extent that the norms established by the Holy Office could no longer be followed, especially the requirement of six months of instruction. The nuncio revealed how much he was aware of the sufferings of the Jews by stating that many Jews, who had no hope for the future and lived under the constant threat of deportation, were seeking to be accepted into the Church.[35] Their hope, of course, was that baptism would save their lives or, at least, improve their situation.

The whole matter had been even more complicated by a rumor that, because of the imminent danger, the Vatican had authorized mass baptisms of Jews with only a brief preliminary instruction. The Romanian bishops had worked out a system with which Cassulo agreed. Those who came to be baptized were given a summary instruction on the points of the Catholic faith, and their family and marital status were examined. After that, they were baptized with the condition that they continue their instruction before being admitted to receive Communion.[36]

The final comments of the nuncio to his superior are noteworthy. The Jews who were converting were professional or business men who were willing to come for their instruction at any time of day. This led him to conclude: "It is clear that human motives cannot be denied, but it is likewise true that Providence also uses human means to arrive at salvation."[37] This is a startling observation that, at best, raises the suffering of the Jews to the level of divine grace and will and, at worst, echoes the traditional Christian view of the Jews as a rejected people.

It would be of great interest to know the number of those baptized under these circumstances. To attract such attention from the government, the number must have been significant. In Bessarabia it was reported that 40,000 Jews, 20 percent of the Jewish population, accepted baptism to escape deportation.[38]

The Romanian government's concern about the baptisms reached its high point in April 1942, when the Romanian minister at the Vatican, Daniel Papp, informed Maglione that his government was suspicious of the rapidly growing number of Jews being converted. So anxious were the Romanian officials that Papp passed on their request that the Pope suspend all baptisms for the duration of the war. It was a petition that could not be granted. Maglione argued that the Church would be contravening its divine mission if it refused baptism to anyone sincerely motivated and adequately prepared. To placate the government, however, he did agree to send Cassulo instructions urging discretion on the part of the clergy.[39]

A few weeks later Cassulo was sent more instructions by the Holy Office. This time he was asked to see if the government would allow Jews during their catechumenate the same rights as those already baptized. If so, it would resolve the problem of hasty baptisms by permitting a longer period for instruction and observation.[40]

Cassulo acknowledged these directives on May 24, 1942, and again he appears to have viewed the conversionary movement as providential, and obstacles to it as contravening the divine will. He wrote in summary:

When the Romanian government in its wisdom and indulgence yielded to our insistence on the recognition of the rights of the Church, especially in that which concerns the education and religious assistance of the newly baptized, the Jews felt themselves efficaciously sustained and comforted, and this has contributed much toward the conversionary movement. It is true that everything could not be obtained, but the fact of being able to call oneself a Catholic is a great recommendation.[41]

JEWS IN TRANSNISTRIA

Between October 1941 and the summer of 1942, 185,000 Jews had been sent to Transnistria, most of them from Bukovina and Bessarabia.[42] German reports at the time announced that there were no longer any Jews left in these provinces, with the exception of 16,000 in the town of Cernauti. Of the 185,000 deported, official reports listed 112,000 as being in Transnistria. Nothing was said about the remaining 73,000, who were presumed dead.[43]

Among the Jews of Cernauti, there were those also who had converted. Their problems with the local authorities had already been brought to the nuncio's attention, for he had written to Mihai Antonescu in June complaining that civil officials there did not recognize their rights as Catholics.[44] Cassulo was convinced that because of the concordat, the marshal, Ion Antonescu, had decided that converted Jews would not be sent away to concentration camps like the others.[45] Thus, any such action by the local authorities would be violating the marshal's decision.

SITUATION OF THE JEWS

The problems of the Jews in Romania were far more serious and extensive than those with which Cassulo busied himself. On March 18, 1942, Richard Lichtheim of the Jewish Agency for Palestine and Gerhart Riegner of the World Jewish Congress had met with Archbishop Felipo Bernardini, the nuncio at Berne. They gave him a memorandum on the situation of the Jews in Central and Eastern Europe. It was sent the following day by Bernardini to Maglione.[46] Its importance in understanding Vatican efforts in Romania cannot be overemphasized. Concerning conditions in Romania, it related:

> Early last year [1941], at the time of the Iron Guard uprising in Romania, several thousand Jews were massacred in the streets of Romanian localities. In Bucharest alone, nearly 2,000 persons—intellectuals, officials of Jewish institutions, merchants and industrialists of repute—were killed. Revolting scenes were enacted, notably at the abattoir in Bucharest, to which the Iron Guard dragged the Jews and there slaughtered them like cattle.
>
> Most of the Jews in Bucovina, numbering 170,000, were forced to leave their homes and were transported, at the beginning of winter, in open freight cars to Russia. By the time they reached the Russian frontier, a quarter of them were already dead. The survivors were marched for six days toward Mogilev. Those who were in no condition to march were shot.
>
> During the reoccupation of Bessarabia by German and Romanian troops, 92,000 Jews were executed by firing squads. A trustworthy report on this subject says that in every town or village Jews were assembled in one place—men, women, children, the aged, the sick, even hospital patients—and having been tortured and starved for several days, were shot.[47]

On July 6, Cassulo discussed the Jewish problem at some length in a report to Maglione. In his own words, the situation of the Jews was difficult and painful, and so complex that he could make no judgment concerning it.[48] He then stated what appears as his apologia:

> With the Romanian government I have not neglected to make my voice heard in the name of charity which embraces all men, and, to tell the truth, the government in various circumstances has listened to me, also in view of the Concordat, in which baptized Jews have a valid support for that which concerns religious matters. Not always, however, are local authorities able or willing to interpret in the same spirit the regulations emanating from the government, which, by itself, while it is inclined to eliminate the abuses of a sad past, would not be so cruel in the measures adopted . . .
>
> Because of the delicacy of such a problem, it is better for me to always proceed cautiously because it might be possible to hurt rather than to be of service to so many unfortunate people whom I must often listen to, comfort and assist. They believe that the Nuncio can do all, on this point. All is done which is possible, so as to make known in these times how the Catholic Church is the only one which can intervene in the name of God on behalf of so many suffering people; a fact which is recognized by all.[49]

PROBLEMS OVER THE BAPTIZED JEWS

Difficulties over baptized Jews developed soon after. During July 1942, inspectors from the Ministry of Religion asked officials of the Bucharest archdiocese to give them their baptismal registers so that they could ascertain the details of the Jewish baptisms. The archbishop of Bucharest, supported by the nuncio, refused, maintaining that in the administration of the sacraments the Church was entirely free and that no governmental or police power had any right to intervene. The archbishop, however, did provide the government officials with lists of names of those baptized.[50]

Another reminder of the Church's liberty in the area of sacraments was sent by the nunciature to the government on August 7, 1942.[51] On August 22, the government reiterated its right and need to exercise control over these conversions. At the same time, the government assured the Vatican diplomats that they should not view these regulations as an attack against the Catholic religion in Romania.[52] This obviously was the way in which the Vatican had interpreted the August 22 decision.

The decision had been issued by the minister of foreign affairs but was actually the result of the efforts of the minister of cults, Ion Petrovici, who was quite hostile to the Vatican. Petrovici was convinced, Cassulo thought, not only that were the Jews using conversion as a means to escape the racial legislation, but also that the Church was encouraging these baptisms against the best interests of the country.[53] In fact, Petrovici had solidified his position by obtaining the agreement of several other ministers to the opinion that the Church had no privileges which would exempt it from the decree of March 18, 1941, forbidding the conversion of Jews.[54]

The confrontation of government and Church became more pronounced when the foreign minister informed the nunciature, on September 30, 1942, that the government would not recognize the baptisms of the Jews of northern Bukovina and Bessarabia that had taken place during the year of Soviet occupation.[55] This was a complete repudiation of the nunciature's statement a few weeks earlier that the baptisms were fully valid in the eyes of the Church.[56]

The Vatican would not accept this restriction. On October 3 the nuncio was ordered to inform the government of the Vatican's regret at this decision. In addition, he was directed to point out that, while the Romanian bishops were obliged to obey the nation's laws, these laws could not violate the articles of the concordat.[57] Again, on October 29, the nuncio was charged with intervening on behalf of the rights of converted Jews.[58]

THREAT OF DEPORTATION

The summer of 1942 was a time of serious danger for the Jews of

Romania. Both Ion and Mihai Antonescu had agreed to the deportation of the Jews of Old Romania and Transylvania, and the Germans had scheduled it to begin on September 10.[59]

PROTEST BY THE NUNCIO

In the middle of August 1942, the minister of the interior had announced that all the Jews would be deported. This news caused great panic among the Jews; and even though the deportations did not actually occur, the Jews were unaware of any change of plans. For months great fear prevailed among them. At this time also, Cassulo, together with the Swiss minister, René de Week, protested to the government in unequivocal terms.[60]

Another sign of the terror that existed among the Jews during these months was a report from the Jewish community of Bucharest to Jewish organizations in foreign countries during September 1942. They used this means to beg their fellow Jews to influence the Vatican and the Red Cross to intervene on their behalf.[61]

After the visit of Lecca, to Berlin, Romanian interest in the deportations appeared to dwindle in spite of pressure from the Germans. As Hilberg writes:

> The finality of the Romanian reversal was not immediately apparent because the frustration of the deportations was not accompanied by an immediate cancellation of all the preparatory measures that had been taken up to the summer of 1942. The Jewish community was still suffocating in the grip of the interrupted destruction process, and that grip was not relaxed. There was even a small deportation across the Dniester in September 1942 . . .[62]

At the beginning of autumn 1942 Safran and his colleagues had no knowledge of such changes. They were convinced that the deportations were imminent and that the whole process was to be completed by the following spring. In desperation Safran appealed to Cassulo, with whom he had maintained close contact. So convinced was the rabbi of the forthcoming catastrophe that he prevailed upon the nuncio to change his ordinary approach to the government and to make a "decisive gesture" which, if successful, could save thousands of lives.

There is no record in the Vatican documents, but according to Safran, Cassulo's dramatic action was a meeting with Ion and Mihai Antonescu, during which he questioned them about their right to make decisions regarding the lives of innocent people. The only concession he obtained from them was the assurance that the question of the deportation of the Jews would be discussed by the ministerial council. Safran also claims that he influenced the nuncio to go to Rome after this to discuss the matter with his superiors there.[63]

FEARS FOR ROMANIAN JEWS

In October 1942, writing to various Jewish organizations from Geneva, Riegner and Lichtheim suggested that public denunciations of Nazi crimes should be encouraged. They were especially insistent that this be done immediately in the case of Romania because of the new anti-Jewish laws and the deportations to Transnistria.[64]

Similar fears were expressed in a report from the nuncio in Switzerland to Maglione at the end of October. Bernardini had been given an account of the sufferings of the Jews of Romania by the leaders of the Swiss Jewish community. He was asked to send the report to the Secretariat of State and to influence the Vatican to intervene to bring about a mitigation of "the barbarous measures taken against non-Aryans."[65] Two months later, on January 14, 1943, a resumé of this report was sent by the secretary of state to Cassulo. He was directed, first, to ascertain the veracity of the report, and, if true, to prudently and charitably intervene "to mitigate such measures so in contrast with the teaching of Christian morality."[66]

It was during this same period, on September 23, that Maglione informed Cassulo that the Vatican had received word that the Jews of Transylvania would soon be deported to Transnistria. His concern, however, was limited to the 3,000 or 4,000 among them who had been Catholics for several years. He authorized his representative to intercede with the government for at least a mitigation of these regulations. Maglione's reasoning is startling.

I again appeal to Your Excellency to please use your good offices once again with the government for the purpose of obtaining at least a mitigation of the provisions feared. Please make clear the particularly unhappy situation which would be created in this matter for those citizens of the Jewish race who had embraced the Catholic religion and were good members thereof.[67]

Cassulo responded to Maglione on October 2 that he expected even harsher racial measures. He blamed the situation on an "Orthodox-nationalist spirit" which was so deeply rooted that it easily ignored the rights of anyone differing with it. For the nuncio, however, the central problem remained the government's usurpation of the right to limit or prevent baptisms.[68]

Cassulo traveled to Rome shortly after and was received by Pope

Pius XII on October 9, 1942.[69] There can be no doubt that he was also involved in consultation with Maglione and other officials.

INTERVENTION BY THE NUNCIO

On his return, the nuncio addressed a long memorandum, dated November 24, 1942, to the minister of foreign affairs. It is disappointing in that it limits itself, except for one remark, to the ecclesiastical question of the rights of baptized Jews. Cassulo wrote:

> Since the time that the Royal Romanian Government has felt obliged to examine the Jewish question in Romania under its different aspects and to provide a solution in the interest of the country, the Holy See, beyond any other consideration, has been occupied with only two things: the respect to be assured to every innocent person, abandoned and without support, and respect and safeguards for the free exercise of the Catholic religion, founded upon divine right, and guaranteed by the first article of the Concordat.
>
> To this effect, when the first dispositions of the laws appeared, the Holy See had believed that it was its duty to examine these measures, *not regarding their civil effects,* but in that which concern the baptism and conversion of Jews to the Catholic faith . . .[70]

Mihai Antonescu did not long delay in replying to the nuncio's complaints. He justified the decision of August 22 as being founded upon the principles of canon law and the statues of the Romanian Orthodox Church. Nevertheless, the Romanian government would give the most careful consideration to the nuncio's remarks because it wished to remain faithful both to Christian principles and to its concordat with the Holy See.[71]

IMPROVEMENT OF CONDITIONS

On December 16, 1942, Cassulo wrote to Maglione and attributed the changed attitude to an intervention by the prime minister himself. He had a wider view of things than the typical Orthodox mentality and was anxious to continue good relations with the Vatican.[72] The nuncio concluded:

> Therefore, it seems to me that, in consequence of the response obtained, it has been possible to put the question of the Jews, whether in part, concerning those baptized, or on the whole, in all its complexity, on a less threatening level.[73]

A report from the Jewish community in Bucharest at the same time echoed this sentiment and described the Jewish situation as "visibly better." The change was attributed to a recent massacre of Jews, the news of which might have made the government more receptive to the pressing diplomatic efforts in their regard, especially those of the Vatican.[74]

Another contemporary report from Romania mentioned three possible explanations for the suspension of the deportations. One explanation was that the Swiss embassy had passed on a note of protest from the United States government threatening grave reprisals against Romania for its anti-Semitic actions. Another version gave the credit to Cassulo, who had intervened with the government. The third possibility was that the government, and especially the marshal, was so disturbed by the news that the earlier deportees had been shot by the Germans that it decided to suspend the deportations.[75]

TRIENNIAL REPORT OF THE NUNCIO

On the last day of 1942 Cassulo wrote his triennial report to Maglione.[76] In it he attributed much of the hostility toward the Jews to the members of the Iron Guard. Again, however, he appears to raise to the level of divine will the atrocities committed against the Jews.

A number of Jews, in view of the fact that there was no escape and that they were in immediate danger of even losing their lives, were determined to become Christians, partially, I believe, for human reasons, partially moved also by supernatural motives because for a time they had already been in contact with Catholics and were only awaiting a propitious moment to embrace the Catholic faith.[77]

As the words of a diplomat, especially of a man who had already served in diplomatic posts on two continents, this statement is baffling. It portrays a naïveté more suitable to a simple and ordinary country priest than to one of ecclesiastical and diplomatic rank. In the same report Cassulo lauded his own activity. Speaking in the third person, he wrote:

It is a fact recognized by all that what has been able to render less harsh the conditions created by the measures taken against the Jews has been the work of the Nuncio, who put himself above every human interest and political consideration, and influenced only by a sentiment of charity, has displayed serene and paternal action in the presence of the government and all others, obtaining that in the area of the interests and rights of the baptized Jews, the consideration might be given them which is due to all Catholic faithful.[78]

1943

Maglione was still apprehensive about governmental respect for the rights of the Church, even after Cassulo's report of December 16. He advised the nuncio, on January 14, 1943, to watch carefully to ascertain whether the government put into practice what it had promised.[79]

MEETING WITH MIHAI ANTONESCU

The cardinal's advice was timely, as Cassulo reported to him a month later. The Ministry of Cults had indeed attempted to impose new restrictions. This time not only did Cassulo send a note of protest to Mihai Antonescu but also arranged a meeting with him on February 13, and through his influence the directives were withdrawn.[80]

The foreign minister's desire to maintain good relations with the Vatican was also evident in a letter to Cassulo of February 19. He described himself as having great appreciation for the work of the Holy See even though he was an Orthodox Christian. He assured the nuncio that the government wanted to remain faithful to the concordat.[81] The letter had a unique importance in the eyes of Cassulo, because, he reported to Maglione, it was a clear declaration of respect for the rights of the Church.[82]

Of far greater importance to Jews, however, was another action of Cassulo during this meeting with Antonescu. He presented him with the report that had come to the Vatican from the Swiss Jewish community.[83] Antonescu informed the nuncio that he himself had been considering aid for the Jews in Transnistria and did not want to appear as their persecutor.[84]

CONTACTS WITH JEWISH OFFICIALS

Of equal interest in Cassulo's report to Maglione are his references to meetings he had with Romanian Jewish leaders. One of them, the president of the Jewish Community of Romania, had visited him twice previously to thank him "for the assistance and protection of the Holy See on behalf of his co-religionists, asking . . . [him] to transmit to the Holy Father the gratitude of all his community that in these difficult times it had in the Nunciature an effective support."[85]

The editors of the Vatican documents indicate in a footnote that the "president" referred to was the chief rabbi of Bucharest, Alexandre Safran. This may be accurate because the chief rabbi and the nuncio had kept in contact. There remains some doubt, however. Two weeks later, Cassulo mentioned Safran by name in a letter to Maglione and identified him as the chief rabbi of Bucharest, who wanted his gratitude and that of his community brought to the attention of the Pope.[86] The lack of such identification in the earlier report, when it would have been expected, might indicate that it was not the same person and that the editors erred.

It could not have been Dr. Gingold, the president of the government-sponsored rubber-stamp Jewish organization,[87] because he is referred to in another context in the same report. It appears, therefore, that the "president" to whom the nuncio referred might have been William Filderman, the long-time president of the Federation of Jewish Organizations in Romania. His federation had been dissolved in December 1941, but he remained an active and outspoken advocate of Jewish rights until his own deportation to Transnistria in May 1943.

Two other facts are pertinent. Early in June, Archbishop Amleto Cicognani, the apostolic delegate to the United States, sent to the Vatican a request from an American Jewish leader, Rabbi Stephen Wise. It was an appeal for intervention in favor of Filderman, who had recently been condemned to forced labor in a concentration camp in Transnistria.[88] The Vatican documents give no specific indication that this matter was brought to Cassulo's attention, but another source records that the nuncio did work for his release.[89]

There is, however, an intriguing reference in the Vatican publication to the case of "Doctor X," who, the nuncio wrote on August 18, was free and living in Bucharest. It did not appear that the government had been too severe on him and, he added, "perhaps his efforts on behalf of his Jewish co-religionists would be more effective if he used less strong and aggressive language in dealing with the government."[90] This could certainly refer to Filderman, but an absolute statement to that effect is not possible. It is possible that the "president" referred to in the dispatch of February 14 and the "Doctor X" of August 18 report are both Filderman.

The second pertinent fact is that there is ample evidence to show that Filderman did appreciate the Vatican's efforts for the Jews. In May 1944 he wrote to the American, British, and Soviet ambassadors in Turkey about obtaining aid for the Jewish refugees in Romania. He especially sought the assistance of neutral countries because, as he wrote:

In the struggle that I have carried on to alleviate the severity of the anti-Jewish measures and to assure the maintenance of the conditions of life for the Jewish community of Rumania, the support of the neutral countries has been of real importance to achieve some of the results obtained. The Jews of Rumania are particularly grateful to His Excellency, Archbishop Andrea Cassulo, the Papal Nuncio, to . . . Minister of Switzerland, and to Messrs . . . delegates of the International Red Cross.[91]

The question of who it was in the Jewish community who expressed gratitude to the Vatican is not an idle exercise. If it was indeed

Filderman, it would be a well-informed and authoritative acknowledgment of the nuncio's assistance by a man whose leadership among Romanian Jews was unchallenged for decades. If it was Rabbi Safran, it remains an impressive tribute, but without the same value.

CALM SITUATION

The situation of the Jews in the early part of 1943 remained fairly calm. This was the information transmitted by Cassulo to Maglione in this same report of February 14. The nuncio had been told this by Gingold, the government-appointed Jewish leader, whom the nuncio described as the official representative of the baptized and unbaptized Jews and, *mirabile dictu,* a baptized Catholic himself for over a year.[92]

A similar assessment of the situation in Romania was sent by Bernardini to Maglione on April 8. He had received a report from Dr. Abraham Silberschein, president of the Committee for the War-Stricken Jewish Population, indicating an amelioration of the condition of Romanian Jewry and attributing this to steps taken by the Vatican.[93] The nuncio himself was described as taking "noble and effective steps ... to relieve the misery of Jews in Rumania."[94]

TRANSNISTRIA

The situation in Transnistria was entirely different, however; the Jews there were in desperate straits. Of the 180,000 originally deported there in October 1941, only 75,000–80,000 remained alive in the spring of 1943. In addition, 8,000 youths had been orphaned.[95]

The deportees in Transnistria were spread out in five areas, in ninety different places. Some lived in labor camps, some in secluded ghettos, and some in relatively free Jewish settlements. They had no possessions, no food, and no money. In some places, twenty or thirty people slept on the floor of one unheated room. Many of the survivors were starving.[96]

On March 1, 1943, Cassulo met with Safran, who presented him with an account and photographs of the Transnistrian situation.[97] By this time the nuncio had received a sum of money from the Vatican to be disbursed during the Easter visit he was planning to make to the camps for prisoners-of-war and civilian internees.[98] This was to be a follow-up to his visits to prisoner-of-war camps in June and July 1942.[99] During his discussion with Safran, the nuncio did not think it opportune to mention either the money or the proposed journey.[100]

TRIP OF THE NUNCIO TO TRANSNISTRIA

On April 6, Cassulo discussed the trip with Mihai Antonescu and final details were arranged. The foreign minister gave the impression of being very pleased with the proposed first-hand opportunity for the nuncio to see personally how conditions were. He did admit, however, that attempts would be made to improve conditions before Cassulo arrived.[101]

The archbishop's journey lasted from April 27 to May 5, 1943. He traveled to Tiraspol, Odessa, Chisinau, Cernauti, and Mogilev.[102] At the prisoner-of-war camp at Tiraspol, he also visited the Jewish section, which he described in this way to Maglione:

It is a task, also this, to which the Romanian government dedicates its attention doing what is possible so that they [the Jews] may have the necessities of life, clothing and health. The activity is reduced and modest, but is not lacking in the care which their condition and the circumstances of the moment demand. I went into all the rooms in the workshops, interesting myself in the needs of the prisoners, whom I later assembled and addressed with words suitable for the occasion, emphasizing that I was there in their midst by the command of the Holy Father who had not forgotten them in his paternal interest, and was anxious to make them aware of his love. I saw on the face of all a ray of true joy and great satifaction.[103]

In his visit to Chisinau, formerly a great Jewish center, the nuncio noted that all the Jewish homes had been burned and destroyed by their owners when they retreated with the Soviet troops. In Mogilev, he met a group of non-Jewish paupers who complained against the Jews administering the town.[104]

It must be admitted that Cassulo's description of his trip is disappointing and hardly appears the work of an astute observer. It should be remembered, however, that the archbishop was a man of seventy-three years at this time. Nevertheless, the journey had several long-range effects other than the immediate purpose of signifying to the Romanian government the Vatican's interest in the welfare of these people.

First of all, the nuncio's trip was a morale-booster for the Jews of Old Romania, who were much impressed by his travels. Cassulo was depicted as one who had undertaken a difficult task to bring both material comfort and moral encouragement to the Jews in Transnistria. One report claimed that all Jews felt profound gratitude toward the Pope and the nuncio. Indeed, in the eyes of some, the nuncio's gesture was seen as an expression of God's own goodness to those who suffer.[105]

JEWISH CHILDREN

A more practical effect of the trip was Cassulo's letter to Mihai Antonescu on May 18, 1943. He asked that the government study the possibility of the emigration of the 8,000 orphans in the province, 5,000 of whom had lost both parents. More than that, the Vatican diplomat requested that in the meantime, while the proposal was being considered, these children be returned to Romania proper and given over to the care of Jewish families.[106]

During May also, Chaim Barlas, the representative of the Jewish Agency for Palestine in Istanbul, sent an appeal to Archbishop Francis Spellman of New York, who was then in Istanbul. Barlas wanted him to encourage the Vatican to approach the Romanian government to grant exit visas for Jews who had the real possibility of settling in Palestine.[107]

About this same time, too, appeals were being issued by the Transnistrian Jews stating that they would be saved only by emigration. They called upon the Holy See and the Red Cross to do all possible for them in this regard.[108]

AGREEMENT REACHED ON BEHALF OF JEWS

Another result of Cassulo's trip was the agreement he reached with Lecca on ten points. They were based on appeals made to the archbishop during his journey and also on requests from Safran. In his report to Maglione on June 6, 1943, the diplomat listed the ten points to which the government consented: the limitation of any more deportations; the transfer of Jews from German-controlled territory in northern Transnistria to Romanian-controlled territory in the west; serious efforts to protect the lives of the deportees; the return of certain privileged persons; expansion of the ghettos; medicine and clothing from the Red Cross; the shipment from Bucharest of food and other products at official prices; freedom to exercise a trade; remuneration for labor; and the right to correspondence. In addition to all of this, Lecca assured Cassulo that a number of orphans would be sent to Palestine.[109]

Unlike many of the other promises, the involvement of the Red Cross in Transnistria does appear to have been realized. In April it was the understanding of the Red Cross that Jews would be permitted to leave Romania if there were a destination to which they could go.[110] This, of course, may have meant only Romania proper, and not the annexed territories. In June the Geneva office of the Red Cross informed its London delegate that it had been informed that assistance could now be sent to the Transnistrian Jews and that it was planning to send representatives there to control the distribution of the aid.[111]

The apostolic delegate in Turkey, Archbishop Angelo Roncalli, also interested himself in the Jews of Romania, sending to the Secretariat of State a list of names of Jewish families in Transnistria who were deserving of help.[112] The list was later sent to Cassulo, who acknowledged receipt of it on July 14, at the same time expressing his thought that little could be done to assist the persons named. In fact, he stated, in the past several days many Jewish families had been transferred from Transnistria across the Bug River to an unknown area.[113] This information must refer to a small group or may actually have been erroneous because such deportations are not mentioned elsewhere.

COMPLAINTS ABOUT THE JEWS

A truly amazing complaint reached Cassulo in July. The bishop of Timisoara, where the majority of people were ethnic Germans, criticized the Information Service of the Vatican as being partial to Jews. The members of his diocese saw this as a sign of hostility to the German people. Cassulo felt constrained to ask Maglione if the service in that area could be suspended to avoid further bad will.[114]

Maglione replied on August 20 that the Vatican's Information Service made no religious or ethnic distinctions in providing its assistance. It was not a question of preference but the simple fact that so many Jews were living or had lived in Romania and their relatives elsewhere were seeking news of them. Actually, the Jewish use of the service was not that one-sided. According to the cardinal, during July and August there were 130 replies to Jews and 117 to others.[115]

It should be noted that the Vatican Information Service as a whole handled thousands of messages to and from Jews. For example, in 1942 there were 48,000 requests for information, and in 1943, 33,000. Conversely, in 1942, 11,000 messages were sent out, with the figure rising to 21,000 in 1943.[116]

CONVERTED JEWS OF CERNAUTI

Two matters concerned the nuncio during the last months of 1943. One was the problem of the converted Jews in Cernauti and other cities, whom the local authorities continued to treat as if they were still Jews. An exchange of letters between Cassulo and Mihai Antonescu in September dealt with this problem.[117] By December the Vatican representative had obtained more reassurance from the government and informed Maglione that he hoped for an end to all problems concerning the baptized Jews.[118]

EMIGRATION OF JEWISH CHILDREN

The second concern of Cassulo involved the removal of Jewish children from Transnistria to Palestine. He had already discussed this with Mihai Antonescu[119] and on September 6 wrote to him again about it. The nuncio had been informed that all was prepared for the transfer and that only governmental permission was lacking. This he requested of Antonescu,[120] who, however, shortly afterwards had to tell him that his information was erroneous. Indeed, no concrete proposals for the emigration of the children had yet been submitted to the government.[121] A few days later Cassulo sent Antonescu another note describing the conditions for the transfer of the children and asked the minister to judge whether they met the governmental criteria or not.[122]

The question of the emigration of the 5,000 orphans had risen earlier, in January 1943, when Zionist leaders in Romania were convinced that the government would allow them to emigrate if they were able to procure entry visas from Great Britain for Palestine, and transit visas from Bulgaria and Turkey.[123] A later report, in July, confirmed that the Romanian government was still prepared to allow the departure, but the Bulgarian government would not grant the transit visas. The writer of the report added that it was absolutely necessary for the Vatican and the Red Cross to intervene directly with Berlin.[124]

The nuncio's involvement in the emigration projects, whether of children or all the Jews in Transnistria, is attested to in various ways. In the summer of 1943, for example, he received a request that "papal passports" be given to the baptized Romanian Jews.[125] In addition, among the proposals presented to the government in November 1943 for the liberation of the Jews of Transnistria was one that they be transported in Romanian ships to their destination. Allegedly, "the papal representative in Romania had agreed to permit the ships transporting the refugees to fly the Vatican flag "as well as the Red Cross emblem.[126] The proposals themselves originated with Lecca, were supported by Gingold, and reportedly had German approval.[127]

Another of the proposals was that the Jews would first be brought back to Bucharest from Transnistria to await their departure. This, at least, was partially accomplished. By February 1944, almost 7,000 Jews had returned to Bucharest.[128] It is Safran's contention that it was Cassulo who brought this problem of repatriation to the attention of the government.

Cassulo, who was a noble friend of our people, did not pause till he had obtained a confirmation of repatriation from Antonescu. It once happened that he appeared before him twice in one day on that same urgent matter, and I remember how, when he returned from Antonescu with "the paper"—a copy of the confirmation—in his hand he showed it to me, he was weeping for joy, and thanked me for having vouchsafed to him the fulfillment of so great a moral duty, so that he could lay up merit in heaven. . . . But after repatriation had begun, Marshal Antonescu revealed signs of changing his mind. "Scoundrels do not repent even on the threshold of hell." But Cassulo still remained undaunted. . . . And a short while later Antonescu fell, and Israel's dignity was restored. [129]

In addition to all his diplomatic efforts, Cassulo was also the intermediary of a sum of money from Pius XII to Mihai Antonescu to be used for the aid of the Jews of Transnistria. [130]

RENEWED FEAR FOR JEWS

The early months of 1944 were a time of renewed fear for the Jews remaining in Transnistria because of the German army's retreat before the Soviets. Rabbi Isaac Herzog in Jerusalem appealed to Roncalli in Istanbul to bring this to the attention of the Vatican. [131] This influenced Roncalli to discuss the situation in Transnistria with Barlas, the representative of the Jewish Agency in Istanbul. Barlas informed Roncalli that in the confusion of the Soviet advance only small groups of Jews had been able to escape. Barlas indicated, moreover, that the Turkish government would supply a ship for 1,500 refugees and assure them of entry into Palestine. The Romanian government, however, would have to organize the transport. Roncalli was asked to use his influence with Cassulo to accomplish this. [132] The Vatican records for 1944 are not available and, therefore, the disposition of these appeals is not known.

There is also evidence that Cassulo, along with the representatives of other countries, served as a mediator in attempting to obtain an armistice during the closing months of the war. Jewish leaders were aware of these efforts and, in fact, Filderman had drawn up a list of Jewish demands. The details of the nuncio's intervention, or the depth of his involvement, however, remain unknown. [133]

Conclusions

The nuncio in Bucharest was possibly the most active of the Vatican diplomats in matters concerning the Jews. The concordat with Romania was used by him numerous times to justify complaints to the government about the treatment of baptized Jews. Like all Vatican representatives, he viewed infringement of the rights of Jews who became Catholics as an offense against the rights of the Church and, therefore, a violation of the concordat.

In dealing with this problem, however, Cassulo betrayed a naïveté, or, perhaps, a narrow-mindedness, that appears rather strange in retrospect. He seemed to sincerely believe that the increasing number of Jewish converts was part of God's plan, even if some human factors were involved. Such an attitude attributed to anti-Semitic legislation and activities some kind of divine stamp of approval as an intermediary of divine grace. Moreover, by his own admission, the nuncio was not particularly concerned about the social aspects of the anti-Jewish legislation but only those areas in which the laws would be harmful to the baptized Jews. [134]

In the summer of 1941, Cassulo knew of the sufferings of the Jews in Bukovina and Bessarabia, and their deportation to Transnistria, but was reluctant to intervene, except for the baptized Jews, for fear of being accused of interference in the internal affairs of the country. Toward the end of 1941, he protested to the foreign minister not on behalf of the Jews, but for the sake of the converted Jews who were not being permitted to exercise their religious rights when grouped together with other Jews in the deportation processes. [135] Again, in the summer of 1942, the nuncio judged the whole situation of the Jews to be so delicate and complex that it was beyond his ability to intervene. [136]

Nevertheless, this same archbishop, who had given evidence of simplicity and obtuseness, did not hesitate to protest openly, in August and September 1942, the impending deportation of the Jews from Romania proper. [137] He did this in response to appeals from Romanian Jewish leaders, with whom he had a great rapport. Similarly, in February 1943 he brought to the attention of the foreign minister a report about the situation of the Jews in Romania which had come from a Swiss Jewish group. [138]

Cassulo visited Transnistria in the spring of 1943. Admittedly, his report was amazingly optimistic, but afterwards he intervened on behalf of several thousand Jewish youths there who had lost one or both of their parents. In addition, he obtained governmental approval for a whole series of steps to be taken on behalf of the Transnistrian Jews. [139]

The nuncio, therefore, was directly involved in Jewish affairs during his tenure in Bucharest. His primary interest was, of course, the Catholic Jews, and this apparently led him to ignore or minimize at times the injustices being committed against the Jews. Moreover, for diplomatic reasons, he was reluctant to become involved, except for Jews who had become members of the Church.

Nevertheless, the nuncio responded effectively and willingly to the appeals of Jewish leaders, particularly when the Jews of Old Romania were threatened. It was these religious and lay officials of the Jewish community who considered him their greatest ally in time of peril, and it was to him that they gave the credit for the safety of the majority of Romanian Jews. In fact, Cassulo's reputation in this regard has led to his being called a "Righteous One of the Nations."[140]

It is an irony of history that the Vatican records reveal less of this activity by Cassulo than do Jewish sources. His Jewish contemporaries might have exaggerated, in those years of crisis, his influence and efforts on their behalf. The fact remains, nevertheless, that Cassulo was able to go beyond the strict lines of ecclesiastical interests and act on behalf of people who were being oppressed.

CHAPTER FIVE

France

Introduction

France had been in a state of war with Germany since September 1939. It was not until the spring of 1940 that Hitler's armies turned to invade the countries to Germany's west. The campaign in France was brief and an armistice was signed on June 23, 1940.

POLITICAL SITUATION

After the armistice with Germany, France was divided into two zones. The northern half of the country and its western Atlantic coast constituted the area occupied by German troops. The rest of the country was under the control of the government established at Vichy on July 2, 1940, with Marshal Henri-Phillipe Pétain as chief of state and Pierre Laval as vice-president.[1]

In November 1942, after the landing of Allied forces in northern Africa, the Germans extended their authority to Vichy France as well. At the same time, Italian troops occupied the southeastern section of the country.

At the beginning of the war, the Jewish population of France was 270,000. After the German conquests of Belgium, Luxembourg, and the Netherlands, 40,000 Jews from these countries fled to France. The division of the country influenced 50,000 Jews to move south to the Vichy territory. The French Jews of Alsace-Lorraine were moved to the unoccupied zone also, as well as 6,000 Jews from the western section of Germany. The final result of these population shifts was that 165,000 Jews remained in German-controlled territory, with 90 percent of them residing in Paris. In Vichy, there were 145,000 Jews.[2]

An important distinction to note here is that out of this total of 310,000 Jews, almost half were foreign-born. In addition to the Jewish refugees from the Low Countries, others from Germany, Austria, Romania, Poland, and Hungary had fled to France. Almost half of these Jews had been deprived of citizenship in their own countries and existed in France, therefore, as "stateless" persons.[3]

It is obvious that those Jews remaining in German-occupied territory were the ones in greater jeopardy. The anti-Jewish measures of the Vichy government were valid for all of France. Thus, the Jews living under German authority had to contend with legislation emanating from two sources, German as well as Vichy. The Jews in the Vichy zone were harassed only by the Vichy regulations, not by the German.[4]

RELATIONSHIP TO VATICAN

Diplomatic relations between France and the Holy See had been resumed in 1921 after a seventeen-year break. The nuncio to France from 1936 to 1944 was Archbishop Valerio Valeri. His predecessor had been Archbishop Luigi Maglione, who had been named a cardinal in 1936. In 1939, Maglione became secretary of state to the newly-elected Pope Pius XII. Valeri's previous diplomatic experience had been as apostolic delegate to Egypt, Palestine, and Arabia from 1927 to 1933, and as nuncio to Romania for the following three years.[5]

Valeri followed the French government in its move to Vichy. There is some evidence that for reasons of status, Pétain and Laval were interested in concluding a concordat between the Vichy regime and the Vatican. Certain French bishops were also in favor of the idea. Valeri, however, urged delay because he believed that the Vichy government was to be short-lived.[6] Nevertheless, the closest relations existed between the Church and the Vichy regime. Attempts were made to obtain subsidies for Catholic schools and to introduce the teaching of religion into the public schools. Pétain himself was also greatly respected and praised by various members of the hierarchy. Moreover, the Vatican gave every evidence of being favorable toward the marshal.[7]

1940–1941

RACIAL LEGISLATION

The first major anti-Jewish legislation in unoccupied France was the law of October 3, 1940. It defined a Jew as someone with three Jewish grandparents, or with two if he was also married to a Jew. In addition, Jews were banned from parliament, governmental positions, the judiciary, the military, and from positions influencing cultural life.[8] A few days before this, the Germans had begun enforcing racial regulations in their zone.[9]

The nuncio wrote to Luigi Maglione, the cardinal secretary of state, on October 4, 1940, indicating that the government was preparing more legislation concerning the Jews. This Valeri attributed to the desire to imitate the totalitarian countries, which had already passed such measures, and also because "without a doubt, unfortunately, the Jews have contributed as much as they could to the outbreak of the war."[10]

Valeri also commented that he expected that the statutes would prevent Jews from entering certain public careers and professions. The fact that the Germans had already enacted such legislation in their area would serve as a stimulus to the Vichy authorities. Moreover, the nuncio revealed to Maglione his hope and his belief that the Vichy anti-Jewish regulations would not be pushed too far. Finally, he claimed that the hierarchy of the country, and he himself indirectly, would make obvious the Christian point of view in the matter.[11]

There can be little doubt that Valeri was referring to the law of October 3, about which he had not yet been officially informed. The editors of the Vatican documents, however, note that the legislation referred to by Valeri was passed on October 18.[12] This does not seem accurate because the October 18 regulations concerned only the occupied zone, and called for the registration and later expropriation of Jewish property.[13]

The Jewish statutes of October 3, 1940 were clarified and refined in the law of June 2, 1941. A Jew was now defined as such if he had three grandparents of the Jewish religion. If he had two grandparents Jewish in religion, and if he himself or his spouse was of the Jewish religion, he was categorized as Jewish. Religion was made the criterion of Jewishness. A person would be considered of the Jewish religion in the absence of proof that his grandparents belonged to the Catholic, Protestant, Orthodox, or Islamic faith.[14]

The statutes of June 2, 1941 also prepared the way for the expropriation of Jewish property, and required a census of Jews and their property. The positions prohibited to Jews were increased and quotas were placed on the areas in which Jews could be employed.[15]

It is noteworthy that the promulgation of the Statute on the Jews was not protested specifically and officially by the French bishops. Xavier Vallat, the commissioner for Jewish affairs at Vichy, claimed that he took this as a sign of tacit consent by the French episcopate and the Vatican to the anti-Jewish measures. During his trial after the war,

Vallat maintained that had any authorized representative of the French hierarchy or of the Vatican approached him with a protest about any of the measures, he would have modified it.[16]

BÉRARD'S LETTER

At the beginning of August 1941, Marshal Pétain wrote to the French ambassador to the Holy See, Léon Bérard, to ascertain whether there would be any objections from the Vatican to the recent or proposed French anti-Jewish legislation. In a preliminary response, Bérard indicated that nothing had been said to him disapproving it. Bérard's definitive and lengthy reply was sent to Pétain on September 2, 1941.[17] It contained five sections and purported to be an exhaustive treatment of the Church's attitudes toward the Jews. Its importance rests not on the accuracy of all its details but on the implication that it removed from Pétain's mind any doubts he might have had about the Christian reaction to the racial legislation.[18]

Bérard's first section was devoted to "The Church and Racism." He informed the marshal that there existed a fundamental conflict between racial theories and Church doctrine, which taught that one Savior died for the redemption of all men, and that all are equally endowed with a soul and called to salvation. Nevertheless, the ambassador concluded, even though the Church condemned racism, it did not follow that it necessarily repudiated every measure taken by particular countries against the Jews. There were certain nuances and distinctions that ecclesiastical authorities made in this regard.[19]

The second part of Bérard's letter was entitled "The Church, the Jewish Problem and Anti-Semitism." Having first acknowledged that there did not exist any well-defined doctrine on the Jews, the ambassador noted that the fundamental principle was, in the view of the Church, that once a Jew was baptized, he ceased to be a Jew. He was then a Christian, with all the rights and responsibilities of that status. Nevertheless, Bérard added, the Church recognized that religion was not the only distinguishing characteristic of Jews, but that there were also certain ethnic, not racial, factors that set them apart as well.

The French ambassador concluded that, historically, the Church's practice and feeling over the centuries had been that Jews should not have authority over Christians. It was legitimate, therefore, to prohibit them from certain public offices and to restrict their entry into universities and professions. He recalled also that ecclesiastical law had required the Jews to wear distinctive garb.[20]

In a third section, dealing with the difficulties between the Italian government and the Vatican over the Jewish legislation, Bérard demonstrated that the problem was a usurpation of what the Church considered its rights over marriage. The concordat between Italy and the Vatican had granted civil recognition of Church marriages. The new racial legislation prohibited marriages between Christians and Jews. The Church felt that it had the authority to perform such marriages, if the Jewish partner had been baptized or if an ecclesiastical dispensation had been obtained. In France, Bérard believed, there would not be similar problems because the circumstances were different.[21]

The fourth part of the letter searched for contradictions between Catholic doctrine and the law of June 2, 1941. Bérard envisioned only one possible conflict. The law of June 2 replaced that of October 3 in attempting to define Jewishness. A Jew with two Jewish grandparents, who had been baptized before June 25, 1940, was legally recognized as a non-Jew. If, however, he had three Jewish grandparents, his conversion would not be recognized and he would remain juridically a Jew. On this point there was, according to the ambassador, a contradiction between Church doctrine and French law.[22]

Bérard's views were reassuring to the marshal. He stated that representatives of the Vatican had expressed two hopes regarding the legislation:

1. That no regulations concerning marriage be added to the law on the Jews. This is the area in which we would run into religious difficulties. Officials at the Vatican were greatly distressed when Romania enacted on this point legislation inspired by, or imitating, Fascist legislation.
2. That the precepts of justice and charity be taken into account in the application of the law. Those with whom I discussed this appeared to me most concerned about the liquidation of businesses in which the Jews have interests.[23]

MEETINGS OF VALERI AND PÉTAIN

On September 14, shortly after he received this letter, Pétain gave a dinner in honor of the diplomatic corps. During the meal he told the nuncio about the report from Bérard and claimed that it indicated that the Vatican, while not pleased with the harshness of some of the racial regulations, was not going to make any comments on them.[24]

By his own description, Valeri was very disturbed by Pétain's remarks, especially because they were uttered in the presence of the Brazilian and Spanish ambassadors. He replied to the marshall "that the Holy See had already made clear its ideas on the racism that lies at the basis of all the regulations taken in regard to the Jews and that, therefore, Bérard could not have expressed himself in such a simple manner."[25] Pétain jestingly retorted that the nuncio was not in accord with the mind of his superiors.[26] In making this statement, he was possibly thinking of his ambassador's claim that he had discussed the matter with Vatican officials.

The question arises, of course, as to the identity of Bérard's sources at the Vatican. According to an office note of Maglione attached to Valeri's report, Bérard had informed him that he had discussed the subject with Monsignors Domenico Tardini and Giovanni Montini, the two principal assistants to the secretary of state.[27] Apparently, Bérard must have had some discussion with these officials and they were the "superiors" of Valeri to whom Pétain referred. That they were as explicit as Bérard said seems doubtful. In a later letter to Valeri, Maglione did verify that the French ambassador had brought up the matter in the Secretariat of State, but he did not reveal to the nuncio the names of Tardini and Montini. In the same context, the cardinal expressed his opinion that Pétain had exaggerated the contents of the letter to help justify his statues against the Jews.[28]

On September 26, the nuncio met with Pétain, who gave him a copy of Bérard's letter. It was forwarded, of course, to the secretary of state with the remark by Valeri that it was far more "nuanced" than Pétain had led him to believe. The nuncio also expressed the opinion that it appeared to be the work of an ecclesiastic.[29]

On the same occasion, Valeri presented Pétain with a note pointing out the grave problems from a religious point of view that could arise from the legislation already in force.[30] Pétain's reply was exculpatory. He himself deplored many of the provisions taken against the Jews and those that might be required by the Germans in the future. He did not see, though, how he could modify or revoke them before peace was reached. Valeri concluded from this that the marshal wanted his ambassador's remarks readily available to use as an argument in favor of the eventual modification of the anti-Jewish legislation.[31]

Shortly afterward, a report came to Vallat from the Information Service that there had been accounts in foreign newspapers that the Pope had sent a handwritten letter to Pétain expressing his disapproval of the French anti-Jewish legislation.[32] The rumors of Vatican disapproval were squelched in a statement issued by the Commissariat for Jewish Affairs on October 14: ". . . from information obtained from the most authoritative sources, there is nothing in the legislation worked out for the protection of France from Jewish influence which is in opposition to Church doctrine."[33]

The subject of the Jews arose again in Valeri's report to Maglione of

December 15, 1941. German soldiers in Paris had been attacked, and the German occupation authorities blamed the incident on Jewish Bolsheviks. The nuncio listed the three forms of reprisal decreed by the Germans: a fine imposed on the Jewish community; deportation of a large number of Jews; and one hundred "Jewish Bolsheviks" to be shot.[34]

The matter was discussed further by the nuncio and the marshal at a meeting on December 17, 1941. Since the incident had occurred in the occupied zone, neither one could do anything. Pétain did inform the archbishop that the hostages had not yet been shot. He claimed that he was trying to dissuade the German authorities from such reprisals because they served to enrage the population and to influence them to greater acts of hostility against the Germans.[35]

1942

DEPORTATIONS

During the early months of 1942 the Germans began their calculations for the deportation of the Jews of France. The first to go were 5,000 stateless Jews in the occupied zone, who were sent to the camp at Drancy. The quota for France was set at 100,000 and was to include Jews in the Vichy zone as well. Severe transportation problems were foreseen, but this in no way weakened the German determination to deport these Jews.[36]

REPORTS TO MAGLIONE

On July 16, 1942, 12,884 stateless Jews in Paris were rounded up for deportation. Valeri reported this to Maglione on July 29, indicating that they were mainly Polish and Czech Jews destined for deportation to the Ukraine. He wrote:

This measure and the cruel way in which it was executed by the occupation authorities, has made a great impression upon the Parisian population, already strongly troubled by an order in force by which all Jews are obliged to wear the star of David on their arm. Above all, that which has affected the people the most was the decision to separate children hardly over two years of age from their parents.[37]

The nuncio added that the French hierarchy had voted against any public protest for fear that the Catholic Action movement, up to then tacitly allowed, would be prohibited. The bishops did decide that Cardinal Célestin Suhard, the archbishop of Paris, should send a letter on their behalf to Pétain.[38]

The letter of the French bishops to Pétain indicated the shock that they felt at the cruel treatment inflicted upon the Jews. They issued their protest, as they said, based on both humanitarian and Christian principles. They also reminded the marshal of the indefeasible rights of all human beings and asked him to listen to their appeal on behalf of the Jews so that charity and justice would be respected.[39]

Valeri attached a copy of this letter to his report to Maglione. The nuncio apparently did not feel that the episcopal statement was a forceful one because he described it as "platonic."[40] It is a surprising designation for what actually was a strong condemnation of the actions taken against the Jews.

One week later, on August 7, the nuncio announced to Maglione that the measures taken against the Parisian Jews were now being extended to the unoccupied zone. Two trainloads of Jews from camps in Vichy France had already left for an unknown destination, which was, he said, generally considered to be Poland or the Ukraine. Valeri added that sick and aged Jews were also being forced to leave, thus contradicting any notion of their being sent away for labor service. This obviously upset the Jewish population.[41]

In this same dispatch, the nuncio reported that a second protest had been made to Pétain. This time, a joint commission of Catholics and Protestants had made known to him their great sorrow over the recent events affecting the Jews. Pétain's only defense was to lay the responsibility upon the Germans.[42]

Valeri concluded his report by reminding the secretary of state that he had already spoken both to the minister of foreign affairs and to the marshal himself about the tragic problem of the Jews. As far as is known, the nuncio had met with Pétain twice, on September 26[43] and December 17, 1941.[44] The latter of these meetings concerned the hostages in Paris; the former was occasioned by the Bérard letter. In his August 7, 1942 report, therefore, he was probably referring to his discussion with Pétain eleven months previously, at which time he had given Pétain a memorandum on the Jews. Given the circumstances of the summer of 1942, the nuncio's recalling of this discussion hardly appears as an adequate expression of concern for the plight of the Jews.

Finally, the nuncio stressed to Maglione:

I have not even neglected at various times to make it known, especially to

South American diplomats, that it is not true that the Holy See is enveloped in silence in the face of such inhuman persecution because many times the Holy Father has made the clearest allusion to condemn it, while on the other hand, the danger of new rigors and an extension of the draconian regulations to other parts of Europe, as, for example, Italy and Hungary, can induce him to prudent delay and enlightened reserve.[45]

RUMORS OF A PROTEST BY THE NUNCIO

At the same time as this dispatch from Valeri, a telegram arrived at the Secretariat of State from Archbishop William Godfrey, the apostolic delegate in London. The British press had asked him for an official confirmation of the rumors that the Pope had protested against the deportation of the Jews of France through the nuncio there. On August 11, Maglione cabled Godfrey that his office had received no such report from the nuncio in France and could not confirm the rumors.[46]

Such rumors appeared elsewhere also. On August 18, the German ambassador at the Vatican, Diego von Bergen, telegraphed Berlin "that the Holy See has approached the Vichy Government through the medium of the Nuncio to secure alleviation of the measures taken against Jews in France."[47]

There seems to have been no factual basis for the Godfrey and Bergen telegrams. There is no indication in the Vatican documents— and indeed there is the denial of Maglione—that Valeri was in touch with the Vichy government in the latter weeks of July or during the first half of August 1942. It may have been, perhaps, the letter of Suhard to Pétain and the protest of the joint commission that gave rise to these rumors.

A further indication that there had been no direct contact is that it was not mentioned in Valeri's report of August 14. In fact, the nuncio wrote that nothing new had developed and that the majority of the Jews remained in deportation centers awaiting further decisions. Valeri added that among all the rumors that were circulating, there was one indicating that the German authorities would allow the children to go along with their parents.[48]

Valeri's August 14 dispatch also contained a report of the recent meeting between Suhard and Laval. Laval had been dismissed from the government in December 1940 by Pétain, but had returned as head of government with wide powers in April 1942. In July, Suhard had written to both Pétain[49] and Laval.[50] The effect of both letters appeared minimal to Laval, for he quoted to Suhard a remark of Ambassador Otto Abetz, the representative of the German Foreign Ministry in

Paris, to the effect that the Pope was expected to speak out about this type of problem.[51]

MEETING OF VALERI AND LAVAL

Eventually, on August 23, the Vatican diplomat did meet with Laval, who blamed the Jews themselves for the measures taken against them. He viewed them as the cause of France's present situation and was anxious to be rid of them. Moreover, he told the nuncio that they were still actively engaged in the black market.[52] Valeri described his response to Laval in these words:

I made it clear to him, of course, that those who did harm to France are not in the concentration camps and that, on the other hand, among them there is also a goodly number of political refugees and Catholics. But I realized that all arguments were useless and that the most we can now achieve is to save some few, as I have already tried to do and successfully.[53]

Laval informed the nuncio that approximately 4,500 Jews had already been deported and that 12,000 or 13,000 remained. He mentioned, too, that Hitler had conceded that children might leave along with their parents. The French leader appeared to be defending Hitler's action when he attributed his decision to gather all the Jews together in one place to a realization that this was the only way to make them cease their anti-German propaganda.[54]

Laval's interest in matters concerning the Jews was again manifested just a few days after this meeting with Valeri. On August 27, 1942, he spoke with Monsignor Carmine Rocco, secretary of the nunciature, representing Valeri, who had become ill.[55] Laval was greatly perturbed by the pastoral letter of Archbishop Jules-Gérard Saliège of Toulouse denouncing the government's measures against the Jews.[56] So outraged was he that he suggested to the Vatican diplomat that Saliège be sent away on a retreat. In addition, he threatened to take action against diocesan organizations in Toulouse. Moreover, Laval repeated his decision to allow the deportation of all non-French Jews. He warned that he would remove by force any of them who were being given asylum in religious houses.[57] These Jews he described as being taken to "a kind of motherhouse in Poland."[58]

This same meeting of Rocco and Laval was also described by Abetz in a telegram to Berlin the following day. It does not appear from the report made to the Vatican of the discussion or from the remarks of Abetz that Rocco made any defense of Saliège, let alone a protest of the government's attitude. Abetz recorded the warning given by Laval to Rocco:

that the French government would not tolerate such interference by the Church in matters concerning the French State. Laval specifically pointed out to Rocco that should the clergy offer to hide the Jews affected by deportation measures in churches and convents, he would not hesitate to have the police round them up there. Besides, anti-Jewish measures were after all no novelty for the Church either, since it had been the Popes who had first introduced the yellow hat to distinguish people as Jews.[59]

MORE RUMORS OF A PROTEST BY THE NUNCIO

Several sources refer to a protest made by the nuncio to the government at this time. The Abetz telegram of August 28 related that Valeri had protested to Laval a few weeks before.[60] The Vatican records contain only a reference to their meeting of August 23, which must have been the one to which Abetz referred. The editors of ADSS write in their introduction:

The reports of Valeri demonstrate that on different occasions, in the course of the following weeks, he discussed the Jewish question with the various officials of Vichy to bring about a change of politics, or at least to obtain certain modifications in the deportation orders.[61]

These Vichy officials were not mentioned by Valeri in his dispatches. There is no reason to doubt that before his illness he spoke to certain authorities, but not to the chief of state himself.

Another source maintains that Valeri intervened directly with Pétain in July 1942 to express to him "his indignation at the attitude of the Laval government and the Vichy police, both of which were accomplices of the Nazis in the inhuman treatment which they were inflicting upon the Jews."[62]

The matter of the reputed protest is even more complex. On September 14, the British minister at the Vatican, Francis d'Arcy Osborne, cabled the British Foreign Office that he had received personal confirmation from Pius XII that Valeri had protested against the persecution of the Jews of France.[63] In December, a deputation of British Jews, in a letter to the foreign secretary, also mentioned as a matter of fact the intervention of the nuncio in France.[64]

On September 14 also, Bergen telegraphed the German state secretary, Ernst von Weizsäcker, that the deportation of the French Jews, and the methods involved in this process, were very disturbing to

Church authorities. Various bishops had protested, but without making reference to the Vatican. Nevertheless, the German ambassador still referred to certain actions taken by the Vatican: "The steps taken by the Holy See with the French government for the mitigation of the anti-Jewish measures have so far been without success."[65]

PROTESTS BY BISHOPS

Concomitant to all this were the reports to Maglione concerning the protests made by various French bishops.[66] In addition to Saliège, the cardinal archbishop of Lyons, Pierre Gerlier,[67] and the bishop of Montauban, Pierre Théas,[68] had issued pastoral letters protesting the government's anti-Jewish measures.[69] It should be noted, however, that in these episcopal protests, and also in those by Protestant leaders, it was not the principle of anti-Jewish legislation which was condemned, but the deportations which violated the basic rights of a human being and his family.[70]

The counselor of the nunciature, Monsignor Alfredo Pacini, acting for the ill Valeri, wrote to Maglione on September 8 informing him that the deportations were continuing. He added that the recent protests by the bishops did not appear to have affected Laval as much as the original one by Saliège. In fact, Laval had met with Henri Chappoulie, the auxiliary bishop of Paris, the preceding day and had complained to him about the attitude of certain members of the hierarchy toward the government. Chappoulie responded that the bishops in the Vichy area would be pleased to discuss the present situation with him. Laval claimed that he was open to suggestions and wanted the bishops to understand that his government was in a difficult and delicate situation.[71]

At the end of August, Chappoulie also met with Julien Weil, the chief rabbi of Paris. The rabbi was seeking the services of the bishop as an intermediary with the Vatican. Perhaps naively, perhaps in despair of any other course of action, Weil's request was only that the Vatican intervene with the German authorities to permit the deported Jews to inform their families of their condition in the east.[72]

INTERVENTION BY ORSENIGO IN BERLIN

Weil's request eventually came to Maglione's attention. On September 28, 1942, the cardinal directed the nuncio in Berlin, Archbishop Cesare Orsenigo, to look into it.[73] Orsenigo did act on the matter, and on

October 15 he brought up the subject with Ernst Woermann, director of the Political Department of the German Foreign Ministry. Woermann described the meeting in a memorandum to Weizsäcker.

Today the Nuncio, with some embarrassment, and without emphasis, brought up the fact that several inquiries had come to the Vatican from Jews who were asking about their relatives who had been forced to leave their previous residences. These inquiries were concerning Jews from France and Lemberg.

I told the Nuncio that I could give him no information regarding this question.

The Nuncio then said that he would report to Rome that he had taken up the matter here, but was unable to obtain any information.[74]

Orsenigo, of course, reported on the meeting to Maglione. His remarks make an interesting contrast to those of Woermann.

Unfortunately, the response was, as always, negative, in the sense that they cannot accept any concern manifested about regions so far distant from the Reich. Someone has suggested to me, however, to advise the interested parties that through the intermediary of a distinguished person, they should insist on the matter with the local authorities at Vichy, who, just as they were responsible for the deportations, are also obliged not to aggravate its consequences.[75]

It should be noted that Orsenigo's ability to intervene with the Berlin government was severely limited. Since the Vatican would not recognize German hegemony in its newly acquired territories as juridically and politically established, the German Foreign Ministry refused to accept any Vatican inquiries concerning people or incidents in these areas.[76]

JEWISH CHILDREN

The situation of the French Jewish children still concerned Maglione. Valeri's July 29 report had indicated that children barely above the age of two were being separated from their parents at deportation. Further information on this reached Maglione from the nuncio in Berne, Archbishop Filippo Bernardini. At the beginning of September, Bernardini wrote that a Swiss interreligious committee had met and was convinced that nothing could be done to assist the adult Jews already deported from France. As far as its members knew, children over the age of sixteen had to accompany their parents; those under that age remained in France. The committee calculated that there were from 3,000 to 5,000 orphaned children in this situation. It wanted to deal with the problem in two steps: first to place the children temporarily in

Portugal for their safety, and then to strive for their permanent placement in the countries of North and South America.[77]

The Vatican's assistance was required in that its nuncios in Portugal and other countries could prepare public opinion to accept the children. The priest who was a member of the committee and whose letter to Bernardini concerning the committee's plans was sent on to Maglione, wrote very poignantly of "these poor Jewish children, who have been separated from their parents in the course of heartrending scenes, parents who, without a shadow of doubt, they will never see again."[78] He also urged ". . . it is absolutely necessary to act quickly; it is a question of days and perhaps of hours."[79]

The cautious diplomacy of Maglione reacted to this appeal in the form of a telegram to Valeri on September 17, 1942, seeking information about the Jewish children in France.[80] Several days later, he telegraphed Bernardini that the Holy Father was greatly interested in the matter and was seeking further information from the nuncio in France.[81] The response from the nunciature in Vichy was telegraphed on September 24: "The Jewish children remaining in France have been brought together in special centers and handed over to various Jewish organizations. Other organizations are also cooperating in assisting them."[82]

The matter of these Jewish children came to the Vatican's attention from two other sources as well. First, a dispatch was received from the Vatican's chargé d'affaires at Port-au-Prince, a diplomat accredited to the governments of Haiti and the Dominican Republic. He passed on the invitation of the president of the Dominican Republic, Rafael Trujillo, to accept 3,500 Jewish children between the ages of three and fourteen from Vichy France. The president, moreover, volunteered to organize and pay for the expenses of their journey.[83]

Secondly, on September 22, Myron Taylor, the personal representative of President Roosevelt to Pius XII, had an audience with the Pope and other officials. He submitted to the Pope a memorandum outlining American efforts on behalf of French Jews. He also mentioned the plight of the children and President Trujillo's recent offer of shelter.[84]

Archbishop Angelo Roncalli, the apostolic delegate to Greece and Turkey, also became involved in attempts to aid the Jews of France. He wrote directly to Valeri from Istanbul on September 18 requesting assistance for a group of Jews living in Perpignan who were anxious to emigrate to Palestine. Roncalli expressed his doubts about the outcome of their efforts but thought that the attempt should be made.[85]

The flurry of diplomatic activity now came to an end. Valeri sent two reports to Maglione during October, both of which referred to anti-

Semitic propaganda in France. On October 9, he informed Maglione that the anti-Semites were using as precedents for their conduct certain examples of anti-Jewish treatment in the papal states. Furthermore, he indicated to the cardinal that ill health kept him confined to his residence, but assured him that he would submit a protest when he became well again.[86] The second report was sent on October 22 and described the situation as one of calm during which the Jewish question and the deportations appeared suspended.[87]

OCCUPATION OF VICHY FRANCE

After the Allied landings in North Africa on November 8, 1942, German troops occupied the rest of France, except for a zone in the southeast taken over by Italy. The peril for the Jews in this changed geographic situation was mentioned by Valeri in his report to Maglione on December 7. The nuncio also passed on a request to the Pope that he intercede with the Italian authorities not to harass the Jews living in their zone of occupation.[88] The Vatican did appeal to Mussolini on behalf of these Jews and was assured that they would not be deported.[89]

It is amazing that for the next several months there are no published reports of Valeri dealing with the subject of the Jews. It was a time during which the situation of the Jews in the former Vichy section of France deteriorated badly. Round-ups and deportations took place in Lyons, Marseille, Toulouse, and Limoges. Moreover, between 10,000 and 30,000 Jews were thought to have fled to the Italian zone.[90]

1943

JEWS MARRIED TO CATHOLICS

In February 1943, Suhard complained to Pétain about the arrests of Jews married to French Catholics. The cardinal said he did not hold the French government entirely responsible, since it was being forced to execute the orders of someone else, but he did express the hope that the carrying out of the orders be done with less severity.[91]

FOREIGN JEWS

The next time that Valeri mentioned the Jews in a dispatch was on July 16, 1943, when he wrote that a German official had confirmed to him that deportation was directed only against foreigners, and especially against foreign Jews. These Jews, he informed Maglione, were ordinarily taken to the camp at Drancy and from there to an unknown destination where all trace of them would be lost.[92] On July 31, the nuncio reported that even the French government knew nothing of the fate of the deportees.[93] Three weeks later, Valeri warned Maglione that intervention on behalf of specific people arrested by the Gestapo could make their situation all the more dangerous.[94]

DIFFICULTIES OF THE NUNCIO

The difficulties which the nuncio faced were most evident in the case of André Baur, president of the Union General des Israélites de France (General Union of the Jews of France). He had been arrested by the Germans and sent to Drancy on July 21, 1943. On October 10, acting on a request from Archbishop Amleto Cicognani, the apostolic delegate in Washington, Maglione wrote to Valeri asking him to intercede on behalf of Baur.[95] Valeri's reply was full of frustration.

I am sorry to have to tell you that, unfortunately, just as in the past, there does not exist any possibility of doing anything on behalf of non-Aryans transferred to the camp at Drancy, and from there, generally taken to Germany. Up until yesterday evening itself these authorities have always replied to me that they are completely ignorant of where and how the persons are located, having never succeeded in finding out anything even remotely precise in this regard.[96]

It is obvious that nothing that Valeri could have done would have been able to save Baur from eventual death in Auschwitz.

During August 1943, the Germans were trying to obtain French approval for a regulation canceling all grants of naturalization made to Jews after 1927. Laval himself was disturbed at the prospect.[97] Pétain was even more opposed. He had received a visit from the auxiliary bishop of Paris, Chapoulie, representing the French episcopate. The bishops wanted the marshal to know that the Pope was perturbed to learn that he was even considering new measures directed against the Jews. Moreover, Chapoulie claimed, the Pope was anxious over the salvation of the marshal's soul.[98]

The opinion of the French hierarchy was later manifested in a letter in late October from Suhard to Kurt Reichl, the secretary to Abetz. The cardinal condemned "the deportation of those Jews against whom there had been no other complaint than their belonging to a determined race."[99]

During August also the Germans were deporting the remainder of the foreign Jews and were trying to isolate the French Jews from the non-Jewish population. Some French Jews were sent to Drancy. Efforts were also made to round up the Jewish children, both those in institutions and those in hiding.[100]

JEWS IN THE ITALIAN ZONE

Of immediate concern in this period were the thousands of Jews who had fled to the Italian-occupied zone of France. On July 25, 1943, Mussolini was over-thrown. The Badoglio government, which followed, signed an armistice with the Allies early in September. Immediately afterward German troops occupied the Italian zone, trapping thousands of Jews.[101] The retreat of the Italian troops from this area had been foreseen as imminent by Jewish officials several weeks previously. At the end of July, Gerhart Riegner, president of the World Jewish Congress in Geneva, appealed to the Congress offices in London and New York to attempt to interest the Vatican in intervening to persuade the departing Italian troops to protect the Jews.[102]

There is no evidence in the Vatican documents that its representatives in Switzerland, Great Britain, or the United States were informed of this appeal or that they passed it on to Rome. It does appear, however, that the apostolic delegate in Washington might have been informed of the matter by the New York office of the World Jewish Congress and then passed on the request to Maglione. An official of the Chancery Office of the Archdiocese of New York informed the World Jewish Congress on September 9 that Maglione had cabled Cicognani, assuring him "that the Holy See had already taken steps to interest itself in the matter of the number of Jews who are being evacuated by Italian troops."[103]

ACTIVITY OF FATHER MARIE BENOÎT

The Jews of France were directly brought to the attention of the Pope during an audience he gave to a Capuchin priest, Father Marie Benoît, on July 16, 1943. The priest used the opportunity to present to the Pope a memorandum dealing with four matters concerning the Jews of France: information about deported Jews, aid for Jews in concentration camps in France, the situation of Jews of Spanish origin in France, and Jews in the Italian-occupied zone.[104]

Pius XII appeared well disposed to all of the priest's requests.[105] This benevolent attitude toward the Jews of France was very reassuring to Jewish leaders.[106] Benoît also described the Pope as being quite surprised by the actions taken by the Vichy police against the Jews. In fact, Pius went so far as to remark that he would never have thought such conduct possible of France.[107]

The Jews living in the Italian-controlled zone were a particular worry to Benoît. They were thought to number from 8,000 to 10,000 but may actually have numbered as many as 20,000.[108] The priest pointed out to the Pope that if the Germans were to take control of this area for any reason, the situation of the Jews would quickly become perilous. Since these Jews were only a few miles from the Italian border, he solicited the help of the Vatican in having them moved into Italy proper.[109]

NEGOTIATIONS FOR EVACUATION

The problem with placing these Jews in Italy was that many Italians themselves had become refugees and Italy had already established camps for 17,000 Jews from Dalmatia, Croatia, and Yugoslavia. Early in August 1943, therefore, negotiations began at the Vatican about the eventual transfer of these Jews to North Africa. Involved in the discussions were Angelo Donati, representing the Badoglio government, Osborne, the British minister to the Holy See, and Harold H. Tittmann, the assistant to Myron Taylor, the representative of President Franklin D. Roosevelt to the Pope.[110]

On August 24, Osborne informed the Foreign Office that he had met several times with Donati, who had proposed that the Jews be evacuated to Algeria, Tunisia, or Morocco.[111] The next day Osborne cabled that there were four Italian ships available which could carry 9,000 people per voyage. The expenses involved in all of this, he said, were to be taken care of by an American Jewish organization, the Joint Distribution Committee. Both the Vatican and the International Red Cross were presumed to be able and willing to help with other arrangements.[112]

On September 6, Osborne notified his government that Italy had given permission for the Jews in the formerly occupied zone to be evacuated to its own territory. The British minister added that if the Donati proposal for the transfer of Jewish refugees to northern Africa were put into effect, the Italian government would be relieved of the obligation of caring for them.[113]

Simultaneously, Tittmann had informed the American State Department of the same proposal.[114] Unlike the British documents, however, the American records do not refer to any eventual assistance from the Vatican. The American reaction was to submit the plan to the Inter-Governmental Committee on Refugees.

Since this committee could not be so quickly convened, an informal consensus of the members available was sought. Their attitude toward the project was pessimistic. They did not feel that the Italians could organize the evacuation of the refugees into Italy and that many of the refugees might not be willing to go into an area of Italy which by that time was also under German occupation. In addition, the members thought that there was no realistic hope of escape from any of the Italian ports.[115]

The role of Vatican diplomacy in these negotiations appears to have been minimal. The British and American diplomats posted at the Vatican were dealing with the Italian government with the knowledge and support of the Vatican. The Vatican's own documents contain no other reference to the proposal than the notes of Father Benoît. He had described the positive reaction of the Pope to his original proposal on July 16, but at that time only the move into Italy was being considered, not the project of transferring the Jews to north Africa.

Donati has written that these negotiations had taken place in Vatican City. He blamed the failure of the whole project on the premature announcement of the Italian armistice by General Eisenhower. This catapulted the Germans into taking actions that originally the Italian and Allied governments had hoped to prevent.[116] Nevertheless, Donati's opinion of Vatican officials was very low: ". . . the Holy See and its high officials never decided on the least initiative, and never did anything to alleviate the situation of the Jews."[117] According to this account, therefore, the Vatican's involvement and assistance must have been minimal.

JEWS OF SPANISH ORIGIN

In his audience with the Pope, Benoît also broached the subject of the Jews of Spanish origin living in France. The government of Spain had already given permission for these Jews to go to Spain, but the bureaucratic aspects of the repatriation process were time-consuming. The Capuchin asked that the Vatican intervene to expedite the procedure.[118]

Maglione forwarded the request to the nuncio in Madrid, Archbishop Gaetano Cicognani,[119] who indicated in his reply of August 23 that the appeal was successful. The Spanish government agreed to grant entry visas to Jews who could prove their Spanish nationality in some way or another, and had given the pertinent instructions to its consuls in France.[120]

It was suggested, moreover, that Father Benoît could help the Jews by working to establish their Spanish nationality. With that proven, they were welcome to enter Spain.[121] Benoît was informed of the success of his appeal to the Pope in a message from Maglione on September 9. Ironically, he was at this time in Rome and in no position to help the Jews remaining in France.[122]

A different picture of the situation for refugees attempting to enter Spain was described by the Spanish ambassador in London. According to him, the border was open to all refugees and no one was sent back to Nazi-occupied France. In fact, he claimed, a reasonably large amount of refugees had managed to reach Spain and, indeed, both the American and British governments were assisting in moving the refugees out. Moreover, the ambassador maintained, there was no Jewish problem in his country and he foresaw the possibility of the Jewish refugees remaining in Spain.[123]

JEWS IN CAMP AT VITTEL

The last Vatican concern involving the Jews of France was occasioned by a dispatch from Cicognani in Washington, dated December 27, 1943. Representatives of the Orthodox rabbis of the United States and Canada had appealed to him to make known to the Vatican the dangers faced by the several thousand Polish Jews interned in the camp at Vittel. Their lives were being threatened because Paraguay had ceased to recognize the validity of the passports which it had earlier issued to them. The possession of these passports had prevented their deportation up to this time. Cicognani asked Maglione to intercede with the Spanish government, which represented Paraguayan interests in Berlin, to attempt to persuade the German officials to defer any decision to deport the Jews from the Vittel camp.[124]

This problem was also discussed at the apostolic delegation in Washington by a representative of the apostolic delegate and Nahum Goldmann of the World Jewish Congress on January 12, 1944. Goldmann was told that the Vatican had already contacted its envoy in Paraguay, who later replied that the Paraguayan government would continue to recognize the validity of the passports.[125]

Bernardini wrote on the same subject to Maglione on December 31, placing the problem in a wider context. Jews who had originally been imprisoned in camps in Germany had paid enormous sums to acquire passports from various Latin American countries. These documents influenced the Germans to transfer Jews possessing them to camps in France, where they were at least, able to survive. Toward the end of 1943, at Paraguay's instigation, the protecting powers were invalidating them.[126] According to Bernardini, "The consequence of all this is that these poor Jews are in imminent danger of being massacred."[127]

The nuncio added that the Red Cross was also prepared to act if the Vatican decided to do so.[128]

On January 24, 1944 the Vatican Secretariat of State cabled its representatives in the various countries concerned to take steps. The eventual outcome of all these efforts was that some countries, including Paraguay, were positive in responding to the Vatican's intervention, some were evasive, and others were totally negative.[129]

Conclusions

The role of Vatican diplomacy during the Holocaust in France remains ambivalent, at best. The anti-Jewish legislation of 1940 and 1941 met with little opposition from the French hierarchy or the Vatican. There is no reason to doubt that Ambassador Bérard's letter to Marshal Pétain was representative of the traditional ecclesiastical attitude toward the Jews.[130] When Archbishop Valeri met with Pétain on September 26, 1941, to discuss the Bérard letter, he handed him a statement pointing out the difficulties in the anti-Jewish legislation already in force.[131] The text is not available, but the most likely interest of the Vatican must be presumed to have been the fact that the Jewish statutes of June 2, 1941 ignored the effects of baptism. No provision for conversion to Christianity was written into the law. Any governmental attitude that did not recognize the rights of the Church was a source of complaint by the Vatican. There is no basis for suggesting that any of the other provisions gave occasion for complaint.

When the deportations began in July 1942, the French bishops protested quietly to Pétain.[132] It was, and is, widely believed that the nuncio also protested the deportations. If so, there is no record of it in the Vatican documents. There is no indication that he dealt with Pétain personally at this time, even though it is generally thought that he did so. One possible explanation for this might have been an implicit association of the nuncio with the letter sent to Pétain by the French bishops through Suhard. The joint Catholic-Protestant protest might also have been implicitly credited to the nuncio.[133] Moreover, Valeri's contacts with lower officials might have led to the notion of a protest to Pétain himself.

Finally, on August 23, 1942, Valeri did meet with Laval, who by this time was the powerful head of government.[134] From the archbishop's own words, it appears that the meeting was very acrimonious, with the nuncio attempting to counterbalance Laval's tirade against the Jews. That the encounter constituted a true protest by an accredited diplomat seems doubtful. The meeting of a lower-ranking member of the

Vatican diplomatic staff with Laval a few days later appears only to have been the occasion for a harangue by Laval against the French bishops.[135]

Later, in November 1942, when German troops occupied the Vichy zone, all of the Allied, Axis, and neutral governments which had maintained diplomatic relations with the Vichy government withdrew. There were only two exceptions, Switzerland and the Vatican.[136] Any Vatican displeasure at the treatment of the Jews of France was not great enough to terminate the diplomatic mission at Vichy at this time. On the contrary, the continuing presence of the nuncio at Vichy was justification enough in the minds of many bishops for their ongoing support of Pétain and his policies.[137]

One is forced to conclude that Valeri concerned himself little with the Jews of France. Even the Vatican's efforts on behalf of the orphaned Jewish children of France were not initiated by him.[138] He did pass on a request that the Vatican attempt to influence Italy to aid the Jews in the Italian-occupied area of France.[139]

There is no doubt that Valeri intervened to assist individual Jews whose cases were brought to his attention. Various of his reports refer to persons making such appeals. Paralleling these efforts of the nuncio were those by Bérard. The ambassador has written that Maglione intervened several times with the French government on behalf of people of various religions who had been treated unjustly.[140] French Jews certainly must have been the subject of some of these appeals.

In August 1942, Valeri had indicated to Rome that the deportation of aged and ill Jews contradicted the notion that the deportations were for the purposes of labor service.[141] A member of his staff, during his illness in September 1942, passed on Weil's request for Vatican assistance in obtaining information about the deportees.[142] The nuncio, therefore, must have felt some suspicion or misgiving about the fate of the deported Jews, from whom nothing was later ever heard. There is nothing to indicate that he expressed these fears or suspicions to the French government.

Valeri wrote nothing and said little to defend the Jews of France. Even if it is admitted that his interventions for specific people could have done more harm than good, this does not necessarily imply that statements or appeals on behalf of all the threatened Jews could have made their fate any worse.

The situation in France is particularly torturous to a student of modern Vatican diplomacy because all indications lead one to conclude that Pétain wanted cooperation with the Church and a strong protest by the papal emissary in France might have dissuaded him from accepting or passing the anti-Jewish measures. Valeri himself once indicated how well received he was in all echelons of the government.[143] The only negative comments which Pétain received were the "nuances" in Bérard's letter.[144] Valeri, as far as it can be ascertained, never made known to Pétain the moral horror involved in the 1942 and 1943 actions taken against the Jews.

It must be admitted, however, that Valeri's options were limited. In the nuncio's own words, the Pope was inclined "toward prudent delay and enlightened reserve."[145] As the Pope's representative in France, he could hardly have been expected to conduct himself any differently. His diplomatic chief, Maglione, gave him no suggestions or orders to protest to the government. In fact, on the contrary, the secretary of state would probably have forbidden any such actions because of the favor which the Vichy government enjoyed at the Vatican.

From a purely diplomatic point of view, Valeri had no particular competence to comment on the laws or treatment accorded to Jews, unless they were baptized Catholics. Moreover, there was no concordat between France and the Vatican spelling out the duties and rights of each. Unlike Romania, for example, there were no large-scale conversions of Jews. Thus, there was no potential source of conflict with the government over the rights of baptized Jews, or legal justification for such Vatican intervention.

Even if Valeri had scant diplomatic competence in regard to the Jews of France, his remarks after the war stressed the uniqueness of Vatican diplomacy. He emphasized that ecclesiastical diplomacy is not limited in the same way as that of ordinary states. Valeri specifically stated that it could and should transcend purely political matters.[146] If Valeri believed this during the years of the Holocaust in France, he would not have needed legal or diplomatic justification, as any other diplomat might have, to intervene on behalf of the Jews.

One comes to the sad conclusion that, in France, Vatican diplomacy chose not to transcend political matters. The Jews of France were of little concern to the nuncio. Those stateless Jews who died, and those French Jews who survived, did so without any intervention on his part. He was well informed, and even suspicious, but his orientation was totally diplomatic and his interest in human suffering minimal. By his own standards, albeit articulated some years later, he failed in that he did not use his unique status as a representative of a moral power to condemn the immorality of all that was done to the Jews of France.

CHAPTER SIX

Slovakia

Introduction

One of the consequences of World War I was the creation of the independent state of Czechoslovakia in October 1918. The Czechoslovakian Republic was a multinational state embracing Czechs, Slovaks, Germans, Hungarians, and other smaller groups. Among its regions was Slovakia, with about 3,000,000 inhabitants.[1]

About 75 percent of Czechoslovakia was Roman Catholic. The 1930 census, for example, listed 11,000,000 Catholics out of a population of 14,500,000. Jews numbered 350,000 in the same census.[2]

Diplomatic relations between the new republic and the Vatican began in 1920.[3] At the end of 1927 a *modus vivendi* was agreed to by Vatican and Czech delegates. In addition to the regulation of territorial and property questions, the *modus vivendi* gave the Czech government the right to veto candidates for the episcopacy. Moreover, the bishops had to swear an oath of loyalty to the state.[4]

POLITICAL SITUATION

After the Munich agreement of September 1938, the then truncated Czechoslovakia entered a period called the Second Republic. During these months, Slovakia agitated for, and became, increasingly more autonomous. The days of the Second Republic were brief. In March 1939, Hitler decided that Bohemia and Moravia, two of the regions of Czechoslovakia, should be severed from that state and become a Protectorate of the Reich. Hungary took control of the region of Ruthenia. Slovakia became an independent state on March 14.[5]

The new Slovak state had a population of 3,000,000 with approximately 90,000 Jews, 3 percent of the total.[6] About 13 percent of the population was Protestant. The remainder were Catholics, thus making Slovakia one of the most Catholic states in Europe.[7]

Moreover, Slovakia was heavily clerically oriented. Not only was the president, Monsignor Josef Tiso, a priest, but many members of the Hlinka Slovak People's Party were priests themselves or pro-clerical. Clergymen were active in both state and party offices, and also served in the cabinet. The Nazi point of view was represented by the radical Vojtech Tuka, the prime minister, and Alexander Mach, the interior minister. The radicals appeared to want direct Nazi intervention in the new state to guarantee their own power; the clericals attempted to lessen direct Nazi influence and dedicated themselves to making Slovakia a "model Catholic state."[8]

The Nazis never intervened strongly enough to upset the balance of power toward the radicals from the clericals. Nevertheless, the clerical party also wanted to earn the confidence of the Nazis. It was in the context of this rivalry for German favor and support that the Jews became involved. Both parties were anti-Semitic and favorable to expelling the Jews from the country. Anti-Jewish measures, as a result, were able to achieve high priority in all governmental programs.[9]

RELATIONSHIP TO VATICAN

Archbishop Saverio Ritter had been named nuncio to Czechoslovakia in 1935. After its dismemberment in 1938, he was transferred to Bratislava, the capital of Slovakia, and arrived there on June 18, 1939 to continue his diplomatic duties.[10] A problem arose immediately between the nuncio and Ferdinand Durkansky, the foreign minister, over the juridic origin of the Slovak state. To the Vatican, Slovakia was not, legally speaking, a new state but the successor to Czechoslovakia, since it was all that remained independent of the former republic. Ritter had originally been accredited by the Vatican Secretariat of State to Prague and this was later extended to Bratislava. Durkansky would not accept such dual accreditation and insisted that the new state deserved its own unique diplomatic accreditation. As a result of the impasse, Ritter was recalled to Rome on June 26.[11]

The question of Vatican recognition of the new state is pertinent. The Holy See has traditionally been reluctant to acknowledge territorial changes during periods of war.[12] Nevertheless, on March 25, 1939 it recognized *de jure* the newly independent Slovakia. This gesture has been interpreted by some as an act of favoritism because of the Vatican's desire to enhance the prestige of the Church in the clerically oriented state.[13] There can be no doubt that an independent Catholic state replacing the secular Czech republic must have been an attraction to Vatican authorities. That the Vatican was consistent with its principles is evident in that Ritter was recalled rather than stripped of his accreditation to Prague. The recognition of Slovakia by the Vatican was not based on the fact that it was juridically a newly formed state, but that it was the successor, and, indeed, the only remnant, of Czechoslovakia.

The diplomatic situation, however, was not quite so simple. Later in the war, the Vatican rejected as premature a request from the Czech government-in-exile in London for diplomatic recognition.[14] In January 1941, Edward Benes, the former president of Czechoslovakia, appealed to the Pope through the apostolic delegate in London, Archbishop William Godfrey, for such recognition. Benes stated:

> The Poles, the Belgians and others continue to have contacts with the Holy See; but since March 1939 there has been no contact with the Czechs. The Slovak Delegate to the Holy See is completely in the hands of the Nazi government.
> Even though I acknowledge the duty of respecting the policy of neutrality of the Holy See, nevertheless it seems to me that non-official contacts, at least for the moment, would be highly desirable.[15]

The response of Cardinal Luigi Maglione, the Vatican's secretary of state, was that such contacts would be premature at the time.[16] Two years later Benes still complained about the Vatican's "recognition" of Slovakia and ignoring of the Czech government-in-exile. In addition, he predicted that this would compromise the Church in Czecho-slovakia in the future.[17]

Monsignor Giuseppe Burzio was appointed chargé d'affaires to Bratislava and arrived there on June 14, 1940.[18] Burzio was a young man of thirty-nine at the time of his posting to Bratislava, and had served in the same position in Lithuania. After the war Burzio served as nuncio to Bolivia from 1946 to 1950 and to Cuba from 1950 to 1954. At that time he left the Vatican diplomatic service and became a canon of the Lateran Basilica in Rome. He died in that position in 1966.[19]

During the summer of 1940, the Vatican was thinking of sending a new nuncio to Slovakia until another diplomatic conflict developed. In August, the foreign minister informed Burzio that Germany, in view of its special relationship with Slovakia, had requested the position of dean of the diplomatic corps for its ambassador rather than for the nuncio.[20] Monsignor Giovanni Battista Montini, Maglione's assistant, saw the German-Slovak decision as a neglect of the traditional rights of the Holy See.[21] Maglione wrote to Burzio on September 17 that the Vatican would not renounce its traditional rights and that such a request would annul the possibility of its considering the appointment of another nuncio to Slovakia.[22]

1939–1941

ANTI-JEWISH LEGISLATION

The first Jewish legislation of the new Slovak government was an ordinance of April 18, 1939 defining a Jew. As would be expected in a religiously dominated state, the determining criterion for Jewishness was religion. Jews baptized after October 30, 1918, however, were still defined as Jews.[23]

At the end of July, Tiso and Tuka met with Hitler and other German officials at Salzburg. One result of the encounter appears to have been an ever-hardening attitude of the government toward the Jews.[24] The Vatican newspaper carried a story announcing that the Slovak constitution was going to be changed to diminish Jewish influence in the country.[25]

REPORT TO MAGLIONE ABOUT JEWS

Burzio's first dispatch concerning the Jews was sent to Maglione on September 5, 1940. He referred to the Salzburg conference and the evident desire for closer relations between the two countries that he saw being manifested afterwards. The diplomat described some of the measures taken against the commercial interests of Jews. For example, they were required to list their enterprises as "Jewish," and also to register all their property. Burzio also expressed the opinion that given the preponderant influence of Jews in Slovak business, some or all of these measures might have been justified, but they had become excessive and gone far beyond the limits of justice. He commented further that the regulations were eliminating Jews from the economic life of the country, but this was benefiting the Germans rather than the Slovaks.[26]

CONCERN FOR BAPTIZED JEWS

Of particular concern to the Vatican diplomat, as it had been for the nuncio in Bucharest, was the provision prohibiting Jewish children from attending middle- and higher-level schools. This could force Catholic children of Jewish origin to leave their Catholic schools to attend Jewish schools. Burzio also mentioned the threat of certain matrimonial legislation which would disturb the Vatican.[27] Maglione's reply of October 5, 1940 was predictable in encouraging the chargé d'affaires to keep him informed about the attitude of the Slovak bishops toward these rules and their efforts to protect the rights of all Christian students, even if Jewish by birth, to a religious education.[28]

Several months later, at the end of March 1941, the converted Jews were still of concern to Burzio. In the event that the Jews were deported to a territory outside of Europe, he expressed the hope that there might be some organization, particularly in America, that could aid the emigration of the Jewish Catholics. Otherwise, they would share the fate of the other Jews.[29]

BURZIO'S REPORT ON THE JEWISH CODE

The Jewish Code was promulgated on September 9, 1941, without the approval of the Slovak parliament or the signature of Tiso. Burzio's lengthy report on September 18 to Maglione described its features.[30] The definition of a Jew now became racial.[31] There were provisions about wearing the star of David, labor service, changes of residence, and prohibited professions,[32] as well as several norms which would assure "their progressive and total elimination from the political, economic and social life of the nation."[33]

Two regulations were of special interest to the Church. Paragraph 9 of the Code forbade marriages between Jews and non-Jews, and between Jews and half-Jews. Paragraph 38 required Jewish students to attend only their own schools or those few permitted by the government.[34]

Burzio also gave Maglione some background material in the same report. Since May, Burzio wrote, when he had first heard rumors of the impending anti-Jewish legislation, he had been urging the Slovak bishops to have an episcopal conference so that they might present a united front to the government in the matter of the Church's rights. They never met. On September 3, with the Code imminent, Burzio tried again, but was told by various bishops that the situation was not as drastic as he thought, and that they had been reassured by Tiso.[35]

According to the chargé, everyone was astonished at the sudden promulgation of the Jewish Code as a governmental decree without the consent of parliament. Burzio had arranged a meeting with Tiso on September 10, the very day that the newspapers announced the Code's existence. As he wrote to Maglione:

There remained to me, in my discussion with Dr. Tiso, only to deplore the matter, expressing my regret that in certain points of the Code the rights of the Church and of Catholics might be disregarded and stating my hopes that the President of the Republic would make use of the power granted to him to repair or to mitigate the more evident injustices.[36]

Burzio's concern at this time was obviously limited to those Jews who had been baptized Catholics. He indicated this specifically by mentioning that 3,000 Catholics would be obliged to wear the star of David. This provision, however, was waived for those who had been baptized before September 10, 1941.[37]

BISHOPS' CONFERENCE

The final point of information in Burzio's report was that early in October there would be a conference of the Slovak hierarchy. This indeed took place at Bratislava on October 7, 1941, and resulted in a statement of the assembled bishops to Tiso.[38] It was not, properly speaking, a diplomatic intervention but is germane because of Burzio's involvement, as well as the fact that it was sent afterwards to the Vatican Secretariat of State.

The bishops' purview was very narrow. Their statement ascribed the origin of the Jewish Code to a theory of racism totally inconsistent with Catholic teaching. The bishops' basic complaints centered on the rights of baptized Jews and the Church's own prerogatives in the regulation of marriages. They concluded with four requests: that baptized Jews be exempted from the effects of the Code; in particular, that Catholic Jews be fully exempted from all ramifications of the Code; that non-Jews, especially members of the clergy, be permitted to intervene on behalf of baptized Jews to testify to their religious and nationalistic dedication; that in the future there should be consultation with ecclesiastical authorities on legislation which pertained to the Church.[39]

INTERVENTION BY MAGLIONE

Maglione himself intervened directly on November 12 with a note to Charles Sidor, the Slovak minister to the Holy See.[40]

With deep sorrow the Holy See has learned that also in Slovakia, a country whose population, in almost its totality, is honored with the best Catholic tradition, there has been published, on September 9 last, a "Government Ordinance," which establishes a particular "racial legislation" containing various provisions in open contrast to Catholic principles.[41]

The secretary of state singled out two provisions as totally unacceptable. Concerning the prohibition of marriages between Christians and Jews, whether baptized or not, he affirmed the right of the Church to marry those who were Catholics, no matter what their ethnic origin was. In fact, the cardinal stated, the Church would be violating divine law if it refused to allow such marriages.[42]

Moreover, Maglione complained about the expulsion of all Jewish youth, even those baptized, from the general schools. Not only did this violate the Church's right to educate its own members, but it was also a source of concern that these Catholic Jews might lose their faith for lack of religious instruction. The cardinal continued:

> The Holy See cannot remain indifferent to the painful situation of so many of its children of Jewish origin, as a result of these and other grave provisions of this ordinance.
> They, indeed, are deprived of not a few rights and segregated from other citizens, in the presence of whom they are in a state of great moral, social and economic inferiority, so great as to practically oblige many of them to heroic actions to remain faithful subjects of the Church and, perhaps, to lead some of them into extreme necessity.[43]

Sidor's response to Maglione's note was not sent until months later.[44] Even before he had received the note, Sidor had discussed the Jewish Code with one of Maglione's principal assistants, Monsignor Domenico Tardini. On that occasion, the minister admitted to Tardini that the regulations in the Code were contrary to Catholic teaching and that they really did not indicate the sentiment of the Slovak people because they were imposed on them by the Germans.[45]

TISO'S REMARKS

Another matter worried the Vatican diplomats at this time. Tiso had recently been quoted as having stated publicly that Catholic social doctrine and Nazism were the same.[46] Tardini and his colleague, Montini, sought clarification of the remarks from Burzio. They were informed that the occasion for the remarks was the consecration of a new church. During the ceremony, Tiso spoke, as he habitually did, without prepared notes. Tiso later explained to Burzio that he meant that National Socialism in the social sphere had put into practice many of the principles contained in the papal encyclicals. Only in that sense did the president see any identity between them. Furthermore, the Slovak version of National Socialism did intend to plan its social reforms in the spirit of the papal encyclicals.[47]

FIRST REPORT OF JEWISH MASSACRES

A startling report on conditions in the east during Germany's invasion of Russia was sent by Burzio to the Vatican on October 27, 1941. Slovak army chaplains were bringing back information on the treatment of prisoners by the Germans: Ukrainian and White Russian soldiers were returned to their homes; Russian soldiers were interned in camps; Jewish soldiers were immediately shot. Furthermore, Burzio reported, it was being rumored that all Jews of any age or sex were being systematically destroyed.[48]

This report of October 27, 1941 appears to be the first time that information reached the Vatican about the massacres of the Jews, at least from one of its own diplomats. Burzio's report was tragically accurate. The *Einsatzgruppen,* or mobile killing units, which followed the German army after the invasion of the Soviet Union in June 1941, had the killing of Jews as one of their primary goals. For example, by October 15, 1941, one of these units had reported to Berlin that it had killed 125,000 Jews. Early in November, another unit stated that it had killed 75,000 Jews.[49]

The Secretariat of State of the Vatican was thus rather well informed. Its reaction to Burzio's dispatch was not one of humanitarian concern for the innocent victims, but of petty and parochial interest to know whether it was Slovaks or Germans who were committing the atrocities. Tardini, for example, in his comments on the Burzio report, appears to criticize him for not being clear on this point.[50] Absent are any words of sympathy or outrage over the contents of the message. Moreover, the Vatican's reaction was extremely slow. It was not until December 20 that Burzio was asked to clarify the role of the Slovak authorities in the matter.[51]

Burzio's reply, dated March 11, 1942, was both definitive and explicit in its tone.

. . . the Slovak authorities are entirely removed from the atrocities committed against the Jews in occupied Russia.

According to information supplied by a Slovak military chaplain, the massacres have been committed by detachments of the S.S. by order of German government authorities. All the Jews of a given place were concentrated at a distance from any inhabited area and killed by machine gun fire.[52]

The Slovak chaplain, it is apparent, described to Burzio very accurately the procedure of the *Einsatzgruppen*.

1942

DEPORTATIONS

In the early months of 1942, German and Slovak authorities were conferring about the deportation of the Slovak Jews, which was to begin on March 26.[53] News of the impending deportation reached the Vatican from various sources. First of all, Burzio cabled Maglione on March 9 that the deportation of all Slovak Jews, without consideration of their age, sex, or religion, was imminent.[54] They were to be sent to Galicia or to the Lublin area.

PROTEST BY BURZIO

Moreover, Burzio indicated that he had protested to the prime minister, Tuka, who confirmed the rumors and strongly defended the legitimacy of such a decision. In fact, Tuka claimed to see nothing inhuman or unchristian in the move.[55] The Vatican chargé d'affaires concluded his report to his superior both poignantly and prophetically: "The deportation of 80,000 persons to Poland at the mercy of the Germans is the equivalent of condemning a great part of them to death."[56]

This concluding remark of Burzio's might, however, have been based more on knowledge than perspicacity. As early as February 1942 Burzio might have known the truth of what was happening to Jews in the east. An official of the German embassy in Bratislava testified that Burzio sent two letters to Tuka during February 1942 denying the veracity of the claim that the Jews were being sent to eastern Poland for labor service and stating instead that Jews were being killed there. At the time German embassy officials in Bratislava queried Berlin about the charge and were told that the Vatican diplomat was in error.[57] Burzio appears to have been convinced that his information was correct because his dispatches to Rome on March 9 and 11 both mention it in some way.

APPEALS TO THE VATICAN

Information about the deportations was also forwarded to the Vatican by its nuncios in Switzerland and Hungary. Archbishop Felippo

Bernardini wrote from Berne on March 10 with an appeal from Jewish leaders that the Pope influence the Slovak leaders to mitigate or cancel the deportation.[58]

Bernardini contacted Maglione again on March 19.[59] He had received from Richard Lichtheim of the Jewish Agency for Palestine and Gerhart Riegner of the World Jewish Congress a description of the conditions of Jews in Central and Eastern Europe.[60] The nuncio sent this statement on and also relayed the Jews' request for papal intervention in Slovakia.

Lichtheim and Riegner had cabled similar information on March 16 to the British office of the World Jewish Congress in London and through it to the New York office. Both offices were encouraged to approach Catholic leaders to influence them to appeal to the Vatican.[61] The Jewish leaders were well aware of the preponderant Catholic influence in Slovakia and hoped that the Pope would use his influence and power to intervene on behalf of the Jews. There is no indication in the Vatican documents that the apostolic delegates in London or Washington were informed of the matter or acted on it.

There is a record of the London office of the World Jewish Congress writing to Cardinal Arthur Hinsley, the archbishop of Westminster. On March 28 the Jewish group informed him that "the entire Jewish population of the Nazi-controlled Republic of Slovakia . . . is to be uprooted and deported to ghettoes near the Polish frontier."[62] Hinsley's disposition of this information is not known.

On March 13, Archbishop Angelo Rotta, the nuncio in Budapest, passed on an appeal to the Pope that he attempt to persuade Tiso to cancel the deportation orders. Included in this plea was a reference to the Catholic Jews who would be included in the expulsions.[63] Attached to Rotta's letter was an appeal from the Jewish community of Bratislava to the Pope.

Most Holy Father!

The Jewry of all Slovakia, 90,000 souls, has recourse to Your Holiness for help and salvation.

We are condemned to destruction. As we surely know, we are to be shipped out to Lublin, Poland. Everything has already been taken away from us (money, linen, clothing, businesses, houses, funds, gold, bank accounts, and all household appliances) and now they want to banish us as Slovak citizens to Poland and send each one, without money or material goods to certain destruction and starvation.

No one can help us. We place all our hope and confidence in Your Holiness as the safest refuge of all the persecuted.

Since the Nuncio of this place is away and we do not know when he will be back, we turn to Your Holiness, through the Nuncio in Budapest, whom we can most easily reach.

Would Your Holiness kindly influence the President of Slovakia, so that he, in the name of mankind and neighborly love, will receive us and not permit our banishment.[64]

A week later Rotta sent a second appeal. This time the chief rabbi of Budapest had asked him to petition the Pope to intervene with the Slovak government "at least to alleviate as much as possible the sad lot of these unfortunate people, among whom there are many women and children, destined in large part to a certain death."[65]

PROTEST BY MAGLIONE

It is not clear whether Maglione had received all this information and the appeals by March 14, but on that day he met with Sidor and presented him with the strongest words of protest so far.[66] The secretary of state did not mention the baptized Jews or the rights of the Church in his complaint. He first recalled his unanswered note of November 12, 1941 and then informed the minister that information had reached his office concerning the deportation of 80,000 Slovak Jews. He concluded:

The Secretary of State would like to hope that such information does not correspond to the truth, not being able to consider that in a country which intends to be inspired by Catholic principles, they had to adopt regulations which were so grave and of such painful consequence to so many families.[67]

JEWISH GIRLS FORCED INTO PROSTITUTION

If the cardinal was worried at this time about the effects of the deportations on families, he was alarmed by even more disturbing news which arrived shortly afterwards. On March 24, Rotta cabled information to the Vatican obtained from the chief rabbi of Budapest. The Germans were planning on sending several thousand Slovak Jewish girls to act as prostitutes for their front-line troops in Russia.[68]

A cable was received from Burzio at the same time stating that many Jewish girls between the ages of sixteen and twenty-five had been rounded up and taken away from their families. It was thought that they were destined for prostitution.[69]

PROTEST TO SIDOR

The Pope himself was so disturbed at this news that he instructed

Maglione to protest again to Sidor and to attempt to dissuade his government from allowing such a horror.[70] Burzio was also authorized by Maglione by cable to appeal to the priestly sentiments of Tiso to prevent it.[71]

Sidor must have been affected by the Pope's directive and complaint because he left soon afterwards for Bratislava. Tuka's instructions to him there were to reply to the Vatican's two written protests with one note based on the argument that the Jews were being sent out of the country for labor service.[72] Sidor also met with Burzio during his sojourn in the Slovak capital.[73]

Burzio's cable of March 24 also indicated that the government had suspended the deportations because of the Holy See's intervention.[74] The tragic inaccuracy of this report was corrected in a second cable received at the Secretariat of State on March 26: ". . . the government has not desisted from its inhuman proposal and is presently in the process of concentrating 10,000 men and as many women as the first contingent. There will be successively other transports until the whole deportation is completed."[75] Attached to Burzio's telegram there was a note written by Tardini calling both Tuka and Tiso "madmen."[76]

The British Foreign Office was also aware of the deportations in Slovakia. It directed the British minister at the Vatican, Francis d'Arcy Osborne, to mention the matter to Vatican authorities to ascertain whether they could do anything to ameliorate the situation. The British officials felt that such efforts by the Vatican might be effective because of the "favorable position of the Church in Slovakia as compared with other countries under German control."[77] Osborne passed on this request to the competent authorities on March 25,[78] and was informed that the Vatican had already tried twice to intervene in Slovakia.[79]

BURZIO'S REPORTS ON THE DEPORTATIONS

In a long report, dated March 31, 1942, Burzio detailed for Vatican officials the events occuring in Slovakia.[80] The Slovak government had decided to deport all its Jews and had actually begun the process on March 25 "in the most cruel manner."[81] In addition, the government took full responsibility for the decision and denied that there had been pressure from Germany. Mach, the minister of the interior, went so far as to say that ecclesiastical authorities agreed with the government's procedure for excluding Jews from Slovak life. Burzio described Mach as deliberately lying in making this statement, although he admitted that certain bishops were quite indifferent to the sufferings of the Jews.[82]

The Vatican diplomat viewed Tuka and Mach as the real powers in Slovakia, after the Germans. Tiso was allowed to remain on as president because of his popularity with the people. Burzio was worried that the whole situation, involving a priest-president and numerous other priests in high offices, could eventually compromise the Church.[83]

Burzio concluded with a vivid description of the deportation process. Jewish girls were brought together in a place near Bratislava, he wrote.

There they are subject to a search, deprived of every object which they have taken along with them (suitcases, purses, rings, earrings, pens, foodstuffs, in sum everything), deprived of personal documents and assigned a simple registration number; if anyone protests or complains or begs that at least some small remembrance of their families be left, she is beaten with kicks and blows . . .[84]

Several convoys had already departed for the German border, Burzio reported. Moreover, there had already been several cases of Catholic girls who underwent the same fate. By this, he explicitly stated, he meant that "these poor children are destined for prostitution or simply for massacre."[85]

Burzio reported again on the deportations on April 9. As they continued, several thousand Jews had escaped to Hungary. Other thousands were attempting to obtain exemptions from Tiso, particularly those who had been baptized. Burzio had been informed that a large number of these exemptions had been granted. He added that the Slovak bishops were preparing a letter on the problem.[86]

The exemptions being sought arose out of Paragraph 255 of the Jewish Code, which gave the president the power to excuse certain Jews from the anti-Jewish measures. Tiso was quite generous in approving the exemptions, especially for Jews who had been baptized, for those who were rich and influential, and for those whose services were needed in a special way. The exact number of dispensations granted by Tiso is difficult to determine, particularly because the exemptions also included all the members of the same family.[87] One author claims that Tiso authorized almost 10,000 exemptions, which would involve, therefore, about 40,000 people.[88] German and Slovak officials during the summer of 1942 were using the figure of 35,000 protected Jews. Many of these, however, had certificates not from Tiso but from various governmental ministries testifying that they were essential to the economy.[89]

MEETING OF MAGLIONE AND SIDOR

Sidor, on his return to Rome, met with Maglione on April 11, 1942. He reported first that Tiso had assured him that he had intervened to mitigate some of the regulations and also to grant exemptions to the baptized Jews. Tuka had instructed him to mention that a response was forthcoming to the Vatican's two notes of November 12, 1941 and March 14, 1942. Maglione, in describing the interview, noted that Sidor had attempted to convince him of the justification for the deportations. The cardinal was very disturbed that young girls were being sent away to serve as prostitutes and thought it was particularly heinous for a Catholic country to be involved.[90]

The Slovak diplomat, however, maintained that the girls were being sent away to work. Maglione's staunch opposition to this defense might have been caused by the fact that Burzio's March 31 report had been read by the Pope himself, who was greatly upset by it. He had just seen the report the day previous to the meeting of the secretary of state with the Slovak Minister.[91] What upset the papal officials was not only the use of Jewish girls for prostitution purposes but also the fact that there were some among them who had been baptized as Catholics.

Maglione expressed to Sidor his opinion that even if the girls were being sent away to work, it was, nevertheless, a heartless thing to separate such youngsters from their families.[92] Shortly afterwards, Maglione informed Burzio of the complaints he had made to Sidor.[93]

EFFECTIVENESS OF VATICAN EFFORTS

From March 26 to the end of June, 52,000 Jews were deported. Those who remained, about 35,000, had exemption privileges.[94] The Vatican's efforts during these months and their effectiveness appear to have been exaggerated in several circles. For example, on April 9, Bernardini wrote to the Secretariat of State expressing the thanks of Jewish officials in Geneva for the intervention of the Holy See with the Slovak government.[95]

A similar sentiment was expressed to the Vatican in a dispatch from Rotta in Budapest on April 17. He sent on to Rome a memoir given to him by a woman involved in relief work stating how appreciated and effective the Vatican's intervention in Slovakia was. The woman also claimed to know how impressed Tiso had been by the Vatican intervention. Moreover, she described Burzio as isolated because people were afraid to approach his office because of police surveillance.[96]

LETTER OF THE SLOVAK BISHOPS

The bishops of Slovakia issued their pastoral letter to the faithful on April 26.[97] Even at a time when thousands of Jews were being deported, it gave them little sympathy or support. Like the earlier letter to Tiso in October 1941, the episcopal statement was not, properly speaking, a diplomatic document, but it is pertinent and important for an understanding of the situation in Slovakia at the time. The bishops first denied the allegations that Jews in large numbers were being baptized Catholics, although they did admit that they had expended particular efforts on behalf of Jews baptized long before, whom they considered true "believers."[98]

The bishops argued from the traditional Christian point of view that the Jews were a cursed people because of their deicide. As they said, "The greatest tragedy of the Jewish nation lies in the fact of not having recognized the Redeemer and of having prepared a terrible and ignominious death for Him on the cross."[99] The hierarchy then delineated its own anti-Semitism.

Also in our eyes has the influence of the Jews been pernicious. In a short time they have taken control of almost all the economic and financial life of the country to the detriment of our people. Not only economically, but also in the cultural and moral spheres, they have harmed our people. The Church cannot be opposed, therefore, if the state with legal regulations hinders the dangerous influence of the Jews.[100]

The bishops tempered their ire by reaffirming the need to act humanely toward the Jews, without violating any divine or civil laws in their regard. They had the right to private property acquired by their own labor and also the right to have their own families.[101]

Burzio had already described one of the Slovak bishops to Maglione as a chauvinist who thought that the hierarchy should not interfere in the government's efforts to rid the country of Jews.[102] There is no doubt, given the tenor of the bishops' letter to their faithful, that his thoughts reflected those of many of his colleagues. Fortunately, however, two other bishops were not similarly inclined. Burzio had asserted that one of them wanted his fellow bishops to take a decisive stand against the governmental measures.[103]

Another bishop, Pavol Jantausch, was known to be unequivocally opposed to the deportation of the Jews and to have intervened at least once to save Jewish lives. It is related that he saved the lives of a rabbi and his wife by driving them around in his car until the deportation train had left.[104]

Some members of the lower clergy also acted on behalf of the Jews.

The Reverend Augustin Pozdech wrote to the Jewish community in Budapest on April 20, 1942, just after the Slovak deportations had begun. Pozdech encouraged them to arouse the conscience of the world against the crimes being committed against the Jews.[105] The priest also intervened numerous times on behalf of Slovak Jews.[106] In addition, a group of priests appealed to Tiso as a brother priest to put a halt to the deportations.[107]

LEGISLATION OF MAY 15, 1942

To retroactively legalize the deportations, the Slovak parliament passed legislation on May 15, 1942 authorizing the deportations, depriving Jews of citizenship, and expropriating their property. This law made two important concessions to the Church. Two groups of Jews were exempted from the measures: those who had been baptized before March 13, 1939, and those married to Christians before September 10, 1941. Jews who had obtained privileges from Tiso were also excluded from the new law's provisions. Burzio described all of this in a report to Maglione on May 23, adding that the priest members of parliament had voted in favor of the law or abstained, but none had voted against it.[108] The cardinal's reply came a few weeks later, expressing the Vatican's displeasure, particularly at the collaboration of the clerical members of the parliament.[109]

REPLY OF SLOVAK GOVERNMENT TO MAGLIONE'S PROTEST

On May 23, 1942, after a six-month delay, the Slovak government finally issued a reply to Maglione's November 12 note, while at the same time ignoring his protest note of March 14.[110] Sidor attributed the long delay to the seriousness of the Jewish question, which occupied so much of his government's attention. It had become clear to the Slovak government, the note stated, that the departure of the Slovak Jews was part of a much wider German plan to move half a million Jews from central and western Europe to the east. Concerning the Slovak Jews, in particular, the government notified the Vatican that

they will be gathered together in various places in the environs of Lublin, where they will remain definitively. The Aryan population will be moved from that area and in its place there will be organized a distinctly Jewish district with its own administration where the Jews can live together and provide for their existence with their own labor. Families will remain united. . . . All the Jews will be under the protection of the Reich.[111]

Moreover, those who were baptized, Sidor claimed, would be taken to a separate area. The minister also denied the allegation that Slovak Jewish girls were being forced into prostitution for German soldiers. He argued that the Nuremberg laws already forbade sexual relations between Aryans and non-Aryans. To defend the government's decision to prohibit marriages between Christians and Jews, Sidor referred to a canonical legal theory justifying such a prohibition.[112]

For the next several months, until March 1943, there is nothing in the Vatican documents from Burzio. During that time period, toward the end of June, the deportations had ceased, and they were only partially resumed in September. It is remarkable that the Vatican diplomat did not report on these matters to his superiors.

MEETING OF BURZIO WITH TUKA

Early in June, however, it appears that Burzio attempted to persuade Tuka to allow a Slovak delegation to inspect conditions of the deported Slovak Jews. Dieter Wisliceny, the Jewish expert at the German legation in Bratislava, went to Berlin at Tuka's request to discuss this proposal. The matter would eventually drag on so long as to be of no effective help to the deported Jews.[113]

RUMORS ABOUT THE TRUE FATE OF SLOVAK JEWS

Except for a brief note by Tardini recalling for Osborne the steps taken by the Holy See on behalf of Slovak Jews,[114] the Vatican documents contain nothing from any source concerning the Jews of Slovakia during the summer and fall of 1942. This is surprising because by the summer of 1942, and ever earlier, rumors about the true fate of the Slovak Jews were circulating in the country. The source of these stories were escapees as well as Hlinka Guard members who were involved in handing over the Jews to the Germans at the Slovak border.[115]

It has been asserted that during July 1942 Vatican officials informed Tiso of the murders taking place in the Lublin area, to which groups of Slovak Jews had been transported.[116] There is no evidence of this in the Vatican documents, as was stated above, and it appears somewhat doubtful because it was not until August that Jewish organizations became aware of German plans for murdering the deportees.[117] All that is known for certain is a brief remark by Archbishop Cesare Orsenigo, the nuncio in Berlin, in a letter to Montini on July 28. Because there was no news from the deportees, Orsenigo stated, all kinds of rumors had developed. Chief among them were stories "of disastrous journeys and indeed massacres of Jews."[118]

In late September 1942, the Italian embassy was in touch with the Vatican about the Slovak situation. According to this information, 70,000 Jews had been deported from March to the middle of August. About 20,000 remained, most of whom had been exempted because they were converts, married to Christians, or had been granted privileges by Tiso. The embassy also referred to some remarks of Tiso questioning the sincerity of Jews seeking baptism.[119]

The figures given by the Italian embassy were slightly inaccurate. Another contemporary source indicated that of the 89,000 Jews in Slovakia, 59,000 had been deported by the middle of August 1942, while 8,000 had escaped to Hungary. About 6,000 were safe because of exemptions or marriage to Christians. Of the remainder it was thought that 6,000 more were soon to be deported.[120]

INFORMATION FROM TAYLOR

On September 26, Myron Taylor, the personal representative of President Roosevelt to Pope Pius XII, passed on to the Vatican information which had come to him from the Geneva office of the Jewish Agency for Palestine. It was specifically stated that Jews from Slovakia were being sent to the east "to be butchered."[121] Maglione's reaction was to ask whether there was any corroborating evidence.[122] In fact, there was. Montini had received similar news from an Italian source several days previously and had noted at the time:

There are in these last weeks two grave facts to note: the bombardment of Polish cities by the Russians and the systematic massacres of the Jews. . . . The massacres of the Jews have reached proportions and forms which are horribly frightful. Incredible killings take place every day; it appears that by the middle of October they wish to empty out entire ghettos of hundreds of thousands of languishing unfortunates . . .[123]

The Vatican's response to the Taylor memorandum was frustrating. Harold H. Tittmann, Taylor's assistant, was informed by the Secretariat of State on October 6 that it had received similar information from various sources but it was not possible to verify its accuracy.[124]

The Vatican was not alone in so slowly putting credence in these stories. Benes, as the leader of the Czech government-in-exile, met with a delegation of officials from the British Section of the World Jewish Congress on September 30, 1942. At that time he urged great caution in accepting the atrocity rumors and saw them as a possible

Nazi propaganda device.[125] On November 11, in a letter to the same officials, Benes stated that "there seem to be no positive indications that the Germans should be preparing a plan for the wholesale extermination of all the Jews."[126] He was all the more convinced of this, he added, because even though many Jews were being persecuted by the Germans, there still remained groups of Jews who had not been affected.[127]

ACTIVITY OF VATICAN

The Vatican had intervened in Slovakia several times, but during the latter months of 1942 it refrained from doing or saying anything, even though aware of the possible atrocities being committed against the deported Slovak Jews. Perhaps the lack of activity was influenced by the Vatican's conviction that, for the most part, the baptized Slovak Jews had been spared deportation. The Slovak law of May 15 had exempted Jews baptized before March 14, 1939 and those married to Christians from anti-Jewish measures.[128] As long as these Jews, officially members of the Church or married to Catholics in ceremonies presumably sanctioned by the Church, were protected, the Vatican appeared content not to intervene. The Italian embassy note of late September 1942 could also have confirmed the Vatican's view that these Jews were relatively secure.[129]

1943

RENEWED THREAT OF DEPORTATIONS

That this was the Vatican's attitude was demonstrated during the early months of 1943, when Slovakia again became an object of grave concern to Vatican officials. In February items began appearing in Slovak newspapers indicating that all Slovak Jews, whether baptized or not, exempted or not, would follow the same course as the Jews of the previous year. Mach himself had stated publicly that in March or April 1943 the transports of Jews would begin again.[130]

BAPTIZED JEWS

This news not only alarmed the Jews but also impelled the Slovak bishops to write to the government on February 17. The bishops, however, specifically limited their concern to Catholic Jews and asked that they not be deported. Amazingly, the bishops were quite defensive in their approach and gave several reasons to justify their intervention, among them that these Jews were sincere converts and had made a complete break with their Jewish background, that they were full members of the Catholic Church, and that it would make a terrible impression if converted Catholics were abandoned by a Catholic state.[131]

BISHOPS' LETTER

The bishops also published a letter which was read in all the churches of Slovakia on March 21, 1943. As Burzio described it, the statement was an attempt to recall the principles of divine and natural law that must be preserved in dealing with the Jews.[132] If the letter to the government several weeks earlier had been defensive in its tone, this pastoral letter contained the strongest language in favor of the Jews issued by the Slovak hierarchy.[133] The bishops complained that people were being harmed by the civil authorities without any judgment being made of individual culpability, and they wanted to solemnly recall the Slovak constitutional guarantees of basic human rights.[134] The bishops also maintained that "our attitude toward people should not be influenced by their linguistic, legal, national or racial connection . . ."[135] Ironically, however, it has been asserted that since the letter was written and read in Latin, whatever effect it might have had was obviously minimized.[136]

On February 26, 1943, Rotta wrote from Budapest to the Vatican indicating that the 20,000 Jews still remaining in Slovakia, half of whom were baptized, were in imminent danger of being deported.[137] This news propelled Maglione to act quickly. On March 6, he ordered Burzio to check the veracity of Rotta's report, and if it was true, to make every effort with the government to prevent the deportation.[138]

BURZIO'S REPORT

At the same time, a long report from Burzio on the Jewish situation in Slovakia was received at the Vatican.[139] He was aware of the rumors about deportations occasioned by Mach's remarks, but he had not been able to verify them because of governmental reticence on the subject. Tiso had tried to reassure him but Burzio described him as doing so unconvincingly. The chargé d'affaires spoke disparagingly of Tiso for not exempting all the baptized Jews. Moreover, he insinuated that there might have been corruption in the president's granting of dispensations because the Jews were willing to pay anything to avoid deportation.[140]

With his dispatch Burzio enclosed a letter from a parish priest in Bratislava. This priest claimed to know for certain that the Jews in Poland were being killed by gas or machine guns and that their bodies were then used to make soap. In fact, the pastor asserted, a German official had "coldly" and "cynically" confirmed the accuracy of this information.[141]

Similar information was brought personally to the Secretariat of State by a Hungarian nun, Sister Margit Slachta, on March 8. She had also heard about the forthcoming deportation of the remainder of the Slovak Jews. Slachta had a particular request for Vatican officials. The Slovak Jews would be interned for a period of time before their deportation. If the Vatican could provide for their sustenance during this internment, then possibly the deportation might be postponed or avoided.[142] The anonymous author of the Secretariat's notes describing Slachta's visit indicated that he assured her that she could have a clear conscience in the matter. In words to be used over and over again, the official said that

the Holy See has done and is doing all that which is in its power on behalf of the Jews, in all the areas where they are the object of odious measures; and particularly, in regard to the case at hand, on behalf of Slovak Jews.[143]

DIRECTIVES FROM MAGLIONE

On March 9, the now even more anxious Maglione cabled Burzio again to say that he had received more information about the impending deportations. As in his cable of three days previously, the cardinal directed his representative to ascertain the truth of the information, and to take all steps, if it were true, to prevent its realization.[144]

Burzio's cable of reply reached the Vatican on the evening of March 11.

The deportation of the last 20,000 Jews remaining in Slovakia is very probable, but does not seem imminent nor is it possible to obtain trustworthy information from governmental authorities who are quite reserved and answer evasively.[145]

JEWISH CHILDREN

On March 13, Archbishop Angelo Roncalli cabled the Secretariat from Istanbul, where he was the apostolic delegate. Chaim Barlas, the representative of the Jewish Agency for Palestine, had appealed to the Vatican to intervene with the Slovak government. The Jewish Agency was particularly anxious that 1,000 Jewish children be permitted to emigrate to Palestine.[146] The reply to Roncalli on May 4 indicated only that the Vatican had intervened several times with the Slovak authorities, and in particular for youth.[147]

TARDINI'S COMMENTS

Roncalli's telegram indicated that the British government would allow the children to settle in Palestine. Godfrey had conveyed a similar message to the Vatican on the same day, except that it referred to Jewish children from all over Europe.[148] Tardini's notes on the Godfrey telegram indicated some interest in the proposal in regard to the Slovak problem. The future ramifications of such a move, however, appear to have given Tardini cause for concern about such a humanitarian project of bringing Jewish children to Palestine. He wrote:

> The Holy See has never approved the project of making Palestine a Jewish home.
> But, unfortunately, England does not yield . . .
> And the question of the Holy Places? Palestine is by this time more sacred for Catholics than . . . for Jews.[149]

On April 7, 1943, Tardini wrote a summary of the Vatican's involvement in Jewish matters.[150] It is an extremely important statement because it reveals the mind of one of the key Vatican officials concerning the Jews. Tardini wrote:

> 1. The Jewish question is a question of humanity. The persecutions to which the Jews in Germany and the occupied or conquered countries are subjected are an offense against justice, charity, humanity. The same brutal treatment is extended also to baptized Jews. Therefore, the Catholic Church has full reason to intervene whether in the name of divine law or natural law.
> 2. In Slovakia the head of State is a priest. Therefore the scandal is greater and greater also is the danger that the responsibility can be shifted to the Catholic Church itself. For these reasons it would appear opportune that the Holy See again issue a protest, repeating—in even clearer form—what was already explained last year, in a diplomatic note to His Excellency, Sidor.
> 3. Since, especially recently, leaders of the Jews have turned to the Holy See to appeal for aid, it would not be out of place to discreetly make known to the public this diplomatic note of the Holy See (the fact of its being sent, the content of the document rather than the text). This will make known to the world that the Holy See fulfills its duty of charity rather than attracting the sympathy of the Jews in case they are among the victors (given the fact that the

Jews—as much as can be foreseen—will never be too friendly to the Holy See and to the Catholic Church).

But this will render more meritorious any charitable efforts.[151]

ANTI-ZIONIST ATTITUDES

The Godfrey telegram of March 13 elicited a response from Maglione on May 4, 1943. He noted once again for the apostolic delegate that the Holy See had done all possible to aid the Jews, and especially Jewish children. In addition, he reminded Godfrey that the Vatican had long opposed the notion of a Jewish homeland in Palestine. The land of Palestine was sacred to Catholics because it was the land of Christ, and, the cardinal worried, Catholics would justifiably fear for their rights if that land were ever to be occupied by a majority of Jews.[152]

This apprehension over Jewish hegemony in the Holy Land was expressed in even greater detail by the secretary of state in a letter to Archbishop Amleto Cicognani, the apostolic delegate in Washington, two weeks later. Maglione thought that there were two problems involved, the first of which was the traditional right of control that Catholics had exercised for centuries over the various holy places and shrines in Palestine.

The second problem concerned Palestine itself. According to Maglione, Catholics all over the world looked to Palestine as a sacred land because it was the birthplace of Christianity. If, however, Palestine were to become predominantly Jewish, then Catholic piety would be offended and Catholics would be understandably anxious as to whether they could continue to peacefully enjoy their historic rights over the holy places.[153] The cardinal continued:

> It is true that at one time Palestine was inhabited by Jews; but how can the principle of bringing back people to this land where they were until nineteen centuries ago be historically accepted?
> . . . it would not seem difficult, in case there is a desire to create a "Jewish Home," to find other territories which would be better suited for that purpose, while Palestine, under a Jewish majority, would give rise to new and grave international problems, would displease Catholics throughout the entire world, would provoke the justifiable protest of the Holy See, and would badly correspond to the charitable concern that the same Holy See has had and continues to have for the Jews.[154]

The secretary of state also encouraged the delegate in Washington to make this opinion known to Myron Taylor, the personal representative of President Roosevelt to the Pope, and cautioned him to alert the American bishops to any change in public opinion in regard to Palestine that might be harmful to Catholic interests.[155]

This fear of a Jewish majority in Palestine was also manifested in a dispatch from Roncalli, the apostolic delegate in Istanbul, to Maglione, on September 4, 1943. He confessed to his superior that he felt uneasy about the attempts of Jews to reach Palestine, as if they were trying to reconstruct a Jewish kingdom. Moreover, he did not think it proper that the charitable activity of the Holy See should be used in this way to help in the realization of any messianic dream that the Jews might have. The delegate concluded that any notions of reestablishing a Jewish reign in Palestine were visionary and utopian.[156]

MEETING OF BURZIO AND TUKA

Burzio's meeting with Tuka on April 7 was very acrimonious.[157] In Burzio's opinion, it was Tuka and Mach who were responsible for the anti-Jewish measures. Tuka accused the Vatican diplomat of meddling in the internal affairs of Slovakia and denied his contention that Slovakia was a Christian state. He affirmed that it was his task to rid Slovakia of the Jews, whom he described as "criminals." To the diplomat's rebuttal that thousands of women and children could not be considered criminals, Tuka replied that in a situation of such national importance he was not going to be concerned about details.[158]

The chargé then mentioned the atrocity stories that were being circulated about the deportees. Tuka denied them but did propose to send an investigation committee to ascertain the truth. If the rumors were indeed true, the prime minister swore, no more Jews would be deported.[159]

Tuka quite remarkably bragged to Burzio that he was a practicing Catholic and attended Mass every day. He claimed to have a clear conscience and the consent of his confessor for what he was doing. These were more convincing to him than any ecclesiastical comments. He claimed that the deportations were carried out at the government's decision and initiative. Baptized Jews would continue to remain exempt.[160]

As Burzio indicated to Maglione, there were some good results from this diatribe. Tiso himself expressed regret at Tuka's remarks. The Council of Ministers also protested the attitude of the prime minister and canceled the deportations of the Jews which he had been preparing. The council also decided that all baptized Jews, no matter what the date of their baptism, would be spared deportation, and that only Jews who were a threat to the state among the remainder would be deported.[161] Maglione's response of May 23 encouraged the diplomat to involve himself in every way to prevent any future deportations of Jews.[162]

The German ambassador also heard of the meeting between Tuka and Burzio. He reported to the Foreign Office in Berlin that the Vatican diplomat had protested the continuation of Jewish deportations, but that Tuka had rejected his protest and pointed out its political aspects.[163]

Sometime toward the end of April 1943, Burzio received more proof of the gas chambers and crematoria at Auschwitz. He was given sketches and plans of the camp and its facilities.[164] The Vatican documents do not indicate this, but it must be assumed that he passed the information on to the Secretariat of State.

PROTEST OF VATICAN TO THE SLOVAK LEGATION

The protest that Tardini had proposed was sent on May 5 to the Slovak legation to the Holy See, although its contents had been discussed four days earlier by Maglione and Sidor.[165] The note indicated the grief of the Vatican on learning that the remaining Slovak Jews would be deported, including women and children, and those who had been baptized Catholic. The note stated quite strongly:

> The Holy See, therefore, would fail its divine mandate if it did not deplore these regulations and measures which strike so gravely at the natural rights of men, for the simple fact of belonging to a particular race . . .
> The sorrow of the Holy See is even more keen considering that such measures have been enforced in a nation of profound Catholic tradition and by a government which declares itself the support and guardian of such tradition.[166]

REPLY OF THE SLOVAK GOVERNMENT

The Slovak government worded its May 28 reply very clearly. First of all, Jews who were a threat to the state would be removed. The remaining Jews who were not a part of the national, cultural, and economic life would be placed in concentration camps, with separate camps for those who had been baptized. Thirdly, those Jews who had received exemptions would not be disturbed. Finally, a committee of four—a priest, a minister, a journalist, and a state official—would be established to check on the conditions of life of the deported Slovak Jews. In what must have been considered a sop for the Vatican, the committee would be charged especially with investigating the way in which the baptized Jews were able to lead their religious lives in the camps.[167]

On the very next day, Maglione recorded that Sidor had asked the Vatican, on behalf of his government, to consider the establishment of a concordat with Slovakia. The cardinal was basically favorable to the notion but refused any action until after the war.[168] Again in December, Sidor brought up the matter and submitted an actual draft proposal for such a concordat, affirming at the same time his government's "devotion" to the Holy See. Again he was told that the time was not opportune for such an agreement.[169]

CESSATION OF THE DEPORTATIONS

The last published dispatches between Burzio and the Vatican were written during June 1943. On June 2, Maglione cabled him asking if the deportations had been suspended and if the government had granted the 1,500 exit visas for the Jewish children.[170] Burzio's reply was received on June 5. The deportations had been suspended, he said, but the proposal of transferring Jewish children out of the country was still only conjecture and not yet decided upon.[171] Burzio's last report was sent on June 11, stating that except for a few rare cases, there was no way of obtaining information about the 50,000 deported Jews.[172]

Burzio was right in informing Maglione that the deportations had been suspended, but the factors that caused the suspension remain open to question. One opinion expressed at the time was that the deportations were suspended three times, twice because of bribery and once because of Church intervention.[173]

At the end of August the Italian embassy contacted the Vatican with the news that an anti-Semitic campaign was apparently beginning again in Slovakia. It had been occasioned by Mach, who cast doubt on the validity of the baptismal certificates and exemptions of many Jews. He threatened to impose severe controls on the documents and dire penalties against anyone possessing them.[174] After this report of August 1943, Slovakia is not mentioned again in the Vatican documents.

The period of calm which the Jews of Slovakia experienced during the second half of 1943 began to be disrupted during December. That month, Tiso, under pressure from the German Foreign Office, agreed that the remaining unconverted Jews should be placed in concentration camps by April 1, 1944. Their number was calculated at 16,000 to 18,000. Later Tuka made an agreement with German officials that the 10,000 baptized Jews would also be placed in special camps of their own. The immediate sign of trouble to the Jews was the order in

January 1944 requiring all the Jews in Bratislava to register with the police.[175]

SLOVAKIA AS A PLACE OF REFUGE

Nevertheless, early in 1944, Slovakia was viewed as a place of refuge, second only to Hungary, for Jews escaping from Poland. World Jewish Congress officials thought it would be helpful to Jews fleeing to Slovakia and Hungary if the Vatican would intervene in their behalf, especially in the light of its influence in both countries.[176] There are no Vatican records available for 1944, but there are several indications that the apostolic delegate in Washington, Archbishop Amleto Cicognani, involved himself in the proposal.

On January 12, 1944, Dr. Nahum Goldmann, an official of the World Jewish Congress, met with a representative of Cicognani. The main topic of their discussion was Hungary, although it may be implied that Slovakia was at least tangentially touched upon.[177] During the latter part of January and February 1944, both Goldmann and Rabbi Maurice Perlzweig of the New York office of the World Jewish Congress were in touch with Cicognani concerning Slovak Jews specifically.

On February 4, Perlzweig informed the delegate of the registration of Slovak Jews that was taking place and their fear of imminent deportation. Cicognani readily agreed to bring this to the attention of the Vatican.[178] On February 15, Cicognani informed Goldmann that he had received word from Maglione "that the apostolic nuncios in Budapest and Bratislava had been notified about the Jewish refugees from Poland to Hungary and Slovakia and have taken an interest in their welfare."[179]

World Jewish Congress officials in New York were very pleased at the Vatican's prompt intervention. Perlzweig was so gratified that he wrote, in a staff memorandum, that the help of the Catholic Church at all levels was so great that a public opportunity should be taken to acknowledge it.[180]

The final statement of Cicognani on the Slovak Jews came in a letter of February 26, 1944 to Edward R. Stettinius, Jr., acting secretary of state of the United States. Maglione had forwarded to him the information received from Burzio in Bratislava. It was reassuring. Cicognani wrote that Burzio

sent a communication to the Secretariat of State to the effect that, although the present condition of the Jews is indeed sad and still uncertain, the census that was taken had only one purpose, the investigation of certain specific suspicions. Furthermore, according to a promise from the President of the Republic, Dr. Josepf Tiso, the Jews will not be persecuted, that is, will not be condemned to severe punishments, but will only be interned and will be given opportunity and facilities to withdraw to some other country. [181]

On February 22, 1944, Sidor and Tardini had a meeting to discuss the establishment of an archdiocese in Slovakia. Tardini, however, used the occasion of their meeting to bring up the subject of the Vatican's displeasure with the way in which Slovakia had attempted to solve the Jewish question. Sidor, in his report to his superiors in Bratislava, indicated that he argued that the Jewish question in Slovakia was primarily social and economic and that the Slovaks themselves had not directly killed even one Jew. [182]

The situation for the Slovak Jews changed radically and tragically at the end of 1944, when German troops put down an uprising sympathetic to the Soviets and took over control of the government. About 13,000 to 14,000 Jews were later rounded up under the pretext of support for the rebels, and most were sent to Auschwitz. [183]

Conclusions

The Vatican's diplomatic activity in Slovakia had three phases: the first occasioned by the passage of racial legislation; the second occurring during the spring 1942 deportations; the third activated by the threat of more deportations in the spring of 1943.

As in other countries, the original Slovak racial laws were protested by the Vatican, not because of any deleterious effects upon the Jews, but because they infringed upon the rights of the Church. Whenever racial regulations did not exempt baptized Jews from the liabilities imposed upon Jews, Maglione and his representatives felt justified in issuing protests.

For example, the expulsion of Slovak Jewish students from the schools, without any exceptions made for baptized Jews, was viewed as vitiating the right of the Church to teach its followers. [184] These Catholic Jewish youths would be forced to attend Jewish schools and thereby possibly lose their contact with the Church.

Another area of concern, one that was considered particularly offensive by the Holy See, was the prohibition of marriages between gentiles and Jews. [185] Ordinarily, interfaith marriages were not permitted by the Church, but if the Jew had become a convert to Catholicism, he was recognized as a full-fledged member of the Church. It was no longer a question of intermarriage, but of the sacrament of marriage between two Catholics. In the realm of the sacraments, the Church

considered itself supreme and would accept no usurpation or diminu-
tion of its rights and responsibilities of control.

Maglione's letter of protest to Sidor on November 12, 1941, should
be seen, therefore, entirely within this context. It did not deal with, nor
did it intend to, the injustices committed against the Jews. Maglione
made it very clear that he was defending the rights of Catholics "of
Jewish origin."[186] His rationale for this limitation is evident and was
based on the narrow view of the Vatican at this time that it concern
itself solely with matters that were justified by canon law or by a
concordat.

A second phase of Vatican diplomatic activity began during the
deportations in the spring of 1942. Maglione protested the deportation
of Jews from Slovakia, but seemed equally concerned that the deportations made no allowance for differences of religion among the
Jews. It might even be argued that the cardinal would have said even
less, or perhaps nothing, if the baptized Jews were not included in the
expulsions. It should be noted, though, that at this time the fate of the
deportees and the atrocities committed against them were not yet
known. Nevertheless, the injustices inflicted upon the Jews by the
expropriation of their property and their deportation should have been
reason enough for a clearly defined protest.

That which outraged Maglione and the Pope the most at the time of
the deportations was the report that Slovak Jewish girls were being
sent away into forced prostitution for German soldiers.[187] Burzio was
specifically directed to intervene to prevent the move, and it must be
presumed that he did, although there is no direct evidence to that
effect.

Maglione, in his meeting with Sidor on April 11, 1942, was more
critical of the deportations than he had been in his letter. He singled out
as particularly opprobrious for a Catholic country the prospect of
forcing girls into prostitution.[188] His vehemence on this occasion was
not typical and must be explained not only by the traditional Vatican
attitudes toward sexual activity outside of marriage, but also by the fact
that Burzio's report concerning this matter had been read by the Pope
just the preceding day. Pius' concern about the information, his
chagrin and ire that such a thing could be permitted in a Catholic
country, must certainly have been transferred to his secretary of state
and experienced by him as well.

If it were not for other sources, it would appear that the Vatican did
nothing else during the height of the deportations. Rumors and
information about the true fate of the deportees had reached Burzio
and in June 1942 he attempted to persuade Tuka to investigate the

conditions faced by the deported Slovak Jews. [189] This was a significant diplomatic intervention although no record of it is contained in the Vatican documents. The absence, of course, can be explained in various ways. Perhaps Burzio did not report it to Rome, possibly his dispatch was lost in transit or the editors chose to omit his report.

The third aspect of Vatican diplomatic activity developed during the threat of new deportations in the spring of 1943. Burzio was instructed to intervene vigorously to prevent any such occurrence. [190] The Holy See's concern, far greater than the previous year, may be traced to two possible causes. The ever continuing reports of what was really happening to the deported Jews made it all the more necessary for the Vatican to intervene to prevent new deportations. Secondly, this wave of deportations would greatly have affected the baptized Jews, and this made the Vatican all the more anxious to do what it could to ward off the deportations.

Thus, the meeting of Burzio and Tuka on April 7, 1943[191] and the letter to the Slovak legation of May 5[192] were far more explicit than previous encounters or statements. Admittedly, the letter did refer specifically to baptized Jews, but it also deplored the steps being taken against innocent people just because they belonged to a certain racial group.

The result of the Holocaust in Slovakia, leaving aside what occurred during the German occupation of the country after August 1944, was that approximately 60,000 Jews, 75 percent of the total, were deported, most during the period from the spring to fall of 1942. For all practical purposes, the deportations were not resumed until late 1944, this time by the Germans themselves.

The Vatican's interventions during this time have been discussed, and, for the most part, they must be judged as being fruitless. No other conclusion can be reached in the face of three-quarters of the Jewish population being deported. Some authors attribute the cessation of the expulsions to Vatican or ecclesiastical influence. [193] It seems more likely that they ended because they had been so effective in ridding the country of the overwhelming majority of its Jewish residents. [194]

The situation in 1943, however, was different. By then, not only was the Vatican aware or, at least, suspicious of the fate of the deportees, but also it realized that the war was beginning to go against Germany. Its intervention was more energetic and apparently effective. For example, deportations scheduled for April 1943 were canceled after Burzio's meeting with Tuka. Tragically, however, the majority of the Jews of Slovakia were already dead.

The Vatican's options were more extensive in Slovakia than in other countries. It was a heavily Catholic country with a priest as president and a prime minister who prided himself on being a practicing Catholic. That anti-Semitism was rampant is evident from the bishops' own statement on the Jews. It was also a country proud of its dedication and loyalty to the Pope. For example, during May and June 1942, various religious celebrations took place in observance of the twenty-fifth anniversary of Pius XII's episcopal consecration.[195]

Yet the Vatican did not act. It issued no threats of excommunication or interdict against the president, the prime minister, or the people. The only action ever contemplated against Tiso occurred in October 1941 after he had made a statement paralleling Catholic social doctrine and Nazism. On that occasion, Pius XII thought that Tiso's name should be removed from the list of prelates and with it, of course, his right to the title of "Monsignor." This was not done because it was discovered that it was unnecessary. Tiso had lost the right to the title with the death of the Pope who had given it to him, since it had not been renewed by his successor.[196]

The failure of Vatican diplomacy in Slovakia must be attributed as much to its own indifference to the deportation of the Jews as to any other factor. The unique conditions presented to the Vatican in the case of this truly Catholic nation were not exploited. German influence in Slovakia and the dependence of the new state upon Germany were factors to be considered by the Vatican diplomatic authorities. Nonetheless, the government was independent. An unambiguous statement from the Vatican condemning the deportation of the Jews would more than likely have affected the nation's leaders. Vatican diplomacy, however, was content to limit itself to the narrow confines of strictly Catholic interests, and an opportunity for a great moral and humanitarian gesture was lost.

CHAPTER SEVEN

Germany

Introduction

The history of Adolph Hitler's accession to power and his consolidation of it are so generally known that they require no lengthy description. He became chancellor of the German Reich on January 30, 1933 and began to put into effect the political and racial policies he had long espoused.

POLITICAL SITUATION

Over the next several years Hitler was able to add to Reich territory Austria, his birthplace, the Sudetenland, and the Wartheland region of Poland (thereafter administered as the Warthegau). Under German administration were the Protectorate of Bohemia and Moravia, the Generalgouvernement area of Poland, the Ukraine, Serbia, and the Baltic countries. Occupied by German troops were half of France, Belgium, the Netherlands, Denmark, Norway, Greece, and part of the Soviet Union. In addition, Hitler was able to set up satellite states in Vichy France, Slovakia, and Croatia, while accepting as allies Hungary, Romania, Bulgaria, and Finland.

The population of the original Reich territory was approximately 60,000,000, about one third of whom were Roman Catholic.[1] In 1933, about 1 percent of the population, or 500,000, were Jews. By 1939 the number had decreased to 200,000.[2]

RELATIONSHIP TO VATICAN

The German constitution of 1871 had bestowed competence in religious matters solely on the state governments, rather than on the central government.[3] Thus it was that by 1933 the Vatican had concluded concordats with Bavaria in 1924, Prussia in 1929, and Baden in 1932.[4] It is noteworthy that in all three cases it was Eugenio Pacelli who signed on behalf of the Vatican, the first two while nuncio in Berlin, and the third as cardinal secretary of state to Pope Pius XI.

CONCORDAT

Six months after Hitler took office, a concordat was signed between the Vatican and the Reich on July 20, 1933. Again, it was Pacelli who led the negotiations and put his signature on the document.[5] The speed with which the treaty was agreed upon raises several questions as to whether one side pushed the other and why each thought it was in its interest to conclude the deliberations so expeditiously.

From one point of view, the Reich Concordat was superfluous since 90 percent of Germany's Catholics lived in the states with which concordats had been previously arranged. Until as late as 1932 the Vatican appeared satisfied with the situation.[6] On the other hand, however, various Weimar governments from 1920 to 1932 had tried to establish a concordat with the Vatican which would have brought about the total regulation of Church-State relations. Pacelli, speaking as Pope Pius XII, shortly after the war, justified the Reich concordat as being the only way that the rights of the Church and of Catholics in Germany could be guaranteed. The individual state concordats could not achieve this.[7]

It was Hitler, obviously for his own domestic and foreign ends, who reopened the discussions with the Vatican. Pacelli was likely a willing partner who saw the Reich concordat as the logical outgrowth of the three earlier agreements.

Each side gained something. The existence and support of Catholic schools throughout Germany was approved.[8] This had long been a sore point for the Vatican. Hitler achieved his goal of removing the clergy from political activity.[9] In addition, the appointment of bishops was subject to government veto, and both hierarchy and clergy were obliged to take oaths of loyalty to the government.[10] Soon afterwards various provisions of the concordat were violated by the Nazis, but at no time was it officially abrogated by either party.[11]

THE NUNCIO, CESARE ORSENIGO

The nuncio who replaced Pacelli was Archbishop Cesare Orsenigo, appointed to the post on February 14, 1930. He had served in a similar position in Holland from 1922 to 1925 and in Hungary from 1925 to

1930. Until June 1934, because of the previously existing concordat with Bavaria, there was also a Vatican diplomat in Munich. The Bavarian representation ceased on May 31, 1934 and the nuncio in Berlin became the sole source of Vatican contact with Germany.[12] Orsenigo remained in Berlin during most of the war. After the nunciature was destroyed in a bombing raid, he moved to Eichstatt in Bavaria. After the collapse of Germany, he returned to Rome. He died while on a private visit to Eichstatt on April 1, 1946.[13]

On February 18, 1946, Pius XII named thirty-two new cardinals, among them two nuncios and several bishops from Germany and other war-ravaged countries. Orsenigo was not elevated to the cardinalate, although the local bishop of Berlin, Konrad von Preysing, was.[14] There can be little doubt that this decision by Pius XII was a deliberate attempt to indicate his displeasure with Orsenigo's activity during the war. In fact, the Jesuit priest Robert Lieber, who had acted as secretary to the Pope, indicated as much. It was Lieber's opinion that Orsenigo's patron had been the previous Pope, Pius XI, who might have made him a cardinal. Piux XII was opposed to honoring him because of "the weak position he had shown toward Germany."[15] There is also the real possibility that Orsenigo was the scapegoat for the errors in Vatican policy toward Germany.

The personalities and opinions of Vatican diplomats are usually difficult to discern, although Orsenigo was an exception and made his feelings known at various times. For example, it is generally believed that the nuncio favored Fascism in general, and National Socialism in particular.[16] Moreover, one author has gone so far as to call him a "collaborationist" of the Nazi government.[17] There is little doubt that Orsenigo's sympathies lay with the Nazis, at least in the sense that the popularity of the regime demanded some support from the clergy and from Catholics. For example, he wrote in April 1940 that he suspected that some priests were against German participation in another war. The nuncio feared that such an attitude would turn the people against the clergy, particularly because of Hitler's popularity at the time.[18]

On the same occasion, the nuncio pointed out that opinions hostile to National Socialism were not viewed as unpatriotic when it was only a question of the internal affairs of the country. When the country was at war, however, such attitudes appeared unpatriotic and, in regard to Hitler, traitorous.[19] Orsenigo himself, at least in the early stages, supported the German war effort. For example, as the German army was approaching Paris, the nuncio made no attempt to conceal his satisfaction.[20] Several months later this would lead him to complain

•

that unlike their Protestant counterparts, only two Catholic bishops had arranged for thanksgiving services in honor of German victories and memorial prayers for those who died in the campaigns.[21]

The German official with whom Orsenigo was most often in contact was Ernst von Weizsäcker, the state secretary. He considered the nuncio a realist who "preferred to avoid making hopeless differences between the Church and the Third Reich into matters of principle."[22] Though Orsenigo was criticized for this even in ecclesiastical circles, it was Weizsäcker's opinion that the Vatican implicitly supported the nuncio's position because of its great reluctance to sever relations with the Reich.[23]

Perhaps the strongest critic of Orsenigo was the bishop of Berlin, Konrad von Preysing. It was this bishop who was one of the Pope's principal sources of information about the Church in Germany. In fact, between 1939 and 1944, Pius XII wrote eighteen letters to Preysing, more than to any other bishop.[24]

Preysing's severest remarks on Orsenigo are found in a letter of his to the Pope on January 23, 1943. He appears to be accusing the nuncio of greater loyalty to the Gestapo than to his fellow Catholics. In addition, he suggested a procedure to minimize the power of the Vatican diplomat.

Still more serious seems to me to be the constantly surfacing effects of the position taken by the Nuncio in ecclesiastical affairs. His almost instinctive position regarding groups loyal to the faith, who come into conflict with the Gestapo has robbed him of practically any sympathy and confidence among Catholics in Germany. Now there comes into question the position he has taken in the matter of the care for deported Poles. . . . To this the Nuncio retorted heatedly that "prudence" is not enough, the clergy must know that the government does not regard Poles as members of a defeated people, but rather as enemies of the State. . . . I fear great damage to Church interests because of such concepts and utterances of the representative of Your Holiness.

Would it not be possible to replace Monsignor Colli[25] with a man of brains, and heart, and once he has been brought in here, to entrust him with charge of affairs, while the Nuncio takes a long vacation? This thought constantly recurs to me because I keep asking myself whether it is good for the exalted person of Your Holiness to be represented at this time (Jewish question, persecutions, etc.) by an Ambassador to the Government.[26]

A somewhat similar opinion of the nuncio was shared by Theodor Innitzer, the cardinal archbishop of Vienna. He considered Orsenigo weak and uninterested in some vital matters.[27]

Orsenigo was not removed; Preysing's suggestions were not followed. The Vatican apparently feared that it would have been very difficult to gain governmental acceptance of a replacement for Orsenigo. Continued Vatican representation at Berlin was the goal of Vatican officials, and every effort was made not to strain relations, even if this meant retaining a nuncio who was lacking the Pope's confidence.

DIFFICULTIES OF ORSENIGO'S POSITION

Orsenigo's situation, it should be noted, was anomalous, and, in some ways, pitiable. As nuncio, he would ordinarily have expected to be the liaison, or conduit, between the Vatican and the German hierarchy. When Pacelli was secretary of state, however, he began the practice of encouraging the German bishops to send their reports and questions on serious matters directly to him, thereby bypassing the nuncio. As Pope, he continued this procedure, going so far as to state immediately after his election that he would deal with all German matters himself.[28] Thus, Orsenigo, for all practical purposes, was ignored, and, it must be concluded, his influence both in Rome and on the German Church was quite limited.

Orsenigo's position vis-à-vis the government was also a difficult one. At the beginning of the war, the nuncio in Warsaw, Archbishop Filippo Cortesi, fled to Romania along with the rest of the diplomatic corps.[29] Because of his absence from the country, Cortesi's faculties were transferred by the Vatican to Orsenigo on November 2, 1939, at least for the part of Poland occupied by German troops.[30] Even though the German ambassador to the Vatican, Diego von Bergen, had assured Maglione that his government wanted religious life in Poland as normal,[31] difficulties arose almost immediately. Orsenigo's position, representing simultaneously the Church of Germany and that of occupied Poland, was practically untenable, and was viewed as bordering on a conflict of interest.[32]

In addition, once German troops occupied Belgium, the Netherlands, and Luxembourg, the Nazi government demanded, in a note of June 29, 1940, that the Vatican diplomats in these countries depart. Orsenigo tried to argue that each nuncio had a twofold task, both diplomatic and religious. The diplomatic functions could be fulfilled by him from Berlin, but someone else would still be needed to oversee the religious life in the countries involved.[33] Orsenigo's contention was not accepted. In the middle of July 1940, both Archbishop Clement Micara, the nuncio to Belgium and Luxembourg, and Archbishop

Paolo Giobbe, the internuncio to the Netherlands, were forced to leave their respective posts and go to Rome, where they attempted to carry out their duties from that distance.[34]

In the case of Belgium, for example, the departure of the nuncio made communications between the Vatican and the Church in Belgium almost impossible. Censorship led to the opening of letters. Whatever contacts came about were as much a matter of stealth and good luck as anything else.[35]

Thus for the first few years of the war, Orsenigo theoretically represented the interests of the Catholics in Germany, the Low Countries, and German-occupied Poland. In August 1941, after the German attack against Russia, the Reich government took the initiative and asked the Vatican to grant it the same rights in the newly acquired territories that it had by virtue of the concordat in the original Reich territory.[36] The Nazi government was particularly anxious to exercise some control over the nomination of bishops.

The Vatican replied to this request on January 18, 1942.

It is, then, for the Holy See itself a norm of enduring practice, of right, or prudence, and of regard, determined by the highest moral and juridic principles, to not proceed, whatever may be the requests for accord or prerogatives on the part of states, with any innovation in the religious life of a country, however occupied or annexed as a result of military operations, until when the hostilities are over, the new state of affairs is formally recognized in peace treaties or by competent international organizations eventually existing.

The Holy See also held to this position during the last world war.[37]

Because the Vatican would not recognize German rights in the new territories, Hitler, in June 1942, decided that his government would reciprocate and deny the Vatican the right to intervene on behalf of the same territories. Hitler continued to acknowledge the concordat as valid, but specifically excluded from the nuncio's competence not only the territories acquired since 1939, but also the others, like Austria, gained before the war.[38] Orsenigo was informed of this decision on June 26.[39] It was a decision of momentous consequence for the Jews, most of whom resided in, or were deported to, the eastern territories. It would develop that not even the least inquiry or informal intervention would be tolerated for anyone, Jew or gentile, living in these territories.

The nuncio in Berlin was a tragic figure, no matter where his sympathies lay. Often ignored by the German bishops and the Vatican Secretariat of State in their direct dealings with each other, on the one hand, his competency in the eyes of the government, on the other hand, was so severely restrained as to almost render him ineffectual.

1939–1941

BAPTIZED JEWS

As would be expected and was paralleled elsewhere, Orsenigo's early communications with Maglione concerning Jews dealt with those who had been baptized Catholic. In May 1939 he indicated that there was a Catholic office in Vienna which was aiding baptized Jews to emigrate.[40] Several months later, in November, he passed on a request for funds for this office.[41] There was also, in these and later exchanges, discussion of the proposal to send the converted Jews to Ethiopia as part of an overall colonization project there.[42] Nothing ever developed of this plan.

APOSTOLIC VISITOR IN POLAND

Of immediate importance to the Vatican after the German victory in Poland was the need for an apostolic visitor to survey the religious situation there. This concern did not directly relate to the Jews, but the failure of the proposal and the absence of any first-hand Vatican observer in Poland contributed to the continuing Vatican reluctance later to believe the atrocity reports. Orsenigo proposed sending a Vatican representative to Poland early in October 1939.[43] On October 14 Maglione ordered him to request German permission to allow Cortesi, the former nuncio, then in refuge in Romania, to return to Poland to watch over the charitable and religious needs of the people.[44]

Ironically, the first to object to the notion of delegating the nuncio to return to Poland in this capacity were the Polish and French ambassadors to the Holy See. They feared that such a mission could be interpreted as a sign of Vatican acceptance of the situation in Poland. They must have argued persuasively because Maglione changed his mind and retracted his order to Orsenigo.[45]

The nuncio, however, had already alerted Weizsäcker to the Vatican request and on October 17 received a note of refusal from him.[46] By this time, Monsignor Carlo Colli, a member of the Berlin nunciature staff, had already returned from a trip to Warsaw to check on the condition of the nunciature there and to arrange for the safekeeping of its archives. He later recounted to Orsenigo all the destruction that he had witnessed in Warsaw.[47] This information made the nuncio all the more anxious to have a Vatican representative on the scene. All he achieved was that he himself was accorded the faculties of the nuncio in Warsaw,[48] but with no assurance that the German government would recognize this extension of his jurisdiction by the Vatican. In fact, in March 1940, Orsenigo was already reporting that the government seemed reluctant to admit that he had any authority to intervene in Poland, except in the case of priests.[49]

The question of an apostolic visitor arose again on March 11, 1940, when Joachim von Ribbentrop, the German foreign minister, visited Rome and had discussions with both the Pope and the secretary of state.[50] Each spoke to the German official about the need to assist the suffering Poles and the desirability of Vatican representation there.[51] As Maglione noted at the time, Ribbentrop's responses were "vague" and "equivocal" to the point of being a refusal.[52]

DEPORTATION OF JEWS

In February 1940, Orsenigo sent to the Vatican his first dispatch dealing specifically with the Jews. He wrote:

> The system of forced transport of less acceptable persons from one region to another, imposed without regard to their age or to the difficulties of such a journey in the most inclement weather, or to the right to safeguard their own household goods, already practiced in the Polish regions, has now also been extended to the regions of old Germany, from where the Jews (men, women, the aged, children) are forced to depart in special trains to shift them to far-off Polish territory in the environs of Lublin.[53]

Maglione's reaction to this information indicated no sympathy for the victims but only a desire to know the nuncio's source of information. At the end of February Orsenigo cabled him that it came from the officially recognized state agency for the Jews. He was probably referring to the Reichsvereinigung der Juden in Deutschland (Reich Association of the Jews in Germany), which was charged with carrying out all governmental decisions regarding the Jews.[54]

Maglione's request for substantiation of the nuncio's report on the movement of the Jews appears needless. The Vatican newspaper itself had already carried various articles in late 1939 and early 1940 announcing and describing the German plans for "The Jewish Reservation of Lublin." For example, the very first of these articles related that the Jews from the Reich, Austria, Bohemia, Moravia, Slovakia, and Poland would be moved to the Lublin area.[55] A later article indicated that the process brought sorrow and tragedy to the Jews involved.[56]

Possibly the cardinal wanted more verification, but the newspaper reports were, as he should have realized, accurate accounts.

The first deportations from Germany occurred in February and October 1940. Over 1,000 Jews from Stettin were sent to Lublin in the first such transfer.[57] The second transport included 7,000 Jews sent to camps in Vichy France.[58] There is no indication that Orsenigo reported on either of these deportations, although the first one was published in the Vatican newspaper. During the rest of 1940 there were no reports from the nuncio concerning the Jews. This, however, is not surprising because during these months anti-Jewish measures in Germany were at a minimum.

PLACES OF REFUGE FOR JEWS

During the years 1938 to 1940, the expulsion of the Jews was considered as a solution to the Jewish problem. The island of Madagascar, to be handed over to Germany in a peace treaty with France, was presented for a time as an ideal place to receive all the Jews of Europe. The Madagascar plan was announced in July 1940, but never came to fruition because the peace treaty with France was contingent on the end of the war with England. Madagascar, as a result, was never ceded to Germany.[59]

The Vatican, too, was involved in the Madagascar plan, although there is no evidence that Orsenigo played any role. Three times during July 1940, the Reverend Alexander Menningen, a priest of the Pallotine order and secretary general of the Raphaelsverein charitable organization, was in touch with both the Pope and Maglione concerning it. Before he was fully aware of the German government's plans regarding Madagascar, Menningen wrote to Pius XII suggesting that the Vatican support a plan to permit the Jews to settle in Alaska. He repeated this request in an audience with the Pope on July 22. The Vatican, of course, had to refuse to consider the request since it was most reluctant to intervene with the United States on such a matter.[60]

On July 31, Menningen wrote to Maglione that the German government intended at a peace conference to definitively settle the problem of the Jews by the transfer of all of them to Madagascar. Officials of the Reichsvereinigung had already indicated to Menningen that they would find this island very unsuitable because of its climate. They were anxious to receive permission from the United States for settlement in Alaska and also for Vatican support of their request. Maglione noted that Menningen himself was aware of the practical impossibility of such an attempt but only wanted the Vatican to make known its encouragement if and when the matter should come to the attention of the American government.[61]

Other possible countries of refuge for the Jews were suggested to the Vatican. In the summer of 1939, and again in January 1940, Angola was discussed, but Vatican officials concluded that the project was totally unrealistic and they refused to intervene in any way with the Portuguese government.[62] The Angola project was to have been a massive one involving all the Jews of Europe. At other times, in addition to the Brazilian visa project,[63] there was some passing interest in Argentina,[64] Venezuela,[65] Ecuador,[66] and Australia[67] for smaller groups of Jews.

There was little overt anti-Jewish activity during 1941 until September. The spring and summer months, however, were momentous for the Jews in that this was the time period during which the idea of the final solution was settled upon. Emigration was now determined to be an impossible option and some other kind of resettlement was felt to be a necessity.[68]

The only incident to occur during the summer of 1941 was announced by Orsenigo in a report to Maglione in July. The Gestapo had closed down the offices of the Raphaelsverein, the charitable association which had done much to aid converted Jews to emigrate.[69]

THE JEWISH STAR

The requirement that all Jews over the age of six wear the Jewish star when they appeared in public was announced on September 1, 1941.[70] Orsenigo reported it to the secretary of state on September 13 as a "painful humiliation for the Jews,"[71] and an even worse problem for the baptized Jews, who were forced to wear it when they worshipped in church. To alleviate their embarrassment, the nuncio mentioned, consideration was being given by ecclesiastical authorities to assigning them special sections in the churches or arranging services solely for them. The minister of religious affairs, Orsenigo indicated, would not permit any exceptions to the law for baptized Jews because churches were public places as envisioned by the ordinance.[72] It is remarkable how acquiescent both the nuncio and the German hierarchy were in the face of such blatant discrimination against their fellow Catholics, albeit of Jewish origin.

A week later the Vatican diplomat gave evidence of his realistic, perhaps fatalistic, approach to the situation in Germany. He had been asked several months previously by Maglione to intercede on behalf of some converted Jews. Orsenigo described the situation in mid-

September 1941 as calm and expressed the fear that any approach on behalf of Jews, even if they were baptized, might stir up the already deep anti-Semitism of the authorities.[73]

ARREST OF LICHTENBERG

The only other pertinent dispatch from Orsenigo during the latter months of 1941 was one on November 12 informing Maglione of the arrest of Monsignor Bernhard Lichtenberg, the provost of the Berlin Cathedral. He had offended the Nazis by his public prayers for the Jews, for prisoners-of-war, and for all those suffering because of the war.[74] German officials had prepared a reply for the nuncio in case he inquired about the priest. They were simply going to say that Lichtenberg had been arrested because he had prayed for the Jews. It is remarkable that they expected that Orsenigo would not object to such a penalty for prayer. Orsenigo, however, did not intervene at this time, but did so only later when it was a question of the priest's health.[75]

1942

EFFORTS ON BEHALF OF BAPTIZED JEWS

There is an interesting note by an anonymous author extant in the files of the Secretariat of State, dated January 25, 1942. For whatever reasons, the Secretariat was interested in three Jews living in the former Czech territory who wanted to obtain passports to emigrate to Honduras. The note does not indicate that they were baptized although that must be suspected to warrant such attention on the part of Vatican officials. The author first recounted that all the relatives of the three had already been deported and they themselves were on the verge of deportation. He then added:

The painful conditions under which this transfer is accomplished, and conditions of accommodations and labor no less grave, and of life in general, which are ordered for Jews transferred to Poland, make the transfer very dangerous for the life of the above-mentioned.[76]

This note served as the basis of a dispatch to Orsenigo, who replied on January 27 that he had acted on the matter. He was, however, very pessimistic about the chances of success, especially because of recent tensions between Germany and the Latin American countries.[77] The identity and eventual fate of the three Jews remain unknown, as also the reason for the Vatican interest in them.

During the latter months of 1941 and early 1942 Orsenigo was attempting to help baptized Jews emigrate. To accomplish this, he had been in contact with Wilhelm Berning, the bishop of Osnabrück, who had been aiding such people after the closing down of the Raphaelsverein in July. The nuncio, on April 15, 1942, announced to both Maglione and Berning that the minister of foreign affairs, for alleged reasons of security, had forbidden German Jews in Germany, Belgium, and Holland to emigrate.[78] This included those who were baptized.

Berning and Maglione themselves had already been in contact. In December 1941 the cardinal had sent the bishop a detailed précis of Vatican efforts on behalf of baptized Jews, especially the expenses involved. It was in this letter that Maglione complained about the conduct and lack of gratitude of the converts who had already been aided.[79]

Several days after Orsenigo, Berning passed on the same information to Maglione. He added a particular plea for $5,000 which would be used, he hoped, to allow some of the Catholic Jews in Belgium and Holland to emigrate.[80] Again, there is no record of Maglione's response or the eventual outcome of the matter.

DEPORTATIONS

The first major transports of Jews from the Reich began in November 1941. From then until the end of 1942, over 200,000 Jews were deported from the Reich, Austria, and the Protectorate. At the beginning of 1943, about 75,000 Jews remained, one-third of whom were partners in mixed marriages.[81]

In January 1942, Orsenigo had interested himself in the situation of three Jews recommended to him by the secretary of state.[82] From then until the beginning of June, with one exception, Jews were not mentioned in his dispatches to Rome. At that time he reported that "The situation of non-Aryans from the beginning of 1942 is always worsening in the sense that they are no longer granted permits to depart."[83] This remark was made in reference to another appeal on behalf of an individual Jew.

Later in June, the nuncio repeated his earlier comment that Jews were no longer permitted to emigrate from Germany, even if they were still free, and that recommendations for this purpose were of no avail.

In fact, he feared that similar interventions could be dangerous because they might antagonize the authorities and influence them to act in cases which they otherwise might have ignored.[84] The nuncio also depicted himself as powerless to act in the case of Catholic priests in the occupied territories sentenced to death.[85]

INQUIRIES ABOUT DEPORTED JEWS

As far as information about the condition of the deported Jews is concerned, Orsenigo had written briefly on May 1 that inquiries about deportees served no purpose because there was no trace of them.[86] On July 28, he wrote more specifically. Concerning all the inquiries from relatives of the deportees, Orsenigo said:

> . . . I must regretfully confess that unfortunately here no one is in any position to obtain secure information about non-Aryans, even worse it is also inadvisable to interest oneself in them because it appears that it is expected with deportation to lose all traces of the deported; that in fact it is already dangerous here to stop along the street to talk with a non-Aryan, wearing the distinctive star . . .
>
> As it is easy to understand, this suppression of news leads to the most macabre suppositions about the fate of the non-Aryans. Unfortunately, also, rumors spread, difficult to check on, of disastrous journeys, and also of mass killings of Jews. Every intervention even if only in favor of the Catholic non-Aryans was till now rejected with the habitual response that baptismal water does not change Jewish blood and that the German Reich is defending itself from the non-Aryan race, not from the religious confession of baptized Jews.[87]

Nevertheless, Orsenigo did make inquiries about deported Jews. On October 15, 1942, at a meeting with Ernst Woermann, director of the Political Department of the German Foreign Ministry, he asked about the Jews deported from France. The only reply he received was a simple denial of knowledge of the situation.[88]

Again on October 19, Orsenigo described his inability to intervene on behalf of the Jews. The foreign minister's response was always that nothing could be done. It was in this dispatch that the nuncio for the first time confronted the problem of the deportations. He wrote to Maglione:

> The antisemitic deportation, witnessed by the diplomatic corps, is being considered here as an incident of internal politics. Unfortunately, the impotence to which even the Holy See is reduced will be badly interpreted and commented upon by some here as if it were negligence on the part of the Church itself. Now, however, they are beginning to be persuaded that the responsibility for these incomprehensible antisemitic measures should be

sought completely elsewhere, and that every intervention of the Holy See, which was repeatedly tried, came to be systematically rejected or turned aside.[89]

DEPORTATION OF INTERMARRIED JEWS

Orsenigo's last dispatch dealing with the Jews during 1942 was dated November 7, and it was his most impassioned one.[90] What upset the nuncio so much was the threat of new laws which would lead to the deportation of Jews, baptized or not, married to Catholics. They had been a privileged class up until then. So disturbed was the papal diplomat that he wrote:

> This outrageous measure will harm not a few good families, will reduce to poverty good Catholic women married religiously to converted non-Aryans or married according to the norms of canon law to non-Catholic non-Aryans, will present agonizing dilemmas to immature children because of their tender filial hearts, and will sow misery and desperation where there had been peaceful and comfortable homes.[91]

In addition, Orsenigo reported to Maglione, the German episcopate was contemplating an appeal to Hitler himself to prevent the deportation of Jews married to Catholics. The nuncio, too, had pointed out the injustice in the proposed regulation to the government authorities.[92]

INTERVENTION BY THE NUNCIO

On the previous day Orsenigo had spoken to Weizsäcker, and it was to him that he was referring in his report to the secretary of state. Weizsäcker's description of his discussion with the nuncio indicated a rather routine conversation.

> As the Nuncio was leaving today, he casually mentioned rumors of an impending intensification of the ordinances concerning mixed marriages. The Nuncio claimed to have heard that in future such mixed marriages would have to be dissolved. Without entering into the dogmatic doctrine of the Catholic Church, he wished to urge me to keep an eye on the impending legislation. I did not get involved in any factual discussion of the subject.[93]

In the same November 7 dispatch the nuncio wrote that he foresaw great reaction on the part of the Catholic population if the deportations were carried out.[94] On this latter point, the nuncio would be proven correct a few months later.[95] The grief of the nuncio on this occasion was well intentioned but obviously one-sided since he apparently felt no similar sympathy for the 100,000 Jews deported from Germany proper by the end of 1942.

PROTEST BY BISHOPS

On November 11, 1942, Cardinal Adolf Bertram, on behalf of the German bishops, did write a letter of protest to the government. It was addressed, however, not to Hitler but to the ministers of justice, of the interior, and of ecclesiastical affairs. Bertram first denied that the bishops' intervention was any indication that they were lacking in patriotism or in a realistic estimation of the harmfulness of Jewish influence on German society. Nevertheless, the cardinal maintained, men of all races should be treated humanely. Furthermore, the proposed legislation would affect thousands of Catholics married according to canon law and, by that token, strain relations between the government and the Church.[96]

DIMEGLIO'S MEMORANDUM

At the end of 1942, a member of the Berlin nunciature staff, Monsignor Giuseppe DiMeglio, prepared and brought to Rome a lengthy memorandum on the Jewish problem in Germany.[97] His comments were principally a review of various anti-Semitic measures taken by the government, but three of his points are noteworthy.

DiMeglio's remarks on the concentration camps were not only accurate but brutally informative.

> Because, as is evident, not all the Jews can find room in the city ghettos, immense concentration camps have been created, where they lead a very harsh life; little food is given to them; they are subjected to extra-ordinarily heavy work: all causes which very quickly bring many to death.[98]

The camps, he added, were in Poland, where the government had decided to group all the Jews. Those being deported were usually removed in the middle of the night so as not to disturb their gentile neighbors. The Jews, DiMeglio reported, were so packed into the railway cars they journeyed on that they could scarcely breathe and, as a result, many died on the way.[99]

DiMeglio's second point expressed praise of the German people. They were quite disturbed at the inhuman burdens placed upon the Jews by being forced to wear the star, he said, and never acted derisively toward them. This kindly attitude outraged the Nazi authorities, who encouraged the people to see in everyone wearing the star someone who had betrayed Germany.[100]

The concluding point of the memorandum was a frank admission that some Catholic priests and lay people were amazed that the

German bishops, unlike their colleagues in other countries, had said nothing about the treatment accorded to the Jews.[101]

SOURCES OF INFORMATION FOR THE VATICAN

During 1942, the Vatican had been informed by several sources about what was happening to the Jews. The memorandum from the World Jewish Congress had been sent to Rome by the nuncio in Switzerland in March.[102] Reports had come from the chargé d'affaires in Slovakia at various times throughout the year.[103] From Belgium, the cardinal archbishop of Malines, Joseph-Ernst van Roey, had written to Maglione both in August and in December about the "inhuman," "brutal," and "cruel" treatment of the Jews.[104] Van Roey was referring only to the deportations from Belgium, but his remarks, in concert with so many others, should have demonstrated a pattern to Vatican officials.

SCAVIZZI'S REPORT

One of the most startling reports came from the Reverend Pirro Scavizzi, the chaplain of an Italian hospital train sponsored by the Order of Malta. He had been in Poland and served as an intermediary between certain Polish bishops and the Vatican.[105] His testimony, one might assume, should have been considered trustworthy by officials of the Secretariat of State. On May 12, 1942, he wrote from Bologna to Pius XII:

> The anti-Jewish struggle is inexorable and is becoming worse, with deportations and mass executions.
> The massacre of the Jews in the Ukraine is by this time complete. In Poland and in Germany, it is equally desired to bring it to completion, with a system of mass killings.[106]

GERSTEIN'S REPORT

Moreover, there was the incident of the visit of Colonel Kurt Gerstein to Orsenigo sometime during August. He had visited the death camps at Belzec and Treblinka and was so affected by what he saw that he wanted to relay the information to neutral authorities. He had been able to speak to a Swedish diplomat, but was rebuffed when he attempted to discuss it with the nuncio in Berlin because of his status as a German soldier. He did, however, make it known later to an official of the Berlin diocese.[107] The Gerstein report plays a central role in *The Deputy*.[108]

POLISH EMBASSY AT THE VATICAN

Moreover, the Vatican had another, very personally involved, source. On October 3[109] and December 19,[110] the Polish embassy at the Vatican gave the Secretariat of State detailed information about the killings. For example, the December report stated that over 1,000,000 Jews had already been killed by the Nazis.[111] These reports will be studied in the chapter on Poland,[112] but are mentioned here to indicate how varied were the Vatican's sources of information.

JOINT DECLARATION OF THE ALLIES

On December 29, 1942, Francis d'Arcy Osborne, the British minister to the Holy See, had an audience with Pius XII and gave him a copy of the joint declaration of Great Britain, the United States, and the Soviet Union, issued on December 17, condemning the German persecution of the Jews. The statement affirmed that "The able-bodied [Jews] are slowly worked to death in labor camps. The infirm are left to die of exposure and starvation or are deliberately massacred in mass executions."[113] The German actions, the statement continued, were part of a "bestial policy of cold-blooded extermination."[114] Osborne appealed to the Pope to approve the joint declaration or, at least, to influence German bishops and Catholics to do what they could to end the atrocities.[115]

Just before Osborne's appeal, Harold H. Tittmann, assistant to Myron Taylor, the personal representative of President Roosevelt to Pius XII, had made a similar request. On December 26, he cabled the State Department that Maglione had indicated that the

Holy See was unable to denounce publicly particular atrocities but that it frequently condemned atrocities in general. He [Maglione] added that everything possible was being done privately to relieve the distress of the Jews. Although deploring cruelties that have come to his attention he said that [the] Holy See was unable to verify Allied reports as to the number of Jews exterminated et cetera.[116]

Osborne tried again on January 7, 1943 to influence the Vatican to associate itself with the joint declaration.[117] In the meantime, he had written to London that the Pope thought his Christmas message contained sufficient condemnation of Nazi crimes against the Jews.[118] Although Osborne indicated that for the Pope it was a strong statement, it was in the context of a much longer speech and, therefore, its impact was minimal.[119]

The British minister spoke again with the Pope on January 5, at which time Pius promised that he would do what he could for the Jews. Because the Pope was so convinced of the strength of his comments at Christmas against the Nazis, Osborne expressed doubt that any other statement would be forthcoming.[120]

Tittmann gave a parallel account of his audience with the Pope on December 30.

> With regard to his Christmas message the Pope gave me the impression that he was sincere in believing that he had spoken therein clearly enough to satisfy all those who had been insisting in the past that he utter some word of condemnation of the Nazi atrocities and he seemed surprised when I told him that I thought there were some who did not share his belief. He said that he thought that it was plain to everyone that he was referring to the Poles, Jews and hostages when he declared that hundreds of thousands of persons had been killed or tortured through no fault of their own, sometimes only because of their race or nationality. He explained that when talking of atrocities he could not name the Nazis without at the same time mentioning the Bolsheviks and this he thought might not be wholly pleasing to the Allies. He stated that he "feared" that there was foundation for the atrocity reports of the Allies but led me to believe that he felt that there had been some exaggeration for purposes of propaganda.[121]

Both the Pope and his secretary of state attributed some lack of objectivity and authenticity to Allied atrocity reports. The sources of information available to them were far more varied than just from the Allies and, as a matter of fact, corroborated the Allied reports. There appears, then, some attempt at duplicity by Pius XII and Maglione in their remarks to the British and American diplomats. By intimating that only Allied sources were passing on such gruesome information, they had a rationale for not acting precipitously because of fears of propaganda.

Maglione also referred to the activity being done "privately" on behalf of the Jews. Except for occasional interventions on behalf of named individual Jews, usually baptized, such activity cannot be verified and must be doubted.

1943

INTERVENTIONS OF THE NUNCIO ON BEHALF OF INDIVIDUALS

During 1943, Orsenigo intervened several times on behalf of certain Jews but always without success. No matter what his personal capabilities or inclinations were, the nuncio's task was a hopeless one.

On one occasion he was told that information about Jews would only be given to the Jewish community organization and not to outsiders.[122] He complained another time in a letter to Maglione that his requests concerning Jews were not even listened to, but were simply refused.[123] He came to realize that the government refrained from giving answers to inquiries about Jews.[124]

An argument used by German officials against the nuncio's intervention was that the person involved, being Jewish, was not German. His case, therefore, was outside the competency of the nuncio.[125] The officials were consistent. On another occasion, when Orsenigo attempted to intervene on behalf of several gentile Dutch Catholics, he was told that such persons were also out of his jurisdiction since they were not German.[126] By a process of elimination, therefore, Orsenigo's powers ostensibly came to be restricted to German Catholics living in the original Reich territory. It was also, of course, a governmental decision that this was the limit of his powers because of Vatican refusal to recognize German hegemony in the newly acquired territories.

ARRESTS OF INTERMARRIED JEWS

In Berlin, during February 1943, the Germans rounded up a number of Jews married to Christians. Several thousands of these Jews had themselves been baptized. The project was a failure because the German wives protested so openly and so bitterly that their Jewish spouses were quickly released.[127] It was to these round-ups that Orsenigo referred in his dispatch to Maglione on March 3, 1943. According to the nuncio, on February 24 Hitler had spoken at a Nazi rally in Munich expressing particularly great hostility toward the Jews. The diplomat added:

Really this past February 28 and March 1 were two particularly cruel days for the deportation of the Jews of Berlin for . . . unknown destinations. Also included were baptized Jews and those married to Germans, thus destroying families.[128]

Orsenigo viewed this deportation as the result of the ordinance about which he had written several months previously.[129]

The papal representative was so affected by this incident that he spoke with Ribbentrop, expressing the distaste of all Catholics at the round-up. For once, the nuncio later recounted, he felt that the minister of foreign affairs listened, but he also feared that no one in German politics was strong enough to oppose the Gestapo in this matter.[130]

PROBLEMS CONCERNING THE *Mischlinge*

Many of the Jews about whom Orsenigo wrote in this report were *mischlinge*, that is, of mixed descent, Jewish and gentile. Many of them were married to Germans and often had been raised as Christians themselves. Certain restrictions had been placed upon them, but generally speaking they escaped the privations and sufferings of the full Jews. *Mischlinge* of the second degree had one Jewish grandparent, and as long as they themselves had been baptized Christian suffered very few liabilities. *Mischlinge* of the first degree were those with two Jewish grandparents who had been raised as Christians or were married to a Christian. This group was always a problem to the Nazis, and tendencies developed to consider them full Jews, which would, of course, have jeopardized their lives.[131]

A report reached the Vatican in April 1943 that *mischlinge* of the first degree were soon to be labeled full Jews by the Nazis. One of the officials of the Secretariat of State took note of this report, with the acknowledgment that such a change of status would lead to their deportation, "which signifies almost certain death."[132] It was a frank admission of the truth. The law was not changed, however, and most *mischlinge*, of both degrees, survived the war.

The person making known this information to the Secretariat of State[133] asked that the Pope act to convince Mussolini to intervene with Hitler to stop any such changes of status. Even though the rumored and proposed change of status would have affected many Catholics, Maglione's response on April 10 was that nothing could be done at that moment.[134]

PROTEST TO RIBBENTROP

The German attitude toward both the nuncio and the secretary of state was revealed in an incident which occurred in March 1943. After several months of deliberations in Rome, Maglione finally decided to send to Ribbentrop on March 2 a long letter full of complaints about how the Germans were treating the Church in the various areas of Poland under their control.[135] Since it dealt primarily with ecclesiastical affairs, Jews were not mentioned in the statement. To avoid the possibility that the German embassy at the Vatican would not forward the cardinal's letter, as had happened with a previous protest concerning the Church in the Warthegau region of Poland,[136] it was decided to send it to Orsenigo with instructions to make sure it reached its proper destination.[137]

On March 15, Orsenigo handed the letter over to Weizsäcker, who assured him that it would go directly to the foreign minister. Two days later, however, Weizsäcker informed the nuncio that he had read the letter, and because it dealt exclusively with the Church in Poland, it was outside the Vatican's competence and, therefore, not acceptable. He thereupon returned the letter to the astonished archbishop.[138]

Weizsäcker maintained afterwards that he was forced to return the letter and described his action as both "discourteous" and "untruthful." He also feared for the nuncio, who was worried that he would be blamed by Vatican officials for the failure of the letter to reach its destination and punished by being recalled to Rome. The Vatican did not react to this diplomatic snub and quite remarkably gave its consent a few weeks later to Weizsäcker's nomination as ambassador to the Holy See.[139]

On April 17, Maglione informed Orsenigo that his office considered the refusal an "unfriendly" gesture toward the Holy See. Furthermore, he would regard the letter as having reached its destination because it was in the possession of German officials for a few days.[140] Orsenigo later addressed a personal note to Ribbentrop on May 5, complaining about the rejection of the letter.[141] The foreign minister defended the government's right not to accept a letter which dealt with a subject on which it thought that the Vatican had no right to intervene.[142]

The incident was viewed by the Vatican as a most serious breach of diplomatic etiquette. At the time that its earlier protest about the Warthegau region had not been acknowledged, the Vatican threatened to depart from its usual attitude of reserve.[143] In March and April 1943, the Vatican did not react. Its lack of action was an indication of the dilemma which it faced. It had made diplomacy and the diplomatic process its chief goals. As a result, to avoid severing diplomatic ties with the Reich, or even straining them, it tolerated actions which it otherwise might not have accepted. It was obvious, too, that even if the Vatican had wanted to make some protest or intervention on behalf of the Jews, it was doomed to failure. If it could not succeed in helping its own faithful, it certainly knew that any effort expended on behalf of the Jews would be in vain.

REQUESTS FROM BARLAS

In January 1943, Archbishop Angelo Roncalli, the apostolic delegate in Istanbul, passed on to the Secretariat of State several requests from Chaim Barlas, the representative of the Jewish Agency for Palestine. Barlas was particularly anxious that the Vatican intervene with the

German government to allow 5,000 Jews, for whom his agency had immigration certificates, to settle in Palestine. Barlas also used the occasion to inform the Vatican that "the slaughter of the Jews . . . goes on intermittently in the occupied countries."[144]

COMMUNICATIONS BETWEEN PREYSING AND THE POPE

Also during the early months of 1943, Preysing, the bishop of Berlin, contacted Pius XII directly on several occasions. On January 17, for example, he informed the Pope that both Catholics and Protestants were concerned about the Jews and that he had been asked "whether the Holy See could not do something in this matter [such as] issue an appeal in favor of the unfortunates."[145] His opinion of the nuncio, expressed in a letter a few days later, would explain why he regularly bypassed him in his communications with the Vatican.[146] On February 26, he communicated to the Pope a Nazi proposal, actually never realized, to dissolve all marriages between Jews and gentiles.[147] Finally, a few days after Orsenigo, Preysing relayed information about the deportation of the Jews of Berlin.[148]

These letters of the bishop of Berlin are less important than the response which Preysing received from Pius XII in a letter of April 30, 1943.[149] The Pope, in this letter, put the burden of protesting upon the local bishops, who could weigh the possibility of reprisals or other punishments resulting from such protests. To avoid a greater evil, the Pope suggested, sometimes an attitude of reserve must be retained.[150]

In the same letter to Preysing, Pius described what he had done for the Jews.

> To non-Aryan Catholics as well as those of the Jewish faith, the Holy See has acted charitably, within the limits of its responsibilities, on the material and moral plane. This action has necessitated a great deal of patience and disinterestedness on the part of the executive arms of our relief organizations in meeting the expectations—one might even say demands—of those asking for help, and also in overcoming the diplomatic difficulties that have arisen. Let us not speak of the very large sums in American money which We have had to disburse on shipping for emigrants. We gave those sums willingly because the people concerned were in distress. The money was given for the love of God, and We were right not to expect gratitude on this earth. Nevertheless, Jewish organizations have warmly thanked the Holy See for these rescue operations.
>
> In Our Christmas message We said a word about the things that are presently being done to non-Aryans in the territories under German authority. It was short, but it was understood. It is superfluous to say that Our paternal love and solicitude are greater today toward non-Aryan or semi-Aryan Catholics, children of the Church like the others, when their outward existence

is collapsing and they are going through mortal distress. Unhappily, in the present circumstances, We cannot offer them effective help other than through Our prayers. We are, however, determined to raise Our voice anew on their behalf as circumstances indicate and permit.[151]

INNITZER'S CONCERN ABOUT INTERMARRIAGES

Another leading Church figure wrote to Pius XII about the same time. Cardinal Innitzer of Vienna had been very involved during 1941 and 1942 in attempting to aid converted Jews to emigrate and had communicated at various times with the Secretariat of State.[152] Finally, on April 3, 1943, he addressed the Pope himself.[153]

Innitzer, like Preysing, was worried about a proposed law which would annul all marriages in which one spouse was Jewish. There were about 5,000 couples in Vienna who would be affected by any such regulation. Once their marriages were dissolved, it was envisioned that the Jewish partner would be deported. The cardinal pleaded with the Pope to do something about the proposed law.[154]

It was Maglione who responded to Innitzer on May 1.

Although such news [of the proposal to dissolve mixed marriages] has arrived here from various places, nevertheless its authoritative confirmation by Your Eminence cannot but deeply sadden the August Pontiff because of the grave moral and material inconveniences which the threatened deportations will bring.

The Holy Father well understands the distress of Your Eminence in this regard and therefore the filial recourse of your heart to His Holiness himself.

It is known to Your Eminence how the Holy See has done and is doing as much as possible to alleviate the sad state of the Jews in various countries and how it has achieved no little results, especially in the area of charity.

As far as concerns the problem of the deportations, the Holy See up to now has not neglected to use all the means in its power, so that in the various countries so many unfortunates might be spared such a cruel fate.

There is no need for me to add that it will continue to be interested with all solicitude, above all when it is a question of those joined in marriage to Catholics.[155]

Maglione's words are most revealing. Even the threat of German dissolution of canonically acceptable marriages did not arouse any protest from the secretary of state. In every other country, any attempt by the state to interfere in marriages already existing, or to prevent marriages which were canonically permissible, brought a stern reaction from the Vatican. It is a moot point, however, because the Nazis did not change the law and most Jews married to Christians survived.[156] In Maglione's response to Innitzer there also appears to have been a subtle reminder that the ordinary procedure was to write to him, not directly to the Pope himself.

In late April, the Jews of Australia, through the apostolic delegate there, appealed to the Vatican to aid the Jews in Germany and the occupied countries, who were, as they said, about to be exterminated.[157] Maglione's patterned response, as always, was that "The Holy See has done and will continue to do all possible for the Jews."[158]

By May 1943, the Reich was officially described as being rid of all its Jews, except those who were married to Germans or of mixed descent and baptized.[159]

FUTILITY OF VATICAN EFFORTS

In July, Maglione instructed Orsenigo to attempt to obtain permission to visit the ghetto at Theresienstadt.[160] Theresienstadt had already been proclaimed a model ghetto. In August 1943, a German Red Cross delegation went there, and in June 1944 a Danish Red Cross commission toured the ghetto.[161] Nevertheless, the foreign minister "categorically" denied the nuncio's request, as Orsenigo informed Maglione on September 28.[162]

Every time that the Vatican intervened on behalf of a non-German, especially a Jew, it was repulsed. A memorandum in the Secretariat of State, dated September 6, 1943, summed up the frustration felt there. It concluded that there were no other options left and, therefore, that requests from relatives about deported Jews could not be answered by the Vatican.[163]

MEETING OF THE NUNCIO AND HITLER

There is some evidence that in November 1943 Orsenigo visited Hitler at Berchtesgaden. According to the account, as soon as the nuncio brought up the subject of the Jews, Hitler turned his back on him and began tapping at the window. His anger at Orsenigo's remarks eventually led him to pick up a glass and throw it on the floor.[164] The whole incident remains doubtful. There is only one source for it, and no record of it in the Vatican publication. It also does not appear plausible that the nuncio would speak so daringly on a subject that he must have known would infuriate Hitler. Moreover, it would be surprising for Hitler even to have allowed such a visit. His attitude toward Orsenigo was, at best, one of mere toleration.[165] It should be noted, too, that the subject of the Jews had only been of minimal interest to the nuncio up to this time. That he would have used the occasion of a meeting with Hitler to discuss it does not appear consistent with his previous lack of interest.

Conclusions

During the war years, Orsenigo intervened repeatedly with governmental authorities concerning Church matters and personnel. In addition:

He made repeated inquiries about other victims of German atrocities, including 33,000 Slovenes who were ejected from their homes in 1941, the Jews expelled from France and Lemberg, and the hostages held in Belgium, Serbia and France in retaliation for attacks on German occupation forces. He made frequent pleas for clemency on behalf of individuals who had been condemned to death by German military tribunals, particularly in Belgium, and, on instructions from the Curia, he interceded on behalf of relatives of members of the former diplomatic corps at the Vatican.... The German authorities were implacable on every count...[166]

The nuncio, therefore, was a strong defender of the rights of certain individuals, groups, and the Church itself. His acts of defense, however, were never extended to the Jews. Concerning the Jews, there appears to have been only one directive from Rome for action on his part in their behalf. The nunciature at Vichy had sent on an appeal to the Vatican to seek information in Berlin about the Jews deported from France.[167]

On October 15, 1942, Orsenigo did speak with Woermann about this matter, doing so, as Woermann later recounted, without any particular emphasis. The nuncio accepted the German official's denial of any knowledge at face value and without any argument.[168] This meeting was only a request for information about the condition and whereabouts of the deportees. It was in no way a protest against the treatment of the Jews. Nevertheless, Orsenigo capitulated without a word of complaint to German intransigence. It could hardly be expected that he would have acted more forcefully, if indeed he would have acted at all, to defend the rights of German Jews.

It is very tempting to blame Orsenigo for the lassitude and indifference he demonstrated toward the Jews. This, however, would be seeking a facile solution to a complex problem. It may be true that the nuncio was, or at least had been, an aficionado of National Socialism, and he may even have had an affinity of some kind for Nazi anti-Semitism. Nevertheless, his failure to act in any way on behalf of the

Jews cannot be entirely and exclusively attributed to him. There are several factors which have a bearing on the situation.

First of all, living as he did in wartime Berlin, with strict censorship, it is not at all certain how many and how secure were his sources of objective information about the German atrocities. Admittedly, there was the contact with Gerstein in August 1942[169] and the nuncio's own remarks in July 1942 about the rumors of the mass killings of Jews.[170] Nevertheless, in his situation, there was always the possibility of wartime confusion and propaganda.

It is true that even the deportations themselves, without any knowledge of what followed, were reason enough for a protest by a man representing a state which claimed that its diplomacy was not limited in the way that the diplomacy of other states was. Except during the period when Jews married to Christians were being threatened with the dissolution of their marriages and being deported themselves,[171] he said nothing. In addition, the absence of any word from those taken away should have made any concerned and objective observer suspicious, but again wartime and a totalitarian state might be mitigating factors in this regard.

A second factor worthy of consideration is Orsenigo's weak position within the power structure of the Vatican diplomatic service. He had been posted to a prestigious capital, but his influence was limited by Pius XII's own personal involvement in German affairs. No diplomat, whether representing the Vatican or any other state, acts independently of the government which he represents. If there is need for tentative or immediate action, the diplomat must decide on the basis of previous governmental practice or decisions. Orsenigo, knowing the autocratic tendencies of Pius XII and his total interest in Germany, would never have presumed to make a move with the government unless directed or encouraged by his superiors in Rome.

Related to this was the nuncio's awareness of how much the German concordat meant to the Pope. He had originally negotiated and signed it in 1933 and was heavily inclined to maintain both the concordat and diplomatic relations at practically any cost. Orsenigo's independence or ability to act was constrained, therefore, by the overwhelming interest of Pius XII, who was confident of his own information about the German scene and not particularly anxious to rely on his nuncio in Berlin.

A third factor which would tend to partially absolve Orsenigo was that his instructions from Maglione, with one exception noted above, never concerned the Jews. The secretary of state had many sources of information consistently and independently referring to German atrocities against the Jews. He never mentioned a word of this to Orsenigo. It may be alleged that he feared that the nuncio, being sympathetic to the government, would not have acted decisively or effectively on such a matter. This, however, was most unlikely because obedience to instructions was certainly part of Orsenigo's training both as a priest and as a diplomat.

Whether aware or not, Orsenigo was indifferent to what happened to the Jews. His superiors in the Secretariat of State, however, were well informed, and yet they manifested no concern for the Jews. He received many instructions from them to intervene on ecclesiastical matters and on behalf of certain individuals, some of whom were Jews, although usually baptized. Regarding the German treatment of the Jews, he was told nothing and received no instructions. If he was treated differently in this regard than his counterparts in Vichy, Bratislava, or Bucharest, it may have been because the officials of the Secretariat of State viewed Germany as a case apart, where interventions on behalf of the Jews were not to be attempted. If this was so, then far more responsibility lies with Maglione than with Orsenigo.

The description of Orsenigo by one recent author seems both pertinent and an effective summary of the man.

If we reconstructed the personality of Mgr. Orsenigo from the large amount of evidence that has come to light in recent years, he would seem to us not so much a tired man who had lost confidence, but a cynic—if we did not know the simple truth that he was a man unequal to his important and crucial task (his nunciature was the most important in the world in those years); and when we reflect on his end, on those last months of his life spent in Rome in an oblivion that was half sought and half imposed, and on his last private visit to Germany which he undertook so as to forget that he had not been elevated to the purple like various colleagues, and during which he died, we cannot doubt that the man who was most hostile to him was perhaps Pius XII himself, his sovereign. But it is nevertheless questionable whether a more gifted diplomat would have been any more successful in such a difficult situation and above all in treating with men so hostile to the Church as the Nazi leaders.[172]

CHAPTER EIGHT

Poland

Introduction

The German invasion of Poland on September 1, 1939 led to the outbreak of World War II. On the 17th of the same month, Russia attacked Poland from the east. By September 28, the two aggressors had overrun the entire country and were able to sign a treaty dividing the country between them.

POLITICAL SITUATION

Germany subdivided its share of Polish territory, incorporating into the Reich that part which lay between Germany proper and East Prussia, the Wartheland. The remainder, the area called the General-gouvernement, was to be occupied and administered by the Germans.[1] It would become the "dumping ground" for Jews expelled from all over Europe.[2] Two million Jews, living in the west of Poland, thus came under German jurisdiction.[3]

RELATIONSHIP TO VATICAN

Diplomatic relations between the Vatican and the Republic of Poland had existed since 1919. A concordat was signed between them in 1925.[4] The nuncio accredited to Warsaw when the war began was Archbishop Filippo Cortesi, who had served there since 1936. Previously, he had represented the Vatican as nuncio in Venezuela from 1921 to 1926, and in Argentina for the following ten years. In 1936, he was appointed nuncio to Spain, but the civil war there prevented him from taking up his duties. He was then, as a result, sent to Poland. Cortesi fled the country with the government after the hostilities began and spent most of the war years in Rome. He retained the title of nuncio until his death in 1947.[5]

Once the war erupted, diplomatic relations between Poland and the Holy See became a problem. Cortesi departed Warsaw on September 5 with the diplomatic corps and eventually reached Romania.[6] On September 19, Monsignor Domenico Tardini, of the Vatican Secretariat of State, communicated to him the Pope's decision that he remain in Romania for the time being to be of assistance to the Poles fleeing there.[7] Cortesi continued this work until March 1940, when he returned to Rome.[8]

PROBLEMS OF REPRESENTATION TO THE GOVERNMENT-IN-EXILE

The counsellor of the Warsaw nunciature, Monsignor Alfredo Pacini, had accompanied the nuncio to Bucharest but for reasons of health left almost immediately for Rome.[9] He was a logical candidate, therefore, to be named chargé d'affaires to the Polish government-in-exile, then located in France. He was appointed to the position in December 1939.[10] After the German invasion of France, the Polish government moved to London in June 1940. Maglione instructed Pacini to follow, but he was unable to arrange transportation and was forced to remain in France.[11]

There was then created the anomalous situation where the Vatican's chargé d'affaires to the Polish government resided at the nunciature in Vichy while the government functioned in London. The Vatican Secretariat of State did nothing about this undesirable situation for two years. On July 1, 1942, Maglione cabled Archbishop William Godfrey, the apostolic delegate in London, announcing his intention to transfer Pacini to London and asking him to inquire whether the British government would grant him the usual diplomatic privileges.[12]

The delegate's reply was received at the Vatican on August 1 and indicated that British officials had denied the request concerning Pacini. The British claimed that they did not want to interfere in matters between the Holy See and Poland, but since the Polish government was functioning in England they were unwilling to admit to the country any diplomats of Italian nationality since there was a state of war between Great Britain and Italy. The government, however, admitted that it would accept a diplomat from an allied or neutral country.[13]

This decision infuriated the Vatican, which responded with a strong note of protest that Vatican diplomats were Vatican citizens and not subjects of their native states.[14] The argument did not dissuade the British.

The Poles, of course, were anxious to have a Vatican representative in close contact with their government in London. The Secretariat of State was just as concerned that it preserve and emphasize its unconditional right to name its own diplomats.[15] The situation remained at an impasse until the first week of April 1943, when it was decided to name Godfrey himself chargé d'affaires to the Polish government. He would retain his position as apostolic delegate while Cortesi would remain the nuncio.[16] This solution greatly pleased the Polish government.[17]

ROLE OF ORSENIGO

In the meantime, however, there was no Vatican representation in Polish territory. Even if Cortesi had not left so quickly at the beginning of the war, it is most likely that the Nazis would have expelled him shortly afterwards, as was the case in Belgium and Holland. There were some attempts in October 1939 to have Cortesi return to Warsaw, not as nuncio, but as apostolic visitor, to oversee the religious situation. This proposal was discouraged by the Polish and French ambassadors at the Vatican, who managed to convince Maglione of their point of view.[18] The faculties of the nuncio in Berlin, Archbishop Cesare Orsenigo, were then extended to cover Poland on November 2, 1939.[19]

The German government, however, never recognized this enlargement of Orsenigo's jurisdiction. Early in the war, as Maglione wrote in March 1940, the government accepted the nuncio's competence when he intervened on behalf of the clergy. Any efforts on behalf of laity were begrudgingly tolerated, and it was made evident to Orsenigo that his duties were not viewed as encompassing Poland.[20]

Nevertheless, until the middle of 1942, Orsenigo's interventions, even though officially discouraged, were accepted. Since the Vatican had denied the German request that it extend the concordat privileges to all of the newly acquired territories, Hitler, in turn, in June 1942, refused to recognize any competence of the Vatican except in the original Reich territory.[21]

In January 1940, Maglione instructed Orsenigo to attempt to obtain permission for Monsignor Carlo Colli, the counsellor of the Berlin nunciature, to visit Poland. Colli had already been in Warsaw for three days during the past October, when he went to check on the condition of the nunciature and the archives there.[22] On this occasion, the cardinal indicated to Orsenigo that it would probably be prudent to mention to the German authorities that the purpose of Colli's visit was to bring the archives back to Berlin.[23] The German authorities acquiesced, provided that Colli did not leave Warsaw and the journey was for the stated specific purpose.[24] On March 8, Orsenigo was able to report to Maglione the success which Colli had in making contacts through various means with a number of Polish bishops and priests.[25]

For the rest of the war, the Vatican did not have an observer of its own in Poland. The Polish embassy at the Vatican, which did not seem to appreciate the stumbling blocks faced by the Vatican in this regard, wrote to Maglione in November 1940 asking him to use all means possible to send a representative to the "disorganized" Church in Poland.[26] As much as possible, Orsenigo attempted to conduct ecclesiastical affairs on behalf of the Polish Church, but his distance from the scene, and the limitations placed upon him by the German government, made his task almost impossible. For example, Orsenigo reported in May 1940 that the German authorities had forbidden all entry into the Generalgouvernement, even to diplomats, including those from Italy. No one from that area was permitted to come to Berlin either.[27] Secure information was difficult to obtain. Individual Polish bishops were occasionally able to communicate directly with the Secretariat of State.[28] In addition, the Polish government-in-exile and the Polish embassy at the Vatican were sources of information.

It would be a matter of conjecture and hindsight to speculate whether the presence of a Vatican representative in Poland would have had any effect on the atrocities committed there against the Jews. Conversely, however, the absence of a trusted observer seems to have made Vatican officials reluctant to accept information about the crimes. It is certain that the Nazis were opposed to there being any Vatican representative in Poland. They feared not only that would he witness and report on their activities, but also that he would become a rallying point for the Polish Church, which they preferred to keep in a subservient position.[29]

1939–1941

REQUESTS FOR PAPAL CONDEMNATION

Toward the end of September 1939, the Vatican's first concern about Poland was to placate those, like the French ambassador to the Holy See, who were urging a papal condemnation of German aggression against Poland.[30] On November 29, 1939, Orsenigo complained to Ernst Woermann, the German undersecretary of state, about the cruelty of the Gestapo in Poland and asked for a governmental investigation. Ironically, however, on this occasion the nuncio emphasized that he was speaking personally and not in his diplomatic capacity.[31] Several days later, he spoke to Ernst von Weizsäcker, the state secretary, about some Poles who had been condemned to death. In what would become a familiar refrain, the German official warned him not to intervene in such cases because it might prejudice the case against those whom he had intended to assist.[32]

COMPLAINTS ABOUT THE JEWS

About the same time as his talk with Woermann, Orsenigo reported to Maglione the information he had received about conditions in the Russian-occupied section of Poland. Reputedly, the best-treated people in this area were the Jews, who had their own schools and military units.[33]

The city of Przemysl was on the border between German- and Russian-occupied territory and divided between the two powers. In November 1939, the local bishop, Francis Barda, described conditions in his diocese in a letter to the Pope. One of the bishop's complaints was that his chancery office building had been made into a dwelling place for Jews. He was even more disturbed that some Jewish women had attempted to enter the episcopal residence where his auxiliary bishop and several priests were living.[34]

Another bishop, whose diocese was in the Russian zone, wrote to Rome on December 26, 1939. The Eastern Rite archbishop of Lwow, Andrea Szeptyckyj, likewise complained about the Jews, a large number of whom had fled to this area to escape the Germans. The archbishop maintained that they had made a bad impression and were attempting to dominate the economic life of the region. He also accused the Jews of avarice and of unethical business dealings.[35]

INFORMATION ABOUT THE WARTHELAND

On November 30, the nuncio reported to Maglione that permission for Bishop Charles Radonski of Wloclawek to return to his diocese had been refused by the German authorities. He was at the time in exile in Budapest. Since the diocese of Wloclawek was part of the Wartheland, Orsenigo suspected that the German decision was based on a desire to Germanize the whole region, and to remove all Poles, including the clergy.[36]

In January 1940, Radonski himself wrote to the Pope about conditions in his diocese. He had been informed that not only had most of the churches been closed and the priests arrested, but also that in a city of

87,000 Poles, all the Poles and the Jews were being ejected from their homes to make way for Germans to move there.[37]

The Vatican authorities had first-hand information about German plans for the Wartheland. They were also aware of German proposals for the remainder of Poland, as Maglione indicated in a letter to Cortesi, still in Bucharest, on January 3, 1940. He gave the nuncio an overview of the situation in Poland and pointed out that the situation in the diocese of Lublin was particularly bad. To make matters worse, he added, the German authorities were thinking of setting aside the Lublin area for Jews from the Reich, the Protectorate, and the rest of Poland.[38]

REPORTS FROM THE POLISH EMBASSY

The Polish embassy at the Vatican, in April 1940, felt the need to comment to Maglione about the pogroms against the Jews taking place in Poland. The German press depicted them as caused by Christian antipathy toward the Jews. The Polish embassy maintained that the raids were organized and financed by the Gestapo. Any stories to the contrary, the embassy affirmed, were attempts by German propaganda to develop hostility between Catholics and Jews.[39]

In May 1940, the Polish embassy reported on the situation in the Russian-occupied area of Poland. In Lwow, in southeastern Poland, the Russian authorities were deporting the Polish population, especially the educated classes. The Catholic Church was being actively persecuted in every way possible. Nevertheless, the embassy revealed, the Jews were spared any of this harassment.[40]

Pius XII received first-hand information about German treatment of the Poles in an audience he gave to an Italian diplomat in May 1940. The official had remained in Warsaw until the end of March. The Pope's own handwritten account of the audience referred to the "cruelty" and "sadism" of the Germans, particularly the Gestapo, whose goal was the destruction of the Polish people.[41]

ORSENIGO'S DUAL ROLE

The difficulties inherent in Orsenigo's dual role of representing ecclesiastical interests both in Germany and in Poland became evident in a complaint from the cardinal archbishop of Cracow, Adam Sapieha, early in September 1940. He claimed that the nuncio was acting in such a way as to give the impression that he thought the geographical and political situation in Poland at the time was the definitive one. In addition, Sapieha lamented the lack of freedom of the Polish bishops to communicate with the Vatican. They also had difficulty reaching Orsenigo, who, the cardinal stated, was not particularly favorable toward them anyhow.[42]

It should be noted that during 1940 and 1941 Orsenigo expended much effort on behalf of the Church in Poland and intervened in its regard on dozens of occasions, generally unsuccessfully. Sapieha's complaint would seem unjustified, therefore. Concerning the Jews of Poland, the nuncio said and did nothing.

Germany attacked the Soviet Union on June 22, 1941. In the territories eventually overrun by German troops, there were about four million Jews. One and a third million of these were residing within the original borders of Poland.[43] Hundreds of thousands of these Jews were quickly killed by the *Einsatzgruppen* that followed after the armies.

BURZIO'S REPORT

The only early information that the Vatican received about these massacres came from the chargé d'affaires in Slovakia, Monsignor Giuseppe Burzio, on October 27, 1941. He informed Maglione that he had been told that Jewish prisoners were immediately shot by the Germans, and that there was also systematic killing of Jewish civilians.[44]

1942

INFORMATION ABOUT THE ATROCITIES
BERNARDINI'S MEMORANDUM

During 1942, the Vatican received information from many sources about the atrocities being committed in Poland. The earliest came from Archbishop Filippo Bernardini, the nuncio at Berne, on March 19, 1942. He sent to his superior a memorandum he had been given by Richard Lichtheim of the Jewish Agency for Palestine and Gerhart Riegner of the World Jewish Congress.[45] It reported two facts about Poland. First, it spoke of the walled ghettos into which masses of Jews had been crowded under conditions so harsh that epidemics were killing a large segment of the population. More startlingly, the document stated:

In addition to the slow and constant extermination brought about by the ghetto system throughout Poland, thousands of Jews in Poland and in the parts of Russia occupied by Germany, have been executed by German troops.[46]

During the visit of the Jewish officials with Bernardini, he told them that "he was aware of the unfortunate fate of the Jews and had already reported on previous occasions to Rome."[47]

SCAVIZZI REPORTS

In May 1942, corroborating evidence came from the hospital train chaplain Pirro Scavizzi, who had been in Poland. He wrote directly to the Pope revealing to him a system of mass killing of the Jews in Poland.[48] Several months later, on October 7, he gave another account of the situation in Poland.

The elimination of the Jews, by mass killings, is almost total, without regard even to nursing babies. Furthermore, civilized life is impossible, and they are all designated with a white wrist-band. They cannot go into a market, or enter a store, get on a trolley or carriage, attend a show, frequent a non-Jewish home. Before being deported or killed, they are condemned to hard manual labor, even if they are of the educated class. The few Jews who remain seem calm, almost showing pride. It is said that over two million Jews have been killed. . . . The Poles are allowed to take refuge in the ghetto homes, which are day by day losing people because of the systematic slaughter of Jews.[49]

BISHOP OF LWOW

At the end of August 1942, Szeptyckyj wrote to Pius XII describing at first-hand conditions in the area of Lwow. The Vatican documents do not reveal how or when this letter reached Rome, but it must be presumed that several weeks passed before it reached its destination. Lwow had originally been under Russian control, but the situation had become worse, according to the archbishop, when the Germans occupied the region. He told the Pope:

For at least a year, there is not a day when there are not committed the most horrible crimes, murders, robberies and rapes, confiscations and injuries. The Jews are the first victims. The number of Jews killed in this small region has certainly passed two hundred thousand. As the army moves east, the number of victims increases.[50]

In the beginning, Szeptyckyj related, the German authorities tried to blame these crimes on others. Later, however, they appeared to lose all shame and killed Jews, and sometimes Christians, right on the street. The archbishop feared, too, that the German overlords might act increasingly more hostile toward the Polish and Ukrainian population because, having become accustomed to shedding blood, they would always be thirsting for more.[51]

ARCHBISHOP OF RIGA

Similar information was sent to the Pope by the archbishop of Riga in Latvia, Anthony Springovics, on December 12, 1942. He told the Pope that most of the Jews of Riga had been killed, and that only a few thousand remained in the ghetto.[52]

WORLD JEWISH CONGRESS

In the middle of August 1942, Riegner informed his World Jewish Congress (WJC) colleagues in London and New York of an alarming proposal of the German authorities. The 3,500,000 to 4,000,000 Jews being deported from all over Europe and concentrated in the east were to be exterminated to resolve definitively the Jewish question in Europe. This news, Riegner added, had not yet been confirmed but was derived from a generally reliable source.[53]

The London office of the WJC then cabled its New York counterpart on September 10, suggesting several steps that could be taken with this information. One of them was that the New York office attempt to approach Vatican authorities.[54] On October 1, the New York office cabled the London office indicating that it had been in contact with Vatican officials, but was awaiting an investigation by the State Department before proceeding any further.[55] There is no record in the Vatican documents of any such contact and nothing more specific in the WJC files. The only Vatican representative in the United States was the apostolic delegate in Washington, Archbishop Amleto Cicognani. Officials of the Jewish organization could have spoken to him or to a member of his staff, or might have availed themselves of the influence of the archbishop of New York, Francis Spellman.

In October 1942, Lichtheim and Riegner issued a more specific memorandum to the WJC office in London. It summed up the Jewish situation in these words:

Four million Jews are on the verge of complete annihilation by a deliberate policy consisting of starvation, the Ghetto-system, slave-labor, deportation under inhuman conditions and organized mass-murder by shooting, poisoning, and other methods. This policy of total destruction has been repeatedly proclaimed by Hitler and is now being carried out.[56]

Again, it is impossible to say how much of this information

specifically reached the Vatican. On November 27, 1942, officials of the British Section of the WJC passed it on to the leading ecclesiastical figures in Great Britain with the request that their memberships condemn the crimes. Arthur Hinsley, the cardinal archbishop of Westminster, was among these churchmen, and he may have informed the apostolic delegate in London. What the clergymen were told by the WJC was that "The Nazis are using Poland as the slaughterhouse for European Jewry. They are seizing and deporting Jews from all the occupied countries to certain areas of Poland organized for the mass murder of Jews."[57]

A week or so later, the London office of the WJC informed New York by cable that Hinsley was planning to make a statement about the Polish atrocities in a sermon which he would shortly deliver. The New York office was again asked to intervene with the Vatican.[58]

MYRON TAYLOR

Myron Taylor, President Roosevelt's personal representative to the Pope, brought most of this information to the attention of Maglione on September 26, 1942.[59] The secretary of state admitted on October 10, in a letter to Taylor's deputy, Harold H. Tittmann, that similar information had reached his office from several sources but said its accuracy could not be confirmed. Nevertheless, he maintained, the Holy See was doing all it could to mitigate the sufferings of the Jews.[60]

POLISH EMBASSY AT THE VATICAN

The Polish embassy at the Vatican sent two reports to the Secretariat of State specifically describing the German atrocities against the Jews in Poland. On October 3, 1942, the embassy spoke of mass killings of Jews by asphyxiation, the depopulation of the ghettos of Vilna and Warsaw, and camps where Jews were gathered and later killed.[61]

On December 19, the Polish embassy communicated the following information to the Secretariat of State:

> The Germans are suppressing the total Jewish population of Poland. It is first of all the aged, the infirm, women and children who are taken away, which is a proof that it is not a case of deportation for work, and which confirms the information, according to which the deportees are put to death by different procedures, in places specially prepared for this. The young and healthy men are often forced to labor so as to make them die of overwork and undernourishment.
>
> As to the number of Jews in Poland killed by the Germans, the estimate is that it has passed one million.[62]

APPEALS TO POPE FROM JEWISH GROUPS

During December 1942 the Pope was besieged by telegrams from the Union of Orthodox Rabbis of the United States and Canada, the chief rabbi of Great Britain, Joseph Hertz, and Jewish groups in Central and South America. All asked that the Pope intervene on behalf of the Jews of Eastern Europe. To all of these appeals, the various apostolic delegates involved were told to answer orally that "the Holy See is doing what it can."[63]

1943

COMPLAINTS OF POLISH CATHOLICS ABOUT THE POPE'S SILENCE

The first two months of 1943 were difficult and embarrassing ones for relations between the Vatican and the Poles. Earlier, in September 1942, a Polish bishop in exile in London, Charles Radonski, had complained to Maglione about the Pope's silence in the face of the suffering of the Poles.[64] Even after Maglione's efforts to placate him in a letter of January 9,[65] Radonski wrote again on February 15 with similar complaints. One of Radonski's arguments in this letter referred to the Jews. The Poles had heard that the nuncio in France had protested the treatment of the Jews there. If that had been done for the Jews, the bishop said, the Catholic Poles should expect at least as much for themselves.[66]

A parallel criticism was heard from Poland itself in March 1943. Bishop Stanislaus Adamski, bishop of Katowice, but residing in Warsaw, wrote at the end of January that there was an opinion shared by many Poles that the Pope had forgotten them.[67]

On January 2, 1943, the president of Poland, Wladislas Raczkiewicz, recalled for the Pope, in a letter from London, the three years of terror experienced by Poland. Among the other crimes, he referred to the scientifically planned mass killing of Jews and of baptized Jews. He bluntly reminded Pius XII of statements made by his predecessors on behalf of Poland and begged him to break his silence.[68]

The president's letter appears to have upset Vatican officials. Maglione was particularly offended, as he wrote to Godfrey on February 3, that Raczkiewicz's letter contained no word of appreciation for all that the Holy See had done for Poland. He requested the delegate to make known to Polish circles in London the various actions taken by the Vatican on behalf of their country.[69]

There was also criticism of the Pope's Christmas message by the

Poles. The Polish ambassador at the Vatican, Kasimir Papee, was charged by his government to tell Maglione that while it appreciated the implicit condemnation of Germany contained in the Pope's Christmas remarks, it wanted more.[70]

The Polish Government is profoundly persuaded that an explicit condemnation of those who sow injustice and death will not only be a support to the Poles in their misfortune, but also that it will recall to reason the masses of Germans in provoking a salutary reflection, and would put a rein on the crimes which the occupying power is committing in Poland.[71]

The Pope's response, sent to Raczkiewicz on February 19, 1943, dealt only with generalities. He described his own sympathy, efforts, and prayers for the Poles but never referred to the country or people who caused all the suffering of the Poles.[72]

Accusations of the Pope's silence about Poland continued to plague the Vatican for several more months.[73] In April, Maglione himself went on the offensive, telling the Vatican diplomats in Washington[74] and Berne[75] what information they might use in refuting the Pope's critics. In addition, on April 20, he wrote to Radonski in London encouraging him to defend the Pope from attacks by Poles living in England.[76] It was also at this time that the decision was made to name Godfrey chargé d'affaires to the Polish government.[77]

At the end of May, a letter from the Pope to the Polish bishops was proposed, prepared, and discussed in papal circles.[78] It was never sent, however, and was replaced by the address which the Pope made annually to the College of Cardinals on his patronal feast day, June 2. This speech received wide distribution and specifically referred to the sufferings of the Poles, while at the same time avoiding any explicit blame for such sufferings.[79] Nevertheless, the Pope's remarks were effective enough to turn public opinion toward him and to earn the gratitude of the Polish president.[80]

APPEALS TO VATICAN ON BEHALF OF JEWS

Concomitant with these difficulties between the Pope and Polish Catholics were the appeals to the Vatican on behalf of the Jews. On March 12, 1943, the Orthodox rabbis of North America again cabled Maglione. They informed the cardinal that the Germans had already begun to liquidate the Warsaw ghetto and that the few hundred thousand Jews still alive there were in immediate danger. They pleaded with the Pope to take some positive action.[81] Cicognani was instructed to answer them in the usual way: ". . . the Holy See has exerted itself and continues to exert itself on behalf of the Jews."[82]

There was an even more urgent appeal forwarded to the Vatican by Cicognani on March 26, 1943. Jewish leaders thought that the Pope could put an end to the deportations and massacres of the Jews by a public statement condemning them.[83] The reply which the delegate was directed to send was again the familiar "the Holy See continues to be occupied on behalf of Jews."[84]

MEMORANDA OF THE SECRETARIAT OF STATE

Before Cicognani was instructed how to reply to this last Jewish appeal, a memorandum was drawn up in the Secretariat of State summarizing its efforts on behalf of the Jews.

> Concerning the steps taken by the Holy See in regard to the deportation of the Jews and the response to be sent to the attached telegram of Archbishop Cicognani.
>
> To prevent the deportations *en masse* of the Jews, which is presently verified in the various countries of Europe, the Holy See has interested the Nuncio in Italy, the Chargé d'Affaires in Slovakia, and the Representative of the Holy See in Croatia . . .
>
> Because the intervention of the Holy See has had, even if only relatively speaking, a certain efficacy, would it not be opportune to give a hint of this, even if only vaguely, in the telegram of reply to the last telegram of Archbishop Cicognani?
>
> An open indication of this would not seem prudent, not only because it is not known what can happen from one moment to another, but also to prevent Germany, learning about the statements of the Holy See, from making even more harsh the anti-Jewish measures in the territories occupied by it and making new and stronger insistences with the Governments belonging to the Axis.
>
> If possible, therefore, respond to Archbishop Cicognani as follows in the attached telegram proposal.[85]

The author of this memorandum was reflecting an attitude in the Secretariat that publicity about the Vatican's diplomatic efforts might deepen the antagonism of the Germans. In countries like Slovakia, Croatia, and Italy, where the Vatican calculated that it had achieved some little success from its efforts on behalf of the Jews, pressure could be brought to bear by Germany on the local officials to take a harsher line toward both the Vatican and the Jews. Two of these states, Slovakia and Croatia, were dependent on German support and recognition and would not have been able to withstand much German pressure.

Another memorandum in the Secretariat of State is dated May 5, 1943. It is demonstrative of the information which the Vatican had at this time.

Jews. Horrendous situation.

In Poland there were, before the war, about four and a half million Jews; it is calculated that now there remain only 100,000 (with the others who came from other countries occupied by the Germans).

At Warsaw a ghetto was formed which contained around 650,000: now there are 20–25,000.

Naturally some Jews have escaped; but it cannot be doubted that the greater part [of the Jews] has been suppressed. After months and months of transports of thousands and thousands of persons, about whom nothing more is known: this can be explained in no other way than death, considering above all the enterprising character of the Jews, who in some way, if alive, show up.

Special death camps near Lublin (Treblinka) and near Brest Litovsk. It is told that they are locked up several hundred at a time in chambers where they are finished off with gas. Carried off in cattle wagons, hermetically sealed, with quicklime floors. In the Warsaw ghetto, even churches were included, which some time later had to be emptied in two hours time. Now these churches serve as stores, etc.[86]

A third memorandum in the Secretariat of State, dated July 7, 1943, was occasioned by information given by a woman who had recently returned from Warsaw. She related to Vatican officials that the ghetto there had been totally destroyed, with the Jewish population killed or deported.[87]

For a period of time in the middle of 1943, there was some anxiety among German officials that the Vatican might share the information it had about German atrocities in Poland with the British. The Germans suspected that the British were going to publish a white paper of some sort on German crimes and would ask the Vatican for its evidence. The Germans were convinced that the Vatican was well informed. To counter any use of Vatican information, German officials discussed the possibility of a propaganda campaign.[88] It was, of course, a moot point because the Vatican had no desire to publicize any of its information and there is no record of any British request for it.

REPORT FROM BERNARDINI

The nuncio in Switzerland, whose position in a neutral country made him readily available to various Jewish leaders, sent to the Vatican, on April 8, 1943, a report which he had just received about the situation in Poland.[89] Bernardini had had several contacts with Abraham Silberschein, head of a relief organization for refugee Jews. It was he who passed on the report to the nuncio along with three secret photographs of the persecution of the Jews.[90]

POLISH JEWS IN ITALY

Polish Jews who had taken refuge in Italy were also a concern to the Vatican. In February 1943, a group of ninety of them, interned in the camp at Ferramonti di Tarsia, were threatened with deportation to Poland. The threat originated with statements made by Fascist officials about removing the foreign population from Italy. The Polish embassy urged the Vatican to use its influence with the Italian government to prevent the deportation. The British minister at the Vatican, Francis D'Arcy Osborne, was instructed by the British Foreign Office to associate himself with these efforts.[91]

A second time, in June, there were rumors that these Jews were to be deported. On June 17, the London office of the WJC cabled the information to the New York office, asking that it approach the State Department and the apostolic delegate about the deportation.[92] Likewise, Osborne was instructed to intervene with the Vatican, since it had been successful in averting the first threat in February.[93]

The British Section of the WJC also wrote to Godfrey about the threatened deportation, which it described as meaning extermination, and asked him to appeal to the Pope to use his influence with the Italian government to prevent it.[94] Several weeks later, on July 19, the WJC repeated this request to Godrey.[95] Not long after, the WJC was assured that Maglione had specifically stated that the Italian government would not deport these Jews.[96]

POLISH JEWS IN THE HOLY LAND

In August 1943, the apostolic delegation in Jerusalem transmitted to Maglione an appeal from Isaac Herzog, the chief rabbi of the Holy Land, and others.[97] Three hundred Polish Jews had escaped to the Holy Land, but had to leave behind their wives and children, numbering about 1,200 people. Originally, there had been an agreement to exchange them for Germans living in Palestine, but the exchange never took place. In the meantime, the husbands and fathers had heard nothing from their families in Poland, but were painfully aware of the rumors about expulsions and massacres in Poland.

The chief rabbi made two requests of the Vatican on behalf of the refugees. He asked the Vatican to intervene with the German government to persuade it to bring together in one place the families involved. Secondly, it was the chief rabbi's hope that the Vatican would encourage the British government to conclude the original agreement on the exchange between the Germans and the Polish Jews.[98]

The Secretariat of State knew well enough the futility of communicating such a matter to the German government. In the meantime, German troops had occupied Rome, which might have increased the ordinary timidity with which the Vatican approached the Berlin authorities. On September 29, however, it did contact the British legation at the Vatican, mentioning its interest in the case and asking for suggestions.[99]

Osborne replied shortly afterwards that in the absence of contacts with his government because of the German occupation, he could not make any concrete proposals.[100] There was some thought in the Secretariat of bringing the matter to the attention of Godfrey, but it was decided to postpone such action because of the conviction that eventually Osborne would communicate with his government.[101] There is no indication that the matter continued after this point.

POLISH JEWS IN SHANGHAI

One last matter concerned the Vatican briefly toward the end of 1943. It involved the 460 members of a rabbinical college in Poland who had fled across Siberia to Japan to escape the Germans. Once the war in the Pacific began, the Japanese transferred them to Shanghai, where they were put into a ghetto with several thousand other Jews. On September 17, Cicognani cabled an appeal to Maglione from the Orthodox rabbis of the United States and Canada. The rabbis asked that the Vatican intervene with the American, British, and Polish governments to work out some kind of exchange with Japan for the rabbinic students.[102]

Maglione's response of September 23 was very sympathetic and appeared to be part of a different approach to Jewish appeals by the Vatican. He instructed Cicognani to discuss the matter with American officials and also to relay the request to British officials, if possible.[103]

Cicognani sent two responses to Maglione's directive. The first, on October 15, indicated that this was a difficult matter for the American government and that possibly the apostolic delegate in Tokyo might be of greater assistance, especially since those involved were clergymen.[104]

Cicognani wrote on the request a month later. The American

government had flatly refused any involvement with the rabbinic students because they were not American citizens. There were many American citizens in similar circumstances, and even for them no exchange procedures had been worked out with the Japanese.[105]

The matter did not end there. The American rabbis prevailed upon Cicognani to appeal again to Maglione. This he did on December 21, 1943, sending along their request that the Japanese ambassador be asked to petition his government to release the students.[106] Maglione later replied that his office had intervened with the Japanese ambassador on behalf of the students.[107] They remained in Shanghai, however, for the duration of the war.

Conclusions

For all effective purposes, Vatican diplomacy did not function in Poland itself. The departure of Cortesi from the country at the beginning of the war and the refusal of the German government to allow any Vatican observer into the country made the diplomatic process impossible. Orsenigo's efforts were always hindered by his distance from the scene, his own attitudes, and the anomaly of his position as nuncio to Germany. If the nuncio in Berlin is to be held responsible for any shortsightedness on his part, or for ignoring the violations of the rights of the Jews, then his accountability must be limited to Germany itself. His ability to act on behalf of Poland was limited at best, and eventually rejected altogether. There is also the question of how much information he had about the atrocities committed in Poland.

Vatican diplomacy did concern itself with the Polish Jews in Shanghai and Italy, and the families of those in the Holy Land. The uniqueness of the Italian situation lent success to its efforts there, but otherwise there was no success. Other than these cases, the Vatican said and did nothing on behalf of the Jews of Poland.

Two aspects of this silence concerning Poland must be kept in mind. Poland itself was one of the chief battlegrounds of the war, and the circumstances attendant on that would have made the ordinary channels of information and communication difficult and sporadic. Moreover, Poland was unique in another way. Vatican nuncios had been expelled from other occupied countries, like Belgium and Holland, but in no other country was the Christian population treated as it was in Poland. In Poland, both Jews and Christians were objects of Nazi oppression and manipulation. Well over 2,000 priests and almost

6,000,000 Poles, Christians and Jews, were killed in Poland, the overwhelming majority of whom died from the cruel practices of the Germans.[108]

A second aspect of this Vatican silence is that it is part of a wider pattern of silence. Pope Pius XII said little and did nothing on behalf of Polish Catholics, whose political and religious leaders appealed to him for some words or for a gesture of support. It was a silence deeply resented by the Polish Catholics and never adequately broken by the Pope, except for some fairly general words in his June 1943 address.[109] Pius XII's silence in regard to the suffering Catholics in Poland is a matter of history; the interpretation of it will be discussed elsewhere.

The Catholics of Poland should certainly have expected that the Pope, who exulted in the title of "father," should have reacted to their suffering by doing all he could to mitigate it, or by condemning those whose aggression caused it. If he refused to act on their behalf, then *a fortiori*, the Jews, no matter how much worse their tribulations were, could hardly expect that he would do anything for them.

The sad conclusion is that the tragic events in Poland were not able to move the Pope or his secretary of state to face the reality of a situation whose cruelty was unparalleled in human history. A more sobering conclusion might be that diplomatic relations with Germany were considered such a premium that no word or deed could be permitted that would endanger them.

CHAPTER NINE

Croatia

Introduction

The Kingdom of Yugoslavia was established in the aftermath of World. War I. Like Czechoslovakia, it was a confederation of diverse peoples—Serbs, Croats, and Slovenes.[1] Great animosity existed between the Orthodox Serbs and the Roman Catholic Croats, who felt that their culture and religion were the objects of discrimination by the Serbs.[2]

Diplomatic relations between the Vatican and Yugoslavia began in 1920. In 1935, a concordat was agreed upon by both parties,[3] but the opposition of Orthodox churchmen prevented its ratification.[4] Archbishop Ettore Felici was appointed nuncio to Belgrade in April 1938, and remained in that post until May 1941, when , after the dissolution of the Yugoslav kingdom, all diplomatic representation ceased.[5]

POLITICAL SITUATION

Yugoslavia's collapse was swift. When the war began, it had attempted to remain neutral, but its geographic location and the political alignment of its neighbors made that impossible. On March 25, 1941, the government joined the Axis, but a coup d'état two days later forced it out of office.[6] The regent, Prince Paul, abdicated and the young king, Peter, assumed the throne in the midst of great demonstrations of Serbian nationalism.

Hitler considered the Yugoslav action a personal affront and decided to crush the nation which had dared to defy him. Within days, German, Italian, Hungarian, and Romanian troops had invaded the country, and it soon ceased to exist as a national entity. On April 10, Croatia was proclaimed an independent state. Serbia, where the revolt against Hitler began, was subjected to German occupation. Other

147

sections of the country went to Bulgaria and Hungary, while the Dalmatian coast came under Italian control.[7]

The independent Croatian state had imprecise boundaries and was occupied by both German and Italian troops. It had a population of over 6,500,000, almost half of whom were native Croats and Roman Catholics. Orthodox Serbs numbered about 2,200,000, Muslims, 350,000, and Jews, 45,000.[8]

The chief of state and prime minister of the new state was Ante Pavelić, called, like Hitler and Mussolini, the "Leader," *Poglavnik* in Serbo-Croatian. He was the founder of the Ustase movement,[9] loyal fascists who differed from the Nazis only in their fanatic Catholicism. Their goal was to purify the new state by eliminating from it any elements not in harmony with their Catholic faith. For various reasons, Muslims and Protestants could be tolerated, but the Orthodox Serbs living in the state were given a choice of conversion to Catholicism or expulsion. In practice, however, it was worse than that for the Orthodox. They were severely persecuted and thousands were killed. The Jews, on the other hand, were no problem for the Ustase. They would not affect the religious unity of the country because they would simply be expelled.[10]

Using Germany as its guide, the Croat government acted speedily in dealing with the Jews. On April 30, 1941, it issued its definition of a Jew and in the next several months continued the process of expropriation and forced labor. In late 1941 or early 1942 discussions and preparations began for the deportation of the Croatian Jews.[11]

RELATIONSHIP TO VATICAN

Relations between the new state and the Vatican did not begin right away. Unlike Slovakia, where the nuncio to Prague was originally transferred to Bratislava, and then replaced by a chargé d'affaires,[12] the nuncio to Belgrade was never assigned to Zagreb. Felici fled to Budapest when the government left, remained there for a time, and then returned to Rome. He retained his title of nuncio to Yugoslavia, while at the same time, Yugoslavia maintained its legation at the Vatican.

The first Vatican contact with the new state occurred in May 1941 during the visit of Pavelić to Rome for discussions with Italian authorities. He requested and received an audience with Pius XII on May 17, but the Vatican took great efforts to insure that the visit was a personal and unofficial one. The Croatian leader was joined by the duke of Spoleto, who had been proclaimed king of Croatia.[13] Pavelić assured the Pope that the "Croatian people wanted all their conduct and legislation to be inspired by Catholicism."[14] In addition, the Croatian leader asked for Vatican recognition of the new state, but the Pope demurred and indicated that the Vatican did not grant such recognition during the time of war.[15]

As a general rule, the Vatican was anxious to have representatives in every nation. Early in June 1941, in an audience with the archbishop of Zagreb, Aloysius Stepinac, the Pope promised that he would send a representative to Croatia.[16] The Yugoslav legation at the Vatican heard that there was consideration of such an appointment and sent a note of protest to the Secretariat of State on June 2.[17] Pavelić, on the other hand, was angry and surprised that the Vatican was thinking only of sending an "observer" since a nunciature had been established in Slovakia.[18]

In July, it was decided to appoint Giuseppe Ramiro Marcone, a Benedictine abbot, as apostolic visitor to Croatia. There was some confusion over the exact title to be given to Marcone. In some of the early dispatches he was called a "legate" or "envoy," but quite soon the Vatican documents consistently refer to him as "apostolic visitor."[19] This was not a diplomatic title, thus indicating the absence of diplomatic relations between Croatia and the Holy See. Marcone's function in Croatia, therefore, was not viewed as primarily diplomatic, but rather as that of an observer of the religious situation.

Maglione, in a letter to Stepinac on July 25, 1941, indicated that Marcone was to take account of the religious needs of the Croat people and to refer them to the Holy See. The cardinal also thought that the envoy would have the opportunity to make some contacts with the government.[20]

At first, Pavelić was offended by the nondiplomatic background and title of Marcone. The situation was worsened by Maglione's hesitation to receive the representative whom Pavelić eventually sent to the Vatican, Nicolas Rusinović.[21] In October 1942, Rusinović was replaced by Prince Erwein von Lobkowicz, who again was accepted by the Vatican only as a private and personal representative.[22]

Marcone, in the meantime, made an ever-growing good impression upon the Ustase government. So favorably was he received that, beginning in February 1942, he was treated as a diplomat by the Croat government, indeed, as the *de facto* nuncio and the dean of the diplomatic corps, albeit small, accredited to Croatia.[23] He was also highly visible at all public ceremonies and given a place of honor.[24] It is apparent that the abbot enjoyed a cordial relationship with Pavelić.[25]

1941

REPORTS ON THE SITUATION OF THE JEWS

Marcone had arrived in Zagreb early in August 1941. His first report to Maglione concerning the Jews was sent on August 23.[26] He indicated that the Jews were obliged to wear the yellow star and added:

This badly tolerated badge and the hatred of the Croats toward them, as well as the economic disadvantages to which they are subjected, often brings about in the mind of the Jews the desire to convert to the Catholic Church. Supernatural motives and the silent action of divine grace cannot be *a priori* excluded from this. Our clergy facilitates their conversion, thinking that at least their children will be educated in Catholic schools and therefore will be more sincerely Christian.[27]

Several days earlier Maglione had received information about the Jews in Croatia which was far more pessimistic than that sent by the abbot.[28] The president of the Union of Jewish Communities, Alatri, writing from Rome, told the cardinal that thousands of Jews in Zagreb and other Croat cities had been arrested without cause and deported. The men were forced to work in salt mines. The Jewish leader also described the dire circumstances in which 6,000 Jews lived.

. . . without means, without clothing, because required to leave carrying only as much as can be contained in a mountain sack, they are forced to live in the open in rocky areas bereft of vegetation, scorched land, with a hot climate, without sufficient water, deprived of every agricultural resource, without a roof in the literal sense of the word.[29]

Alatri asked that the Vatican intervene with the Croatian government to attempt to end the Jewish deportations and to bring about a modification of the forced labor. He also requested that his agency be permitted to assist these Jews.[30] There is no record of a Vatican reply.

Maglione's response to Marcone on September 3 was extremely complimentary and contained several pieces of advice.[31] One of them was that the abbot should confidentially and unofficially do what he could "to recommend moderation concerning the treatment of Jews residing in Croat territory."[32]

REPORT FROM ROZMAN

Three days later, the subject of the Croatian Jews came to Maglione's attention again. The archbishop of Ljubljana in Slovenia, Gregory Rozman, made an appeal on behalf of the baptized Croatian Jews who had come into his diocese. This part of Slovenia was under Italian control, and the archbishop asked that the baptized Jews be allowed to remain there rather than be forced to return to Croatia, where they were threatened with what he described as grave penalties.[33]

This was really a matter for the Italian government and, in this regard, Maglione often used the services of Pietro Tacchi-Venturi, a Jesuit. Tacchi-Venturi knew Mussolini well and was respected by Fascist officials. He had originally acted as an intermediary between the Vatican and Mussolini during the concordat discussions of 1929 and had often served in a similar capacity on other occasions.[34] His intervention in response to Rozman's telegram was most effective. He spoke to the head of the Italian police, who agreed that the Jews might remain in the province of Ljubljana.[35]

Early in October 1941, Maglione again heard from Rozman, who asked on this occasion that the converted Jews be placed in their own camps, if it should happen that they were forced to go to concentration camps.[36] Again, Tacchi-Venturi was asked to intervene with the Italian government, which agreed. In fact, the Jesuit indicated to Maglione his hope that these Jews could be transferred to the camp in Italy at Ferramonti di Tarsia.[37]

BISHOPS' CONFERENCE

The bishops of Croatia met in conference from November 17 to 20, 1941. Marcone was present for the first of their sessions. Stepinac reported their deliberations to Maglione on December 3.[38] The bishops were primarily concerned about the conversions of the Serbian Orthodox to the Catholic Church. The Serbs were being treated so badly by the Ustase that great numbers of them were seeking relief through conversion. The second item on the bishops' agenda concerned those who were suffering. In this regard they sent a letter to Pavelić urging him to treat the Jews as humanely as possible, considering that there were German troops in the country. The bishops were particularly concerned about the rights of those Jews who had been baptized.[39]

Maglione acknowledged the report in a letter to Marcone on February 21, 1942. He praised the bishops' efforts "to obtain humane treatment for the citizens of Jewish origin."[40]

1942

A Jewish leader in Trieste appealed to the Vatican in December 1941 on behalf of the Croatian Jews whose relatives had heard nothing from them for a long period of time. Maglione sent Marcone a list of the names he had received and directed him to take the necessary steps with the government to find out something about these Jews.[41]

Marcone gave the names to the Croat foreign minister, but had to wait until the end of March 1942 for a reply. He was informed that the majority of the persons named were revolutionaries or Communists or were outside the country. In addition, the abbot told Maglione, the authorities were very reluctant to give any response on matters dealing with the Jews.[42] Marcone reiterated this point several months later when he described the Croat authorities as "closed up in inexplicable silence"[43] whenever information about Jews was sought.

APPEALS ON BEHALF OF YOUNG CROATIAN JEWS

An appeal from the Jewish community of Zagreb reached Maglione in a letter from Stepinac dated January 9, 1942.[44] The Jews were deeply concerned about 200 young people, most of whom had been orphaned and were living in great misery because of the anti-Jewish laws. They asked the Vatican to intervene with the Italian authorities to obtain permission for them to go to Italy, where they could be cared for by the local Jewish community.

Maglione acted immediately on this request and sought the advice of Tacchi-Venturi. The Jesuit responded that in this case the Vatican's intervention would fail. The Italian government had previously refused entry into Italy to students who had close relatives in the country and who could have been saved from deportation if they had been admitted. Tacchi-Venturi did not judge the authorities to be too receptive to a similar request for 200 students from Zagreb.[45]

The secretary of state informed Stepinac, on January 23, 1942, that he had brought the case to the attention of an authoritative person who thought that the government would not permit the entry of these youths. He did suggest to the archbishop, however, that the Italian minister at Zagreb might be able to render some help.[46]

A similar appeal on behalf of young people was made toward the end of 1942 in a report from Marcone, dated December 15. The chief rabbi of Zagreb, Miroslav Shalom Freiberger, asked that the Holy See help in the transfer of fifty or sixty Jewish children from Zagreb to one of the Jewish community groups in Italy.[47]

In February 1942, the apostolic delegate in Washington, Archbishop Amleto Cicognani, in a dispatch to Maglione, asked about the situation of the Jews in Croatia. Cicognani's request was prompted by efforts made by World Jewish Congress officials to enlist the services of Francis Spellman, the archbishop of New York. Spellman had been asked to solicit Vatican assistance for the Jews in the Croatian camps.[48] In his reply on April 21, 1942, Maglione stated that Marcone had intervened several times on behalf of the Jews and that the abbot's secretary had been able to visit some of the concentration camps to bring the Jews some solace. Moreover, the cardinal informed Cicognani that he had obtained permission for any Jews who escaped to Italian-controlled territory to remain there and not be sent back to their country of origin.[49]

DEPORTATIONS

By the summer of 1942 the Jews of Croatia were ready for deportation.[50] Marcone announced this in a report to Maglione on July 17, 1942.

The German government has ruled that within a period of six months all the Jews residing in the Croat State must be transferred to Germany, where, according to what [Eugene] Kvaternik [chief of the Croat police] himself told me, two million Jews have been recently killed. It appears that the same fate awaits the Croat Jews particularly if old and incapable of work.

Since this news has also spread among the Jews, I am continually beseeched to do something for their salvation. Also the Chief Rabbi himself of Zagreb comes to see me and to inform me of new misfortunes.

I have appealed to the Chief of Police, who, following my suggestion, retards as much as possible, the execution of this order. He also will be pleased if the Holy See can intervene for the repeal of this ordinance, or at least to propose that all Croatian Jews be concentrated on an island or in an area of Croatia, where they could live in peace.[51]

JEWISH CHILDREN

In addition, the visitor related to Maglione that the chief rabbi had been assured that Turkey would accept fifty Jewish infants from Croatia. The problem was that these infants would have to travel through Hungary, Romania, and Bulgaria, only the last of which had given permission for the transit. The rabbi wanted the Vatican's assistance to influence the Hungarian and Romanian governments to give the required permission.[52]

On August 14, the secretary responded to the rabbi's concern, directing the nuncios in Budapest and Bucharest to intervene with their governments for a solution to the transit problem.[53] Archbishop Andrea Cassulo wrote the foreign minister in Bucharest on September 5 asking for transit visas for the children.[54] There is no indication of the eventual outcome in Romania. The nuncio in Budapest, Archbishop

Angelo Rotta, wrote to Maglione on August 28 that the Hungarian foreign minister was receptive to the request.[55]

Two months after Maglione's directive to the nuncios, Jewish leaders in Zagreb were surprised to learn that even though the Hungarian government had expressed its willingness to cooperate in the transit project, nothing further had been done about it.[56]

In a report to Maglione at the same time, on October 14, 1942, Marcone indicated that Freiberger had told him that the delay was caused by the refusal of the Croatian police to issue the proper documents for the departure of the children.[57]

Nevertheless, eventually some of the children were able to go to Turkey. On February 23, 1943, Marcone reported to Maglione the gratitude of Freiberger for the Vatican's assistance in arranging the transfer. Among those moved out of Croatia was the rabbi's own son.[58]

APPEAL TO POPE

As was seen above, during the month of July, the chief rabbi appealed to Marcone for assistance. On August 4, Freiberger wrote directly to Pius XII. He began by thanking the Pope for the kindness shown toward the Jews by his representative in Croatia. His words to the Pope were full of supplication.

> Now at a moment when the last remnants of our community find themselves in a most critical situation—at a moment when decisions are being made about their lives—our eyes are fixed upon Your Holiness. We beseech Your Holiness in the name of several thousand women and abandoned children, whose supporters are in concentration camps, in the name of widows and orphans, in the name of the elderly and the feeble, to help them so that they may remain in their homes and spend their days there, even if necessary, in the most humble circumstances.[59]

Marcone was instructed by Maglione to answer the rabbi's plea in a way he thought "fitting" and with "prudence" and "tact." The traditional formula was to be used: ". . . the Holy See, always desirous of bringing help and relief to the suffering, has not neglected to involve itself on several occasions in favor of the recommended persons."[60]

Marcone acknowledged the secretary of state's directive on September 30, 1942.[61] He mentioned that he had had several contacts with Freiberger, who was grateful for the Vatican's efforts on behalf of the Jews. The abbot also indicated that he was frequently in touch with the chief of police, Eugene Kvaternik, but with only partial success.

> Unfortunately, we have not been able to bring about any change in the

course of events. Nevertheless, many exceptions proposed by us in the deportation of the Jews have been granted and the families, on the basis of mixed marriages between Jews, even though not baptized and Catholics, have been spared without exception.[62]

Marcone's contacts with the chief of police were not only unsuccessful in preventing the deportation of the Jews, but it was the police who were preventing the fifty Jewish children from leaving the country. In July, Marcone had depicted Kvaternik as being concerned about the fate of the Jews;[63] in October he attributed to the police the denial of exit documents for the Jewish children.[64]

CROATIAN JEWS ON THE DALMATIAN COAST

Yugoslavia still maintained its legation at the Vatican even with the destruction of the state. The legation had been in contact with the Secretariat of State earlier in 1942 concerning the financial affairs of Yugoslav Jews interned at Ferramonti di Tarsia.[65] On August 14, 1942, the legation brought an urgent problem to the attention of the Secretariat. It was similar to the problem presented by Rozman in September 1941.[66] According to the Yugoslav diplomats, many Croatian Jews had fled to the Dalmatian coast to be in territory under Italian control. They suffered badly in this situation but had, at least, a certain degree of security.[67]

The Croatian government had already allowed its Jews to be deported by the Germans. The 5,000 Jews who had reached the Italian-occupied area were spared this deportation, but became an object of great concern to the Germans. The Italian authorities, however, would not consent to their deportation, and the German Foreign Office, in August 1942, declined to intervene with its counterpart in Rome.[68]

Nevertheless, there was real fear among these Jews that the Italian authorities would eventually permit them to be sent back to Croatia and from there, of course, to deportation. The legation informed the Vatican that fifty Jews had already been sent back to Croatia. The legation added:

Since the sad experiences of their brothers in Croatia, where a large number of Jews have been exterminated in such an inhuman manner, remain in the memory of all, the news of this recent deportation [of the fifty] has plunged all the Jews into the greatest anxiety. There are some of them that, to escape a long agony in the concentration camps and cruelties of all kinds, have killed themselves.[69]

The Yugoslav diplomats asked the Holy See to intervene with the Italian authorities to prevent the extradition of any Jews from territory under their control.[70]

The nuncio to Italy, Archbishop Francesco Borgongini Duca, was informed of the request. His reply, on September 11, 1942, contained the welcome information that there was no agreement between Italy and Croatia to send back the Croatian Jews. Italy did not want these Jews living in its own territory, but would allow them to remain in those areas of Yugoslavia under Italian control.[71]

WORSENING SITUATION FOR CROATIAN JEWS

In November, it appears that Germany again wanted to deport 2,000 to 3,000 Jews from Italian-controlled areas. The matter, therefore, was not as settled as Borgongini Duca's report indicated. The Italian ambassador to the Holy See, Bernard Attolico, was asked by Maglione to intervene with his government to prevent any such transfer of the Jews.[72]

On November 13, Maglione also instructed Borgongini Duca to act on behalf of the Jews.[73] Just a few days previously, the cardinal had received a memorandum stating that there were about 1,700 Jews in this area, among them many women and children. Maglione's informant indicated that the Jews were in danger of being expelled, which would probably mean death for the majority of them.[74] It was, no doubt, this information that led Maglione to deal with Attolico and Borgongini Duca.

The matter had also been brought to Marcone's attention. He responded to Maglione on November 8[75] and depicted himself as doing all he could "to alleviate the sad condition of the Croat Jews."[76] He had also spoken about them to Pavelić and the chief of police, but felt that very little had been gained. The concluding words of his report were ominous. There was a new chief of police, who

has ardently deplored with me the excesses committed in Croatia against the Jews, but who has openly admitted to me that he cannot substantially change the provisions adopted against these unfortunate people and that sooner or later all must be transported to Germany.[77]

On October 6, 1942, Maglione specifically directed Marcone to intervene with the Croat government on behalf of the Jews. It is noteworthy that he indicates, in the same dispatch, that many pieces of information and appeals had come to the Secretariat of State on behalf of Croatian Jews.[78]

About this same time, the World Jewish Congress office in Geneva issued a report on the status of the Jews in Europe. Of the 30,000 Jews in Croatia, the Jewish officials calculated, 4,000 had escaped to Italian-held territory, and "Nearly all the others have either been killed or imprisoned in labor camps where they are starving."[79]

Marcone's reply to Maglione's directive, dated December 1, 1942, described the steps he had taken.

In my visits with Pavelić and in my contacts with the other civil authorities, especially with the Chief of Police, I have always insisted on a benevolent treatment of the Jews. The responses have always been the same: "The Jews must leave Croatia; it is not the intention of the government to treat them harshly." Pavelić has also given orders in this regard.

As this Government does not have the power to make itself obeyed, it is easy, it is even certain that the inferior authorities, instead of obeying superior orders, give themselves over so many times to deplorable excesses.[80]

1943

CROATIAN JEWS IN ITALIAN-OCCUPIED TERRITORY

The Croat Jews who had taken refuge in Italian-occupied territory were again a cause for concern early in 1943. The Yugoslav legation at the Vatican had informed Maglione that 1,700 of these Jews were to be transferred.[81] The cardinal directed Borgongini Duca to take the necessary steps with the competent Italian authorities to prevent such a transfer.[82] Several weeks later, on March 21, the nuncio was able to relay to Maglione the news that the dire warning of the Yugoslav legation was not accurate.[83]

It appears, however, that it was Borgongini Duca whose information was incorrect. During March 1943, the Germans were indeed prepared to deport another 2,000 Jews from Croatia and put particular pressure upon the Italian authorities to hand over the Jews in their territories.[84] Maglione himself was aware of this new German insistence, as he wrote in his office notes on March 13, 1943.[85]

Maglione confided to Francis D'Arcy Osborne, the British minister to the Holy See, that Mussolini himself, at Vatican urging, had made efforts to prevent the deportations from Croatia.[86]

Maglione must have had in mind the cable he had received just the week before from the apostolic delegate in Washington. Myron Taylor, President Roosevelt's representative to Pius XII, had been asked by the president of the World Jewish Congress, Stephen S. Wise, to seek the delegate's aid in making known to the Vatican some startling information. The Jewish authorities believed that 15,000 Yugoslav Jews living in Italy proper or in the areas occupied by its troops would be handed over to the Germans for deportation to Poland. Cicognani added that such a transfer was the equivalent of condemning these Jews to death.[87]

The British Section of the World Jewish Congress was also active at this time to forestall the threatened deportation. On March 15, it was in touch with the apostolic delegate in London, Archbishop William Godfrey, informing him of the danger that the Yugoslav Jews in Italy would be handed over to the Nazis. They asked him to solicit the assistance of the Vatican to prevent this, a task which Godfrey readily agreed to fulfill.[88] Also, the British Foreign Office had assured the World Jewish Congress officials that it had instructed its minister at the Vatican to intervene on behalf of the Jews.[89]

THREAT TO THE JEWS IN CROATIA

Maglione's response to Cicognani on March 17 indicated only that the Holy See was continually involved on behalf of the Jews.[90] On that same day, however, he also directed Tacchi-Venturi to intercede on behalf of the Jews living in Croatia who were threatened with deportation.[91] It appears that it was Cicognani's request, along with others, that influenced Maglione to enlist Tacchi-Venturi's aid, even though the original cable of Cicognani concerned a far greater number of Jews.

Tacchi-Venturi's entrée to the highest government circles was again put to good use. He discussed the subject of Italian racial politics with the undersecretary of the Ministry of Foreign Affairs, Giuseppe Bastianini. In a long report to Maglione on April 14, 1943,[92] the situation in Croatia was referred to. In Bastianini's opinion, the Italian government could do nothing for the Jews of Croatia and the parts of Slovenia occupied by the Germans. The secretary saw as proof of this the fact that several requests by Italy in this regard were not even accepted.[93]

Finally, on March 30, 1943, Maglione made known his fears about the Jews of Croatia to Marcone. He had had contacts with or information from Cicognani, the Yugoslav legation, the British minister, and possibly others. He had instructed Tacchi-Venturi to deal with the Italian government. Only after all this did he send instructions to his representative in Zagreb. The cardinal made it clear that the threat of deportation hanging over the Jews remaining in Croatia particularly concerned him because 80 percent of them were baptized. He directed Marcone to ascertain the veracity of this report and, if it was found to be true, to take "whatever steps which were possible and opportune to impede such grave measures."[94]

Marcone replied to Maglione's telegram the very next day, stating that he was continually watching over the situation and that the Jews themselves kept him well informed. He had been told by high government officials that nothing had changed concerning the Jews. Furthermore, he assured the cardinal, Jews who had been baptized or were married to Catholics were safe. Nevertheless, Marcone admitted, he had some doubts about the assurances which had been given to him and had written to Pavelić to receive confirmation of the government's position toward this category of Jews.[95] Concerning his other activities on behalf of the Jews, the visitor reminded Maglione that he had sent him a more detailed report earlier in March.[96] On that occasion he wrote:

> Many times I have had to involve myself on behalf of the Croatian Jews with the Head of State [Pavelić], with various ministries and with the Chief of Police. At every moment of alarm the Jews crowd around my residence.
>
> Repeatedly, both orally and in writing, I have insisted to Pavelić that above all families resulting from mixed marriages and, in general, all the baptized Jews, not be molested. Pavelić has always promised me to respect the Jews who had become Catholics or were married to Catholics.
>
> In these last days there has been another alarm in Jewish circles because of a notice from the police which requested these unfortunate people to come to the offices of public security. Prompted by a desire to save at least the Catholic Jews, not be molested. Pavelić has always promised me to respect the Jews Moreover, I reminded him that I, basing myself on his promises, had already given assurances in this regard to the Holy See. I did not desire to find myself in contradiction with the facts.
>
> In the meantime I came to know that Pavelić one day, in the presence of certain authorities, stated clearly to the minister of the Reich that he did not intend to persecute the baptized Jews, having already given assurances in this regard to the representative of the Holy See to the hierarchy [Marcone]. But by means of an official, a good Catholic attached to the German embassy, I have been now informed that the minister of the Reich . . . a Protestant and a fanatical Nazi, after the posting of the notice regarding the Jews, had exclaimed: "The Holy See is beginning to become too powerful in Croatia; I want to see if this time it wins or I do." I pray to the Lord that He grant to Pavelić the strength to resist.[97]

The archbishop of Zagreb also complained to Pavelić about the notice requiring the Jews to report to the police. It appears that because of Stepinac's and Marcone's interventions, the police order was rescinded, much to the chagrin of the Germans.[98]

The Vatican Secretariat of State in its office notes seems to take credit for this decision in listing its efforts on behalf of Jews facing deportation.[99] There is little doubt, however, that the interest of the Vatican in the Jews of Croatia was directed primarily toward those who had become Catholic or who had been married according to Church rules. It was only in the spring of 1943 that these Jews were in jeopardy, occasioning the directive of Maglione to Marcone to intervene. Assurances that these Jews would be spared were accepted very willingly, and indeed proudly, by the officials of the Secretariat of State.

Given such a limited perspective, it is surprising that, in March 1943, the chief rabbi of Zagreb wrote to Pius XII again, through Marcone, to congratulate him on the anniversary of his coronation and to thank him for the charitable activity of the Holy See.[100]

DEPORTATIONS

There exists some disagreement among historians about the number of Jews deported from Croatia during 1942 and the first half of 1943. One source admits that the statistics for this period are incomplete and lists just under 5,000 Jews as being deported in 1942, with other smaller groups being sent away during 1943. Another 2,000 were deported in March 1943.[101] Another author believes that 9,000 were already removed by August 1942 and that the deportations continued in smaller numbers throughout the rest of 1942 and 1943.[102]

It would appear that several thousand Jews remained in Croatia during the spring of 1943. Many of these—if Maglione is to be believed, as many as 80 percent[103]—were baptized.

May of 1943 was a fateful month for the Zagreb Jews. Heinrich Himmler had visited the capital early in the month. According to Marcone, in a report to Maglione on May 10, Himmler's arrival occasioned the arrest and deportation of the last Jews remaining there. The number given by Marcone, however, was only 600, although he added that there were still a few in hiding.[104]

Both Marcone and Stepinac protested to the minister of the interior, Andrija Artukovic,[105] who claimed that he had strongly defended the Jews in the presence of Himmler.[106] All that Artukovic could obtain, according to Marcone, was that Jews married to Catholics would be spared. The fear remained that these Jews would also be deported, especially in the light of the fact that among the 600 rounded up there were a number of baptized Jews.[107]

Marcone sent similar bad news to Maglione two weeks later, on May 24.

. . . I am extremely saddened to inform you that, except for now, at least, mixed marriages, all the Jews, including those who had already been baptized for years, have been arrested and transported to Germany . . .

The scene of arrest of these unfortunate people was truly pitiful: During the night, while they were peacefully asleep, agents of the police came to their homes, and without any regard for their age, social condition, or baptism, arrested them. Several of the more elderly ones died of fright.[108]

On the last day of May, Marcone once again reported on the Jewish situation to Maglione. He had received a letter for the foreign minister stating that mixed marriages in Croatia were considered protected and no measures were being contemplated against them. The abbot also described the tears of gratitude in the eyes of the Jews involved in these marriages who came to his residence to thank the Holy See, "who alone in these very sad times is also taking care of these unfortunate sons of Israel."[109]

Maglione's response on June 12 was not typical of him. He admitted his pleasure at the foreign minister's decision about Jews married to Catholics, but indicated that he would be happier if the government would refrain from all regulations against Jews, not just those married to Catholics.[110]

It is startling to note that on the very same day, May 31, that Marcone was writing about the safety of Jews in mixed marriages, an urgent telegram was received from the apostolic delegate in Istanbul, Archbishop Angelo Roncalli, concerning the Croatian Jews. The Jewish Agency for Palestine had informed Roncalli that among the 400 Jews recently deported from Croatia were the president of the Jewish Community, Ugo Kon, and the chief rabbi himself. The Jewish Agency was asking Vatican assistance for precise information because there was a possibility of transferring them to Palestine.[111]

Marcone's apparent ignorance of Freiberger and Kon's deportation is truly amazing. Not only was he on the scene in Zagreb, but also he had claimed to have frequent contacts with Jewish officials. Maglione cabled him immediately upon receipt of the information from Roncalli asking if anything could be done about the situation.[112] This would seem to have been Marcone's first information about it. The matter is all the more perplexing because on August 15, Maglione had to repeat his request for information to Marcone, and asked what steps he had taken about the matter.[113] There is no record of any reply by Marcone to either of these telegrams.

Toward the middle of June, Roncalli received a note of gratitude from a Jewish relief official in Istanbul, Meir Touval-Weltmann.[114] Attached to Roncalli's letter was a memorandum by Touval-Weltmann concerning Stepinac, in which he acknowledged that the archbishop had done all possible for the Jews of Croatia. He also asked Stepinac's aid for the recently arrested Kon and Freiberger as well as his intervention with governmental authorities to allow the remaining 2,500 Jews to leave Croatia for other countries.[115]

ISLAND OF RAB

During March 1943, under German pressure, the Italian government began sending Jews from the Dalmation coast to the island of Rab (Arbe) off the coast of Croatia.[116] The safety of these refugees was temporarily assured several months later when the island was captured by Yugoslav partisans. Another 4,000 Jews were transferred there by September mainly through the efforts of the British Section of the World Jewish Congress.[117] The Congress officials were very grateful to Godfrey and the Vatican for their efforts in assisting this move.[118]

The last communication of Marcone with the Vatican for the next several months was the report of May 31. Presumably there was one in late November or early December, because Maglione referred to it in extending Christmas greetings from the Pope to the prisoners-of-war and other interned people in Croatia in a dispatch to Marcone dated December 13, 1943.[119]

It was not published in the Vatican documents, but it appears doubtful that it dealt with the Jews.

Conclusions

The Vatican's relationship with Croatia had diplomatic aspects unlike those in its dealings with any other nation during this period. From the Vatican's point of view, diplomatic relations did not exist between Croatia and the Holy See. For this reason, the Secretariat of State took great pains to insist in May 1941 that Pavelić's visit to the Pope was private and personal.[120] Again, in May and June 1943, when it was possible that Pavelić would be coming to Rome for discussions with Mussolini, Vatican officials agreed among themselves that any visit of the Croatian leader with the Pope be totally unofficial and that he not meet with Maglione, whose office was primarily diplomatic.[121]

In attempting to assay the role of Vatican diplomacy in Croatia, certain conditions must be kept in mind. First of all, Croatia's creation as a state in April 1941 came in the midst of a world war that had changed the map of Europe and in two months would explode into the German attack on the Soviet Union. Not only did the young state face the problems of governmental and political organization, but it had to do so in the context of war and with heavy dependency on its Fascist supporters, Germany and Italy.

Croatia, of course, was a creature of Hitler and, as such, accepted both his Fascist principles and anti-Semitism. Croatia was heavily involved with Italy also. Not only had the Dalmatian coast been ceded to Italy, but the crown of Croatia had been offered to the Italian House of Savoy.

Formal diplomatic relations between Croatia and the Holy See were never established. The Croatian leaders were originally disappointed and angry at the Vatican policy of not recognizing territorial changes during time of war, which, therefore, prevented any formal acknowledgment of the new state. Nevertheless, the Vatican's desire to have representatives in the various capitals of Europe led it to appoint an apostolic visitor, whose role was to be an observer of the religious scene in Croatia and to serve as a liaison between the Croatian hierarchy and the Holy See.

Marcone did not arrive in Zagreb until August 1941. He had not been a member of the Vatican diplomatic corps and was never given diplomatic status by the Vatican. Nevertheless, he achieved such good relations with the Croat authorities that they extended to him *de facto* diplomatic status, even if not reciprocal. Histories and accounts of Croatia during this period, for example, often picture him in the company of high government officials at various state functions.[122]

Moreover, it has been seen that on several occasions Maglione implicitly acted toward Marcone as he did toward the formal diplomats. He was given tasks that required him to deal with governmental authorities in ways that would normally be within the purview of established diplomatic personnel. He reported to Maglione, the Vatican's chief diplomatic official, through ordinary diplomatic channels. One has to conclude, therefore, that Marcone's role, although not officially diplomatic, was such in practice. The Croat government treated him in that way, and there appears to have been an implicit acquiescence by Maglione to that fact. Marcone, for example, had far more contacts with the government and greater accessibility to it than many apostolic delegates would have.

This point is argued because it might be objected that one cannot speak of Vatican diplomacy in regard to Croatia, let alone attempt to judge the role of the Vatican representative there. Admittedly, Marcone's task was not specifically diplomatic, but by mutual consent, explicit of Croatia, and implicit of the Vatican, he frequently served a diplomatic function.

Several times during 1941, 1942, and 1943, Marcone made some efforts to assist the Jews of Croatia. As early as September 1941, Maglione instructed him to advise the government to be more lenient toward the Jews.[123] In July[124] and September 1942,[125] in dispatches to Maglione, the abbot mentioned his contacts with the chief of police. In December 1942, he referred to a personal appeal which he made directly to Pavelić.[126] In October 1942[127] and again in March 1943,[128] Marcone was specifically instructed by Maglione to intervene with governmental officials on behalf of the Jews.

In all of these contacts, however, with one possible exception, there is no evidence of a protest against or condemnation of the actions taken by the authorities against the Jews. Requests for humane or benevolent treatment of the Jews were made, it is true, but no indictment was given of the whole process that was attempting to remove all Jews from Croatia in ways that were both cruel and unjust.

Moreover, there is an underriding current in all of Marcone's efforts that appears to limit his interest and activities to those Jews who had been baptized Catholic or who had married Catholics in ecclesiastically approved ceremonies. In his very first report to Maglione about the Jews, in August 1941, he saw spiritual benefits in the conversion of the Jews to Catholicism, even if they were motivated to do so to escape the penalties of the racial legislation.[129]

In March 1943, he defended the rights of these Jews to Pavelić, who assured him that Jews who were baptized or married to Catholics would not be harmed.[130] In May, Marcone singled out these Jews as expressing their deep gratitude to the Vatican for his efforts on their behalf.[131] In May 1943, on the occasion of the deportation of some baptized Jews, he made what might have been considered a protest on their behalf.[132] His strong words on this occasion were doubtlessly caused by Maglione's own fears, expressed earlier, that the baptized Jews would also be deported.[133]

One could argue that such a limited perspective of particular concern for Jews who became members of the Church or were married to Catholics is justified. Such a narrow focus for humanitarian efforts, however, appears without merit in the face of the information passed on to the Vatican by Marcone in July 1942 that 2,000,000 Jews had already been killed in Europe and a similar fate was anticipated for the Jews of Croatia, especially those not able to work.[134]

It must be concluded that Marcone's activity in Croatia was only minimally concerned with the Jews. His influence with the government was never fully utilized to help them or alleviate their sufferings, and the few efforts he made on their behalf seem perfunctory. He could, and did, claim success in aiding the Jews of Croatia, but only those who had been baptized Catholics or were married to Catholics.

The record of Croatia on the Jews is particularly shameful, not because of the number of Jews killed, but because it was a state that proudly proclaimed its Catholic tradition and whose leaders depicted themselves as loyal to the Church and to the Pope. The Holy See's representative in the country was honored, but his presence was not enough to deter the Ustase from the goal of ridding the country of all its Jews. Marcone made few efforts to defend the Jews and failed to use his personal and ecclesiastical prestige to aid them.

CHAPTER TEN

Italy

Introduction

Italy, in 1939, was a Fascist state whose leader, Benito Mussolini, was drawing it more and more into partnership with Nazi Germany.

POLITICAL SITUATION

In November 1937, Italy joined the Anti-Comintern Pact, which had been concluded the previous year between Germany and Japan. In December 1937, Italy withdrew from the League of Nations, while at the same time the German government announced that it had no intention of joining the League.[1]

The most obvious sign of Italian interest in participating in Germany's policies were the racial laws enacted in November 1938, even though there was no racial problem in the country at the time.[2] Jews were well assimilated in Italian society and numbered only 57,000, about 0.1 percent of the total Italian population.[3]

RELATIONSHIP TO VATICAN

In 1939 the formal relationship between Italy and the Vatican was only of ten years duration. The unification of Italy in 1870 had resulted in the loss of the Papal States. The Popes from that time on refused to recognize the Kingdom of Italy or have any dealings with it because of what they considered a unilateral aggrandizement of territory at the expense of the Holy See. Both Mussolini and Pius XI came to power in 1922, and both seemed anxious to put an end to what had been called for decades the "Roman Question."[4]

The Lateran Treaty, signed by the Italian government of Mussolini

166

and the Holy See on February 11, 1929, established the sovereignty of the Vatican State over 108.7 acres in Rome, as well as 160 acres of extraterritorial buildings and institutions.[5] On that same date a concordat was concluded regulating the relations between Italy and the new state of the Vatican.[6]

The treaty and the concordat were ratified on June 7, 1929, and, on the same day, Archbishop Francesco Borgongini Duca was appointed the first nuncio to the Kingdom of Italy. Borgongini Duca was well received by the Italian government because he had been involved in the concordat negotiations and had also openly demonstrated his support of Fascism.[7] Moreover, the nuncio was considered in Fascist circles to be an anti-Semite.[8] Borgongini Duca remained as nuncio to Italy for twenty-four years, until January 1953, when he was named a cardinal.[9]

Borgongini Duca, of course, was the official liaison between the Vatican and the Italian government, but paralleling his activity were the efforts of the Jesuit priest Pietro Tacchi-Venturi. The Jesuit often acted as an intermediary between the two parties because he was thought to have some influence over Mussolini, dating back to the days of the treaty negotiations, and he was generally respected by other Fascist officials.[10]

1939–1942

Unlike the other nations of Europe, where the usual pattern was anti-Jewish laws followed by deportations, Italy never went beyond the stage of anti-Jewish legislation. Only after September 1943, when the northern half of the country was occupied by German troops, were the Italian Jews subject to deportation. Thus, most of the Vatican diplomatic activity in Italy was focused on the racial legislation.

The racial laws of November 17, 1938 not only established a definition of Jewishness but also excluded Jews from the civil service, the armed forces, and the Fascist Party. There were restrictions on Jewish ownership of certain industries, real estate, and farm property. Marriages between Jews and Italians were prohibited.[11]

PROTESTS AGAINST RACIAL LEGISLATION

The racial laws were considered objectionable by the Vatican principally because there was no recognition of the rights of baptized Jews, whom the Vatican considered Catholics. In addition, the regulations were viewed as usurping the Church's right to decide who was eligible to be married. Pope Pius XI had immediately branded the prohibition of intermarriage as contrary to the concordat.[12]

Two of the provisions detailing Jewish identity also caused the Vatican difficulty. According to the law, the offspring of a Jewish parent and a non-Italian parent was considered Jewish, regardless of whether the child or either of his parents had been baptized. Another provision classified as Jewish the child of an Italian parent and a Jewish parent not baptized before October 1, 1938.[13]

During the first several months of Pius XII's reign, many attempts were made by Maglione, enlisting at various times the services of Borgongini Duca or Tacchi-Venturi, to have the racial legislation changed. As early as March 28, 1939, for example, just weeks after Pius XII became Pope, Tacchi-Venturi relayed to Mussolini the appeals coming to the new Pope from converted Jews. According to the Jesuit, they were devoted sons of the Church, even if of Jewish blood. Among his proposals to the Duce was one asking that the children of mixed marriages, baptized in infancy, be recognized as Aryan, even if one parent was non-Italian. Another proposal he made was that membership in the catechumenate rather than actual baptism be recognized as being effective before the October 1, 1938 deadline.[14]

Shortly afterwards, Borgongini Duca was instructed by Maglione to encourage the government to accept the catechumenate as a sign of being a Catholic.[15] Since the catechumenate, or preparation time for baptism, might last for several months, more Jews would be recognized as Catholics by the law. The nuncio reported to Maglione, on April 19, 1939, that the government would only accept baptism as proof of Church membership. In addition, he relayed to the cardinal the complaints and suspicions of government officials that there were some efforts to falsify dates on baptismal certificates.[16]

During May another matter concerned Maglione. He had already heard that another racial law was in preparation,[17] which would severely affect baptized Jews. They would be forbidden by this law to exercise their professions except with Jews. Borgongini Duca was instructed to intervene with the government to obtain an exception in the law for baptized Jews.[18] In the middle of June the nuncio had to acknowledge that his efforts had not succeeded. He had been told that he had intervened too late and that the law had already been approved. His request for modification of the law was likewise rejected.[19]

The fear that the nuncio would be unsuccessful influenced Maglione to delegate Tacchi-Venturi also to intervene on behalf of converted

Jews who were professional people. The cardinal admitted that it was a difficult assignment, but praised the priest's ability to accomplish it.[20]

This concern about Jews who had converted to Catholicism or who had intermarried was statistically justified. The ordinary rate of conversion of the Italian Jews was approximately 10 percent.[21] After the 1938 racial laws, it was thought that 4,000 Jews left Judaism to become Catholics.[22] The rate of intermarriage was also high, and during the decade before the war 30 percent of Italian Jews married gentiles.[23]

There is little doubt that the Vatican's exclusive focus on converted Jews was narrow, but at the same time it was an obvious denial of the whole rationale underlying the racial legislation. The Church did not consider race or ethnic background in determining its membership. As Monsignor Domenico Tardini, one of Maglione's assistants, noted, the Church's interest and activity on behalf of baptized Jews were motivated by the conviction that they were Catholics, like all other Catholics.[24]

A similar point of view was expressed by Borgongini Duca in an argument with Roberto Farinacci, the anti-Vatican and anti-Semitic editor of the *Regime Fascista*. The archbishop tried to convince him that Jews baptized Catholics should no longer be considered Jews, but Catholics, with the same rights as other Catholics.[25]

In August the prerogatives of baptized Jews were again of interest to the Secretariat of State. Tacchi-Venturi had suggested two goals for the Vatican to consider: baptized Jewish children should be permitted to attend Catholic schools, and baptized Jews should be allowed to marry Italians with full civil recognition of their marriages.[26] Maglione instructed Borgongini Duca on August 23 to consult with Tacchi-Venturi and attempt to achieve these goals.[27]

On August 29, the very eve of the outbreak of the war, the nuncio met with Guido Buffarini, the undersecretary in the Ministry of the Interior. Buffarini argued that international Judaism was against Italy, and with war imminent it was not the time to discuss the issue. Borgongini Duca suggested the contrary in what appears to be an amazing combination of logic and naïveté. If baptized Jews were recognized as Catholics by the government, he argued, then they would join the army, from which they were excluded as Jews. Furthermore, if the effective date for Church membership were pushed back from October 1, 1938 to the end of 1939, then many more Jews would join the Church and could prove the sincerity of their conversions by risking their lives in defense of Italy as members of the armed forces. The minister did not accept the argument. The nuncio later wrote to Maglione that both he and Tacchi-Venturi were agreed that no improvements in the marrige legislation were possible at that time.[28]

In the same dispatch, Borgongini Duca indicated that both he and Tacchi-Venturi, given the text of the regulation, saw no problem with baptized Jewish children attending religious schools.[29]

EFFORTS ON BEHALF OF MIXED FAMILIES

During 1940, the Vatican's efforts were directed toward "mixed" families where one spouse was Italian and the other Jewish, often baptized. In December 1939, Maglione asked Tacchi-Venturi to describe for government officials the sad situation of many of these families.[30]

In February 1940 the Secretariat of State sent a lengthy appeal on behalf of mixed families to the Italian embassy at the Vatican. The Vatican statement pointed out, first of all, that, according to the law, the Jewish partner in a mixed marriage was inferior to the other and this could be destructive of family unity and stability. The regulation prohibiting professional services by Jews to non-Jews, soon to take effect, was also mentioned as being detrimental to mixed families, particularly when the father was Jewish. The Secretariat asked the embassy to use its good offices to have all the members of mixed families recognized as fully Aryan.[31]

During May 1940, there were rumors that the racial laws were being changed so that children born of a baptized Jew and an Italian would be considered Aryans.[32] On May 25, Tacchi-Venturi was charged by Maglione to work toward achieving this change in the law.[33]

During July, it was thought in the Vatican that the racial laws were being modified so that the head of a family, if a baptized Jew, would be exempted from the prohibitions directed against Jewish professionals.[34] On July 25, Maglione wrote to Tacchi-Venturi expressing his pleasure that such a change was being considered. He encouraged the priest to do what he could to bring about this modification, describing it as an asset both to the Church and to the state.[35]

At the end of 1940, Tacchi-Venturi was still reporting to the secretary of state that changes in the racial legislation, whereby all the members of mixed families would be considered Aryans, were being proposed. The officials involved were depicted as only awaiting an opportune moment to present them to Mussolini.[36]

Five months later, in May 1941, Tacchi-Venturi was still striving to gain some mitigations in the racial laws.[37] Toward the end of that month, Edvige Mussolini, the sister of the Italian leader, made known to one of the Roman cardinals that changes in the racial laws were indeed being contemplated. She suggested that discussions on this subject should be conducted with Fascist officials, not by the nuncio or Tacchi-Venturi, but by the highest officials of the Secretariat of State.[38]

Tardini's reaction to the proposal was realistic. He noted that the Italian government was already well informed of the Vatican's wishes in regard to the racial legislation and that further discussions would not add anything. Moreover, Tardini felt that the German influence in Italy would not permit any mitigation of the regulations concerning the Jews. For this reason he felt that any intervention by the Holy See, at whatever level, was already doomed.[39]

Pius XII, however, directed Maglione to discuss the matter with the Italian ambassador, Bernardo Attolico. In a meeting on June 3, 1941, Attolico told the cardinal that he was aware that a law in favor of mixed families was being prepared, but he suspected that it would not be promulgated until after the war.[40]

In November 1941, Maglione indicated in a letter to Borgongini Duca how preoccupied the Vatican was with the racial legislation, especially since the provisions were contrary to Catholic doctrine and the marriage rights guaranteed to the Church by the concordat.[41]

Even during 1942, when deportations of Jews from all over Europe were in full swing, racial law discussions were going on in Rome. On March 6, Maglione himself met with Buffarini only to be informed that the decree labeling as Aryan all the members of mixed families was being postponed.[42]

In October 1942, Maglione once again indicated to Tacchi-Venturi how the delay in announcing the racial law changes was affecting the converted Jews. He authorized the Jesuit to appeal directly to Mussolini if he thought it opportune.[43]

AID TO BAPTIZED JEWS

In attempting to aid the baptized Jews, the Vatican came into contact with Delasem (Delegazione Assistenza Emigranti Ebrei), the Jewish organization whose principal task was to assist Italian Jews to emigrate. In May 1941, the organization wrote directly to the Pope asking him to use his influence with the Portuguese government to grant transit visas to Jews departing from the port of Lisbon.[44] At the beginning of 1941, Portugal had changed its regulations and had made the process of obtaining visas far more difficult and time-consuming than it had been. This delay effectively prevented many Jews from leaving because the validity period of their other documents would expire. The Delasem asked that the Portuguese consul in Rome be authorized to grant the transit visas.[45]

The problem had already been brought to the Pope's attention in February by the Reverend Franz Hecht, the representative of the Raphaelsverein in Rome. This group was chiefly concerned with the needs of baptized Jews and in particular, at this time, those with visas for Brazil.[46] Hecht expressed the same fear that the lengthy delay in obtaining the transit visas would invalidate the time period stated in the Brazilian visas.[47]

The Vatican apparently did not react to either of these appeals because, in June 1941, another Roman representative of the Raphaelsverein, the Reverend Anthony Weber, made what was the third attempt to obtain Vatican influence with the Portuguese government.[48] The Vatican finally responded and on July 1 cabled the nuncio in Lisbon to work on the matter.[49] It was not until October 1 that he informed Maglione that the Portuguese government had agreed to grant the visas expeditiously.[50] It was unfortunately too late for many Jews whose visas had expired.

About this same time, the Delasem made it very clear to the Vatican, through Borgongini Duca, that it was in no position financially to offer assistance to the baptized Jews. In July 1941, the Jewish organization wrote to the nuncio asking him to suggest a group or an office to which it might send baptized Jews who required aid.[51] Bongongini Duca's reply was that his nunciature had already done all that it could to assist Jews of whatever religion and that the Holy See had paid the traveling expenses of many Jews.[52]

INTERNMENT CAMPS

Shortly after Italy entered the war in June 1940 as an ally of Germany, concentration camps were set up throughout the country to house enemy aliens. Several thousand Jews of non-Italian nationality were interned in them, as well as a few hundred Italian Jews.[53]

These Jews would eventually become subjects of great interest to both the Italian government and the Vatican. The nuncio visited several of the camps during the spring of 1941 and again toward the end of 1942.[54] That his visits were appreciated is evident in the letters from Jewish officials thanking both the nuncio and the Vatican for their interest.[55]

The camp at Ferramonti di Tarsia appears to have been the one with which the Vatican was most involved.[56] Borgongini Duca reported that during his visit there in May 1941 there were over 1,100 foreign Jews, of whom 85 had been baptized.[57] According to him, most of them were of German or Polish origin.[58] Included also were 500 Slovakian Jewish refugees who had been shipwrecked near the island of Rhodes, and taken by the Italian navy to Ferramonti.[59]

To assist the needs of the baptized Jews in the camp, a Capuchin priest, the Reverend Calliste Lopinot, was sent there as chaplain. His services, however, were directed toward all the Jews interned in the camp. For example, in March 1942, at the height of the deportations throughout Europe, Lopinot wrote to Borgongini Duca on behalf of the Jews whose relatives were being deported. They asked that the Vatican intervene with the Italian government to accept their relatives into the Italian camps. They naïvely thought that Germany would give permission for these Jews to leave and that the main obstacle to such a procedure was the Italian government. The nuncio noted very realistically that the number of Jews involved was over 6,000 and that neither the German nor the Italian government would cooperate in such a venture.[60]

Several months later, in September 1942, Lopinot related to the nuncio the terror that was spreading throughout the camp because of the news about the deportations. On behalf of all the interned Jews, he begged Borgongini Duca to work toward preventing such measures from being enacted in Italy.[61]

The Vatican also donated money for the upkeep of the Jews in Ferramonti both through Lopinot[62] and through the nuncio.[63]

The Jews interned at Ferramonti survived the war, although there was an alarming report in August 1943, shortly before the German occupation, that all the refugees in Ferramonti had been moved to similar camps in northern Italy. This would, obviously, have been a grave threat to the Jews. The British Foreign Office, which heard the report, asked its minister at the Vatican, Francis D'Arcy Osborne, to check. He replied to the Foreign Office on August 25 that the information had not been accurate.[64]

Two other matters concerned the Vatican during 1942. Tacchi-Venturi made several attempts to obtain entry into Italy for non-Italian Jews whose lives were threatened in other countries. The consistent governmental reply was that such Jews would no longer be allowed into the country.[65]

The other matter, of little importance in view of the total Holocaust, but interesting, nonetheless, was the reaction of the Vatican to a complaint brought to its attention by Harold H. Tittmann, the chargé d'affaires of the United States. He wrote in June 1942 that he found it "degrading" and "appalling" that some Roman Jews were being forced to do manual labor quite close to St. Peter's Basilica.[66] Maglione immediately asked the Italian ambassador to do something about it.[67]

Tacchi-Venturi was also asked to use his services. A week later he informed the cardinal that the Jews working along the Tiber were of the working class and that no Jews of the professional classes were engaged in such labor.[68]

The forced labor of the Jews was also discussed by Borgongini Duca in a meeting with Buffarini in November 1942. The nuncio had inquired whether there would be any improvement in the situation of the Jews. The undersecretary replied that it personally repelled him to send educated Jews to do heavy labor and only a few were involved in such work. The Grand Council of Fascism, he added, wanted to defend the race, not to persecute the Jews.[69]

TRIENNIAL REPORT OF THE NUNCIO

The situation at the beginning of 1943 was summed up by Borgongini Duca in his triennial report to the secretary of state for the years 1940, 1941, and 1942.[70] As he wrote:

The state of war has brought an exacerbation of the racial question. Many Jews have fled from the territories occupied by Germany, preferring to come to Italy, even taking the risk of being interned. Afterwards they have called upon this Papal Nunciature to obtain the possibility of going abroad especially to America. Through our intervention many have obtained the necessary visas from the various consulates, and also [visas] for transit and the Holy Father, in his inexhaustible charity, has provided for many not insignificant funds for their journey.

The Nunciature has also succeeded, but only in the rarest cases, in obtaining from Count [Galeazzo] Ciano [Italian foreign minister] entry visas for the kingdom for Jews who were in danger of being deported.[71]

1943

FOREIGN JEWS IN ITALY

The foreign Jews who had been interned in camps were to be the source of much Vatican activity during 1943. Those in greatest jeopardy were the Jews from Poland and Yugoslavia. In February 1943, the Polish embassy at the Vatican informed the Secretariat of State that the Polish Jews at Ferramonti were in danger of being repatriated and handed over to the German authorities.[72] This influenced Maglione to instruct

Borgongini Duca on February 17 to verify the report and take appropriate action.[73] The nuncio responded ten days later that there had been no German demand up to that time for the return of the Polish Jews.[74]

The Yugoslav Jews were in even greater danger. There were 15,000 of them, some of them in camps, but most in areas occupied by Italy, with the potential threat of being subjected to the Germans. Maglione was first alerted to the threat in a cable from the apostolic delegate in Washington, Archbishop Amleto Cicognani, on March 7, 1943. He had been asked to refer the matter to the Vatican by Myron Taylor, President Roosevelt's representative to the Vatican. Stephen S. Wise, the president of the World Jewish Congress, had been the source of Taylor's information that the Yugoslav Jews would be handed over to the German government at its request and deported to Poland. As Cicognani wrote, possibly quoting one of his sources, "This signifies their condemnation to death."[75] The only response that was sent to Cicognani at this time was the vague information that the Holy See was involved on behalf of the Jews.[76]

The British Section of the World Jewish Congress was also active at this time. On March 15, 1943, the office was in touch with the apostolic delegate in London, Archbishop William Godfrey, relating to him the threat of deportation hanging over the Yugoslav Jews living under Italian control. The Jewish group asked him to intervene with the Pope to prevent any such deportation from occurring.[77] There is no record in the Vatican documents, but Godfrey did indicate that he would communicate with the Vatican on the matter.[78]

The London office of the World Jewish Congress also informed the British Foreign Office of the impending danger and received assurances that the British minister at the Vatican would be given pertinent instructions.[79] On March 20, the British legation asked the Vatican's assistance in preventing any such measure from being carried out.[80]

After having received requests from Cicognani, the British legation, and, perhaps, Godfrey, the Secretariat of State finally reacted on April 10. Monsignor Giovanni Battista Montini, one of Maglione's assistants, sent instructions to Borgongini Duca telling him to investigate the accuracy of the threat and to take appropriate action if necessary.[81] The nuncio replied immediately that the rumor was without any foundation.[82]

During May and June the Yugoslav and other Jews were again a source of worry. The Yugoslav legation at the Vatican petitioned the Secretariat of State on May 29 to protect its citizens.[83] Maglione once again asked Borgongini Duca to look into the matter to ascertain the attitude of the government toward the Yugoslav Jews.[84] The nuncio repeated his earlier assurances that there was no change in the government's attitude toward these Jews and none of them would be handed over to the German authorities.[85]

In the middle of June 1943 reports began to circulate that all the foreign Jews in Italy, numbering 10,000, were being concentrated in the camp at Ferramonti as a prelude to their deportation.[86] This news led the Jewish Agency for Palestine, as well as the Polish and Czechoslovak embassies in London, to bring the matter to the attention of the Foreign Office. The immediate fear of the Foreign Office was whether the Italian government, under threat of invasion by Allied forces, might change its mind and deliver the Jews to the Germans. Accordingly, on June 24, Osborne was instructed to "request the Vatican authorities to be good enough to intervene urgently with a view to causing deportation if intended to be delayed or avoided altogether."[87]

A similar appeal came toward the end of June from the chargé d'affaires at the apostolic delegation in Cairo, the Reverend Arthur Hughes, writing at the request of the chief rabbi of the Holy Land Isaac Herzog.[88] The response to Hughes on July 3 stated confidently that the Vatican's efforts to prevent the deportation of foreign Jews had been successful.[89]

Nevertheless, the concern for these Jews continued during July 1943. Twice during that month the British Section of the World Jewish Congress was in touch with Godfrey concerning them.[90] On July 20, Godfrey sent to the Vatican a memorandum that he had received from Alexis L. Easterman, the political secretary of the British Section of the World Jewish Congress.[91] With the anticipated advance of the Allied troops in Italy, after their landing in Sicily earlier in the month, there was a new fear of what would happen to the Jews in Italy during whatever hostilities might develop. Easterman asked that the Vatican intercede with the Italian government to have the Jews of northern Italy moved to the south, where they would presumably be secure in the event of an Allied invasion from Sicily.[92]

On July 23, Cicognani cabled a similar appeal from Washington, again at the request of Wise.[93] By the time the response to Cicognani had been formulated, Mussolini had fallen from power (July 25) and the urgency of the matter had lessened. Nevertheless, on July 26, Cicognani was informed that the Holy See was doing all it could to prevent any harm coming to the foreign Jews in Italy.[94]

Easterman, after his memorandum to Godfrey, later telegraphed the Pope directly on August 2. It was again a plea for help in transferring the Jews of northern Italy to the south.

World Jewish Congress respectfully expressing gratitude to Your Holiness for your gracious concern for innocent peoples afflicted by calamities of war appeals to Your Holiness to use your high authority by suggesting Italian authorities may remove as speedily as possible to Southern Italy or other safer areas twenty thousand Jews refugees and Italian nationals now concentrated in internment camps and residing in Northern Italy vicinity Trieste, Fiume, Parma, Modena and so prevent their deportation and similar tragic fate which has befallen Jews in Eastern Europe. Our terror-stricken brethren look to Your Holiness as the only hope for saving them from persecution and death.[95]

The response to Easterman's appeal was made through Godfrey, who was told on August 6 to make known to the Jewish official that the Holy See would continue to do what it could on behalf of the Jews.[96]

World Jewish Congress officials in the United States were also active and asked Cicognani to cable a similar plea, which he sent on August 20.[97] He was advised in reply several days later that the Holy See had already been involved on behalf of these Jews.[98]

Maglione did contact the Italian embassy concerning the Jews in northern Italy. The reply on August 12 was very reassuring in its tone and stated that there were no concentration camps in the north.[99] The text of Maglione's communication with the embassy has not been published. As a result, it is not known whether he specifically inquired about the possibility of transferring the Jews in the north to the south. The embassy's response did not deal with this issue, but simply denied the existence of any camps.

Paralleling these activities on behalf of foreign Jews in Italy were discussions with government officials on their attitude toward the Jews. In April, Tacchi-Venturi met with Bastianini,[100] who summarized the Italian attitude toward the Jews as "separation, not persecution."[101] The Fascist official claimed that the government did not want to act as executioners toward the Jews and that the desire to be separated from the Jews was inspired by the traditional Church practice.[102]

It is not so clear, however, whether foreign Jews were included in this moderate tolerance. Contrary to the embassy's assertion that there were no camps for Jews, most of the foreign Jews in the country were already interned and no more were being permitted to enter the country. Already in May it was apparent to Tacchi-Venturi that all efforts to allow foreign Jews to remain free were doomed to futility.[103]

During July, Maglione involved himself in a matter of narrow and insignificant focus. It concerned the mandatory labor service. The cardinal complained to the nuncio that no provisions had been made for separating baptized Jews from Jews during their work. He thought this was humiliating for the converts and asked Borgongini Duca to seek the separation of the two groups.[104]

The converted Jews had other problems too. Maglione received a letter from a group of them in mid-August explaining to him their grave financial situation. They pointed out that Delasem would not aid baptized Jews or Jews who had intermarried and they feared that similar relief organizations would act in the same way.[105] There is no record or indication whether the converted Jews worked separately or not, or whether any aid was given to the group who wrote to Maglione.

RACIAL LEGISLATION UNDER THE BADOGLIO GOVERNMENT

After the fall of Mussolini on July 25, 1943, the racial legislation was still in effect. Tacchi-Venturi thought that it was an opportune time to approach the new government of Pietro Badoglio to discuss modifications in the regulations. He asked Maglione on August 10 for authorization to do so.[106] This Maglione gave him, of course, while at the same time agreeing to the three problems on which the Jesuit should concentrate his efforts: that all members of mixed families be considered Aryans, that the catechumenate be recognized as proof of membership in the Church, and that marriages celebrated ecclesiastically between Italians and Jews be acknowledged as civilly valid.[107] Toward the end of August Tacchi-Venturi met with the new minister of the interior, who appeared favorably disposed to the proposals.[108] These efforts, unfortunately, were all in vain since shortly afterwards German troops took control of Rome and all of the nation north of it.

GERMAN OCCUPATION OF ROME AND NORTHERN ITALY

Thus, the situation of the Jews in the northern half of Italy changed radically after September 1943. The Secretariat of State took note of its own fears on September 17 when one of its members wrote that regulations against the heads of Jewish families were soon to be issued. There appeared to the Vatican diplomats only one course of action, to recommend to the German ambassador, Ernst von Weizsäcker, that the rights of the entire civilian population, no matter what race, be respected.[109] This was discussed by the Pope himself with Montini as a course of action to be studied, but there is no indication that such a recommendation was made.

Also on September 17, the Jewish lawyer Ugo Foa, president of the Jewish community organization in Rome, visited the Secretariat of

State. He was concerned about a group of 150 non-Italian Jews who had been afraid to flee south with other Jews because of their inability to speak Italian. They were then living in a Jewish school and could easily be arrested by the Germans. Foa asked the Vatican to allow them to move into some of the religious houses in Rome. The request was denied, and it was recommended that the 150 Jews flee from Rome in small groups led by an Italian-speaking Jew.[110]

The problem of Jews lodging in religious houses was discussed on October 1 by the Pope and Montini. A Jewish family had asked to stay with a group of nuns, who were willing to accept them except for the husband. Montini authorized the nuns to accept the male member of the family because he was elderly and needed the attention of his wife.[111]

On September 26, Foa was called to the headquarters of the S.S. and told by Major Herbert Kappler that within thirty-six hours the Jewish community of Rome must hand over to him 50 kilograms of gold or 200 of them would be deported.[112] The Pope offered to lend the Jewish community whatever they would need, but they were able to collect the entire amount themselves.[113] The Jews did ask, however, that they be permitted to bring such a request to the Vatican in the future, if it were necessary.[114]

On October 11, Vatican officials were told of some rumors that 3,000 S.S. troops had been requested by the German military commander in Rome to be used for a house-search operation in Rome to begin on October 18.[115] Some of these facts were erroneous and Jews were not even mentioned in the rumor. Nevertheless, unknown to the Vatican, Kappler had been ordered to prepare for the deportation of 8,000 Jews from Rome. Both German military and diplomatic officials in Rome attempted to have the order rescinded, but on October 9 the German Foreign Ministry told them not to become involved and to leave the matter to the S.S.[116]

Unfortunately, the Jews of Rome did not appreciate the danger of their position. They were relieved after they delivered the 50 kilograms of gold and readily and naïvely accepted Kappler's word that no harm would come to them.

The Jews of Rome also felt a certain sense of security because they doubted that the Germans would commit any actions that might arouse the ire of the Vatican. Moreover, the Jews of Rome knew little about the total scope of the Nazi campaign against the Jews. They had heard about the atrocities being committed against eastern Jews, but could not conceive of such actions occurring in a civilized state like Italy.[117]

RAID OF OCTOBER 16 AND VATICAN REACTION

On Saturday morning, October 16, 1943, beginning around 5:30 A.M., an S.S. force suddenly surrounded the Roman ghetto and began to round up the Jews living there.[118] Before the raid ended in the early afternoon, 1,259 people had been arrested. They were taken to the Collegio Militare, where most of those of mixed descent or involved in mixed marriages were later released. Two days later, 1,007 of them were shipped to Auschwitz.

The reaction of the Pope to this event has become one of the most confused and controversial issues in the study of the Vatican's reaction to the Holocaust. A principal contributor to this was Weizsäcker, whose reports to Berlin were written in such a way as to obfuscate the situation in Rome and minimize any reaction by the Pope or the Vatican.[119]

The first news of the raid was brought personally to the Vatican early Saturday morning by the Princess Enza Pignatelli Aragona Cortes, who had been informed of it by someone who resided near the ghetto. She immediately sought and received an audience with the Pope, who was surprised at the news because he had believed the German promise not to harm the Jews. He immediately instructed Maglione to intervene.[120]

Maglione and Weizsäcker met that same day, at the bidding of the secretary of state. He recorded the details of their discussion.

Having learned that this morning the Germans made a raid on the Jews, I asked the Ambassador of Germany to come to me and I asked him to try to intervene on behalf of these unfortunates. I talked to him as well as I could in the name of humanity, in Christian charity.

The Ambassador, who already knew of the arrests, but doubted whether it dealt specifically with the Jews, said to me in a sincere and moved voice: "I am always expecting to be asked: Why do you remain in your position?"

I said: No, Ambassador, I do not ask and will not ask you such a question. I say to you simply: Your Excellency, who has a tender and good heart, see if you can save so many innocent people. It is sad for the Holy See, sad beyond telling that right in Rome, under the eyes of the Common Father, so many people have been made to suffer only because they belong to a particular race.

The Ambassador, after several moments of reflection, asked me: "What will the Holy See do if events continue?"

I replied: The Holy See would not want to be put into the necessity of uttering a word of disapproval.

The Ambassador observed: For more than four years I have followed and admired the attitude of the Holy See. It has succeeded in steering the ship in the midst of rocks of every kind and size without colliding and, even if it has greater confidence in the Allies, it has known how to maintain a perfect balance. I ask myself if, at the very time that the ship is reaching port, it is fitting to put everything in danger. I am thinking about the consequences which such a step of the Holy See would provoke. . . . The order came from the highest source. . . . "Your Eminence will leave me free not to report this official conversation?"

I remarked that I had asked him to intervene appealing to his sentiments of humanity. I left it to his judgment to make or not make mention of our conversation which was so amicable.

I wanted to remind him that the Holy See, as he himself has perceived, has been so very prudent so as not to give to the German people the impression that it has done or wished to do the least thing against Germany during this terrible war.

But I also had to tell him that the Holy See should not be put into the necessity of protesting: if ever the Holy See is obliged to do so, it will rely upon divine Providence for the consequences.

"In the meantime, I repeat: Your Excellency has told me that you will attempt to do something for the unfortunate Jews. I thank you for that. As for the rest, I leave it to your judgment. If you think it more opportune not to mention our conversation, so be it."[121]

Weizsäcker may also have spoken to Montini on the occasion of his discussion with Maglione. In a conversation with Gerhard Gumpert, a diplomat in the service of General Rainer Stahel, the military commander of Rome, he affirmed that he had warned Montini of the dire consequences that might result from any papal protest.[122]

Whether the German ambassador spoke to Montini or not, and one historian denies it,[123] or whether in conversation he inadvertently mixed up the two Italian names, and was actually describing his discussion with Maglione, his motivation was clear. He appeared genuinely to fear the effects of any protest by the Vatican, leading him to write reports to Berlin which are ambiguous at best, and deceitful at worst.

Weizsäcker reported on developments in Rome in a telegram to Berlin on October 17. He did not mention that he had been summoned to see Maglione or that the cardinal had mentioned the possibility of a protest. He cabled:

I can confirm the reaction of the Vatican to the removal of Jews from Rome, as given by Bishop Hudal.[124] . . . The Curia is dumbfounded, particularly as the action took place under the very windows of the Pope, as it were.[125] The reaction could perhaps be muffled if the Jews were employed on work in Italy itself.

Circles hostile to us in Rome are turning the action to their own advantage to force the Vatican to drop its reserve. It is being said that in French cities, where similar things happened, the bishops took up a clear position. The Pope, as Supreme Head of the Church and Bishop of Rome, could not lag behind them. Comparisons are also being made between Pius XI, a much more impulsive person, and the present Pope.

Our opponents, in their propaganda abroad, will certainly seize upon the present action in the same way in order to sow discord between us and the Curia.[126]

This telegram has served as one of the main causes of the accusation that the Vatican was silent even in the face of the deportation of the Roman Jews. As well-intentioned as Weizsäcker may have been, and zealous for the safety of the Pope and Rome,[127] his report gave a distorted view of the events of these days to posterity.[128]

On the 17th, a priest official of the Secretariat of State, Igino Quadraroli, visited the Collegio Militare, where the arrested Jews were being kept. He was not permitted to speak to any of them, but was able to leave a package of food for one family. The priest was told that since their arrest the previous day they had not received any food or drink. Among those being detained, he mentioned, he had seen Jews who had been baptized, confirmed, and married in the Church.[129]

The Vatican's efforts on behalf of these converted Jews were partially successful. Over 200 of those arrested were set free. The Secretariat of State specifically requested the release of twenty-nine people in a note to Weizsäcker on the 18th.[130] These were doubtlessly among those let go, while the remainder were people involved in intermarriages, whom the Germans would have been reluctant to take.

On October 22, another list containing five names were sent to the German ambassador.[131] Five more names were added the next day,[132] and several more times during November and December the Secretariat of State sent notes to the German embassy requesting the release of certain Jews, some of whom were baptized, but most were not.[133] It is not likely that these interventions were fruitful, since the Jews had already been transported north.

Appeals came simultaneously to the Vatican from the relatives of those arrested.[134] At a meeting of the Pope with Montini on October 18, it was decided to say, as a response to these requests, that the Vatican was doing what could be done.[135]

There was never again any large-scale arrest of Jews in Rome. Himmler apparently gave orders shortly after the October 16 raid that, because of the Vatican's position in Rome, all such arrests should be suspended.[136]

There was an embarrassing rumor that the Vatican had to deal with at the same time that it was taking these steps. According to this story, a woman who had protested the arrests of the Jews was told by a German official that several days previously, when the Pope met with the German ambassador, he told him that if Jews had to be deported from Rome, it would be best to do it quickly. Nothing was actually done to deny the rumor although there was concern in the Secretariat of State because there were witnesses to the statement and it was feared that the story would be spread.[137]

The fate of the Roman Jews would haunt the Vatican for the next few months. For example, on October 25, it was informed that the deported Jews had passed through Padua, a city in northeastern Italy, several days previously.[138] On the 28th, word reached the Secretariat that the Jews had passed through Vienna.[139]

Tacchi-Venturi also involved himself with their fate. It would appear that he was disturbed not only by the sufferings of the Jews, who had so often appealed to him in the past, but also by the lack of action by Vatican officials. He wrote to Maglione on October 25 that the recent cruel treatment of the Jews by the Germans had led to an ever-increasing number of entreaties to him. He added:

> In a special way I have been begged to arrange that the Holy See make some urgent intervention so that at least it might learn where so many Jews, even those Christian, men and women, young and old, children and babies, will end up, [Jews who were] transported barbarously like beast for slaughter last week from the Collegio Militare. . . .
>
> A step of this kind taken by the Holy See, even if unfortunately it does not obtain the desired effect, will be worthwhile without a doubt to increase the veneration and gratitude toward the August Person of the Holy Father, always the avenger of suppressed rights.[140]

A sentiment similar to Tacchi-Venturi's was expressed to Montini by the Swedish minister to Rome. He was not accredited to the Vatican, but was well thought of there. It was his opinion that if the Holy See should make some public statement condemning the recent events involving the Jews of Rome, it would be well received.[141]

Tacchi-Venturi wrote again to Maglione the day after his last report on October 26. He told the cardinal about one of the arrested Jews, who had been baptized for over thirty years and had been prepared for confirmation by the Jesuit himself.[142] The plea led to an intervention by the Secretariat of State with the German embassy, but with no evidence of any success.[143] Again, on October 29, Tacchi-Venturi brought to Maglione's attention the entreaties from Jews who were anxious for news about the deportees.[144] There is no evidence of any response or reaction to this letter of Tacchi-Venturi.

In addition to appeals for the release of certain individual Jews, the Secretariat of State was also in contact with the German embassy seeking information about the whereabouts and condition of other individual Jews. For example, on December 1[145] and December 29[146] lists of names were sent to the embassy with requests for information about the persons. There is no indication that the embassy could or did respond to any of these interventions by the Vatican.

A very moving cry for aid was sent directly to the Pope himself on October 27 by Rabbi David Panzieri, who was taking the place of the chief rabbi of Rome, who was in hiding.[147] There is unfortunately no evidence that any response was made to the rabbi's plea.

It may have been a coincidence or possibly there was a relationship between Panzieri's letter and the lead article in the previous day's edition of L'Osservatore Romano, the Vatican newspaper. The article was headlined "The Charity of the Holy Father" ("La carità del Santo Padre"). It glowingly depicted the Pope's charitable activity as universal in its perspective, and not bound by nationality, religion, or race.[148] Such a prominent article might have influenced the rabbi to appeal to the charity of the Pope for his besieged people.

The Jewish community of Rome also planned a direct petition to the Pope. It was to have been a memorandum drawn up by the Jewish leaders, Dante Almansi and Settimio Sorani, and presented to the Secretariat of State by a member of the Yugoslav legation to the Holy See, Cyril Kotnik. Sorani, however, was arrested by the Gestapo on October 28 as he entered Kotnik's residence to give him the memorandum.[149] It never reached Vatican officials.

On October 28, Weizsäcker again telegraphed Berlin. He appeared quite pleased to announce to officials there the continuing silence of the Pope regarding the arrests.

> By all accounts, the Pope, although harassed from various quarters, has not allowed himself to be stampeded into making any demonstrative pronouncement against the removal of the Jews from Rome. Although he must count on the likelihood that this attitude will be held against him by our opponents and will be exploited by Protestant quarters in the Anglo-Saxon countries for purposes of anti-Catholic propaganda, he had done everything he could, even in this delicate matter, not to injure the relationship between the Vatican and the German Government or the German authorities in Rome. As there will presumably be no further German action to be taken in regard to the Jews here in Rome, this question, with its unpleasant possibilities for German-Vatican relations, may be considered as liquidated.
>
> On the Vatican side, at any rate, there is one definite indication of this. L'Osservatore Romano of October 25/26 gives prominence to a semi-official communique of the Pope's loving-kindness which is written in the characteristically tortuous and obscure style of this Vatican paper, and says that the Pope lavishes his fatherly care on all people, *regardless of nationality, religion or race* [emphasis in the text]. The manifold and increasing activity of Pius XII (it continues) has been intensified of late because of the augmented suffering of so

many unfortunate people. No objection can be raised to this public statement, the less so as its text . . . will be understood by only very few people as having special reference to the Jewish question.[150]

It seems reasonable to assume that Weizsäcker's motivation in this and his earlier telegram to Berlin was to assure officials there that the Vatican was not going to protest. Moreover, he indicated that this policy of silence would continue if there were no further actions against the Jews of Rome. That he did not tell the complete truth in either of these reports is evident, but his rationale was well intentioned: to protect the Pope and the Vatican.

Some diplomats posted to the Vatican were convinced that the Pope had intervened with the German authorities on behalf of the Jews. The fact that some of the arrested Jews were later freed and that there were no later deportations were attributed to a strong papal complaint.[151] Obviously, Maglione's meeting with Weizsäcker could have been considered a diplomatic protest, but the secrecy that surrounded it made it ineffectual. The diplomats gave too much credit to the Vatican in assuming that it would take strenuous steps in the face of such an action against the Jews.

On the first day of November the Secretariat of State heard indirectly from a German police official that the deported Jews would not be returning to their homes.[152] It was perhaps this information, as well as the various appeals coming to the Secretariat of State, that influenced Maglione to write a confidential letter to Weizsäcker on November 6.

The nobility of soul of Your Excellency encourages me to ask you if it is possible for you to accede to the desires of many relatives and friends of the non-Aryans recently arrested in Rome, who would like to have news of their dear ones, and to send them, eventually, some material aid.

Numerous appeals, indeed, have arrived and continue to arrive at the Holy See for this purpose, so that a step, in this sense, by Your Excellency with higher authorities, might give the same Holy See a way to bring solace to so many families.[153]

Weizsäcker did not respond to this confidential communication in writing, but did inform Montini in conversation that little or nothing could be done for these Jews. It was not even possible to obtain news about them.[154] This was, of course, the typical response of all German officials when questioned about deported Jews. The ease with which the Vatican diplomats accepted Weizsäcker's evasiveness is all the more surprising and blameworthy at this late date when so much information about German atrocities against the Jews had come into the Vatican. It is impossible to imagine that Maglione did not suspect the worst for these Jews, but he never indicated such to the German ambassador. One could easily conclude that the cardinal and the ambassador were playing games, each one knowing the truth but performing all the diplomatic niceties, while realizing the futility of such efforts on behalf of people already unequivocally doomed.

Of the 1,007 Jews deported from Rome, only fourteen remained alive at the end of the war.[155] The rest were killed at Auschwitz, but are said to have been confident to the end that they would be rescued and freed through some papal action.[156]

The Vatican's efforts on behalf of these Jews failed, principally because the steps taken were so slight as to be out of all proportion to the crime committed. Concomitant, however, with these actions was the more successful and spirited defense of the Jews remaining in Rome. Many Jews, of course, had fled south to the security of the Allied area of control, but thousands of Jews were still residing in Rome. Apprehension centered mainly on the foreign Jews among them. For example, on October 21, Tittmann asked Vatican help for 470 non-Italian Jews who had come to Rome after the armistice.[157]

JEWISH REFUGEES IN THE RELIGIOUS HOUSES OF ROME

The most obvious way that the Vatican could help the Jews of Rome was by using the hundreds of religious houses in Rome as places of refuge. Some of these had extraterritorial status as part of the property of the Vatican City state. As a matter of fact, the Vatican did suspend the rules of enclosure and cloister which prevented lay people from entering monasteries and convents, except for certain public areas.[158] Over 4,000 Jews were housed in the various religious houses of male and female religious orders, and received financial aid from both the Delasem and the Raphaelsverein.[159]

There was, however, fear for these Jews too. It was generally thought that the German military authorities would respect the inviolability of these institutions and not enter them. The S.S. troops, on the other hand, were suspected of being all too eager to invade any of these institutions for their own purposes.[160]

Even this act of charity was criticized in some Church circles. The Vicariate of Rome, which gave permission for the lodging of Jews in the monasteries and convents, was accused of being misguided in this decision because it was feared that great harm could come to the Church and to the refugees themselves.[161]

Jews were housed in these institutions continuously during the period of danger. It is noteworthy that the highest officials of the Secretariat of State were involved in efforts to find refuges for Jews. On October 29, for example, Montini asked a convent to take in eight refugee Jews.[162] The Pope himself received a request from a baptized Jewish woman seeking lodging in Vatican City itself or in a convent. Montini was directed to help find her a place.[163] In December, Maglione received a similar request.[164]

German officials were suspicious that such steps were being taken. Weizsäcker related to Montini that it was being said in Germany that Vatican City was taking in political refugees, soldiers, and Jews. Montini replied diplomatically that the allegation was not accurate.[165] It was an evasive rejoinder, but could be justified in that officially there were no such residents in Vatican City.

The refugee Jews in hiding in religious houses were also indirectly involved in a discussion that took place in another context on November 4. The Reverend Pancratius Pfeiffer, superior general of the Salvatorians, had often served as an intermediary between Stahel and the Vatican, and was well known to the various German officials in Rome. On November 4, he was at the German embassy in Rome and met the assistant to the S.S. chief in Rome, Erich Priebke. The priest dared to broach to the S.S. official the subject of rumors to the effect that the S.S. was going to search religious houses for refugees. Priebke denied this but added that an accusation had been made that there was a commission in the Vatican which concerned itself with seeking places of refuge. He did not believe this to be true, he admitted, but did suspect that certain priests in the Vatican were engaged in making such arrangements. Pfeiffer responded that if there were such priests, they were acting without official authorization.[166]

Pfeiffer concluded his remarks by informing Priebke of his past services to Stahel and offering to be of similar assistance to the S.S. officer. The priest described him as being receptive to the suggestion and added in his note to the Secretariat of State that he thought it was beneficial to maintain close contacts with the S.S.[167]

The activities of the French Capuchin priest Father Marie-Benôit must also be considered at this point.[168] He was much concerned about 499 Jews of various nationalities who had fled the Italian zone in France for refuge in Rome, and were in great jeopardy because of the German occupation. Benôit's first thought was to provide these Jews with documents from both Italian and German authorities, although not acknowledging them to be Jews. To accomplish this he needed the recommendation of the Holy See, which he requested on November 5 from Montini.[169] He was dissuaded, however, from dealing with German officials because the Secretariat of State viewed any such contacts as potentially dangerous for the Jews.[170]

The Polish Embassy at the Vatican was also worried about these 500 Jews, most of whom it thought were Polish citizens. The Polish ambassador was assured by Maglione that he would look after them.[171]

Benoît's attempts to provide documentation for the Jews almost resulted in his arrest. One of the officials in the Secretariat of State was informed that the priest was about to be accused of falsifying signatures and stamps on ration cards. The Vatican diplomats had urged Benoît to be cautious in these actions on behalf of the Jews but at the same time made every effort to assure that the charge was not leveled against him.[172]

JEWS IN NORTHERN ITALY

All the Jews in the northern half of Italy were in peril after the German occupation and the proclamation of the shadow Salo Republic under Mussolini. German officials and agencies moved into Italy. By September 25, 1943 it had been announced to the pertinent authorities that the deportation of the Italian Jews would be taking place.[173] It began in Rome in the middle of October with the deportation of 1,007 Jews, but after the first arrests the process was not repeated there. This was not to be the case, unfortunately, in the other major cities of the Salo Republic.

The Vatican was also involved in this. On November 26, Maglione wrote to Weizsäcker on behalf of the Jews in the area of Trieste. The local bishop, Antonio Santin, had informed him that the German authorities there had arrested certain Jews without making any distinction between those who had been baptized Catholics and those who had not. Also included in the round-ups were Jews married to Catholics. In addition, the property of these Jews was confiscated. The cardinal asked the ambassador to intervene to correct the situation,[174] but there is no evidence of any response to his letter.

Santin came to Rome soon afterwards to personally inform Maglione of the situation in the Trieste area. He described the Jews who had remained in the city as being the older and poorer ones because all the others had fled. Their fate was a cause of alarm to the entire citizenry, who shared in their suffering. It would be a great error, the bishop thought, for the Germans to arrest these Jews. Again, however, like so many others, Santin was willing to accept restrictions against the Jews as long as those baptized or married to Catholics were left undisturbed.[175]

These activities were, doubtlessly, a prelude to the law announced on December 1 by Mussolini requiring all Jews to be sent to concentration camps and their property confiscated.[176] This law caused great consternation in many circles not so much because it was grievously offensive to Jews but because it was feared that it would include converted Jews and those married to Catholics.

On December 6, Maglione learned of the situation in Venice from its patriarch, Cardinal Adeodato Piazza.[177] The Venetian cardinal feared that the new law would classify Catholic Jews as Jews, but expressed confidence that the Vatican would do all possible to help the Jews.[178]

Piazza, moreover, discussed the law with the German consul in Venice, Hans Koester, and suggested to him that moderation be exercised in the implementation of the ordinance. Koester's response, although admitting his interest in the problem, was obviously noncommital.[179]

Later in December, it was the archdiocese of Ferrara whose archbishop, Ruggero Bovelli, asked the Vatican to intervene on behalf of the Jews there, especially those in mixed marriages.[180]

Vatican officials judged that it would not be prudent to directly or formally approach the republican government of Mussolini. They thought, however, that the services of Tacchi-Venturi could be utilized.[181] On December 19, Maglione instructed the Jesuit to indicate to the competent authorities, if he found the opportune moment, the concern of the Holy See over the rights of mixed families in the enforcement of the recent law.[182] Tacchi-Venturi's intervention became superfluous, however, because on the same day Maglione had been assured that Mussolini had decided not to disturb mixed families.[183]

Maglione doubtlessly felt relieved that the mixed families would be exempted from the confiscation and deportation involved in the law of December 1. Yet he was willing to accept a situation where thousands of Jews would be arrested and their property taken, a procedure he must have known had been a prelude to deportation in every other European country.

A week after the December 1 law was passed, stories began to circulate outside of Italy that 60,000 Jews had already been arrested and their property expropriated by the German occupation authorities. Moreover, it was believed that the Pope had personally protested these measures to Weizsäcker.[184] The rumors themselves were obviously exaggerated, but so also was the belief that the Pope could not possibly be silent in the face of such crimes. The most that the Vatican was willing to do was to quietly approach certain authorities through the mediation of Tacchi-Venturi, but only to defend the rights of Jews who had been baptized or were married to Catholics. There is no hint in the documents that any other form of protest against this law was made or even considered.

JEWISH CHILDREN

Early in 1944, it was made known to the British Section of the World Jewish Congress that the Vatican was exhausting the funds it had available for the support of Jewish children in Italy whose parents had been deported by the Germans. A request for $50,000 was made.[185] A cable had been sent from the London office of the World Jewish Congress to its New York counterpart asking it to provide the funds.[186] Nahum Goldmann, an official of the World Jewish Congress, brought the matter to the attention of the apostolic delegation in Washington. Monsignor Romolo Carboni of the delegation staff agreed to cable the Vatican to see whether funds were indeed needed and to help in transmitting them if they were.[187] In a memorandum presented to Carboni on this same occasion, the Jewish group wrote:

> The World Jewish Congress seizes this opportunity, on behalf of the entire Jewish Community, to express once again its profoundest gratitude for the protecting hand extended by His Holiness over the persecuted Jews in this trying period.[188]

It must be assumed that some money was sent because a letter from Cicognani to Goldmann on February 15, 1944 indicated that the Vatican was very willing to accept such donations.

> His Eminence, the Cardinal Secretary of State, requests me to inform the representatives of the World Jewish Congress that in response to a recent appeal[189] various donations for victims of war have been given to the Holy Father. The Holy See will continue, as she has in the past, to assist also the Jewish victims of war in the best manner that lies within her means. If offerings are entrusted to His Holiness by the World Jewish Congress, the Holy See will not fail to increase her assistance to Jewish sufferers.[190]

Conclusions

The primary focus of the Vatican's activity on behalf of the Jews of Italy was the racial laws. There is no evidence that the officials of the Secretariat of State were concerned about the restrictions placed upon the Jews. Their ongoing complaint was that the laws did not recognize the changed status of a Jew who converted to Catholicism.[191] To lay burdens upon baptized Jews was considered an affront to the Church, which considered all the baptized as equal, no matter what their background. Worse than that to the Vatican was the government's usurpation of what the Holy See judged to be one of its most inviolable rights—the right to decide who may or may not be married in the Church. The racial laws, prohibiting intermarriage between Italians and Jews, whether baptized or not, directly contravened this basic right of the Church.[192]

Thus, the Vatican protested this infringement of ecclesiastical independence and authority. It is true that in many ways these objections may have helped the baptized Jews. The motivation, however, behind the interventions appeared directed more toward defending and championing the prerogatives of the Church than assisting any of its members. Any help to the baptized Jews was tangential to the diplomatic process of claiming for the Church the rights which it believed to be its own.

This concern over the racial laws continued even after the fall of Mussolini and the accession of the Badoglio government. The officials of the latter government were also asked to alter certain provisions of the racial ordinances,[193] but there was still no attempt to protest the basic rationale of the laws or their penalties against the Jews. Jews who remained faithful to Judaism were ignored in all of the efforts made to revise the racial laws. The suffering which they endured because of these laws and the total injustice of the Fascist treatment of the Jews were neither discussed nor considered.

The baptized Jews were also aided financially through the Raphaels-verein.[194] In addition, special efforts were made to secure for them the necessary papers for emigration to Brazil.[195]

There is much evidence that the Vatican was concerned about Jews confined in camps throughout Italy. Some distinction again was made between the baptized and the unbaptized, but the Secretariat of State, through the nuncio, offered assistance to all who were interned in the camps. The nuncio, in fact, claimed to have made over a hundred visits to these various facilities.[196]

The activity of the Vatican diplomats during 1943 on behalf of foreign Jews in the camps threatened with deportation was both praiseworthy and successful. Borgongini Duca was instructed several times to verify the accuracy of the reports that Polish or Yugoslav Jews would soon be deported, and to take the appropriate preventive steps if the information was correct.[197] In each case, the reports were inaccurate.

There was a drastic change in September 1943, when German troops took control of Rome and all of Italy to the north. The Vatican must have known that this action would jeopardize all Jews caught under German occupation. For example, early in October 1943, rumors were heard of an impending S.S. action in Rome. Although it was not related as being directed against the Jews, the Vatican diplomats must certainly have suspected the worst for them.

The activity of the Vatican during this period is ambivalent. On the one hand, official sanction and assistance were given to the lodging of thousands of Jews in the religious institutions of Rome, and all canonical restrictions were suspended. These efforts, no doubt, saved thousands of Jews. Yet, on the other hand, the Vatican reaction to the deportation of 1,007 Jews from the Roman ghetto was so minimal as to be disappointing and, possibly, shameful.

This statement is made with the knowledge of the meeting between Maglione and Weizsäcker, which took place at the cardinal's bidding.[198] According to Maglione's notes, it was a diplomatic protest by the Holy See, but one which the German ambassador felt free to ignore and even gained the secretary of state's assent to do so. Maglione indicated his reluctance to utter any word of protest which might offend the German people.

It is easy to suspect that Weizsäcker felt relieved by this admission of consideration for the feelings of his countrymen. In fact, he felt so confident that the reluctance of the Vatican to alienate the Germans would influence it to remain silent that he neglected to mention his meeting with Maglione in his report to Berlin.

Weizsäcker's motivation in all of this was quite possibly very laudable. At issue, however, is the motivation of the secretary of state, who, having made a statement to the German ambassador expressing concern for the deported Jews, did not pursue the matter and apparently felt that he had done his duty. It is true that Maglione later made several requests of Weizsäcker for the release of certain Jews, and for information about them, but these requests, couched in diplomatic terminology, lacked the urgency and force of action at the time of arrests.

Tacchi-Venturi must have felt that the Vatican's response to the deportation was inadequate.[199] He suggested that the Vatican do something, and that such an intervention, even if it did not succeed, would be greatly to the credit of the Holy See. The Jews of Rome likewise pleaded for similar intervention, but no action was taken.

The Vatican heard in November that these Jews would not be returning to their homes. In addition, Montini was told by Weizsäcker that nothing could be done for the deported Jews, nor could information about them be obtained.[200] Maglione accepted this evasiveness, while at the same time praising the noble qualities of the ambassador.[201] For all practical purposes, therefore, one must conclude that even though efforts were expended on behalf of the Jews of Rome who were taking refuge in religious houses, no similar steps or interest were taken for the deported Jews.

The Jews in the other cities of northern Italy were also of interest to the Vatican during the latter months of 1943.[202] Local bishops had informed the Secretariat of State of actions taken against the Jews. These actions were seen as a prelude to, or the result of, the law of December 1, interning all the Jews and confiscating their property.[203] It is notable that even at this late date, even after the deportation of the Roman Jews, Tacchi-Venturi was directed to intervene discreetly,[204] not to protest the intrinsic injustice of the measures, but on the basis that the rights of baptized Jews and Jews married to Catholics were being infringed upon.

Vatican diplomatic activity in Italy was, therefore, twofold: protesting racial legislation, and protecting Jews in the camps or taking refuge in the religious houses of Rome. In the face of the October 16 raid, however, this diplomatic process did not function.

It is regrettable that, during the two days that the Jews were sequestered in Rome before being transported north, there was no word of protest or sign of solidarity with them. A staff member of the Secretariat of State had visited the place of detention and related his experiences to his superiors.[205] The secretary of state, therefore, knew almost every detail of the Nazi action, knew obviously of all the other charges made against the Germans about Jewish atrocities, and yet did nothing except speak to the German ambassador, permitting him to keep their conversation secret.

It can be argued that the Vatican diplomats feared that open criticism of German actions in this regard could have resulted in further raids throughout Rome against the Jews and violation of the sanctuary of the religious houses. There was every reason to believe that the S.S. would not have respected custom or regulation. From this point of view, silence was the best policy, an opinion with which Weizsäcker obviously concurred.

Moreover, the Vatican attitude may be seen as echoing that of many Judenrat leaders who were willing to choose certain members of their communities for deportation, while hoping by this gesture to save the majority. Many of them sought and received rabbinic justification for their decisions, although there were contrary rabbinic opinions that a part of the Jewish people could not be sacrificed to save the whole.

The greatest fault of Vatican diplomacy in the face of the October 16 raid was not so much that it remained silent, because that point of view can be argued, but that the German officials involved felt rather assured at this late date in the war that the Vatican would do nothing to jeopardize its relations with Germany. They had witnessed, likewise, a lack of concern by the Vatican for the fate of the Jews who had been deported from all the other countries. To deport Jews from Rome itself, under the eyes of the Pope, was risky, but they took the chance and in so doing proved that their impressions of Vatican diplomacy were correct.

The greater tragedy, therefore, is not the death of a thousand innocent people, but that the diplomats of the Vatican, which claimed such a unique and spiritual status for their diplomacy, concurred by their silence. This was a concurrence which the Germans had come to expect and, in the most daring move of all, proved would also be forthcoming in Rome.

CHAPTER ELEVEN

Conclusions

Any attempt to judge the effectiveness of Vatican diplomacy during the Holocaust and to draw conclusions concerning it must include looking at the distinct levels of this diplomacy. The lowest level were the nuncios and other Vatican representatives, the men on the scene in the various European capitals, to whom directives were sent from the Secretariat of State and from whom a myriad of reports was received. The next level was the secretary of state, the chief diplomatic official of the Holy See. The highest level, of course, was the Pope himself, the head of state, whose representatives were the nuncios, and whose executive officer was the secretary of state.

The Nuncios

According to canon law, the functions of the nuncio were quite clearly defined: to oversee the religious situation of the Church in the country to which he was assigned and to serve as a liaison between the government of that nation and the Holy See.[1] These were his minimal duties according to ecclesiastical law, and as such they parallel the responsibilities of civil diplomats. The Vatican, however, has consistently claimed that the role of its nuncios goes beyond the narrow confines of law. The nuncios were depicted as men practicing an ideal form of diplomacy, not dedicated solely to the interests of the Vatican which they represented, but devoted to the needs of all the people in their host country. Theirs was to be a mission of justice and charity. The Vatican, therefore, prided itself that its representatives acted not only as overseers and links but also that they served humanitarian purposes. Moral, social, and cultural concerns were to be a part of their task as diplomats. Three criteria, therefore, were established by the Holy See itself for its emissaries.[2]

There is little doubt that the nuncios performed their canonical duties by their involvement in the religious affairs of the various nations and their representation to the governments. It is, however, the third criterion, humanitarian concern, that is of issue here. The Jews, with few exceptions, were not members of the Church, but they were indeed an oppressed people living in the same countries, whose needs should have been encompassed by the humanitarian concern of the nuncios.

This study of the Vatican and Jewish sources has revealed little evidence that the nuncios manifested any consistent humanitarian concern about the sufferings of the Jews during the years 1939 to 1943. This research has indicated that the Vatican diplomats only rarely acted on behalf of Jews as Jews, and this usually only for specific individuals. They sometimes had words of sympathy for the Jews, but little action followed from these words.

The only consistent pattern of reaction by the diplomats was focused on the racial laws enacted in the various countries. Usually, these statutes failed to recognize the effects of baptism and continued to consider as Jews even those baptized for long periods of time. Intermarriage between Christians and Jews was prohibited, educational restrictions placed on Jewish students, and commercial and professional limitations enacted against the Jews. Since these ordinances were often harmful to baptized Jews, the nuncios protested to the governments on behalf of people whom they considered full-fledged Catholics. The regulations against intermarriage and those forbidding the conversion of Jews to Catholicism were particularly obnoxious to the Vatican because they struck at the exclusive sacramental structure of the Church.

The nuncios continually intervened on behalf of baptized Jews and filed protests with the governments. They were legally and canonically justified in doing this, because not only were the rights of Catholic Jews at stake, but also the unique prerogatives and independence of the Church were being threatened by governmental interference. The nuncios had added support for their intervention in those nations with which the Holy See had signed concordats.

Moreover, the Vatican was generous in helping converted Jews financially and arranging in many cases for them to emigrate. The Brazilian visa project[3] and the work of the Raphaelsverein[4] demonstrate this. The nuncios were usually involved in these activities.

There can be no argument raised against such interest on the part of the Vatican and its delegates in defending the rights of Church members. Indeed, the Vatican's championing of the rights of baptized Jews implicitly denied the premises of all the racial legislation. Racial theories self-avowedly proclaimed inherent and permanent racial traits, which, in the case of the Jews, were considered intrinsically inferior. Every statement or action by a Vatican diplomat on behalf of baptized Jews, therefore, can be interpreted as contradicting such notions and enunciating the traditional Christian ideal that all the baptized are equal and free in the grace of Christ.

Nevertheless, an embarrassing problem remains that centers on the baptized Jews. For centuries the Church has tried to convert the Jews. Members of the Church, often self-righteous and blinded by their own prejudices, have not been reluctant to use moral and physical pressures and threats to attempt to convince the Jews of the veracity and superiority of Christianity. The history of the Jews of Europe is replete with examples of these efforts. Some of the preachers of the Gospel did not hesitate to accept into the Church those Jews who chose baptism as an alternative to death or exile. Fortunately, the inherent incongruity of such conversions was obvious to some ecclesiastical authorities, who condemned conversions that were not motivated by sincere convictions.

Echoes of this conversionary attitude, regretfully, were not absent from the minds of at least two Vatican representatives.[5] They suspected that some Jews were seeking baptism to escape the effects of anti-Jewish persecution or even to save their lives, but, nevertheless, they welcomed the conversions. They felt that divine grace might have been using such human motivation to accomplish providential purposes.

Without attempting to deny the presence or effect of God's grace on men, such views must be challenged. They must be challenged not only because of their inherent naïveté, but also because they appear to give some kind of divine approval to Nazi racial practices. Moreover, such an attitude was denigrating to the Jewish people and religion. Worse, it must be suspected that a diplomat who imagined that he saw the hand of God in some of the anti-Semitic legislation and activity might not be as inclined to react too hostilely to it.

There is no attempt being made here to exaggerate or accuse all the nuncios of this viewpoint. Two of them specifically indicated such attitudes. That some others may have had similar feelings, at least in the sense that the conversions of the Jews were welcome, no matter what the cause, cannot be proven from the documentation available. That it may be a logical corollary, however, would not be an unreasonable assumption.

The first conclusion, therefore, is that the nuncios were greatly concerned about the rights of baptized Jews and expended many efforts on their behalf. Such actions were viewed as beneficial both to the individuals involved and to the Church of which they were members.

One early historian of the Holocaust suspected that instructions had been sent from the Vatican to ecclesiastical officials in the various countries because of certain similarities in their reactions to the persecution of the Jews.[6] Research in the Vatican's own records and elsewhere, however, does not demonstrate this. There are no data to support the thesis that such directives were issued concerning the problems of the Jews. Moreover, the only pattern of conduct of the nuncios that can be determined was their activity on behalf of the baptized Jews.

Concerning the Jews who remained faithful to Judaism, there are two possible topics for study: the racial laws and the deportations. The nuncios repeatedly complained about the racial laws as they affected the baptized Jews, but there is no evidence to show that they attacked the basic injustice that motivated this legislation. In fact, on the contrary, some of them felt that certain aspects of the anti-Jewish legislation would be beneficial in minimizing Jewish influence in countries where it was considered harmful to Christian society.[7] These diplomats viewed the Jewish badge, and regulations affecting Jewish professions, commerce, and education, as having merit in that they restrained Jewish activity in those areas.

Such an opinion, like the conversionary attitude mentioned above, has a historical echo in the age-old Christian view of the Jews as "the witness people." According to this theory, the Jews rejected and killed Christ and by so doing incurred the anger of God. Because they were deicidists, the Jews were destined by God to suffer. One aspect of their suffering was to be their low status in Christian society, with all kinds of legislation to that effect. It was thought that this servile posture would serve as a witness or testimony to Jewish inferiority and Christian superiority in the mind of God.

It can be concluded, therefore, that the racial laws restricting the Jews were not protested by the Vatican diplomats. Some of the nuncios might have asked that the principles of justice be followed in the application of the laws, but nowhere is there evidence to indicate that these harmful regulations were a source of grief to the Vatican representatives. The corollary, unfortunately, may be that some aspects of the legislation were welcome.

The racial legislation was the Nazis' first step in their campaign against the Jews. It was followed in every country by deportations. From all over the continent the nuncios reported to the Secretariat of

State the deportations from their countries: from Bukovina and Bessarabia to Transnistria in December 1941,[8] from Bratislava in March 1942,[9] from Zagreb in July 1942,[10] from Paris also in July 1942,[11] and from Berlin in October 1942.[12]

The response of the nuncios to these events has been the primary focus of this research. It is true that the diplomats reacted in some way, some more than others, but it is difficult to establish any consistent pattern in their reactions. Certainly, Archbishop Andrea Cassulo in Bucharest and Monsignor Giuseppe Burzio in Bratislava interceded valiantly on behalf of the Jews, but unsuccessfully and, perhaps, ineffectually. In Cassulo's case, there was equal, if not greater, worry that the baptized Jews would also be involved in the deportations.[13] Burzio's intervention was joined with the twofold repulsion that this action was being permitted in a staunchly Catholic country and was not worthy of it, as well as the fear that many of the girls being deported would be forced into prostitution.[14]

Archbishop Valerio Valeri's reaction was different, and must be partially attributed to historical circumstances. There was no concordat between France and the Holy See. Moreover, the whole existence of the Vichy state was contingent on maintaining the good will of the Germans occupying the other half of the country. His own illness might also have been a factor. His intervention, therefore, appears to have been minimal and, at best, constituted an acrimonious meeting with Pierre Laval, the head of the French government.[15]

The nuncio in Berlin had so many restrictions placed on him by the German government that even if he were inclined to do so, he could not have done much on behalf of the Jews. Words of protest, however, even if unsuccessful in achieving their end, could have served as a testimony to the Church's concern for the Jews. The diplomat did intervene when the deportation of Jews in mixed marriages began.[16]

The apostolic visitor in Croatia, accepted as a diplomat by the government, claimed to have done all that he could on behalf of the Jews and had spoken to the head of state himself.[17] Because of the lack of regular diplomatic relations between Croatia and the Holy See, his interventions had to be on an informal and personal basis. How forceful his comments might have been cannot be specifically established. The good rapport he maintained with the Croatian authorities casts some doubt on the strength of the criticism he might have brought to their attention.

There is no evidence that the nuncio in Rome reacted to the deportation from there. At the time Rome was an occupied city and the Italian government was divided, casting doubt on his diplomatic status. Moreover, the matter was handled directly by the Secretariat of State.[18]

The circumstances in which each nuncio found himself were, admittedly, quite different one from the other. Various steps were taken by the nuncios, but there does not appear to have been any fixed attitude or approach underlying these efforts. In fact, it would not be difficult to suspect that in most of the cases of diplomatic involvement, the nuncios had other purposes in mind, in addition to the condition of the Jews. The value of the efforts of these men is not negated by the presence of these other purposes, but the integrity and sincerity of their commitment to humanitarian values could be questioned.

The nuncios were men of charity and sympathy. On countless occasions, they intervened on behalf of individual Jews, not necessarily baptized. Most had good relations with the local Jewish communities, the leaders of which did not hesitate to appeal to them for aid. The numerous expressions of gratitude from Jewish officials give ample proof that they appreciated their contacts with the nuncios and their efforts on behalf of the Jews.

There is no doubt that the nuncios were personally grieved at the treatment accorded to the Jews at the time of the deportations. They made efforts to translate this into action by intervening in various ways with governmental authorities. That any of their steps was particularly successful is problematic and highly doubtful because the deportations continued.

The issue, unfortunately, is not whether the efforts of the Vatican diplomats succeeded in preventing the deportations, or in making them cease after they had started. Many other aspects of the history of those years indicate that nothing, even military needs, would have deterred the Nazis from their genocidal campaign against the Jews. The issue, rather, is whether these men used the full weight of their diplomatic positions as representatives of the great moral and religious power that the Holy See claimed to be, in their efforts on behalf of the Jews. One must sadly conclude that they did not. While highly active in defense of Church rights, their involvement in the Jewish problem was tangential at best, and minimal at worst. By a lack of total response to the Jews in their hour of greatest need, the nuncios failed to live up to the high calling that they proclaimed for themselves.

Whatever failings they had do not seem to have been those of malevolent men, but rather those of well-intentioned men unable to cope with circumstances beyond their ordinary experience and requiring a commitment to specifically human, rather than institutional, values. They could not make this commitment because they were captives of a profession that bound them more to the institution of the Church than to the ideals of brotherhood which it averred.

The conclusion, therefore, is that the Vatican diplomats did indeed intervene with governmental authorities in vain attempts to prevent the deportations or to ameliorate the conditions associated with them. The nuncios, however, did not bring the full weight of their offices and position to these efforts. Their interventions were sporadic and reluctant, at times apologetic, and lacking the force of condemnation that the circumstances required. They had acted otherwise when Church rights were at stake, but they were unable to go beyond this narrow purview of their diplomatic functions. As a result, they missed the opportunity, not to save the Jews, which would have been impossible in any case, but to give witness to the humanitarian commitment which they proudly claimed as the hallmark of Vatican diplomacy.

The Secretary of State

The conclusion that the Vatican diplomats did not do all that their positions warranted for the Jews in their tragic circumstances and, in that sense, failed to live up to the criterion of humanitarian concern which they had set for themselves, reflects not only on them, of course, but also on the Vatican's secretary of state, Luigi Cardinal Maglione. In fact, his responsibility is all the greater because he was the man exclusively entrusted with the direction of papal diplomacy and it was to him and from him that all the diplomatic dispatches were sent.[19]

This research has indicated that Maglione directed and supported the nuncios in their defense of the rights of the Church and baptized Jews. In fact, he intervened himself on occasion to protest limitations on the rights of baptized Jews to be treated like other Catholics.[20] In this regard, he made it very clear that he did not accept the rationale of the racial laws.

Like the nuncios, however, Maglione refrained from any direct criticism of the basic injustice of the regulations. It was said, in the case of the anti-Jewish statutes passed by the Vichy government, that the Vatican was unhappy with some of them, which it considered harsh and inhumane, but it was not going to comment on them.[21] Maglione did not repudiate this comment or its implicit association with his two assistants, Monsignors Domenico Tardini and Giovanni Battista Montini.

Thus it was that neither the secretary of state nor his emissaries ever attacked the racial laws on the whole, while, at the same time, frequently complaining about certain of their provisions which were considered injurious to Church interests.

Concerning the Jews and the deportations, no clear pattern can be discerned in Maglione's responses. He directed the nuncio in Romania, in January 1943, to act on behalf of baptized Jews threatened with deportation.[22] He instructed the nuncio in Berlin, in September 1942, to solicit information about the condition of the deported French Jews.[23] He intervened personally, in March and April 1942, to condemn the deportation of young Slovak Jewish girls who were to be used as prostitutes, and ordered the chargé d'affaires in Bratislava to do likewise.[24] His instructions to the apostolic visitor in Croatia, in September 1941, were to act confidentially and unofficially to recommend moderation in the treatment of the Jews, with similar advice repeated the following year.[25] Moreover, the cardinal met with the German ambassador to Rome, in October 1943, to protest the deportation of Jews from that city.[26]

Other efforts of Maglione along these lines have been revealed throughout the course of this research. Nevertheless, it cannot be concluded from all of this that the secretary of state was particularly concerned about the sufferings of the Jews. In most of the cases in which he issued instructions to the nuncios to act, there were other factors involved as well: danger to baptized Jews, embarrassment to the Church, the evil of prostitution. It is true that he was besieged by all kinds of problems caused by the war, his attention to which is well documented in the Vatican records. Even in the midst of all these human tragedies that made so many demands upon him, however, it could be expected that he would have dealt with the unique aspects of the Jewish situation. This unparalleled catastrophe was given little attention.

The seriousness of this charge against Maglione is heightened by two facts: the information that came into his office about the atrocities, and the appeals for action that followed. Information came from the Vatican's own diplomats. For example, as early as August and December 1941, the nuncio in Bucharest sent descriptions of what was being done to the Jews in Transnistria.[27] From Bratislava, in October 1941, came a report from Burzio relating rumors from Russia that the Germans were killing all the Jews there.[28] Archbishop Cesare Orsenigo, writing from Berlin in July 1942, spoke of allegations of mass killings of all the deported Jews.[29] The memorandum from a member of the Berlin nunciature at the end of 1942 described the harsh treatment of the Jews by the Germans.[30]

Other sources in the Church sent information to the secretary of state. In May 1942, a hospital train chaplain, Pirro Scavizzi, related that all the Jews in the Ukraine had been killed and that plans to do the same in Poland were underway.[31] Several months later, he informed the secretary of state that 2,000,000 Jews had been killed in what he termed a "systematic slaughter."[32] Late in the summer of 1942 a bishop in eastern Poland calculated that 200,000 Jews had been killed in his region.[33] Similar information came from Latvia at the close of 1942.[34]

There were, of course, other sources. The memorandum given to the nuncio in Berne in March 1942 by officials of the World Jewish Congress and the Jewish Agency for Palestine described the total Nazi plans against the Jews and referred to the murder of thousands of Jews in eastern Europe.[35] The Polish embassy at the Vatican, both in October and December 1942, spoke of the mass killing of Jews by asphyxiation, and estimated that a million Jews in Poland alone had already been killed.[36] British and American diplomats reported similar facts.[37]

Nevertheless, two times in 1942, in October and December, Maglione specifically stated that the accuracy of all these reports could not yet be verified.[38] Moreover, he insinuated that they might have been motivated by Allied propaganda efforts and, thus, must be treated cautiously. The cardinal gave the impression that he was wary of being duped. Nevertheless, it appears that the ever-accumulating body of facts did have some effect because internal notes of the Secretariat of State, written in May 1943, referred to the suppression of millions of Jews and even to the gas chambers.[39]

The secretary of state was well informed. Numerous and poignant appeals, moreover, poured into his office. Polish Catholics begged for a word of support for them in their horrible sufferings; Allied diplomats warned the secretary of state that the Vatican's prestige would suffer if it did not condemn the German atrocities; Jewish groups pleaded for interventions and protests that they supposed would save the Jews. Maglione, informed as he was, was not moved to act by any of these appeals, at least not in the way that the petitioners asked.

To the Jewish groups, or to those who spoke on their behalf, the cardinal's constant response in some form or other was that the Vatican had done, was doing, and would continue to do all possible for the Jews. Nuncios and apostolic delegates all over the world were instructed to use this or a similar response in replying to appeals on behalf of the Jews. That the secretary of state did something for the Jews is certainly verified in this research. That he and the Holy See, whose agent he was, did all that was possible must be unequivocally denied.

Admittedly, the only options available to the Vatican's diplomatic

service were diplomatic. That the Pope may have had other alternatives is not pertinent here. The only viable diplomatic choices available
to the Holy See were a diplomatic protest, unambiguous in its
condemnation of the crimes against the Jews, or the cessation of
diplomatic relations. The former of these, the protest, if publicized,
might have been an effective means to show the humanitarian concerns of Vatican diplomacy.

More highly effective, however, would have been the suspension or
cessation of diplomatic relations with the countries which carried out
such policies against the Jews. The Vatican traditionally had been
reluctant to initiate such a rupture in relations between it and a
particular country. Nevertheless, there had been a recent precedent for
such an action in the interruption of diplomatic relations with
Czechoslovakia in 1925 as a protest against a governmental decision to
which the Vatican objected.[40]

The officials of the Secretariat of State had to weigh two factors in
considering a decision to recall the nuncios: the desirability and need to
have representatives in as many European capitals as possible versus
the Vatican's obligation as a self-proclaimed moral and religious power
to protest the immoral decisions and actions of the various governments against the Jews. This research has produced no evidence that
the second factor was even considered.

The nuncios were allowed to remain in their posts, lending, in some
ways, the prestige of their presence to the governments involved. So
firm must have been this decision to retain the nuncios in place that
even the diplomatic discourtesies of the German government toward
the Holy See and the complaints of bishops about him were not
enough to persuade the Secretary of State to recall the nuncio in Berlin.
The same was true of the nuncio in Vichy, who remained at his post
even though all the other diplomats had departed when the Germans
occupied the Vichy territory.

There was, without a doubt, a great value for the Vatican in having
these representatives in the various countries. Their first concern was
to protect the Church and its members in these nations. If joined to this
there had been any consistent effort on behalf of the Jews, then their
presence would have been beneficial. That was not the case, unfortunately, and their continued presence in the midst of the crimes against
the Jews, while not to be seen as a condonation, could not be taken as
disapproval or condemnation either.

The Vatican had a strong weapon in its diplomacy. That it felt
justified in using it to intervene for humanitarian purposes is evident
from a memorandum written by Tardini in April 1943. The Vatican

official described the German treatment of the Jews as an offense not only against justice and charity, but also against humanity. He concluded that for reasons of both the divine and natural law, the Church had the right to intervene.[41]

This justification notwithstanding, Maglione did not decide to use the full power of Vatican diplomacy in confronting the Jewish problem. In fact, he dealt with it only minimally. This point of view must be assumed to have reflected that of the Pope. Setting such a policy, without papal approval, was not entirely within Maglione's competence.

The secretary of state must certainly have concurred with the Pope's decision. The nuances of their approach to such a decision are beyond the scope of this research. There must have been a resolution constantly reinforced, to keep diplomatic relations, and the Church interests thereby involved, as a priority. The logic of such a decision could not be criticized except for the claim that Vatican diplomacy was also destined for wider, humanitarian, interests.

Two other points must be kept in mind in assessing the role of the secretary of state in his executive control of Vatican diplomacy. The overwhelming majority of the Jews killed during the Holocaust were from Eastern Europe, Poland, the Soviet Union, and the Baltic countries. If there had been Vatican diplomats in these countries, they had been expelled and all direct contacts lost. There was nothing that the secretary of state could do, except through the nuncio in Berlin, who was, practically speaking, powerless, because of the geographical distance involved and the government's restrained view of his competence.

It should be remembered, therefore, that the ability of the Vatican to intervene, even if it wanted to, was limited to states where the Jewish population was proportionately lower than it was in Eastern Europe. If every one of the Jews in these nations had been spared, several million, nonetheless, would have been killed in the east. This fact is often overlooked by those who would give the impression, simplistic and unrealistic as it is, that the Vatican could have saved the Jews of Europe by a few words or actions.

The possibility of anti-Jewish attitudes in the Secretariat of State should also be discussed. The research has indicated little in this regard. In December 1941, because of their continuing demands, Maglione did express annoyance at the baptized Jews who had emigrated.[42] Maglione and other members of the Secretariat of State also appeared to feel that the Jews were basically unfriendly and ungrateful to the Church.[43]

Anti-Zionist attitudes, however, prevailed among the Vatican diplomats. Maglione, for example, in two diplomatic dispatches, decried Zionism.[44] Tardini, in a memorandum, argued against the notion of a Jewish homeland.[45] The apostolic delegate in Ankara, Archbishop Angelo Roncalli, expressed similar sentiments,[46] which were most likely shared by members of the diplomatic corps.

Anti-Zionist feelings are not automatically equivalent to anti-Semitism, but such opinions expressed in the midst of the Holocaust were thoughtless and narrow-minded. They made no allowance for the devastation that was wiping out the Jewish people. It is striking to read, for example, that Tardini, who could speak of the offenses against charity, justice and humanity in the German treatment of the Jews, could also, a few weeks earlier, dismiss the notion of a Jewish homeland. Maglione reacted to Jewish pressures for assistance in the escape of some Jews to Palestine as a threat to Catholics and as a sign of Jewish ingratitude for all that the Holy See had done for them. The records show that these attitudes were manifested in the middle of 1943, at a time when the Vatican was well informed about the German actions against the Jews. There is no humanitarian concern evident in such a begrudging attitude of the Vatican diplomats toward the surviving Jews, many of whom were still in danger.

Thus, the interest taken in the Jews by the secretary of state was minimal. At best, his feelings toward them were indifferent; at worst, they were hostile. Their Zionist aspirations were not only unappreciated but also feared and scorned; their lack of gratitude for the efforts of the Holy See on their behalf was accepted as a given fact.

The conclusion, therefore, is that the needs and sufferings of the Jews were of little importance to Maglione in the face of his overriding concern for other priorities. Chief among these was the desire to maintain relations with all the nations of Europe. Maglione himself admitted that this was the case with Germany, and *a fortiori*, it would be true for the other states.

In his meeting with the German ambassador while the Jews of Rome were being rounded up, in October 1943, Maglione gave the *raison d'être* of Vatican efforts up to that point. He claimed that the Holy See had been very prudent in all that it had said and done, "so as not to give to the German people the impression that it has done or wished to do the least thing against Germany during this terrible war."[47]

The prudence to which the secretary of state referred was such that it dictated the preservation of diplomatic relations with Germany lest offense be given to the German people. The effort was successful, too, for the nuncio in Berlin remained there for the duration of the war, as did the German ambassadors at the Vatican. Even when information about the full dimensions of the Holocaust came from everywhere, joined with appeals from, or on behalf of, so many suffering people, nothing was said or done that would sever this rapport. If, in the midst of all this, the secretary of state found justification for retaining Orsenigo at his post in Berlin, then it would have been all the easier to justify maintaining all the other nuncios in their positions.

Maglione made his choice: diplomatic presence and relations with Germany and the other states rather than the use of Vatican diplomacy as a moral and humanitarian agent in defense of the Jews.

The Pope

The head of the Vatican State was Pope Pius XII, who possessed full temporal authority in the Vatican State and full spiritual authority in the Church. He was the former Eugenio Cardinal Pacelli, who had served as secretary of state to Pope Pius XI and as nuncio to Germany before that. This research has rarely focused directly on the Pope because Vatican diplomacy was principally conducted under the auspices of the secretary of state. Nevertheless, it is known that the Pope and Maglione were in daily contact. Moreover, many of the diplomatic records studied indicate that the subject matter contained in them had been discussed with the Pope.

The only written sources that came directly from the Pope and have been part of this research are some of his speeches and his letters to the bishop of Berlin.[48] The former were specifically designed for publication; the latter may not have been. The only private, contemporaneous remark by the Pope about his attitude toward the war is contained in one of these letters.[49] Otherwise, there are no written sources directly from his hand.

The link between the Pope and Maglione is evident. There is no doubt that the decisions of Maglione and the instructions he gave to the nuncios were the result of the leadership and orders of the Pope. The daily audiences, Pius' own experience as a diplomat, and his concept of the power of the papacy, would all lend themselves to a harmony of views between the Pope and the secretary of state.

It was the Pope's point of view that ultimately determined that certain provisions of the racial laws violated the rights of the Church or its members, and were, therefore, a legitimate source of complaint. It was his tolerance that allowed the rationale underlying the racial legislation to go unchallenged. In the final analysis, it was he, with decades of experience as a Vatican diplomat, who set the tone and pace of Vatican diplomacy during these years. As head of state, that was his right and, in fact, obligation. What is surprising, however, is that having relied upon Vatican diplomacy so much, he failed to utilize its full potential when confronted with the Jewish catastrophe.

As head of the Church, the Pope had other options that he might have used in dealing with the crimes committed during the war. For example, he could have imposed ecclesiastical sanctions on the guilty parties or nations or he could have spoken out as the Vicar of Christ to condemn those who perpetrated such atrocities against their fellow men. Appeals from all over, including the papal court,[50] came to him to utter these words of chastisement. That the Pope did not chose any alternative other than diplomacy is a historical fact. Any hypotheses about the other alternatives are not within the scope of this research.

Pius XII decided to rely on diplomacy and maintained the Vatican's diplomatic network throughout the entire war. The only interruptions of diplomatic relations were those caused by the Germans or Russians in their occupation of certain countries. Diplomatic relations were never suspended by the Holy See and must have been a highly valued premium in the eyes of the Pope. The preservation of relations with the various nations, particularly Germany, at almost any cost, is the only verifiable explanation for the way in which Pius XII conducted the Vatican's diplomacy.

It appears that the criterion of this diplomacy was to avoid offense to any nation. That Germany was of special concern is evidenced not only by the remarks of the secretary of state but from many other sources, not touched upon in this research, which indicate the special affection and loyalty the Pope felt for Germany. Maglione himself stated that the Holy See had maintained an attitude of reserve during the war so as not to hurt the German people in any way.[51] This approach was praised by the nuncio in France as "enlightened reserve."[52]

The Pope himself, in April 1943, in a letter to the bishop of Berlin, justified this reserve as a way of avoiding possibly greater evils. He thought that the local bishops, who could weigh all the aspects of a situation better, were in a stronger position to decide upon a protest than he was.[53] This, unfortunately, is a pastoral rather than a diplomatic record, but it is the only contemporary source dealing with the Pope's attitude at the time.

Thus, reserve and prudence were the criterion of papal diplomacy, according to both the Pope and his secretary of state. It was a criterion that could not coexist with humanitarian concern. To avoid offending Germany, and to maintain prudent reserve, the Vatican had to act, or neglect to act, in ways that ignored the depth of suffering that was so widespread among both Christians and Jews.

No argument is raised here against Pius XII's concentration upon diplomacy. The Vatican's diplomatic system was such that it could have been an effective means to demonstrate humanitarian concern for all the victims of the war. That it was not was the responsibility of Pius XII, who chose to emphasize diplomacy, then decided not to use it to its full effectiveness. An attitude of reserve and prudence, joined with a desire to offend no nation, particularly Germany, placed a straitjacket on Vatican diplomacy and made it little different from the diplomatic practices of civil states.

The Pope, in defining and restraining Vatican diplomatic practice in this way, failed not only the Jews but also many members of the Church who suffered brutal treatment from the Germans. Moreover, he caused Vatican diplomacy to fail, by forcing it to make a mockery of its claims that it was an ideal form of diplomacy dedicated to justice, brotherhood, and other similarly exalted goals, when in practice it made little attempt to work toward any of them.

The nuncios could have vigorously protested the rationale behind the racial laws as a violation of justice. Likewise could they have condemned the deportations that followed. These protests might have led to the severing of diplomatic relations with particular countries. No matter what their results, these efforts of the nuncios would have made clear that the Church and its diplomatic service were concerned for all men and opposed to injustice of any kind.

The Pope did not give such direction to the Vatican diplomats. He chose reserve, prudence, and a diplomatic presence in all the capitals over any other goal or needs. This approach does not seem to have been motivated by malevolence or anti-Semitism, but was caused by an inability to depart from cherished ecclesiastical or personal concepts to confront the evils besetting Europe and the Jewish people.

It must be concluded that Vatican diplomacy failed the Jews during the Holocaust by not doing all that it was possible for it to do on their behalf. It also failed itself because in neglecting the needs of the Jews, and pursuing a goal of reserve rather than humanitarian concern, it betrayed the ideals that it had set for itself. The nuncios, the secretary of state, and, most of all, the Pope share the responsibility for this dual failure.

APPENDIX A

Diplomatic Representatives of, and to, the Vatican

As of January 1, 1940, the Vatican had accredited representatives, possessing diplomatic status, in the following countries.[1] Most of them were papal nuncios.

Argentina	Latvia
Belgium	Liberia
Bolivia	Lithuania
Brazil	Luxembourg
Chile	Nicaragua
Columbia	Netherlands
Costa Rica	Panama
Cuba	Paraguay
Dominican Republic	Peru
Ecuador	Poland
Estonia	Portugal
France	Romania
Germany	San Salvador
Guatemala	Slovakia
Haiti	Spain
Honduras	Switzerland
Hungary	Uruguay
Ireland	Venezuela
Italy	Yugoslavia

As of January 1, 1940, the following states had accredited diplomatic representatives at the Vatican.[2]

Argentina	Estonia
Belgium	France
Bolivia	Germany
Brazil	Great Britain
Chile	Guatemala

Columbia
Costa Rica
Cuba
Dominican Republic
Ecuador
Latvia
Liberia
Lithuania
Monaco
Nicaragua
Panama
Peru
Poland
Portugal

Haiti
Honduras
Hungary
Ireland
Italy
Romania
San Marino
San Salvador
Slovakia
Spain
Uruguay
Venezuela
Yugoslavia

In addition, the Vatican assigned representatives without diplomatic status to the following countries.[3] Most of them were apostolic delegates.

Africa
Albania
Australia
Belgian Congo
Bulgaria
Canada
China
East Indies
Egypt and Arabia
Great Britain
Greece
India

Indochina
Iran
Iraq
Italian East Africa
Japan
Mexico
Philippines
South Africa
Syria
Turkey
United States of
    America

APPENDIX B

Memorandum from Richard Lichtheim, Jewish Agency for Palestine, and Gerhart Riegner, World Jewish Congress, to Archbishop Filippo Bernardini, the Nuncio in Switzerland, March 18, 1942

1. The multiplicity of measures, dictated by violent anti-Semitism, which have been taken in the past few years against the Jews living in Germany and the territories annexed to Germany are more or less well known to public opinion. They consist in the absolute exclusion of Jews from all professions, all trades and all economic activity in general, except for incorporation in the system of forced labor adopted to meet the needs of war. They consist also in the confiscation of almost all the Jews' worldly goods and, in countless cases, of persecution in various forms, such as arrest, internment in concentration camps or mass explusion of Jews—stripped in advance of all they possess—either to Poland or to concentration camps in France. Through the forced emigration which was pursued up to the outbreak of the war and by reason of the privation and persecution they have endured, the number of German and Austrian Jews has fallen from around 800,000 to about 200,000.

The remainder of the Jewish population in what was once Czechoslovakia, now living in the "Protectorate of Bohemia-Moravia" and numbering some 70,000 have been the victims, since the country was occupied of similar measures, and are at this moment on the point of being concentrated *en bloc* in a ghetto established at Theresienstadt.

2. Analogous measures, less rigorous in certain cases but even more rigorous in others, have fallen upon the Jews in all the countries occupied during the war by the German Army, such as Belgium, Holland, the Occupied Zone of France, Yugoslavia, Greece, the Baltic countries and notably Poland, where concentration of masses of Jews in ghettos surrounded by unscalable walls has created indescribable misery and caused epidemics which, at this moment, are literally decimating the population.

3. Germany's allies, imitating the example set by the Reich, have

followed the same course and introduced anti-Semitic legislation, or launched violent persecution, aimed at the total dispossession or even the physical extermination of the Jews. This is notably the case in Romania, in the newly created states of Croatia and Slovakia and, to a certain degree too, in Hungary, where preparations are now afoot to incorporate all Jews from 18 to 50 in forced labor units.

4. Among the most striking illustrations of such persecution, we would quote the following:

a. The establishment in Occupied France of reprisal camps at Drancy and Compiègne, near Paris, where approximately 6,000 to 7,000 Jews, who were arrested in the streets or in their own homes in August last, are literally dying of hunger and being used by the military authorities as hostages.

b. The establisment of concentration camps in Unoccupied France; for example, at Gurs, at Récébédou, at Noé, Vernet, Rivesaltes, etc., where several tens of thousands of Jews of all nationalities, who were already living in France or took refuge in France in consequence of the advance of the German armies into Belgium, have been herded—the women and children separated from their husbands and fathers—into sordid huts surrounded by barbed wire, where they have been vegetating for more than two years in unimaginable misery. To these camps, Germany has also sent 9,000 German Jews who had been established for centuries in Baden and the Palatinate.

Apart from these camps, there are also "foreign workers' units" and "social reclassification centers" which are being used under various labels for the purpose of employing on forced labor a group of Jews, many of whom served under the French colors during the war.

c. Among the cruelties perpetrated in the occupied countries by Germany, we would cite the example of several hundred young Dutch Jews who, without any charges being levelled against them, were sent to the concentration camps at Buchenwald in Germany and Mauthausen in Austria, where virtually all of them perished within a few weeks.

d. Apart from the slow and steady extermination associated with the ghetto system throughout Poland, thousands of Jews in Poland and in the parts of Russia occupied by Germany have been executed by German troops.

e. Eighteen thousand Jews located in Hungary (a number of whom were Hungarian Jews, the others, Jews of different nationalities) have been expelled by order of the government and transported in revolting conditions to Eastern Galicia, where they were delivered into the hands of the German authorities who shot them all, with few exceptions.

f. Early last year, at the time of the Iron Guard uprising in Romania, several thousand Jews were massacred in the streets of Romanian localities. In Bucharest alone, nearly 2,000 persons—intellectuals, officials of Jewish institutions, merchants and industrialists of repute—were killed. Revolting scenes were enacted, notably at the abattoir in Bucharest, to which the Iron Guard dragged the Jews and there slaughtered them like cattle.

g. Most of the Jews in Bucovina, numbering 170,000, were forced to leave their homes and were transported, at the beginning of winter, in open freight cars, to Russia. By the time they reached the Russian frontier, a quarter of them were already dead. The survivors were marched for six days toward Mogilev. Those who were in no condition to march were shot.

h. During the reoccupation of Bessarabia by German and Romanian troops, 92,000 Jews were executed by firing squads. A trustworthy report on this subject says that in every town or village Jews were assembled in one place—men, women, children, the aged, the sick, even hospital patients—and, having been tortured and starved for several days were shot. Among the victims was the Chief Rabbi of Kishinev.

i. In Croatia—where, after the dismemberment of Yugoslavia, there were 30,000 Jews—several thousand families were either deported to desert islands on the Dalmatian coast or incarcerated in concentration camps. After a while, all the male Jews in Croatia (as happened in Serbia under German occupation) were sent to labor camps where they were assigned to drainage or sanitation work and where they perished in great numbers as a result of inhuman treatment or through lack of food and clothing. The Croatian Government has not even allowed relief parcels to be sent to them, and it is almost impossible to establish contact with the internees. At the same time, their wives and children were sent to another camp where they, too, are enduring dire privations.

j. In Slovakia, anti-Semitic legislation was promulgated in the course of last year which, like the German legislation, regulates every detail of Jewish life. At the beginning of this month, grave anti-Semitic disturbances broke out. At the same time the government promulgated new decrees aiming at "concentration" of the whole Jewish population of Slovakia, amounting to 90,000 souls. According to reports received in the last few days, this concentration is to be effected as follows: every Jew is authorized to bring a suit, one shirt, and a pair of shoes, all his other property being confiscated by the Hlinka Guard. Preparations have been made to send the Jewish population into camps or ghettos near the Polish frontier between now and March 23. It is feared that they will be sent from there into Poland itself where they will suffer the same fate as the masses of Jews expelled from Romania.

5. It should be noted that among the Hungarian, Romanian and Slovakian Jews, there are several hundred families who are in possession of immigration visas for Palestine or some of the American countries. Above and beyond the steps that can be taken to secure general alleviation of the fate of persecuted and threatened Jewish populations, it is likewise a matter of great urgency to attempt approaches to the competent authorities, notably (for those emigrating to America) to the Italian Government, with a view to obtaining transit visas or, eventually, arranging specially organized convoys to enable the emigrants to reach their ports of embarkation.

APPENDIX C

Triennial Report of the Nuncio in Romania,
Archbishop Andrea Cassulo, to the Secretary of State,
Luigi Cardinal Maglione

Bucharest, December 31, 1942

The gravest problem which I have had to confront in the second half of
1941 and the months following has been that of the Jews. These people,
I would say, have taken control of business in Romania and have taken
residence in the capital, in the cities of the country, especially at
Cernauti, where they constitute 60 percent of the population, in
Chisinau, in Otin, in Bessarabia. Since the Romanians are rather given
to the good life, to ceremonies of honor, they have left almost all
business affairs: commerce, minor jobs and professions, in the hands
of others. Eventually they have therefore been suffocated by the Jewish
pressure and influence, which has infiltrated everywhere. The founder
of the legionnaires [Horia Sima] who had noticed such abnormality for
some time, with the intention of purging the country and returning
things to a normal state, opened a strong campaign against the Jews,
supported by Professor Cuza of the University of Jassi, from whom he
was later alienated.

Public opinion at the time, aroused by the legionnaires, developed
into ferocious aversion, which burst forth later like a flame, leading to
very sad consequences. A number of Jews, in view of the fact that there
was no escape and that they were in immediate danger of even losing
their lives, were determined to become Christians, partially, I believe,
for human reasons, partially moved also by supernatural motives
because for a time they had already been in contact with Catholics and
were only awaiting a propitious moment to embrace the Catholic faith.
They, in fact, are being instructed and it is to be hoped that a good
number of them having passed into the Church, will persevere and be
exemplary Catholics.

The attendence at religion classes has been continuous and numer-

216

ous, and in general the clergy has done its duty. There have been but a few who have shown themselves not equal to their duties. There were some moments of great anger, and the Nuncio had to intervene with the bishops and parish priests, giving them the norms received from the Holy Office.

The government in the meantime has published its repressive laws against the Jews and has considered placing its hand also on the rights foreseen in the Concordat. It thought that it could also prohibit priests from administering baptism to the Jews under penalty of imprisonment.

The Nuncio naturally has intervened with the Government reporting to the Holy See what occurred. As a result of the remonstrances made the Marshal has given formal assurances that the liberty of the Catholic Church will not be touched and afterwards also gave assurances in this regard, defining better what the Holy See has asked to be clarified. In the succeeding months the mentality of the State is not maintained in the precise terms contained in the Note received from the Minister of Foreign Affairs, and is beginning to take a not so good route. The Holy See, made aware of the fact and of the threat, asked the Nuncio to make, in the best way, his remonstrances. The terms of these remonstrances and the reassuring response of the Minister, M. Antonescu, are contained in the Notes exchanged between the Nuncio and the Minister, sent to the Holy See with the relevant report in December 1942.

It is a fact recognized by all that what has been able to render less harsh the conditions created by the measures taken against the Jews has been the work of the Nuncio, who put himself above every human interest and political consideration, and influenced only by a sentiment of charity, has displayed serene and paternal action in the presence of the government and all others, obtaining that in the area of the interests and rights of the baptized Jews, the consideration might be given them which is due to all Catholic faithful. They have indeed been admitted to Catholic schools, even to those recognized by the State, and many families threatened with being transferred elsewhere, have been left in place.

Lately, after some very sad events, it is known, and all speak of it, that the Holy See and the Nunciature with its authoritative influence has been able to obtain that certain rigors be mitigated or suppressed. In this period of time a great part of it was absorbed by action carried out in favor of the Jews. I do not want to linger further on the work accomplished at the end of 1941 and 1942, because volumes would be necessary to deal only with the questions treated.

Among the other activities which were the object of our diligent attention and solicitude in the preceding year, a year which has been, I would say, one of peace and of good relations with the government, because the gravest difficulties have been overcome, is that of visits to prisoners-of-war and the naming of a sufficient number of military chaplains in the army for Catholic soldiers of the Latin rite, because those of the eastern rite have already been provided for.

Visit to Prisoners-of-War

The visit to prisoners-of-war, accomplished happily thanks be to God, since the Holy Father desired it, occupied me from December 1941 to July 1942. Discussions with the Government were long. Having to enter an Orthodox camp, the government while kindly welcoming the proposal of the Holy Father, feared that the Orthodox bishops and clergy would create difficulties. In various conferences held with the Marshal and with Minister Antonescu, I explained and always repeated what the purpose of the visit was. Finally my words and the Notes sent obtained their effect and the result is well known from the reports, after the visit was completed, sent by me to the Holy See, and accompanied by an album and a film which the government has sent, as a gift to the Holy Father.

Le nonce à Bucarest Cassulo au cardinal Maglione

Bucarest, 31 décembre 1942

Il problema piú grave che ho dovuto affrontare nel secondo semestre del 1941 e mesi seguenti è stato quello degli ebrei. Questo popolo, direi, si era impadronito degli affari della Romania e aveva preso residenza nella Capitale, nelle città di provincia, specialmente a Cernauti, ove formava il 60% della popolazione, a Chisinau, a Otin, in Bessarabia. Essendo il rumeno piuttosto portato a vivere bene, alle funzioni onorifiche, aveva lasciato presso chè tutti gli affari: il commercio, gli uffici minori e professioni in mano di altri. Col tempo si è trovato quindi soffocato dalla pressione e influenza ebrea, che si era infiltrata dappertutto. Il fondatore dei legionari che si era accorto da tempo di tale anormalità, nell'intento di epurare il paese e rocondurre le cose ad uno stato normale, aprì una campagna forte contro gli ebrei, appoggiato dal prof. Cuza, dell'università di Jassi, dal quale poi si distaccò.

L'opinione pubblica da tempo eccitata dai legionari, diventò avversione feroce, che divampò poi come fiamma, portando a coseguenze dolorosissime. Un numero di ebrei, visto che non c'era più una via di scampo e che erano in pericolo prossimo di perdere anche la vita, si sono determinati di farsi cristiani, parte credo per ragioni umane parte mossi da motivi anche soprannaturali, perché da tempo erano già in relazione coi cattolici e non aspettavano che il momento propizio per abbracciare la fede cattolica. Essi, infatti, si sono fatti istruire e giova sperare che una buona parte passati alla Chiesa, ora perseverino e siano cattolici esemplari.

L'affluenza al catechismo è stata continua e numerosa, e in generale il clero ha fatto il suo dovere. Pochi sono stati quelli che si sono mostrati non all'altezza dei loro doveri. Ci furono dei momenti di parossismo, e Monsignor Nunzio ha dovuto intervenire presso i vescovi e parroci, dando loro le norme ricevute dal S. Offizio.

Il Governo nel frattempo emanava le sue leggi di repressione contro gli ebrei e credeva di mettere la mano anche sui diritti contemplati nel Concordato. Esso credeva di poter interdire anche ai sacerdoti di amministrare il battesimo agli ebrei sotto pena di carcere.

Monsignor Nunzio naturalmente è intervenuto presso il Governo riferendo alla Santa Sede quello che avveniva. In seguito alle rimostranze fatte il Maresciallo ha data assicurazione formale che la libertà della Chiesa Cattolica non sarebbe stata intaccata e appresso dava anche assicurazioni al riguardo, precisando meglio quello che la Santa Sede domandava che fosse chiarito. Nei mesi successivi la mentalità dello Stato non si mantenne nei termini precisi contenuti nelle Note ricevute dal Ministero degli Affari Esteri, e si cominciava a prendere una via non buona. La S. Sede fatta consapevole del fatto e della minaccia, pregò mons. Nunzio di fare, nel modo migliore, le sue rimostranze. I termini di tali rimostranze e la risposta rassicurante del Ministro M. Antonescu, si hanno nelle Note scambiate fra il Nunzio e il Ministro, inviate alla S. Sede con relativo rapporto nel dicembre 1942.

È un fatto da tutti riconosciuto che chi ha potuto rendere meno grave la condizione creata dalle misure prese contro gli ebrei è stata l'opera di Monsignor Nunzio, che si è messo al disopra di ogni umano interesse e considerazione politica, e mosso soltanto da un sentimento di carità, ha spiegato un'azione serena, paterna, presso il governo e presso tutti, ottenendo che sul campo degli interessi e diritti degli ebrei battezzati, fossero usati quei riguardi che erano dovuti ai fedeli cattolici. Essi sono stati quindi ammessi alle scuole cattoliche, anche a quelle riconosciute dallo Stato, e molte famiglie minacciate di essere trasferite altrove, sono state lasciate al loro posto.

Ultimamente, poi, dopo fatti dolorosissimi, si è saputo, e tutti lo dicevano, che la S. Sede e la Nunziatura con la sua autorevole influenza ha potuto ottenere che certi rigori venissero mitigati o soppressi. In questo periodo di tempo gran parte ne fu assorbito dall'azione svolta a favore degli ebrei. Non credo di indugiarmi più oltre sul lavoro compiuto sullo scorcio del 1941 e 1942, perché occorrerebbero dei volumi per accennare soltanto a tutte le questioni trattate.

Fra le altre attività che furono oggetto della nostra diligente attenzione e sollecitudine nel decorso anno, anno che è stato direi di pace e in buona relazione col governo, perché le difficoltà più gravi erano state superate, è quella della visita ai prigionieri di guerra e la nomina di un sufficiente numero di cappellani militari nell'esercito per i soldati cattolici di rito latino, poiché quelli di rito orientale già ne erano provvisti.

Visita ai prigionieri di guerra

La visita ai prigionieri di guerra, riuscita grazie a Dio felicemente, quale il Santo Padre la voleva, mi ha occupato dal dicembre 1941 al luglio 1942. Lunghe sono state le trattative col Governo. Dovendo entrare in campo ortodosso, il governo pur accogliendo benevolmente la proposta del Santo Padre, temeva che i vescovi ed il clero ortodosso creassero difficoltà. In varie conferenze avute col Maresciallo e col Ministro Antonesco, ho spiegato e ripetuto sempre quale era lo scopo della visita. Finalmente le mie parole e le Note inviate hanno ottenuto il loro effetto e il risultato è ben conosciuto dai rapporti, a visita compiuta, da me trasmessi alla S. Sede, ed accompagnati da un album e da un film che il governo ha inviato, come omaggio al Santo Padre.

APPENDIX D

Letter of Luigi Cardinal Maglione, Secretary of State, to Charles Sidor, Minister of Slovakia to the Holy See

Vatican, November 12, 1941

The undersigned Cardinal Secretary of State has the honor to communicate to His Excellency the Minister of Slovakia the following:

With deep sorrow the Holy See has learned that also in Slovakia, a country whose population, in almost its entirety, is honored with the best Catholic tradition, there has been published, on September 9 last, a "Government Ordinance," which established a particular "racial legislation" containing various provisions in open contrast to Catholic principles.

In fact, the Church, which is universal by the will of its Divine Founder since it welcomes into its bosom persons of every race, thus views with maternal solicitude all of mankind, to provoke and develop among all men sentiments of fraternity and love, according to the explicit and categorical teaching of the Gospel.

To this universal character of the Church and its doctrine, Article 9 of the aforesaid Ordinance is totally opposed, because it prohibits marriages between Jews and non-Jews, and between Jews and half-Jews.

On this important point it is well known what is the doctrine of the Church and what is the resulting canonical practice.

To remove from its children the danger of losing the inestimable gift of the faith, the Church has forbidden marriages between Catholics and non-Catholics, but she has, and intends to preserve intact, the right of dispensing from this prohibition, when such a dispensation is called for by the demands of conscience. Practically, the Church permits those marriages only in the rarest cases, for serious reasons and always when well defined conditions have been verified and solid guarantees offered.

But when it is a question of two Catholics free from canonical impediments, but only of different races, the Church cannot be

221

opposed to their marriage without failing its sanctifying mission and violating higher divine laws, not omitting, however, discouraging marriages between persons belonging to races too heterogeneous, in view of the dangers to which their children can be exposed.

In view of the principles recalled above, there cannot be any doubt that the aforesaid Article 9 is in opposition to Catholic doctrine because it prohibits in an absolute and general way marriages between Jews and non-Jews and between Jews and half-Jews.

Moreover, the government Ordinance, with Article 38, excludes children whom it considers as belonging to the Jewish race, even if Catholic, from every kind of study in all the schools and institutes of instruction, except from elementary schools and from courses specially organized for them.

It is evident that this greatly impedes the Church from the exercise of one of its more important and sacred rights, that of the Catholic education of its youth, and hinders also in various ways its apostolic activity. Furthermore, such a provision can only be the cause of serious preoccupation for the Church, because so many of its faithful are thus exposed to the danger of losing their sincerely embraced faith and of failing the solemn tasks assumed before God.

The Holy See, moreover, cannot remain indifferent to the painful situation of so many of its children of Jewish origin, as a result of these and other grave provisions of this Ordinance.

They, indeed, are deprived of not a few rights and segregated from other citizens, in the presence of whom they are in a state of great moral, social, and economic inferiority, so great as to practically oblige many of them to heroic actions to remain faithful subjects of the Church and perhaps to lead some of them to extreme necessity.

Finally, the Holy See considers that the dispositions of Article 33 about the participation of Jews in public assemblies do not prohibit Catholics of Jewish origin from taking part in religious manifestations: if such were not the case, a reassuring official declaration would be necessary.

The writer, the Cardinal Secretary of State, even though he finds it an unpleasant necessity to recall the attention of the Minister of Slovakia to the matters which he has explained, nourishes the confidence that the Slovak government will not neglect to appropriately modify the Ordinance in question, removing from it whatever is in opposition to Catholic principles.

In this regard it has been noticed with satisfaction how up to now, in Article 255, there have been decreed norms which while far from dissipating the worries of the Holy See, attribute to the Slovak government the intention of mitigating in practice the rigor of the published provisions.

Therefore, the Holy See is quite confident that the Slovak government, until such time as the above-mentioned Ordinance is revoked or altered, would be willing to interpret and apply the regulations in such a measure and way as to render them as least harmful as possible to the demands of the Catholic conscience.

Le cardinal Maglione
au ministre de Slovaquie Sidor

Vatican, 12 novembre 1941

Il sottoscritto Cardinale Segretario di Stato ha l'onore di comunicare a Sua Eccellenza il signor Ministro di Slovacchia quanto appresso:

Con vivo dolore la Santa Sede ha appreso che anche in Slovacchia, in un paese, cioè, la cui popolazione, nella quasi totalità, si onora della migliore tradizione cattolica, è stata pubblicata, il 9 settembre u.s., una "Ordinanza Governative" la quale stabilisce una particolare "legislazione razziale" contenente vari provvedimenti in aperto contrasto con i principi cattolici.

Infatti, la Chiesa, universale per volere del suo Divin Fondatore, come accoglie nel suo grembo persone di qualsiasi stirpe, così riguarda con materna sollecitudine l'umanità intera, per suscitare e sviluppare fra tutti gli uomini sentimenti di fraternità e di amore, secondo l'esplicito e categorico insegnamento del vangelo.

A tale carattere universale della Chiesa e della sua dottrina, si oppone innanzitutto l'articolo 9 della citata Ordinanza, con cui si proibiscono i matrimoni fra ebrei e non ebrei, come pure fra ebrei e incroci ebraici.

Su questo importante argomento è noto quale sia la dottrina della Chiesa e quale la conseguente prassi canonica.

Per allontanare dai propri figli il pericolo di perdere l'inestimabile dono della fede, la Chiesa ha proibito i matrimoni fra cattolici e acattolici, ma essa ha e intende conservare integro il diritto di derogare dall'accennata proibizione, quando tale deroga sia reclamata da imperiose esigenze di coscienza. Praticamente, la Chiesa permette quei connubi soltanto in casi rarissimi, per gravi ragioni e sempre che si verifichino ben definite condizioni e si offrano solide garanzie.

Ma quando si tratta di due cattolici liberi da impedimenti canonici, sia pure di stirpe diversa, la Chiesa non potrebbe opporsi al loro matrimonio senza venir meno alla sua missione santificatrice e violare superiori leggi divine, benché non tralasci di sconsigliare matrimoni tra persone appartenenti a stirpi troppo eterogenee, in vista dei danni a cui può essere esposta la prole.

Di fronte ai principi qui sopra ricordati, non può esservi dubbio che il citato articolo 9 sia in contrasto con la dottrina cattolica, poiché proibisce, in modo assoluto e generale, i matrimoni fra ebrei e non ebrei e fra ebrei e incroci ebraici.

Per di più, l'Ordinanza governativa, con l'articolo 38, esclude i giovani che essa considera appartenenti alla stirpe ebraica, anche se cattolici, da qualsiasi studio in tutte le scuole e in tutti gli istituti d'istruzione, fuorché dalle scuole elementari e dai corsi specialmente per loro organizzati.

È evidente che in tal modo viene, in gran parte impedito alla Chiesa l'esercizio di uno dei più importanti e sacri suoi diritti, quello dell'educazione cattolica della gioventù, e ne viene, in vari modi, inceppata l'attività apostolica. Di più, un tale provvedimento non può non essere motivo di grave preoccupazione per la Chiesa, anche perché tanti suoi fedeli sono così esposti al pericolo di perdere la fede sinceramente abbracciata e di venir meno a solenni impegni assunti davanti a Dio.

Né può, inoltre, la Santa Sede rimanere indifferente alla penosa situazione di tanti suoi figli d'origine ebraica, in seguito a queste e ad altre gravose disposizioni dell'Ordinanza su detta.

Essi, invero, sono privati di non pochi diritti e segregati dagli altri cittadini, nei cui confronti vengono a trovarsi in uno stato di grande inferiorità morale, sociale ed economica, tale da obbligare, praticamente, molti di loro ad atti eroici per rimanere sudditi fedeli della Chiesa e da condurre forse parecchi in estrema necessità.

La Santa Sede, infine, ritiene che le disposizioni dell'articolo 33 circa la partecipazione degli ebrei a pubbliche adunanze, non vietino ai cattolici d' origine ebraica di prendere parte alle manifestazioni religiose: così non fosse, occorrerebbe una rassicurante dichiarazione ufficiale in proposito.

Lo scrivente Cardinale Segretario di Stato, mentre si trova nella spiacevole necessità di richiamare l'attenzione del signor Ministro di Slovacchia su le considerazioni qui esposte, nutre fiducia che il Governo slovacco non mancherà di opportunamente modificare l'Ordinanza in parola, togliendo da essa quanto è in contrasto con i principi cattolici.

A questo proposito è stato rilevato con soddisfazione come, fin da ora, nell'articolo 255, siano state sancite delle norme che, pur essendo ben lontane dal dissipare le apprensioni della Santa Sede, attestano nel Governo slovacco il proposito di mitigare nella pratica il rigore degli emanati provvedimenti.

Perciò la Santa Sede confida assai che il Governo slovacco, fino a che non venga revocata o rimaneggiata detta Ordinanza, vorrà interpretarne ed applicarne le disposizioni in misura e in modo tale da renderle meno che sia possibile lesive delle esigenze della coscienza cattolica.

APPENDIX E

Report of the Chargé d'Affaires at Bratislava,
Monsignor Giuseppe Burzio, to Luigi Cardinal
Maglione, Secretary of State

Bratislava, March 31, 1942

As I have already had the honor of informing Your Eminence, the Slovak government has decided to deport all the Jews: the operations involved commenced on the 25th and are being conducted in a most brutal manner.

The plan for the deportation was developed in total secrecy in agreement with the German authorities; but it would have been impossible to hold secret the immediate preparations and already at the beginning of the current month the proposals of the Government were leaked out and there was also known the date on which the plan would be placed into execution.

In the face of the reaction of public opinion and as a result of various interventions and appeals, among which there was not lacking one from the Slovak episcopate, the Government finally realized that it must make a statement. This was done by Alexander Mach, the Minister of the Interior and Vice-President of the Council, in the presence of the representatives of the Slovak and foreign press, on the 27th. Permit me to enclose the text of the statement, as it was communicated to the newspapers by the Slovak press agency.

With this statement the Slovak government assumes full responsibility before the entire world for its action and expressly proclaims that there had been no pressure from Germany. The Minister of the Interior, with impudent cynicism and contrary to the truth of the facts that all know, declares that the measures in course are legitimate, that the procedure is not inhuman, nor is it in opposition to natural law. With a deliberate lie, Minister Mach, to disorientate and confuse the conscience of the people, looks to compromise the Church and declares: "In the session of the Council of State of yesterday I was

226

convinced by a most responsible person that the ecclesiastical authorities are in accord with the proceedings of the Government in the
question of excluding Jews from Slovak life."

I cannot say that the attitude of all the bishops is spontaneous and
energetic, nevertheless, Minister Mach knew full well that the episcopate had presented to the Government an appeal, to deplore and
condemn the measures projected against the Jews. It seems, though,
that the Minister had, if not a reason, at least a pretext for such a
statement, supporting himself with the attitude of the Bishop of
Scepusio, who, as is known to Your Eminence, is a member, even
Vice-President, of the Council of State. I have been told that during the
session in which the deportation of the Jews was discussed, Bishop
Vojtassak, instead of rising up against this inhuman project, had
retained a totally passive attitude, limiting himself to objections of little
substance. Afterwards, speaking with another bishop, he would have
him understand that, according to his opinion, it would be better that
ecclesiastical authorities remain out of the question, that it not create
obstacles for the Government and for the President of the Republic,
that the Jews are the worst enemies of Slovakia, that in any case things
would have followed their course . . . and so forth. It is difficult to
know the truth as to what has been done and said in the State Council; I
know that Bishop Vojtassak passes for a great chauvinist; for my part I
am convinced of it because the one time that I was in his company, at
the request of His Excellency, Bishop Sapieha, on behalf of certain
Polish parish priests, whom he had ejected from their parishes, I heard
him respond: "Our kindness (toward these priests) would almost be
sinful." One cannot expect him to have greater kindness toward the
Jews.

More direct and, I would say, clear-sighted, is the position of His
Excellency, Bishop Carsky, who, writing to a colleague on the necessity of taking a decisive attitude, concluded: "If we remain passive now
when they are taking away the children of the Jews, what will we do
when they take away the children of our people?" It is a fact that now
Catholics, especially after the statement of Minister Mach, are awaiting
a clear word from their leaders.

In the meantime, it is evident that the position of Dr. Tiso, the Chief
of State, of the Bishop of Scepusio and of numerous other ecclesiastics
in the Council of State and in the parliament, begins to seriously
prejudice the Church. The recent events demonstrate that President
Tiso is placed in a bind and that the true masters of Slovakia, after the
Germans, are the President of the Council, Dr. Tuka, and the Minister
of the Interior, Mach. The former is called a sphinx-man; it is not

known what precise purposes he pursues; the members of the Hlinka Party and particularly Tiso accuse him of intrigue, especially after Colonel Snacky (until a short while ago the military attaché at the Slovak legation at the Quirinal), friend and prison companion of Dr. Tuka, has fled to Budapest and placed himself at the disposition of the Hungarian government. Mach is a man capable of anything, ready for any instruction of the Germans; full of ambition he aspires to be the President of the Council, while the aspiration of Dr. Tuka is to become President of the Republic. Both struggle against Tiso and seek to create for him an untenable position. This serves also to explain their tenacity, in carrying to its full consequences the persecution against the Jews. The Germans are delighted with them: they leave Tiso in his position because of his popularity and for the purposes of their foreign propaganda; at the same time they give all their support to Dr. Tuka and Mach, knowing their zealous execution of their orders.

From a certain indication I have had, I am inclined to believe that Dr. Tiso would like to get away from this unpleasant situation, probably with a dramatic gesture, to save his own honor, that of Hlinka and that of Slovakia. But his followers and friends dissuade him from it and say that the word of order should be: "Do not get provoked." But perhaps they do not understand that with this conduct, they favor the game plan of their adversaries, who, being without scruple, will equally bring to completion their projects and at the opportune moment they will get rid of Tiso and his friends.

I said above that the measures against the Jews are being carried out in the most brutal fashion. Concerning the treatment inflicted upon Jewish girls, from secure and controlled information it turns out that, after they are taken by force from their families—(the raids, which began the 25th and continue every night, are accomplished by the police and the militia of the Hlinka Guard)—they are concentrated in the locale of a building of "Patronka," which is located in the outskirts of Bratislava. There they are subject to a search, deprived of every object which they have taken along with them (suitcases, purses, rings, earrings, pens, foodstuffs, in sum everything), deprived of personal documents and assigned a simple registration number; if anyone protests or complains or begs that at least some small remembrance of their families be left, she is beaten with kicks and blows. This entire infamous affair is carried out by men of the lowest class, under the direction of an inspector from the Reich. The unfortunates are then gathered together in the places and there, thrown on a little bit of straw, without receiving anything to eat, they wait their turn to be loaded on to the cattle wagons that transport them to the German border. Several convoys have already departed. This is what is happening in Bratislava; news from the provinces is not different, and it is already known that several Catholic girls have undergone the same fate.

All this demonstrates that account must be taken of the statements of Minister Mach; besides, no one puts any stock in them and one is of the opinion that these poor girls are destined for prostitution or simply for massacre.

His Excellency Minister Sidor departs tomorrow for Rome, and I must leave incomplete the present report to make time to deliver it to him.

Le chargé d'affaires à Presbourg Burzio
au cardinal Maglione

Presbourg, 31 mars 1942

Come già ebbi l'onore di riferire a Vostra Eminenza reverendissima, il Governo slovacco ha deciso di deportare tutti gli ebrei; le operazioni relative sono cominciate il 25 corrente e vengono condotte nel modo più brutale.

Il piano di deportazione era stato elaborato in tutta segretezza, d'accordo con le autorità tedesche; ma sarebbe stato impossibile tenere nascosti i preparativi immediati e già al principio del corrente mese i propositi del Governo erano trapelati e si conosceva perfino la data in cui il piano sarebbe entrato in esecuzione.

Davanti alla reazione dell'opinione pubblica e in seguito a vari interventi e ricorsi, tra i quali non è mancato quello dell'episcopato slovacco, il Governo si sentì finalmente in dovere di fare delle dichiarazioni. Ciò avvenne per bocca del Ministro dell'interno e Vicepresidente del Consiglio, signor Alessandro Mach, davanti ai rappresentanti della stampa slovacca ed estera, il giorno 27 corrente. Mi permetto di allegare il testo della dichiarazione, quale fu comunicato ai giornali dell'agenzia stampa slovacca.

Con questa dichiarazione il Governo slovacco assume davanti al mondo intero la piena responsabilità del suo operato e proclama espressamente che non c'è stata pressione alcuna da parte della Germania. Il Ministro dell'Interno, con sfacciato cinismo e contro la verità dei fatti che tutti conoscono, dichiara che le misure in corso sono legittime, che non si procede in modo inumano, né in contrasto col diritto naturale. Con deliberata menzogna, il Ministro Mach, per gettare disorientamento e confusione nella coscienza del popolo, cerca di compromettere Chiesa e dichiara: "Nella seduta del Consiglio di Stato di ieri, mi sono convinto dalla bocca stessa dei più responsabili in merito, che le autorità ecclesistiche sono d'accordo coi procedimenti del Governo, nella questione dell'esclusione degli ebrei dalla vita slovacca."

Non posso dire che l'atteggiamento di tutti i vescovi sia spontaneo ed energico, tuttavia il Ministro Mach sapeva benissimo che l'episcopato aveva presentato al Governo un ricorso, per deplorare e condannare le misure progettate contro gli ebrei. Sembra, però, che il Ministro abbia avuto, se non una ragione, almeno un pretesto per simile dichiarazione, fondandosi cioè sull'atteggiamento di Monsignor vescovo di Scepusio, il quale, come è noto a Vostra Eminenza, è membro, anzi Vicepresidente, del Consiglio di Stato. Mi è stato riferito che, durante la seduta in cui venne discussa la deportazione degli ebrei, Monsignor Vojtassak, invece di insorgere contro l' inumano progetto, avrebbe tenuto un atteggiamento del tutto passivo, limitandosi ad obbiezioni di poca entità. In seguito, parlando con un altro vescovo, avrebbe lasciato capire che, secondo la sua opinione, sarebbe stato meglio che l'autorità ecclesiastica rimanesse al di fuori della questione, che non creasse ostacoli al Governo e al Presidente della Repubblica, che gli ebrei sono i peggiori nemici della Slovacchia, che tanto le cose avrebbero seguito il loro corso . . . e così via. È difficile sapere la verità su quanto si è fatto e detto al Consiglio di Stato; so che Monsignor Vojtassak passa per un grande sciovinista; per parte mia ne sono convinto, perché una volta che ero intervenuto presso di lui, dietro preghiera di S.E. Monsignor Sapieha, in favore di alcuni parroci polacchi, che egli aveva cacciato dalle loro parrocchie, mi sentii rispondere: "humanitas nostra (verso quei sacerdoti) esset fere peccaminosa." Non si può pretendere che abbia maggior tenerezza verso gli ebrei.

Più netta e, direi, chiaroveggente, è la posizione di S.E. Monsignor Carsky, il quale, scrivendo a un suo collega sulla necessità di prendere un atteggiamento deciso, conchiudeva: "se restiamo passivi ora che rapiscono le figlie degli ebrei, che cosa faremo quando prenderanno, le figlie del nostro popolo?" Sta di fatto che ora i cattolici, specialmente dopo le dichiarazioni del Ministro Mach, attendono una parola chiara da parte dei loro pastori.

Intanto, è evidente che la posizione del Dr. Tiso a capo dello Stato, del vescovo di Scepusio e di altri numerosi ecclesiastici nel Consiglio di Stato e nel parlamento, comincia ad essere di serio pregiudizio per la Chiesa. Gli ultimi avvenimenti dimostrano che il Presidente Tiso è messo in un canto e che i veri padroni della Slovacchia sono, dopo i tedeschi, il Presidente del Consiglio, Dr. Tuka, e il Ministro dell'Interno, signor Mach. Il primo è chiamato l'uomo-sfinge; non si sa che scopi precisi egli persegua; gli uomini del Partito di Hlinka e particolarmente Tiso lo accusano di macchianazioni, specialment dopo che il colonnello Snacky (fino a poco tempo fa Addetto militare alla Legazione slovacca presso il Quirinale), amico e compagno di carcere del Dr. Tuka, è fuggito a Budapest e si è messo a disposizione del Governo ungherese. Il signor Mach è un uomo disposto a tutto, pronto ad ogni cenno dei tedeschi; pieno di ambizione, egli aspira alla Presidenza del Consiglio, mentre l'aspirazione del Dr. Tuka è di diventare Presidente della Repubblica. Enttrambi lottano contro Tiso e cercano di creargli una posizione insostenibile. Questo serve anche a spiegare il loro accanimento, nel portare alle ultime conseguenze la persecuzione contro gli ebrei. I tedeschi ne godono: lasciano Tiso al suo posto per la sua popolarità e ai fini della loro propaganda all' estero; allo stesso tempo danno tutto il loro appoggio al Dr. Tuka e al signor Mach, sapendoli zelanti esecutori dei loro ordini.

Da qualche indizio avuto, sono inclinato a credere che il Dr. Tiso vorrebbe uscire da questa ingrata situazione, magari con gesto clamoroso, per salvare il suo onore, quello di Hlinka e della Slovacchia. Ma i suoi fautori ed amici ne lo distolgono e dicono che la parola d'ordine deve essere: "non lasciarsi provocare." Ma forse non capiscono che, con questa condotta, favoriscono il gioco degli avversari, i quali, essendo senza scrupoli, condurranno ugualmente a compimento i loro propositi e al momento opportuno si sbarazzeranno di Tiso e dei suoi amici.

Ho detto più avanti che le misure contro gli ebrei vengono eseguite nel modo più brutale. Per quanto riguarda il trattamento inflitto alle ragazze ebrei, de informazioni sicure e controllate risulta che, dopo essere strappate a viva forza dalle loro famiglie—(le razzie, che sono cominciate il 25 corrente e continuano ogni notte, sono compiute dalla polizia e da miliziani della Guardia di Hlinka)—esse sono concentrate nei locali di un fabbricato detto "Patronka," che si trova nella periferia di Bratislava. Quivi sono sottoposte ad una perquisizione, sono spogliate di ogni oggetto che portano con sé (valigie, borsette, anelli, orecchini, penne, generi alimentari, insomma ogni cosa), sono private dei documenti personali e contrassegnate da un semplice numero di matricola; se qualcuna protesta o si lamenta o prega che le sia almeno lasciato qualque piccolo ricordo di famiglia, viene brutalmente percossa a calci e bastonate. Tutta questa infame bisogna è eseguita da uomini della più bassa lega, sotto la direzione di un ispettore venuto dal Reich. Le infelici sono quindi ammassate nei locali e lì, buttate sopra un po' di paglia, senza nulla ricevere da mangiare, attendono il loro turno per essere caricate sui vagoni-bestiame, che le trasporteranno alla frontiera tedesca. Parecchi convogli sono già partiti. Ciò è quanto accade a Bratislava; le notizie dalle provincie non sono diverse, e si sa già di parecchi casi di fanciulle cattoliche che hanno subito la stessa sorte.

Tutto ciò dimostra che conto si deve fare delle dichiarazioni fatte dal Ministro Mach; del resto nessuno vi presta fede e si è della convinzione che quelle povere fanciulle siano destinate alla prostituzione o semplicemente al massacro.

S.E. il Ministro Sidor riparte domani per Roma, e devo lasciare incompleto il presente rapporto, per fare in tempo a consegnarglielo.

APPENDIX F

Letter of the Minister of Slovakia to the Holy See, Charles Sidor, to Luigi Cardinal Maglione, Secretary of State

Rome, May 23, 1942

The undersigned Extraordinary Envoy and Minister Plenipotentiary of the Slovak Republic to the Holy See has the honor of communicating to His Eminence, the Cardinal Secretary of State of His Holiness, that the Minister of Foreign Affairs of the Republic of Slovakia in response to the Note of the Secretariat of State of His Holiness of November 12, 1941 (#8355/41) with its note of May 8, 1942 (#8325/1/42) has made known to our Legation the following statement:

A response to the Note of the Secretariat of State of His Holiness of November 12, 1941 (#8355/41) could not be given right away for the following reasons:

The solution to the Jewish question is a very serious problem toward which the competent authorities of the Slovak state had to devote their total attention. It was planned that the President of the Council and Minister of Foreign Affairs several days after having received the *Note Verbale* (in December) would go to Rome and also the Chargé d'Affaires of the Holy See, Monsignor Burzio, during his discussions with the President of the Council was of the same opinion that instead of exchanging formal notes it would be much better to discuss orally the problem of the condition of the Jews in Slovakia and to give right away exact clarifications of the various and detailed questions in its regard.

For various reasons the journey to Rome of the Minister President was postponed to January 1942 and then to March.

But during this period of time there occurred a change concerning the solution of the Jewish question. Long negotiations took place between the Slovak and German governments about the solution of the Jewish problem in Europe and it was considered that the emigration of the Slovak Jews is only a part of a much vaster total program.

233

Actually a half-million Jews will be sent from Europe to east Europe. Slovakia will be the first state whose inhabitants of Jewish origin will be accepted by Germany. At the same time the emigration of the Jews of France (the occupied zone), Holland, Belgium, the Protectorate, the Reich, is taking place. So also has Hungary indicated that it is ready to send away 800,000 Jews as was said in a speech by the President of the Council, Dr. Kallay on April 20.

The Slovak Jews will be gathered in various places in the environs of Lublin, where they will remain definitively. The Aryan population will be moved from that area and in its place there will be organized a distinctly Jewish district with its own administration where the Jews can live together and provide for their existence with their own labor. Families will remain united. A certain amount of alarm developed from the fact that a certain Jewish girl and several men of Jewish origin fit for work were forced to emigrate before their families; but this procedure was only determined so that they could make the necessary preparations for the other Jews, especially the women, the old, the sick, and the infants. The emigration of the remaining members of the Jewish families had already begun so that soon all the Jewish families will be reunited. All the Jews will be under the protection of the Reich.

We have received the promise of the Reich government that Christians of Jewish origin will be gathered together in a separate area.

According to our law those considered Christians of Jewish origin are those who had been baptized before September 10, 1941, namely before the Jewish law was put into effect. This exception, therefore, is not valid for Jews recently baptized because they received baptism for opportunistic reasons. That these baptisms received practically at the eve of emigration were sought for material interests we can show from the following statistics: at Zilina a certain Calvinist pastor, Stefan Puskas, baptized in one day 180 Jews, the following day 110, and the third day 40, for a total of 330 Jews baptized in three days. He has received from each Jew baptized thousands and thousands of Slovak crowns. In the parish of Vrutky 86 were baptized and at Zvolen 160 Jews. At Nitra another Protestant pastor baptized 80 Jews. At Bratislava, a Protestant pastor baptized 276 Jews in one day. At Trencin the Protestant pastor baptized 50 Jews in one day, at Ruzemborek 28, at Presov 46, at Spisska Novaves 87, at Tranava 107, at Hlochovec 29. The majority were baptized by Protestant pastors.

It has been communicated to us by the German government that the Jews will be treated humanely.

The Extraordinary Envoy and Minister Plenipotentiary to the Holy See, Karl Sidor, during his recent visit to Bratislava, referred to the rumor which the Holy See has heard, according to which the Slovak government had ordered that all young girls of Jewish origin be seized and taken to the front lines and then put at the disposal of the German soldiers. Such a thing has not and cannot occur because according to the Nuremberg laws such a deed is severely punished. Officially it was told to us that some German soldiers who had relations with women of Jewish origin were condemned by a military tribunal to execution.

In Slovakia after the present emigration of the Jews there will remain only a small minority of these so that the objections raised in the aforementioned note, perhaps, will not be current even in a single marriage case.

Concerning Article 9 of the government Ordinance, which prohibits marriages between Jews and non-Jews, may we be permitted to call attention to the book of Cardinal Gasparri: *Tractatus Canonicus de Matrimonio*—published in 1932, part I, page 143, where it says: "The ruler . . . can in some circumstances for an urgent reason of public good prohibit marriage for a time or determine other conditions to be fulfilled by those who wish to be married." Also, "Because natural right in this case does not oblige under pain of nullity, a marriage initiated against civil law is valid (and also licit): and therefore the civil authority can deny civil effects separable to this marriage but not however inseparable."

Slovak law therefore establishes: an impediment "improperly so-called," that is, which prohibits marriages of this kind and punishes couples who dare to contract marriages against this law. Besides that, the Minister of the Interior can dispense even these in exceptional cases and for serious reasons.

According to Article 38 of the government Ordinance students belonging to the Jewish race have not been excluded from schools where they can obtain instruction necessary for their religious life. Likewise it is not forbidden to Catholics of Jewish origin to take part in religious manifestations, Mass, pilgrimages, processions, Marian congresses, etc.

Le ministre de Slovaquie Sidor au
cardinal Maglione

Rome, 23 mai 1942

Il sottoscritto Inviato straordinario e Ministro plenipotenziario della Repubblica Slovacca presso la Santa Sede ha l'onore di comunicare a

Sua Eminenza Reverendissima il Cardinale Segretario di Stato di Sua Santità che il Ministero degli Affari Esteri della Repubblica Slovacca in risposta alla Nota della Segreteria di Stato di Sua Santità n. 8355/41 del 12 novembre 1941 con sua nota del 8 maggio 1942 n. 8325/1/42 ha fatto sapere alla nostra Legazione la seguente dichiarazione:

La risposta alla Nota della Segreteria di Stato di Sua Santità del 12 novembre 1941 n. 8355/41 non poteva essere data subito per le seguenti ragioni:

La soluzione della questione ebraica è un problema molto grave sul quale le competenti autorità dello Stato slovacco dovevano portare tutta la loro attenzione. Era in progetto che il Presidente del Consiglio e Ministro degli Affari Esteri alcuni giorni dopo aver ricevuto la succitata Nota verbale (nel dicembre) si recasse a Roma e anche l'Incaricato d'Affari della Santa Sede Mons. Burzio durante i colloqui con il Presidente del Consiglio era della stessa opinione che invece di scambiare Note formali sarebbe molto meglio trattare a voce il problema della condizione degli ebrei in Slovacchia e dare subito gli esatti chiarimenti sulle diverse e dettagliate questioni in proposito.

Per varie ragioni il viaggio a Roma del Ministro President è stato prima rimandato al mese di gennaio 1942 e poi al mese di marzo.

Ma in questo periodo di tempo avvenne un mutamento circa la soluzione della questione ebraica. Fra il Governo slovacco e il Governo tedesco ebbero luogo trattative sulla soluzione del problema ebraico in Europa e fu considerato che l'emigrazione degli ebrei slovacchi è soltanto come una parte di un più vasto programma integrale. Attualmente un mezzo milione di ebrei sarà mandato dall'Europa in Europa Orientale. La Slovacchia sarebbe il primo Stato i cui abitanti d' origine ebraica sarebbero accettati dalla Germania. Contemporaneamente si realizza l'emigrazione degli ebrei dalla Francia (dalla parte occupata) dall' Olanda, dal Belgio, dal Protettorato, dal territorio del Reich. Così anche l'Ungheria ha manifestato di essere pronta di mandare via 800,000 ebrei come ha detto nel suo discorso il Presidente del Consiglio Dott. Kallay il 20 aprile a.c.

Gli ebrei slovacchi saranno collocati in diversi posti nei dintorni di Lublino dove resteranno definitivamente. La popolazione ariana sarà trasferita de quei territori e al suo posto sarà organizzato un distretto esclusivamente ebraico con sua propria amministrazione dove gli ebrei potranno vivere insieme e provvedere per la loro esistenza col proprio lavoro. Le famiglie resteranno unite. Un certo allarme provenne dal fatto che qualche ragazza ebrea e alcuni uomini d' origine ebraica abili al lavoro furono spinti ad emigrare prima delle loro famiglie; ma questo provvedimento fu solo determinato dal fine di fare da essi preparare le cose nécessarie agli altri ebrei specialmente alle donne, ai vecchi, ai malati ed ai bambini. L'emigrazione dei rimasti appartenenti alle famiglie ebraiche è già incominciata cosicché fra poco tutte le famigle ebraiche saranno riunite. Tutti gli ebrei saranno sotto la protezione del Reich (Schutzbefohlene).

Noi abbiamo ricevuto la promessa da parte del Governo del Reich che i cristiani d'origine ebraica saranno collocati in una zona separata.

Secondo la nostra legge sono considerati come cristiani d'origine ebraica coloro che sono stati battezzati prima del 10 settembre 1941 cioè prima che entrasse nel vigore la legge ebraica. Questa eccezione quindi non vale per gli ebrei recentemente battezzati poiché essi hanno ricevuto il battesimo per le ragioni di un certo opportunismo. Che questi battesimi ricevuti proprio alla viglia dell'emigrazione siano stati determinati da interessi materiali lo vediamo dalla seguente statistica: A Zilina un certo parroco calvinista Stefano Puskas ha battezzato in un giorno 180 ebrei, il giorno seguente 110 e il terzo giorno 40, complessivamente 330 ebrei sono stati battezzati in 3 giorni. Costui ha ricevuto da ogni ebreo battezzato migliaia e migliaia di corone slovacche. Nella parrocchia di Vrutky furono battezzati 86 e a Zvolen 160 ebrei. A Nitra un altro pastore protestante ha battezzato 80 ebrei. A Bratislava in un giorno furono battezzati da un pastore protestante 276 ebrei. A Trenchin il parroco protestante ha battezzato in un giorno 50 ebrei, a Ruzomberok 28, a Presov 46, a Spisska Novaves 87, a Trnava 107, a Hlohovec 29. La maggior parte fu battezzata dai pastori protestanti.

Da parte del Governo tedesco ci fu comunicato che gli ebrei saranno trattati umanamente.

L'Inviato straordinario e Ministro plenipotenziario presso la Santa Sede Karol Sidor durante la sua recente visita a Bratislava ha riferito a voce che la Santa Sede avrebbe ricevuto delle informazioni secondo le quali il Governo slovacco avrebbe dato ordine di catturare tutte le giovani d'origine ebraica e di esportarle al fronte militare e poi porle alla libera disposizione dei soldati tedeschi. Una cosa simile non è mai stata e non può avvenire mai perché secondo le leggi di Norimberga un tale fatto è severamente punito. Ufficialmente ci fu comunicato che alcuni soldati tedeschi i quali avrebbero avuto relazione con donne d'origine ebraica furono condannati dal tribunale militare alla fucilazione.

In Slovacchia dopo l'attuale emigrazione degli ebrei resterà soltanto una piccola minoranza di questi cosicché le obiezioni esposte nella Nota succitata forse non saranno attuali nemmeno in un unico caso matrimoniale.

Per quanto riguarda l'articolo 9 della Ordinanza governativa, con cui si proibiscono i matrimoni fra ebrei e non ebrei, ci sia permesso richiamare l'attenzione sul libro del cardinale Gasparri: Tractatus canonicus de matrimonio—pubblicato 1932 Pars I. p. 143 dove dice: "Princeps . . . potest in nonnullis circumstantiis ratione boni publici urgendo naturae ius matrimonium ad tempus prohibere vel aliquas determinare conditiones ab illis implendas qui volunt matrimonium inire." Poi: "Quoniam vero ius naturae in casu non obligat sub poena nullitatis, hinc matrimonium forte initum contra legem civilem est validum (imo quandoque licitum); et ideo auctoritas civilis potest huic matrimonio negare effectus civiles separabiles non autem inseparabiles."

La legge slovacca dunque stabilisce: impedimentum improprie dictum cioè proibisce i matrimoni di questo genere e punisce quegli sposi i quali osassero contrarre il matrimonio contro questa legge. Oltre ciò il Ministero dell-Interno in casi eccezionali e per ragioni gravi può permettere anche questi.

Secondo l'articolo 38 dell'Ordinanza governativa i giovani appartenenti alla stirpe ebraica non sono esclusi da quelle scuole dove possono ottenere l'istruzione necessaria per la loro vita religiosa. Come anche non è vietato ai cattolici d'origine ebraica prendere parte alle manifestazioni religiose, alla s. Messa, pellegrinaggi, processioni, congregazioni mariane etc.

APPENDIX G

Report of the Chargé d'Affaires at Bratislava,
Monsignor Giuseppe Burzio, to Luigi Cardinal
Maglione, Secretary of State

Bratislava, April 10, 1943

Following my respectful report # 1517 of March 7 last, I have the honor to inform Your Eminence that the feared measures of new deportations of Jews from Slovakia have not yet been put into effect, but nevertheless the danger has not disappeared, and it seems that it may only be a question of time and means.

During this situation of inquietude and anxiety caused by the statements of the Minister of the Interior, about whom I explained in my last report, and the letter of the Bishop of Nitra sent to the Head of the Government remaining without a response or apparent effect, the Slovak episcopate thought it necessary to publish a collective statement, to confirm one more time the principles of natural and divine law in regard to the Jewish question and to the measure of deportation of the Jews.

The document in question, a copy of which in translation I am enclosing, was read in all the churches of Slovakia on the Second Sunday of Lent (March 21), also radio listeners would have heard it read from the station at Presov, which transmits religious services every Sunday. As I have been told, the President of the Republic himself, as pastor of Banovce, read the letter of the bishops to the faithful.

As it was foreseeable that the printed reproduction of the document might have been impeded by censorship, the copies of it sent to the parishes were reproduced by polygraph, also with the intention of preventing certain indiscretions which could have compromised the good results of the matter.

Nevertheless, the Minister of the Interior had knowledge of it four days before the date determined for the letter; also he had in his possession a German translation of the document, with the text somewhat altered, inasmuch as it was told to me, transmitted to him by one of the legations. The same day the Bishop of Nitra received a telephone call from the Minister of the Interior who asked him to order that the reading of the collective statement of the bishops not take place. Bishop Kmetko wrote immediately to the auxiliary Bishop of Tirnavia, Bishop Buzalka, charging him to personally see the Minister to clarify the matter. Taking cognizance of the original text of the document and hearing the explanation of the aforesaid Bishop, the Minister of the Interior seemed satisfied and did not raise any more objections to the reading of the bishops' statement, which took place on the established date and made a very good impression on Slovak public opinion.

As I had the honor of pointing out above, although the threat of new deportations, announced in the speech of the Minister of the Interior, has up to now not been carried out, this does not signify that the proposal of the government has changed. (Permit me to emphasize that, when I speak of the government, I mean to refer principally to the Head of the Government and Minister of Foreign Affairs, Dr. Adalbert Tuka, and to the Minister of the Interior, Mr. Alexander Mach: they bear the greater responsibility for that which has been done in Slovakia against the Jews.) A week ago, I was informed confidentially that the Head of the Government had convened a meeting of the various functionaries dependent upon him to discuss the measures to be taken for the next deportations.

Therefore, I thought that the opportune moment had arrived to execute the venerable instructions given to me by Your Eminence in dispatch #1376/43 of March 6 last, namely that I make efforts with the government so that the Jews still living in Slovakia be spared the cruel fate of deportation. I sought an audience with the Minister of Foreign Affairs; it was granted to me for the 7th of this month, at 11:00 A.M.

There is nothing more unpleasant and humiliating than to maintain a conversation with this person, whom some call a sphinx, others a maniac, others a cynical hypocrite. When I explained the purpose of my visit, he changed visibly and said dryly: "Monsignor, I do not understand what the Vatican has to do with the Jews of Slovakia. Make known to the Holy See that I reject this step." I did not react to the discourteous and vulgar response and I made known to him that the Holy See is not involved in, and does not intend to be involved in, the internal affairs of Slovakia; I asked him to consider the step that I undertake as a delegate of the Holy See as uniquely dictated by motives of humanity and Christian charity; I added that it did not seem to me an inopportune intrusion to speak of humane and Christian sentiments to the rulers of a state, which, according to the words of its constitution, "brings together on the basis of natural law all the moral and economic forces of the people in a Christian and national community."

"The State is not and cannot be Christian!—decreed Dr. Tuka—there is no article of the constitution which declares Slovakia a Christian state. And then, when it is a matter of Jews, it is useless to invoke principles of Christianity and humanity. I do not understand why they try to prevent me from bringing to completion my mission, which is to rid Slovakia of this plague, this band of malefactors and gangsters."

I observed to the Minister that it was unjust to consider and treat as evildoers the thousands of women and innocent children, who made up a part of the deportations of last year.

"When it is a matter of such importance and range for the nation, the government cannot split hairs. The Jews are an asocial and inassimilable race; they are a pernicious and deleterious element, whom it is necessary to eradicate and eliminate without regard. But, in sum, Monsignor, I would ask if the Church or the Holy See ever protested when our Slovak people, brutalized and reduced to misery by Jewish profiteers, were forced to emigrate en masse to America? And why did they not protest when there was an exchange of Italian and German populations of the Tyrol and in other similar cases? Also the bishops and the Slovak clergy are meddling beyond what is necessary in this affair and take up the defense of the Jews; this demonstrates that the Jewish element is still very influential in Slovakia and it is one more reason to put an end to it once and for always."

"Your Excellency, without a doubt, is aware of the sad news that is spread about the atrocious fate of the Jews deported to Poland and the Ukraine. Everyone speaks of it. Admitting for a moment that a state can prescind from the norms of natural law and of the dictates of Christianity, it does not seem to me that it can, for its own prestige and for the future well-being of the nation, disassociate itself from international opinion and from the judgment of history."

"I have no direct information which authorizes me to believe such rumors, diffused by Jewish propaganda. However, it is my plan to send a commission to ascertain the condition of the Jews deported from Slovakia. If this news of atrocities proves to be true, I will not permit one more Jew to cross the Slovak border. You have pointed out the judgment of history: if history speaks someday of present-day Slovakia, it will recall that there was at the head of the government an honest and courageous man, who had the strength to liberate his homeland from the greatest of scourges. As far as international opinion is concerned, we know that it is divided into two currents: one does not trouble me and the other does not interest me, because directed or influenced by Jewish propaganda. I regret—he had the impudence to add—that even the Vatican is not altogether immune from such influence."

Is it worth the trouble to continue to explain to Your Eminence the rest of my conversation with a demented man? Nor can one hope that with such a superman arguments touching on conscience can have any force. He foresees it and repeats what he also said to me, who would have avoided touching that point: "I know that some things are good and some evil; I am a convinced and practicing Catholic; I attend holy Mass every day and receive Communion quite frequently; and I am at ease in my work; for me the supreme spiritual authority, more than the bishops, more than the Church, is my conscience and my confessor."

I asked him a final question: "May I at least, this being the opinion, indeed the current conviction, communicate to the Holy See that the deportation of the Jews of Slovakia did not occur through the initiative of the Slovak government, but under external pressure?"

"I assure you on my honor as a Christian that it is our will and our initiative. This, yes, is true, that I was offered the possibility of realizing my plan, and I certainly did not refuse it."

He then added that the Jews baptized before the date determined by the law will not be deported; those elements useful to the state and those who have obtained exemptions will also not be deported. Concerning these last, however, they must reapply for the concession, because many documents have been falsified and there has been not a little corruption.

Then he wishes to emphasize again his absolute conviction that to liberate Slovakia from the "Jewish plague" there is no other means than forced and massive deportation. Having commented to him that for delinquents there are laws, tribunals, penalties, and prison, but that it is a fundamental and inviolable right of each man not to be punished without a previous trial or for the crimes of others, he responded to me: "Prison is not enough, prisons do not better anyone, believe me, because I had the experience of it for nine years." Without intending it, Tuka said the greatest truth and the only sincere thing in all the discussion.

Finally, with true relief, I was able to leave, accompanied by these words of dismissal: "As a functionary of the Vatican, you have done your duty and I will do mine; let us remain friends, but the Jews will depart."

Nevertheless the effort has produced a certain good effect. The first to react was the President of the Republic who, informed of the discussion, called me and expressed to me his regret about the attitude and response of the Minister of Foreign Affairs. He made me also a certain confidential statement, which he asked me right away not to communicate in writing but eventually only orally.

This morning the Minister of Religion sent to the Papal Nunciature his representative to inform me that yesterday Dr. Tuka in the meeting of the Council of Ministers referred to his discussion with me and that all the ministers protested and said that they considered the intervention of the Holy See an honor for Slovakia. I was told also that the Council of Ministers decided at once to suspend the deportation of 4,000 Jews for whom the Minister of the Interior had already given the pertinent dispositions; that baptized Jews, no matter what the date of baptism, will not be deported; and that concerning the other Jews one must proceed with discernment and send away only those elements truly harmful to the state. I hope that the facts will confirm this information.

Le chargé d'affaires à Presbourg Burzio
au cardinal Maglione

Presbourg, 10 avril 1943

Facendo seguito al mio rispettoso rapporto nr. 1517 del 7 marzo u. s., ho l'onore di riferire a Vostra Eminenza Reverendissima, che le temute misure di nuove deportazioni di ebrei dalla Slovacchia non sono ancora state portate ad effetto, ma che tuttavia il pericolo non è scomparso, anzi pare che sia solo questione di tempo e di mezzi.

Perdurando la situazione di inquietudine e di ansia causata dalle dichiarazioni del Ministro degli Interni, di cui ho riferito nel mio precedente rapporto, ed essendo rimasta senza risposta o apparente effetto la lettera inviata al Capo del governo dal vescovo di Nitra, l'episcopato slovacco credette necessario di emanare una dichiarazione collettiva, per ribadire ancora una volta i principii del diritto naturale e della legge divina in rapporto alla questione ebraica e alle misure di deportazione degli ebrei.

Il documento in parola, di cui allego copia con traduzione, fu letto in tutte le chiese della Slovacchia la seconda Domenica di Quaresima (21 marzo), anzi gli ascoltatori della radio hanno potuto sentirne la lettura dalla stazione di Presov, che ogni domenica trasmette le funzioni religiose. Come mi è stato riferito, il signor Presidente della Repubblica, come parroco di Banovce, ha letto lui stesso ai fedeli la lettera dei vescovi.

Siccome era prevedibile che la riproduzione tipografica del documento sarebbe stata impedita dalla censura, le copie da rimettersi alle parrocchie furono riprodotte col poligrafo, anche allo scopo di prevenire possibili indiscrezioni, che avrebbero potuto compromettere il buon esito della cosa.

Tuttavia, il Ministro dell'Interno ne ebbe conoscenza quattro giorni prima della data fissata per la lettura, anzi ebbe nelle sue mani una traduzione tedesca del documento, col testo alquanto alterato, a quanto mi si disse, trasmessogli da una di queste Legazioni. Lo stesso giorno il vescovo di Nitra riceveva una telefonata dal Ministro dell'Interno, che lo pregava di impartire ordini, perché la lettura della dichiarazione collettiva dei vescovi non avesse luogo. Monsignor Kmetko scrisse subito al vescovo ausiliare di Tirnavia, monsignor Buzalka, incaricandolo di recarsi personalmente del signor Ministro per chiarire la cosa. Presa conoscenza del testo originale del documento e udite le spiegazioni date dal prelodato monsignor vescovo, il Ministro dell'Interno sembrò soddisfatto e non sollevò ulteriori obbiezioni alla lettura della dichiarazione dei viscovi, la quale ebbe luogo alla data stabilita e produsse ottima impressione nell'opinione pubblica slovacca.

Come ebbi l'onore di accennare più sopra, sebbene la minaccia di nuove deportazioni, annunziata dal discorso del Ministro dell'Interno, sia rimasta fino ad oggi incompiuta, questo non significa che il proposito del governo sia mutato, (Mi permetto di sottolineare che, quando parlo di governo, intendo riferirmi principalmente al Capo del governo e Ministro degli Affari Esteri, dr. Adalberto Tuka e al Ministro degli Interni, signor Alessandro Mach: essi portano la maggiore responsabilità di quanto è stato fatto in Slovacchia contro gli ebrei). Una settimana fa, fui informato confidenzialmente che il Capo del governo aveva convocato presso di sé una riunione di vari funzionari da lui dipendenti, per trattare delle misure da prendersi per le prossime deportazioni.

Pertanto, credetti giunto il momento opportuno per eseguire le venerate istruzioni datemi da Vostra Eminenza, con dispaccio nr. 1376/43 del 6 marzo u. s., e cioè di adoperarmi presso questo governo, affinché sia risparmiata agli ebrei ancora dimoranti in Slovacchia la dura sorte della deportazione. Chiesi un 'udienza al signor Ministro degli Affari Esteri; mi fu accordata per il giorno 7 c. m., alle ore 11.

Non c'è cosa più antipatica e umiliante che sostenere una conversazione con questo personaggio, che altri chiama sfinge, altri maniaco, altri fariseo cinico. Quando gli ebbi esposto l'oggetto della mia visita, si alterò visibilmente e disse seccato: ''Monsignore, io non comprendo che ha da vedere il Vaticano con gli ebrei della Slovacchia. Fate comunicare alla Santa Sede che io respingo questo passo." Non reagii alla scortese e volgare risposta e gli feci presente che la Santa Sede non si immischiava e non intendeva immischiarsi nelle cose interne della Slovacchia; lo pregai di considerare il passo, che io compievo per incarico della Santa Sede, come dettato unicamente da motivi di umanità e di carità cristiana; aggiunsi che non mi sembrava inopportuna intromissione parlare di sentimenti umani e cristiani ai dirigenti di uno Stato, il quale, secondo le parole della sua stessa Costituzione, "riunisce sulle basi del diritto naturale tutte le forze morali e economiche del popolo in una comunità cristiana e nazionale."

"Lo Stato non è e non può essere cristiano!—sentenziò il dr. Tuka—non c'è nessun articolo della Costituzione che dichiari la Slovacchia uno Stato cristiano. E poi, quando si tratta di ebrei, è vano invocare principii di cristianesimo e di umanità. Io non comprendo perché mi si vuole impedire di portare a compimento la mia missione, che è quella di sbarazzare la Slovacchia da questa peste, da questa banda di malfattori e di gangsters."

Osservai al signor Ministro che non era giusto considerare e trattare come malfattori le migliaia di donne e bambini innocenti, che fecero parte delle deportazioni dello scorso anno.

"Quando si tratta di provvedimenti di tanta importanza e portata per una nazione, il governo non può andare per il sottile. Gli ebrei sono una razza asociale, inassimilabile; sono elementi perniciosi e deleteri, che bisogna sradicare e eliminare senza riguardi. Ma, insomma, mi dica, monsignore, se mai la Chiesa o la Santa Sede hanno protestato, quando il nostro popolo slovacco, abbrutito e ridotto alla miseria dagli sfruttatori ebrei, fu costretto ad emigrare in massa verso le Americhe? E perché non hanno protestato, quando vi fu lo scambio delle popolazioni italiane e tedesche del Tirolo e in altri casi consimili? Anche i vescovi e il clero slovacco si sono immischiati oltre il bisogno in questo affare e prendono le difese degli ebrei; questo dimostra che l'elemento ebraico è ancora molto influente in Slovacchia ed è una ragione di più per farla finita una volta per sempre."

"Vostra Eccellenza è, senza dubbio, a conoscenza delle tristi notizie che corrono sulla sorte atroce degli ebrei deportati in Polonia e Ucraina. Tutto il mondo ne parla. Ammettendo per un istante che uno Stato possa prescindere dalle norme del diritto naturale e dai dettami del cristianesimo, non mi pare che possa, per il proprio prestigio e per il bene futuro della propria nazione, disinteressarsi dell' opinione internazionale e del giudizio della storia."

"Io non ho informazioni dirette che mi autorizzino a credere a simili dicerie, diffuse dalla propaganda ebraica. Però, è mio proposito di inviare una commissione a informarsi di presenza della condizione degli ebrei deportati dalla Slovacchia. Se queste notizie di atrocità risultassero vere, non permetterei che un ebreo di più varcasse la frontiera slovacca. Avete accennato al giudizio della storia: se la storia parlerà un giorno della Slovacchia attuale, ricorderà che vi fu alla testa del Governo un uomo dabbene e coraggioso, il quale ebbe la forza di liberare la sua patria dal più grande dei flagelli. Quanto all'opinione internazionale, sappiamo che è divisa in due correnti: l'una non mi preoccupa e l'altra non mi interessa, perché diretta o influenzata dalla propaganda ebraica. Lamento—ebbe l'impudenza di aggiungere—che anche il Vaticano non sia del tutto immune da simlie influsso."

Vale la pena che io continui a riferire a Vostra Eminenza il seguito della mia conversazione con un demente? Né è da sperare che con tal superuomo possano valere argomenti toccanti la coscienza. Egli li previene e ripete quello che disse anche a me, che pure mi sarei guardato di toccare quel punto: "So che cosa è bene e che cosa è male; sono cattolico convinto e praticante; assisto ogni giorno alla Santa Messa e mi comunico con molta frequenza. E sono tranquillo del mio operato; per me la suprema autorità spirituale, più che i vescovi, più che la Chiesa, è la mia coscienza e il mio confessore."

Gli posi un'ultima questione: "Posso almeno, essendo questa l'opinione anzi la convinzione corrente, comunicare all Santa Sede che la deportazione degli ebrei dalla Slovacchia non avviene per iniziativa del governo slovacco, ma sotto una pressione esterna?"

"Vi assicuro sul mio onore di cristiano, che è nostra volontà e nostra iniziativa. Questo, sì, è vero, che mi è stata offerta la possibilità di realizzare il mio piano ed io, per certo, non la ho rifiutata."

Aggiunse, poi, che gli ebrei battezzati prima del termine fissato dalla legge non saranno deportati; così pure non saranno allontanati gli elementi utili allo Stato e quelli che hanno ottenuto la discriminazione. Che, però, per quanto riguarda questi ultimi, si dovranno rivedere le concessioni, perché sono stati falsificati molti documenti e vi è stata non poca corruzione.

Poscia, volle ancora sottolineare la sua assoluta convinzione, che per liberare la Slovacchia dalla "peste ebraica" non vi è altro mezzo che la deportazione forzata e in massa. Avendogli osservato che per i delinquenti vi sono le leggi, i tribunali, le condanne e il carcere, ma che è diritto primordiale e inviolabile di ciascuno di non essere punito senza previo giudizio o per delitti di altri mi rispose: "La prigione non basta, la prigione non migliora nessuno, creda pure a me che ne ho fatto l'esperienza per nove anni." Senza volerlo, il signor Tuka disse la più grande verità e l'unica cosa sincera di tutto il colloquio.

Finalmente, con vero sollievo, potei andarmene, accompagnato da queste parole di commiato, che riassumono l'esito dell'intervista: "Come funzionario del Vaticano, avete fatto il vostro dovere ed io farò il mio; resteremo amici, ma gli ebrei partiranno."

Tuttavia il passo ha prodotto qualche buon effetto. Il primo a reagire è stato il Presidente della republica il quale, informato del colloquio, mi fece chiamare e mi espresse il suo rammarico per l'atteggiamento e risposta del Ministro degli Esteri. Mi fece anche qualche dichiarazione confidenziale, che però mi pregava istantemente di non comunicare per iscritto ma eventualmente solo di viva voce.

Questa mattina il Ministro dei Culti ha inviato alla Nunziatura Apostolica un suo rappresentante per comunicarmi che ieri il dr. Tuka riferì nella riunione del Consiglio dei Ministri circa il colloquio avuto con me e che tutti i Ministri protestarono e dissero che consideravano un onore per la Slovacchia lo intervento della Santa Sede. Mi riferì pure che il Consiglio dei Ministri ha subito deciso che sia sospesa la deportazione dei 4000 ebrei per la quale il Ministero degli Interni aveva già dato le relative disposizioni; che gli ebrei battezzati non saranno più deportati qualunque sia la data del battesimo; e che per quanto riguarda gli altri ebrei si dovrà procedere con discernimento e allontanare solo gli elementi veramente nocivi allo Stato. Spero che i fatti confermeranno queste informazioni.

APPENDIX H

The Jewish Problem: A Report Written by Monsignor Giuseppe DiMeglio, a Member of the Staff of the Nunciature in Berlin, and Brought to the Secretariat of State, December 9, 1942

During the years 1941 and 1942 the National Socialist Government has given an extraordinarily wide-ranging impetus to the struggle against the Jews. Thus, while there continues a continuous and progressive application of the National Socialist program against its three classic enemies: Jews, Christians, and Masons, nevertheless, it is, at this moment, an indication also of the base sentiments of vengeance and anger, which animate the chiefs of the Reich by the unexpected and very strong Russian resistance, attributed by them to the clever Jewish commissars, and also for the entry of the United States into the war, attributed by them to international Jewish high finance.

Numerical Estimates

To prescind, however, from these rather contingent motives, it is evident that, at the present moment, the Jewish problem must become of primary importance, in the internal political camp, if National Socialism really wishes to carry out the progressive purification of Germany of Semitic blood.

The number, in fact, of Jews residing at present in the Reich or in the countries occupied by it, or subject to its political domination, is today very large.

According to data supplied by the press, Jews residing in Germany in 1939 numbered about 500,000. After the Russian-German partition of Poland, those residing in the areas which now form the General-gouvernement were numbered at two million. Many Jews live in Hungary, Romania, Slovakia. After the beginning of the war with

248

Russia, there fell under German domination about a million and a half Jews, living in the regions of Poland which had been granted to Russia; and 260,000 living in the Baltic regions.

In the area of Russia proper, according to data furnished in 1939 by the Soviet government, three and a half million live; of these, at least a million and a half reside in the Russian territories now occupied by Germany.

Because very many fled before the arrival of the German troops from the Polish regions subject to the Russians and from the Russian territory proper, it is estimated that now, both in the Reich and in the occupied territories, also in the Protectorate of Bohemia and Moravia, there are more than four million Jews, namely, a quarter of the total world Jewish population.

Measures

The principal measures taken against the Jews are the following:

1. INSTITUTION OF GHETTOS

Entire quarters of certain cities have been set aside for Jews, as their permanent residence, with right of administration, police, and their own means of communication.

Of the ghettos established up to now, the most important are those of Lodz and Warsaw. Several ghettos have also arisen in the Baltic countries and also in the occupied Russian territories.

2. CONCENTRATION CAMPS

Because, as is evident, not all the Jews can find room in the ghettos of the cities, there have been created immense concentration camps, where they lead a very harsh life; little food is given to them; they are subjected to extraordinarily heavy work; all causes which quickly lead many to death.

It is said that such concentration camps have till now risen in Poland, which leads one to think that the eastern regions, particularly Poland, have been established, in the plans of the German government, as the definitive place of residence for the Jewish population of Europe.

In general, so as not to draw too much attention from the population, they have been obliged to leave in the middle of the night; they can take with them very few personal garments and a small sum of money.

3. THE STAR

Beginning in the month of September 1941, a sign of recognition has been made obligatory for every Jew; a yellow star, with six points, to be worn on the chest, with "Jew" written in the center.

The sight of these unfortunate people who, pallid and emaciated (the food rations for them are much reduced compared to the Germans; certain food products are completely excluded for them), crowd the city streets, at a set hour of the day, or else, when traveling, huddle in a corner, arouses a feeling of deep revulsion and pity.

The Reaction of the German Population

The German people—may it be said to their honor—in spite of their vivid nationalistic sensitivity, have shown themselves, however, externally very indifferent toward such provisions. There is never noted a gesture of derision or even of simple irony regarding the Jews; such external indifference presupposes a very notable internal resentment because of the inhumanity of the measures, which—the Germans themselves well understand it—cannot redound to the advantage of a civilized people, above all, when it is a question of people who claim to be the highest *kulturträger* ("pillar of culture") in the world!

The Counter-Reaction of the Party

A sign of the unpleasant reaction provoked in the population by the regulation of the star, is a flier recently passed around by the party, in which it is expressly stated that the Jews should be considered enemies of the fatherland.

Goebbels, in a violent article, after having disapprovingly set in relief the excessive humanitarian sense, "innate in the German spirit," exhorted the citizenry to see in each person wearing the yellow star, the authentic betrayer of the German people, of its morals and of its culture.

Inhuman Treatment in the Occupied Regions and in the Countries Politically Subject to Germany

An Italian journalist, recently returned from Romania, gave me, some time ago, a long account concerning the brutal methods against the Jews, adopted in that country, above all through German instigation.

He recounted to me that an entire train was filled up with Jews; every opening was then carefully blocked up, in such a way that not even a breath of air could pass through. When the train reached a preestablished destination, the survivors were very few, namely those who finding themselves near an opening, not completely closed up, were able to breathe a little bit of air.

Of these unfortunates, not only is their end wished, but also they want to enjoy, with satanic pleasure, the slow and very cruel death of the others.

The same journalist noted that the most grave element, the aspect truly tragic, of this anti-Jewish action, is the absolute coldness of spirit with which the responsible authorities communicate orders and the indifference of the officers who attend executions smoking cigarettes.

The "Institute for the Investigation of Jewish Influence on German Life"

This Institute was opened a year ago with a speech by Alfred Rosenberg entitled "The Jewish Question as a World Problem."

This Institute has—as Reichswart indicated—as its principal purpose to demonstrate the intimate union existing between Christianity and Judaism, through which the deleterious effects of Judaism on the German soul are to be attributed also to Christianity.

In the above-mentioned speech, Rosenberg stated: "For Germany the Jewish question will only be solved when the last Jew has left greater Germany."

Recently there took place at Nuremberg the third plenary session of the members of the Institute. Among others the following topics were discussed: "Paul, Jewish emissary and apostle of Christ; Jesus' mother tongue." The development of spiritual elements, proper to Germanism, are supposed to have been impeded by a "Jewish coordinated system" of Pauline theology. Jesus Christ is a reformer in the internal camp of the Jews. This has been demonstrated sufficiently by the Dane, Grenbach; now Professor Odeberg has brought in new personal scientific results in its regard.

The President of the Institute has given a conference at the University of Berlin under the title "The Work of the Institute in the Religious Struggle of the Present" in which he developed the ideas expressed above.

The Jewish Question and the German Episcopate

Certain ecclesiastics and lay Catholics have noted with amazement that till now the German episcopate has made no collective manifestation on the question of the grave mistreatment afflicted upon the Jews, while the French episcopate right away took a position against the racial legislation in France, introduced by Marshal Pétain; also voices of protest were raised in other nations.

Notes de la Nonciature à Berlin

Rome, 9 décembre 1942

Negli anni 1941 e 1942 il Governo nazionalsocialista ha dato alla lotta contro gli ebrei un impulso straordinariamente ampio. Ciò, mentre costituisce una graduale e progressiva applicazione del programma nazionalsocialista contro i suoi tre classici nemici: ebrei, cristiani e massoni, tuttavia è, in questo momento, indice anche dei bassi sentimenti di vendetta e di ira, che animano i capi del Reich per l'imprevista, durissima resistenza russa, da essi attribuita agli abili commissari ebraici, nonché per l'entrata in guerra degli Stati Uniti, attribuita essa pure all'alta finanza ebraica internazionale.

Valutazioni numeriche

A prescindere, però, da questi motivi, piuttosto contingenti, è evidente che, nel momento attuale, il problema ebraico doveva divenire di primaria importanza, nel campo politico interno, se il nazional-socialismo voleva realmente attuare la progressiva purificazione della Germania dal sangue semita.

Il numero, infatti, degli ebrei, oggi residenti nel Reich e nei paesi occupati dal medesimo, o sotto posti alla sua dominazione politica, è oggi ingentissimo.

Secondo i dati, forniti dalla stampa, gli ebrei residenti in Germania erano, nel 1939, circa 500.000. Dopo la divisione russo-tedesca della Polonia, quelli residenti nelle regioni, che ora formano il General-gouvernement era valutato at 2 milioni. Molti ebrei vivono nell'Un-gheria, Romania, Slovacchia. Dopo l'inizio della guerra con la Russia, cadevano sotto la dominazione germanica circa un milione e mezzo di ebrei, abitanti nelle regioni della Polonia, che erano state attribuite alla Russia; e 260.000 appartenenti alle regioni baltiche.

Nelle regioni propriamente russe, secondo i dati forniti nel 1939 dal governo sovietico, ne abitavano tre milioni e mezzo; di essi, almeno un milione e mezzo risiedevano nei territori russi, ora occupati dalla Germania.

Poiché moltissimi fuggirono, prima dell'arrivo delle truppe germaniche, dalle regioni polacche sottoposte ai russi e da quelle propriamente russe, si valuta, che attualmente, sia nel Reich come nei territori occupati, nonché nel Protettorato della Boemia e Moravia, si trovino oltre 4 milioni di ebrei, cioè, un quarto di tutta la popolazione ebraica mondiale.

Misure

Le principali misure stabilite contro gli ebrei sono le seguenti:

1. ISTITUZIONE DEI GHETTI

Interi quartieri di alcune città sono stati destinati agli ebrei, come loro stabile dimora, con diritto di amministrazione, forze di polizia, e mezzi di comunicazione proprii.

Dei ghetti, finora istituiti, i più importanti sono quelli di Lietzmannstadt (Lodz) e di Varsavia. Alcuni ghetti sono sorti anche nei paesi baltici nonché nelle regioni russe occupate.

2. CAMPI DI CONCENTRAMENTO

Poiché, com'è evidente, non tutti gli ebrei possono trovar posto nei ghetti delle città, sono stati creati immensi campi di concentramento, dove essi conducono una vita durissima; vien loro dato poco cibo; sono sottoposti a un lavoro straordinariamente pesante: cause tutte che ben presto conducono molti alla morte.

Si dice che tali campi di concentramento siano finora sorti in Polonia, il che lascia pensare che le regioni orientali, particolarmente la Polonia, siano state, nei disegni del Governo germanico, stabilite come luogo definitivo di residenza per le popolazioni ebraiche dell'Europa.

In genere, per non richiamare troppo l'attenzione della popolazione, essi sono obbligati a partire nel cuore della notte; possono portare seco pochissimi indumenti personali ed una somma di danaro lievissima.

3. LA STELLA

A partire dal mese di settembre 1941, e stato reso obbligatorio per ogni israelita un segno di riconoscimento: una stella gialla, a sei punte, da portarsi sul petto, con nel contro la scritta: Jude!

La visione di questi infelici, che, pallidi e macilenti (le razioni alimentari sono molto ridotte rispetto a quelle dei tedeschi; alcune derrate alimentari sono per essi del tutto escluse) affollano le vie cittadine, in determinate ore del giorno, oppure, viaggiando, si raccolgono in un angolo, desta un senso di profondo raccapriccio e commiserazione.

La reazione del popolo germanico

Il popolo germanico—sia detto a suo onore—nonostante la sua viva sensibilità nazionale, si dimostra tuttavia anche esternamente molto indifferente verso tali provvedimenti. Non si nota mai un gesto di scherno o anche di semplice ironia riguardo agli ebrei; tale indifferenza esterna presuppone un risentimento interno molto notevole per l'inumanità di questa misura, che—i tedeschi stessi ben lo comprendono—non può ridondare a vanto di un popolo civile, soprattutto, poi, quando si tratti di un popolo che afferma di essere il più alto Kulturträger del mondo!

La contro-reazione del partito

Segno della non felice reazione suscitata nel popolo dal provvedimento della stella, è un foglio volante, recentemente diffuso dal partito, in cui si dice espressamente che i giudei devono essere considerati come nemici della patria.

Il signor Göbbels, in un violento articolo, dopo aver messo in rilievo, disapprovandolo, l'eccessivo senso umanitario, "innato nell'anima germanica," esortava i cittadini a vedere in chiunque porti la stella gialla, il traditore autentico del popolo germanico, della sua morale e della sua cultura.

Inumani trattamenti nelle regioni occupate e nei paesi sottoposti politicamente alla Germania

Un giornalista italiano, reduce dalla Romania, mi fece, tempo fa, una lunga relazione circa i metodi brutali, adoperati in quel paese, soprattutto per istigazione germanica, contro gli ebrei.

Egli mi raccontava che era stato riempito di ebrei un treno intero; ogni fessura fu poi accuratamente otturata, in modo che non passasse un filo d' aria. Quando il treno giunse alla localitá prestabilita, i superstiti erano pochissimi, quelli, cioè, che, trovandosi vicino a qualche fessura, non completamente chiusa, avevano potuto respirare un po' d'aria.

Di questi infelici non si vuole solo la fine; ma si vuole assaporare anche, con satanico gusto, l' altrui morte lenta e atrocissima.

Lo stesso giornalista notava che l'elemento più grave, l'aspetto veramente tragico, di tale azione antiebraica è l'assoluta freddezza di spirito con cui le autorità responsabili impartiscono gli ordini e l'indifferenza degli ufficiali, che assistono alle esecuzioni, fumando la sigaretta.

L' "Institut für Erforschung des judischen Einflusses auf das deutsche Leben"

Tale Istituto è stato aperto lo scorso anno, con un discorso di Alfredo Rosenberg, del titolo "Di Judenfrage als Weltproblem."

Tale Istituto ha—come avverte il "Reichswart"—come scopo principale di dimostrare l'intima unione esistente tra il cristianesimo e il giudaismo, per cui gli effetti deleteri del giudaismo sull'anima germanica sono da attribuirsi anche al cristianesimo.

Nel surriferito discorso, il signor Rosenberg dichiarava: "Für Deutschland ist die Judenfrage erst dann gelöst, wenn der letzte Jude den groBdeutschen Raum verlassen hat."

Recentemente ha avuto luogo in Norinberga la terza seduta plenaria dei membri dell'Istituto. Tra gli altri sono stati discussi i seguenti temi: "Paulus, Judensendling und Christusapostel; de Muttersprache Jesu." Lo sviluppo degli elementi spirituali, propri del germanesimo, sarebbe stato impedito da un "judisches Koordinatensystem" della teologia paolina. Gesù Cristo è un riformatore nel campo interno dei giudei. Ciò era stato dimostrato sufficientemente dal danese Grönbach; ora il professore Dr. Odeberg ha recato nuovi personali risultati scientifici in proposito.

Il presidente dell'Istituto ha tenuto nell'università di Berlino una conferenza dal titolo "Die Arbeit des Instituts im religiösen Ringen der Gegenwart," nella quale ha sviluppato le idee sopra espresse.

La questione ebraica e l'episcopato germanico

Alcuni ecclesiastici e laici cattolici hanno notato, con meraviglia, come finora l'episcopato germanico non abbia fatto alcuna manifestazione collettiva sulla questione dei gravi maltrattamenti inflitti agli ebrei, mentre l'episcopato francese ha subito preso posizione contro la legislazione razziale in Francia, introdotta dal Maresciallo Pétain, nonché voci di protesta sono state elevate anche in altre nazioni.

APPENDIX I

Triennial Report of the Nuncio in Italy, Archbishop Francesco Borgongini Duca, to the Secretary of State, Luigi Cardinal Maglione

Rome, January 31, 1943

The triennial period 1940, 1941, 1942 concerning which I have the honor to report as to how the activity of this Nunciature has developed, is characterized by a cruel war which is still raging.

· The conflict has given new forms to such activity, due above all to the apostolic charity of the Holy Father.

As soon as the war broke out, this Nunciature was obliged to assume the protection of the diplomatic representatives accredited to the Holy See, whose countries were at war with the Axis. Hence it affixed seals to the British Legation, the French, Belgian, Polish Embassies, and has had the charge of protecting the ecclesiastics involved and the religious personnel of all of these countries.

The state of war has brought an exacerbation of the racial question. Many Jews have fled from the territories occupied by Germany, preferring to come to Italy, even taking the risk of being interned. Afterwards they have called upon this Papal Nunciature to obtain the possibility of going abroad, especially to America. Through our intervention many have obtained the necessary visas from the various consulates, and also [visas] for transit, and the Holy Father, in his inexhaustible charity, has provided for many the not insignificant funds for their journey.

The Nunciature has also succeeded, but only in the rarest cases, in obtaining from Count [Galeazzo] Ciano [Italian Foreign Minister] entry visas for the kingdom for Jews who were in danger of being deported.

The conflict having become worse, many refugees have come to Italy in the most pitiable condition, especially from Poland. His Holiness has deigned to place at my disposal notable sums to assist them; and thus with the aid of the Ursuline Sisters, this Nunciature has been able to place with religious institutions Polish girls and women, more or less abandoned, and to provide for unemployed men. We have also entered into correspondence with the other Polish refugees spread throughout Italy, without neglecting the internees, who in a certain way are in better condition, because they have bread and a roof assured. It is indeed known to Your Eminence that the Holy Father has deigned to accept the very humble proposal of this Nunciature to open a "hearth" for the women, and this has been entrusted to the Ursulines of the Dying Heart with excellent results and is still functioning regularly.

Not only from Poland, but also from all the other fronts, there have poured into Italy Greeks, Orientals, Maltese, Italians fleeing from Tripoli and from Cyrenaica, Italians expelled from France, Slovenes, Croats and Serbs, and for all the Holy Father, with apostolic action, has opened the not too rich treasure of the Roman Church; hence the Nunciature has been charged with distributing the subsidies, both to those who come to the Nunciature, and to those scattered throughout Italy or in various concentration camps.

The distribution of the money is done, normally, after having received from the priests of the places of residence, verification of the moral life and poverty of the petitioners. The question of religion has never been raised, because the charity of the Pope embraces all; but for all I have striven to obtain authoritative assurances of good conduct.

To date of this respectful report the Apostolic Nunciature has distributed from the beginning 625,816.56 lire to the Poles and 307,705.80 lire to the other refugees.

Because of the war the Royal Government has been obliged to establish many concentration camps for foreign civilians more or less suspect and also to create camps for prisoners captured in combat. The former camps are generally operated under the authority of Public Security and the latter under military authorities.

The Holy Father has expressed the august desire that the Apostolic Nuncio go personally to visit the interned people and to bring them with His Blessing the comforts of His august charity.

To the date of this humble triennial report, the visits completed by the undersigned have been in total 106. The camps are located all over Italy, from Bolzano and Udine to Apulia and Calabria, and on the island of Sardinia. The visits completed by the secretaries of the Apostolic Nunciature on their own amount to five.

I have discovered that generally the prisoners and civilians are treated humanely. The Nunciature has paid special attention to religious assistance. At our suggestion the government has named a permanent chaplain in the internment colony of Pisticci. Another (who speaks various languages) for the camp of Ferramonti Tarsia, where the charity of the Holy Father has also furnished the temporary church and donated a harmonium. A chaplain of the Chinese language has been assigned to the camp of the Chinese, Tossicia in the Province of Teramo, and at present the island of Gran Sasso. The good chaplain has zealously instructed the poor Chinese pagans, printing also a catechism with Chinese letters. After a year of instruction and trial about fifty of the catechumens were admitted to baptism and as many the year following. I myself went twice to the sanctuary of St. Gabriel, on Gran Sasso, for the solemn ceremonies, attended by the Chief Constable of Teramo, the Inspector of the Ministry of the Interior, and local authorities.

Other conversions have been verified just about everywhere especially among the women, also among the Jews. The Ursuline Sisters continually instruct such women and young girls, and more than one baptism has been celebrated. Steps have been taken to regularize not a few marriages in Rome and elsewhere.

The occupation of Dalmatia has brought about the confinement in Italy of about 50,000 Slovenes and Croats, who have been interned in Tuscany, in Venice, and on the island of Arbe.

I have visited the camp of Gonars in Friuli; as the Apostolic Nunciature has also been concerned about the improvement of the conditions of all these deported people, who suffer from the upheaval of displacement, which has taken place right in the midst of a civil war. This improvement is being obtained from the government, and by order of Your Eminence, soon I will also visit those confined on the island of Arbe. Meanwhile His Holiness has accepted the humble suggestion of this Nunciature to take at his own expense into the Illyrian Pontifical College of Loreto two hundred young Slovenes and discussions are underway with the Minister of Foreign Affairs (of rather long duration because of the burdensome bureaucracy of the war) for the purpose of putting into effect the desire of the Pope.

Moreover, the Apostolic Nunciature has become the organ of liaison between the Information Office of the Secretariat of State and the Italian Red Cross, for the transmission of messages to prisoners in Italian hands and to their families abroad, and also for shipment to these same prisoners of manuals of prayer and catechisms, published by the Vatican Press, as well as some readers that the Secretariat of State is sending them.

For Italian prisoners in foreign lands, this Nunciature has a special office for the receipt of messages from their families, which it transmits to the Vatican office, as well as under the direction of the Secretariat of State, it has overseen the consignment to the Red Cross of 16,000 volumes collected by the Secretariat of State for Italian prisoners.

The war has indeed brought about an infinite number of requests of every kind from those suffering, directed to the Holy Father (military exemptions, bringing soldiers nearer, pensions for families, liberation of those interned, penalties even for small infractions and related requests for pardon, permissions for marriage to those impeded by racial or military laws, the promotion of employees, transfers, and the like); all these proceedings which flow into the Nunciature, transmitted by the Secretariat of State or also directly sent to us by the interested parties, are looked after, as much as it is possible and effort is made to give a response to each.

The correspondence with the interned merits special mention, because all, or almost all, these unfortunates, without exception, seek the involvement of this Nunciature with the police authorities, who receive our interventions with much deference. In our archives every interned person has his file . . .

Le nonce en Italie Borgongini Duca
au cardinal Maglione

Rome, 31 janvier 1943

Il triennio, sul quale ho l'onore di riferire come si sia svolta l'attività di questa Nunziatura, è caratterizzato dall'immane guerra che ancora infierisce.

Il conflitto ha dato a tale attività nuove forme, dovute sopratutto all'apostolica carità del Santo Padre. Appena scoppiato il conflitto, questa Nunziatura ha dovuto assumere la protezione delle rappresentanze diplomatiche accreditate presso la Santa Sede, i cui paesi erano in guerra coll'Asse. Quindi ha apposto i sigilli alla Legazione britannica, alle Ambasciate francese, belga, polacca ed ha avuto l'incarico di proteggere gli interessi ecclesiastici ed il personale religioso di tutti questi paesi.

Lo stato di guerra ha portato un inasprimento della questione razziale. Molti ebrei sono fuggiti dai territori occupati della Germania, preferendo di venire in Italia, sia pure correndo il rischio di essere internati. Qui poi hanno interessato questa Nunziatura Apostolica per avere la possibilità di recarsi all'estero, specialmente in America. Molti hanno ottenuto per il nostro intervento i visti necessari dei vari consolati, anche per transito, e il Santo Padre, nella sua inesauribile carità, ha provveduto per molti le spese non indifferenti di viaggio.

La Nunziatura è riuscita pure, ma solo in pochissimi casi, ad ottenere dal conte Ciano il visto d' ingresso nel regno ad ebrei che erano in pericolo di essere deportati.

Aggravandosi il conflitto, molti profughi sono giunti in Italia nelle più pietose condizioni, specialmente dalla Polonia. Sua Santità si degnò di mettere a mia disposizione delle notevoli somme per soccorrerli; e così con l'aiuto delle suore Orsoline, questa Nunziatura poté collocare presso istituti religiosi le ragazze, e signore polacche, più o meno abbandonate, e provvedere agli uomini senza lavoro. Siamo anche entrati in corrispondenza con gli altri profughi polacchi sparsi per l'Italia, senza trascurare i confinati, che in certo modo sono in migliori condizioni, perché hanno un pane e un tetto assicurati. È noto poi a Vostra Eminenza che il Santo Padre si è degnato di accogliere l'umilissima proposta di questa Nunziatura, di aprire un "focolare" per le donne, e questo fu affidato alle Orsoline del Cuore Agonizzante con ottimi risultati e esso ancora funziona regolarmente.

Non solo dalla Polonia, ma da tutti gli altri fronti, sono piovuti in Italia greci, levantini, maltesi, italiani sfollati da Tripoli e dalla Cirenaica, italiani espulsi dalla Francia, sloveni, croati e serbi, e per tutti il Santo Padre, con gesto apostolico, ha aperto il non molto ricco tesoro della Chiesa Romana; quindi questa Nunziatura è stata incaricata di distribuire i sussidi, tanto a quelli che si presentano alla Nunziatura, quanto agli altri dispersi per l'Italia o nei vari campi di concentramento.

La distribuzione del danaro si fa, normalmente, dopo aver ricevuto, dai parroci dei luoghi di dimora, attestazioni della moralità e povertà dei riccorrenti. Non si è mai fatta questione di religione, perché la carità del Papa abbraccia tutti; ma per tutti mi sono studiato di richiedere assicurazioni autorevoli di buona condotta.

Alla data di questo rispettoso rapporto la Nunziatura Apostolica ha distribuito dal principio, per i polacchi, Lire 625.816,56 e per gli altri rifugiati Lire 307.705,80.

A causa della guerra il Regio Governo ha dovuto costituire molti campi di concentramento per i civili stranieri più o meno sospetti e anche creare dei campi di prigionieri catturati in combattimento. I primi campi generalmente sono tenuti dalle autorità di Pubblica Sicurezza e i secondi dalle autorità militari.

Il Santo Padre ha espresso l'augusto desiderio che il Nunzio Apostolico si recasse personalmente a visitare gli internati e portare loro con la Sua Benedizione i conforti della Sua augusta carità.

Alla data di questo umile rapporto triennale, le visite compiute dal sottoscritto sono state complessivamente n. 106. I campi si trovano dislocati in tutta Italia, da Bolzano e Udine fino alle Puglie e alla Calabria, e nell'isola di Sardegna. Le visite compiute dai segretari della Nunziatura Apostolica da soli ammontano a 5.

Ho trovato che generalmente i prigionieri ed i civili sono trattati con umanità. Un'attenzione speciale la Nunziatura ha avuto per l'assistenza religiosa. Su nostro suggerimento il governo ha nominato un cappellano permanente nella colonia confinaria di Pisticci. Un altro (che parla varie lingue) per il campo di Ferramonti Tarsia, ove la carità del Santo Padre ha arredato anche la chiesa provvisoria e donato un harmonium. Un cappellano di lingua cinese è stato dato dei Cinesi, Tossicia in Provincia di Teramo, ed ora Isola del Gran Sasso. Il buon padre cappellano con molto zelo ha istruito i poveri cinesi pagani, stampando anche un catechismo con i caratteri cinesi. Dopo un anno d'istruzione e di prova furono ammessi al battesimo una cinquantina di catecumeni e l'anno seguente altrettanti. Io stesso mi recai nelle due volte al santuario di s. Gabriele, sul Gran Sasso, per la solenne cerimonia, cui assistettero il Questore di Teramo, l'Ispettore del Ministero dell'Interno e le autorità locali.

Altre conversioni si sono verificate un po' dappertutto, specialmente nell'elemento femminile, anche tra gli ebrei. Le suore Orsoline istruiscono in continuazione tali signore e signorine, e più di un battesimo è stato celebrato. Si è provveduto pure a regolarizzare non pochi matrimoni in Roma e fuori.

L'occupazione della Dalmazia ha provocato il confinamento in Italia di circa 50.000 sloveni e croati, che sono internati nella Toscana, nel Veneto e nell' isola di Arbe.

Ho visitato il campo di Gonars nel Friuli; come pure la Nunziatura Apostolica si è interessata per il miglioramento delle condizioni di tutti questi deportati, che risentono del tumultuario sfollamento, avvenuto in piena guerra civile. Qualche miglioramento si sta ottenendo dal governo, e per ordine di Vostra Eminenza, prossimamente mi recherò a visitare i confinati anche nell'isola di Arbe. Intanto Sua Santità ha accolto l' umile suggerimento di questa Nunziature di prendere a sue spese nel pontificio collegio illirico di Loreto 200 giovani sloveni e sono in corso trattative con il Ministero degli Esteri (abbastanza diuturne per la pesante burocrazia di guerra) allo scopo di portare ad effetto il desiderio del Papa.

Inoltre la Nunziatura Apostolica è divenuta organo di collegamento tra l'Ufficio informazioni della Segreteria di Stato e la Croce Rossa italiana, per la trasmissione dei messaggi ai prigionieri in mano italiana e alle loro famiglie all'estero, come pure per l'invio ai medesimi prigionieri dei manuali di preghiera e catechismi, editi dalla Tipografia vaticana, nonché dei libri di lettura che la Segreteria di Stato manda loro.

Per i prigionieri italiani all'estero, questa Nunziatura ha una speciale sezione di raccolta dei messaggi delle famiglie, che trasmette all'Ufficio vaticano, come pure, per incarico della Segreteria di Stato, ha curato la consegna alla Croce Rossa dei 16.000 volumni raccolti dalla Segreteria di Stato per i prigionieri italiani.

La guerra poi ha provocato un'infinità di domande di ogni genere di sofferenti, dirette al Santo Padre (esoneri di militari, avvicinamento dei soldati, pensioni alle famiglie, liberazione di confinati, condanne anche per piccole infrazioni e relative domande di grazia, permessi di matrimonio agli impediti dalla legge razziale o militare, avanzamenti d'impiegati, trasferimenti, e simili); tutte queste pratiche che affluiscono alla Nunziatura, trasmesse dalla Segreteria di Stato o anche direttamente inviate a noi dagli interessati, sono curate, come è possibile, e si cerca per ognuna di dare una risposta.

Speciale menzione meritano le corrispondenze cogli internati, perché tutti, o quasi tutti, tali disgraziati, senza eccezione, chiedono l'interessamento della Nunziatura presso le autorità di polizia, che accolgono con molta deferenze i nostri interventi. Nel nostro archivio ogni internato ha la sua posizione . . .

APPENDIX J

Letter from Alexis L. Easterman, Political Secretary of the British Section of the World Jewish Congress, to Archbishop William Godfrey, Apostolic Delegate in London, July 19, 1943

May we again invite Your Grace's kind assistance in relation to the Jews in Italy, Nationals as well as Refugees?

These Jews, numbering about 20,000 are now chiefly concentrated either in internment camps or otherwise in Northern Italy and notably in the regions of Fiume and Trieste, Milan, Como, Bologna, Modena and Parma. It will be apparent to Your Grace that as the war develops in the Italian peninsula, the position of these Jews will become progressively precarious. Should the Allied invasion of Italy progress, there is every danger that these Jews may be either subject to persecution, similar to that which has befallen Jews in other Axis-occupied countries, or that they may be deported to Eastern Europe, where they may suffer the same fate of extermination as the many hundreds of thousands who have already perished there at the hands of the Nazis.

There is only one hope for our people in Italy—that they be removed as speedily as possible to Southern areas of Italy where, in the event of an Allied invasion, they may come under the protection of the Allied Forces.

We would therefore ask, as a matter of extreme urgency, if Your Grace would be so kind as to communicate with the Holy See with a view of His Holiness's intervention with the Italian Government to secure the removal of the Jews from the danger areas of Northern Italy to the South where there are already a considerable number of Jewish refugees, for example in the internment camp at Ferramonti.

We take the opportunity, also, of asking Your Grace's intervention in the case of 2,500 Jews who are now concentrated in the Yugoslavian coast areas . . . These places are in an area constituted since the Italian

263

occupation as "Croatian" territory, but they are under Italian military control.

These Jews, also are in imminent peril as the military position in Italy deteriorates. Should Italy capitulate to the Allies, they are likely to be left to the mercy of the Axis-controlled "Croatian" authorities who are notoriously anti-Semitic.

Our suggestion, for the sympathetic consideration of Your Grace, is that these Jews may also be removed to the Southern part of Italy, so that they may have some chance of escape from persecution and probably murder.

In this case, also, may we ask Your Grace's aid in communicating with the Holy See.

APPENDIX K

Notes Written by the Reverend Igino Quadraroli of the Secretariat of State

Vatican, October 17, 1943

For His Excellency Monsignor, the Substitute [Montini].

This morning October 17 acceding to the requests of good persons I succeeded in entering the Collegio Militare where many poor Jews of humble condition are located. I was not permitted to speak to any of them, but I was able to leave a package of food with an indication of those for whom it was destined, among whom there is a gentleman of eighty years.

The person who sent me told me that these poor people could not have either food or drink yesterday.

I saw them from a distance sheltered in the halls, then put in line to have some bread. I noticed a poor woman make a sign to an S.S. guard that her baby needed to leave the line. I saw the guard bluntly refuse. I likewise saw a car depart with several doctors of the Holy Spirit Hospital who had come to give medicine to those unfortunates who have been stricken. In departing, I learned that a poor woman suffered a premature delivery and in fact shortly after that I met the obstetrician from the hospital who had been urgently summoned, and who asked me how she could go about getting in.

It seems, in the words of some who were outside and knew some of the arrested, that there were also there persons already baptized, confirmed, and canonically married.

It is not allowed to the arrested to have clothing but it is only permitted to provide them with food and, also, a few lines of correspondence, which, it is understood, can represent a trap.

Notes de la Secrétairerie d'État

Vatican, 17 octobre 1943

Per S. E. Mons. Sostituto.

Stamane 17 ottobre accendendo alle preghiere di buone persone sono riuscito ad entrare nel Collegio Militare dove si trovano molti poveri ebrei, di umile condizione. Non mi hanno fatto parlare con nessuno di essi, ma ho potuto lasciare un pacco di cibarie con le indicazioni dei destinatari, fra cui vi é un signore di 80 anni.

Chi mi mandava me ha detto che quei poveretti non hanno potuto avere ieri né bevanda né nutrimento.

Li ho veduti da lontano ricoverati nelle aule, poi metterli in fila per aver un pane. Ho notato una povera donna far cenno ad una sentinella S.S. che la sua bimba aveva bisogno di appartarsi. Ho veduto la sentinella negarlo recisamente. Ho veduto parimenti uscire una macchina con alcuni medici di S. Spirito recatisi per medicare quei poveretti che sono stati percossi. Nell'uscire ho appreso che una povera donna soffriva per un parto prematuro e difatti di lì a poco mi sono incontrato con l'ostetrica dell'ospedale, chiamata d'urgenza, la quale mi ha chiesto come poteva fare per entrare.

Sembra, a detta di alcuni che erano al di fuori e conoscevano degli internati, che vi si trovano anche persone già battezzate, cresimate, e unite con matrimonio canonico.

Non è concesso ai reclusi poter avere indumenti, ma è ammesso solo provvederli di cibarie ed anche qualche rigo di corrispondenza, che si capisce, può rappresentare un'insidia.

BIBLIOGRAPHY

Acta Apostolicae Sedis: Commentarium Officiale [Acts of the Apostolic See: Official Commentary].

Alfieri, Dino. *Dictators Face to Face.* Translated by David Moore. London: Elek Books, 1954.

Annuario Pontificio per l'Anno 1940 [Pontifical Yearbook for the Year 1940]. Vatican City: Tipografia Poliglotta Vaticana, 1940.

Aron, Robert. *Histoire de Vichy, 1940–1944* [History of Vichy, 1940–1944]. Montreal: Le Cercle du Livre de France, 1955.

Barlas, Chaim. הצלה בימי שואה [Rescue during the Holocaust]. Tel Aviv: Hakibbutz Hameuchad Publishing House, 1975.

Bauer, Yehuda, ed. *Guide to Unpublished Materials of the Holocaust Period.* Introduction by Joseph Kermish. Jerusalem: Yad Vashem Martyrs' and Heroes' Remembrance Authority, 1975.

Bérard, Léon, "Ambassade au Vatican" [Embassy at the Vatican]. In Hoover Institute of War, Revolution and Peace, *La Vie en France sous l'Occupation (1940–1944)* [Life in France under the Occupation (1940–1944)], pp. 695–697. 3 vols. Paris: Crété, 1957.

Binchy, Daniel A. *Church and State in Fascist Italy.* London: Oxford University Press, 1941.

Brezzi, Paolo. *La Diplomazia Pontificia* [Pontifical Diplomacy]. Milan: Istituto per gli Studi di Politica Internazionale, 1942.

British Foreign Office Documents, Public Record Office, London.

Cardinale, Hyginus [Igino]. *The Holy See and the International Order.* Gerrards Cross: Colin Smythe, 1976.

Cardinale, Igino. *Le Saint-Siège et la Diplomatie: Aperçu Historique, Juridique et Pratique de la Diplomatie Pontificale* [The Holy See and Diplomacy: A Historical, Juridical, and Practical Survey of Pontifical Diplomacy]. Paris: Desclee et Cie, Editeurs, 1962.

Carp, Matatias. *Cartea Neagra: Suferintele Evreilor din Romania* [Black Book: Sufferings of the Jews of Romania]. 3 vols. Bucharest: Societatea Nationala de Editura, 1947.

Cavalli, Fiorello. "La Santa Sede contro le Deportazioni degli Ebrei dalla Slovacchia durante la Seconda Guerra Mondiale" [The Holy See against the Deportations of the Jews from Slovakia during the Second World War]. *La Civiltà Cattolica* 112, no. 3 (1961): 3–18.

Centre de Documentation Juive Contemporaine, Paris.

Chabod, Federico. *A History of Italian Fascism.* Translated by Muriel Grindrod. New York: Howard Fertig, 1975.

Chadwick, Owen, "Weizsäcker, the Vatican and the Jews of Rome." *Journal of Ecclesiastical History* 28, no. 2 (April 1977): 179–199.

Charles-Roux, François. *Huit Ans au Vatican, 1932–1940* [Eight Years at the Vatican, 1932–1940]. Paris: Flammarion, 1947.

Chevalier, Jean. *La Politique du Vatican* [The Politics of the Vatican]. Paris: Planete et S.G.P.P., 1969.

Ciano, Galeazzo. *Ciano's Hidden Diary, 1937–1938.* Translated by Andreas

Mayor. Introduction by Malcolm Muggeridge. New York: E. P. Dutton & Co., 1953.

Ciechanowski, Jan. *Defeat in Victory*. Garden City: Doubleday & Co., 1947.

Codex Iuris Canonici [Code of Canon Law]. Vatican City: Typis Polyglottis Vaticanis, 1956.

Conway, John S. *The Nazi Persecution of the Churches, 1933–1945*. New York: Basic Books, 1968.

Dank, Milton. *The French Against the French*. Philadelphia: J. B. Lippincott Co., 1974.

Dawidowicz, Lucy S. *The War Against the Jews, 1933–1945*. New York: Holt, Rinehart, & Winston, 1975.

DeFelice, Renzo. *Storia degli Ebrei Italiani sotto il Fascismo* [History of Italian Jews under Fascism]. Turin: Einaudi, 1972.

deMarchi, Giuseppe. *Le Nunziature Apostoliche dal 1800 al 1956* [Apostolic Nunciatures from 1800 to 1956]. Rome: Edizioni di Storia e Letteratura, 1957.

Deschner, Karlheinz. *Mitt Gott und den Faschisten: Der Vatikan im Bunde mit Mussolini, Franco, Hitler und Pavelic* [With God and the Fascists: The Vatican in League with Mussolini, Franco, Hitler, and Pavelic]. Stuttgart: Hans E. Gunther Verlag, 1965.

Deutsch, Harold C. *The Conspiracy Against Hitler in the Twilight War*. Minneapolis: University of Minnesota Press, 1968.

Documentation Catholique [Catholic Documentation].

Duclos, Paul. *Le Vatican et la Seconde Guerre Mondiale: Action Doctrinal et Diplomatique en faveur de la Paix* [The Vatican and the Second World War: Doctrinal and Diplomatic Action in Favor of Peace]. Paris: Editions A. Pedone, 1955.

Duquesne, Jacques. *Les Catholiques Francais sous l'Occupation* [French Catholics under the Occupation]. Paris: Editions Bernard Grasset, 1966.

Ecclesia: Revista Mensile a Cura dell'Ufficio Informazioni [Church: A Monthly Review Published by the Information Office].

Ehler, Sidney Z., and Morrall, John B., eds. and trans. *Church and State through the Centuries: A Collection of Historic Documents with Commentaries*. Westminster, Md.: Newman Press, 1954.

Enciclopedia Cattolica [Catholic Encyclopedia]. 12 vols. Vatican City: Ente per l'Enciclopedia Cattolica e per il Libro Cattolico, 1953.

Encyclopaedia Judaica. 16 vols. Jerusalem: Keter Publishing House, 1972.

Falconi, Carlo. *The Silence of Pius XII*. Translated by Bernard Wall. Boston: Little, Brown, & Co., 1970.

Farmer, Paul. *Vichy: Political Dilemma*. New York: Columbia University Press, 1955.

Feingold, Henry L. *The Politics of Rescue: The Roosevelt Administration and the Holocaust, 1938–1945*. New Brunswick, N.J.: Rutgers University Press, 1970.

Foreign Relations of the United States: Diplomatic Papers, 1942. 7 vols. Washington: United States Government Printing Office, 1961.

Foreign Relations of the United States: Diplomatic Papers, 1943. 6 vols. Washington: United States Government Printing Office, 1963.

Friedländer, Saul. *Kurt Gerstein: The Ambiguity of Good*. Translated by Charles Fullman. New York: Alfred A. Knopf, 1969.

———. *Pius XII and the Third Reich: A Documentation*. Translated by Charles Fullman. New York: Alfred A. Knopf, 1966.

Giordani, Igino. *Vita contra Morte: La Santa Sede per le Vittime della Seconda Guerra*

Mondiale. [Life Against Death: The Holy See on Behalf of Victims of the Second World War]. Rome: Arnolde Mondadori, 1956.

Giovanetti, Alberto. *Roma Città Aperta* [Rome, Open City]. Milan: Editrice Ancora, 1962.

Gottschalk, Louis. *Understanding History: A Primer of Historical Method.* New York: Alfred A. Knopf, 1950.

Graham, Robert A. *Vatican Diplomacy: A Study of Church and State on the International Plane.* Princeton: Princeton University Press, 1959.

————. "La Strana Condotta di E. von Weizsäcker Ambasciatore del Reich in Vaticano" [The Strange Behavior of E. von Weizsäcker, Ambassador of the Reich at the Vatican]. *La Civiltà Cattolica* 121, no. 2 (1970): 455–471.

Graubart, Judah L. "The Vatican, and the Jews: Cynicism and Indifference." *Judaism* 24, no. 2 (Spring 1975): 53–64.

Guariglia, Raffaele. *La Diplomatie Difficile: Memoires 1922–1946* [Difficult Diplomacy: Memoirs 1922–1946]. Translated from the Italian to French by Louis Bonalumi. Paris: Librairie Plon, 1955.

Guerry, Emile Maurice. *L'Église Catholique en France sous l'Occupation* [The Catholic Church in France under the Occupation]. Paris: Flammarion, 1947.

Harrigan, William M. "Pius XII's Efforts to Effect a *Détente* in German-Vatican Relations, 1939–1940." *Catholic Historical Review* 49, no. 2 (July 1963): 173–191.

Hausner, Gideon. *Justice in Jerusalem.* New York: Harper & Row, 1966.

Hilberg, Raul. *The Destruction of the European Jews.* Chicago: Quadrangle Books, 1967.

Hill, Leonidas E., III. "The Vatican Embassy of Ernst von Weizsäcker, 1943–1945." *Journal of Modern History* 39, no. 2 (June 1967): 138–159.

————, ed. *Die Weizsäcker—Papiere 1933–1950* [The Weizsäcker Papers, 1933–1950]. Frankfort on Main: Verlag Ullstein GmbH, 1974.

Hitler, Adolph. *Conversazioni Segrete* [Secret Conversations]. Arranged and edited by Martin Bormann. Translated into Italian by Augusto Donaudy. Naples: Richter & Co., 1954.

Hochhuth, Rolf. *The Deputy.* Translated by Richard and Clara Winston. Preface by Albert Schweitzer. New York: Grove Press, 1964.

Holtkamp, Jürgen. "Werde Katholisch—Oder Stirb" [Become Catholic—or Die]. *Stern,* October 17, 1965, pp. 80–86.

Hoptner, Jacob B. *Yugoslavia in Crisis, 1939–1941.* East Central European Studies. New York: Columbia University Press, 1963.

Institute for Jewish Affairs, Files for 1942, 1943, 1944. World Jewish Congress, British Section, London.

Jelinek, Yeshayahu. *The Parish Republic: Hlinka's Slovak People's Party, 1939–1945.* East European Monographs, no. 14. New York: Columbia University Press, 1976.

————. "The Vatican, the Catholic Church, the Catholics, and the Persecution of the Jews during World War II: The Case of Slovakia." In Bela Vago and George L. Mosse, eds., *Jews and Non-Jews in Eastern Europe, 1918–1945,* pp. 221–255. New York: John Wiley & Sons, 1974.

Katz, Robert. *Black Sabbath.* New York: Macmillan Co., 1969.

Kent, George O. "Pope Pius XII and Germany: Some Aspects of German-Vatican Relations, 1933–1943." *American Historical Review* 70, no. 1 (October 1964): 59–78.

Kirkpatrick, Ivone. *Mussolini: A Study in Power*. New York: Hawthorn Books, 1964.

Lapide, Pinchas E. *Three Popes and the Jews*. New York: Hawthorn Books, 1967.

Leclef, Edmond F. *Le Cardinal van Roey et l'Occupation Allemande en Belgique* [Cardinal van Roey and the German Occupation in Belgium]. Brussels: A. Goemaere Editeur, 1945.

Leiber, Robert. "Pio XII e gli Ebrei di Roma, 1943–1944" [Pius XII and the Jews of Rome, 1943–1944]. *La Civiltà Cattolica* 112, no. 1 (1961): 450.

Levin, Nora. *The Holocaust: The Destruction of European Jewry, 1933–1945*. New York: Thomas Y. Crowell Co., 1968.

Lewy, Guenter. *The Catholic Church and Nazi Germany*. New York: McGraw-Hill Book Co., 1964.

Lichten, Joseph L. "Pius XII and the Jews." *Catholic Mind* 57, no. 1142 (March–April 1959): 159–162.

Mandel, Louis. *The Tragedy of Slovak Jewry in Slovakia*. New York: American Committee of Jews from Czechosolovakia, n.d.

Martini, Angelo. "La Santa Sede e gli Ebrei della Romania durante la Seconda Guerra Mondiale" [The Holy See and the Jews of Romania during the Second World War]. *La Civiltà Cattolica* 112, no. 3 (1961): 449–463.

———. "Silenzi e Parole di Pio XII per la Polonia durante la Seconda Guerra Mondiale" [Silences and Words of Pius XII for Poland during the Second World War]. *La Civiltà Cattolica* 113, no. 2 (1962): 237–249.

Matley, Ian M. *Romania: A Profile*. New York: Praeger Publishers, 1970.

Mercati, Angelo, ed. *Raccolta di Concordati su Materie Ecclesiastiche fra la Santa Sede e le Autorità Civile* [Collection of Concordats on Ecclesiastical Matters between the Holy See and Civil Authorities]. 2 vols. Vatican City: Tipografia Poliglotta Vaticana, 1954.

Mikus, Joseph A. *Slovakia: A Political History, 1918–1950*. Translated from the French by the author and Kathryn D. Wyatt. Milwaukee: Marquette University Press, 1963.

Morse, Arthur D. *While Six Million Died: A Chronicle of American Apathy*. New York: Ace Publishing, 1968.

Muggeridge, Malcolm, ed. *Ciano's Diary 1939–1943*. London: William Heinemann, 1947.

Nagy-Talavera, Nicholas M. *The Green Shirts and the Others: A History of Fascism in Hungary and Rumania*. Stanford: Hoover Institution Press, 1970.

Neumann, Jirmejahu Oskar. *Im Schatten des Todes: Ein Tatsachenbericht vom Schicksalskampf des Slovakischen Judentums* [In the Shadow of Death: An Actual Report of the Fateful Struggle of the Slovak Jews]. Tel Aviv: Edition "Olamenu," 1956.

New Catholic Encyclopedia. 15 vols. New York: McGraw-Hill Book Co., 1967.

Nichols, Peter. *The Politics of the Vatican*. New York: Frederick A. Praeger, 1968.

Nuremberg Trials Evidence. NG (Nuremberg, Government), Documents pertaining to the Activities of the Reich Ministries. Archives of Yad Vashem and Centre de Documentation Juive Contemporaine.

L'Osservatore Romano [The Roman Observer].

Pallenberg, Corrado. *Inside the Vatican*. New York: Hawthorn Books, 1960.

Papeloux, L. "La Diplomatie Vaticane et la Belgique (Juin 1940–Octobre 1942)" [Vatican Diplomacy and Belgium (June 1940–October 1942)]. *La Vie Wallonne* 47, no. 344 (Fall 1973): 215–224.

Paris, Edmond. *Genocide in Satellite Croatia, 1941–1945: A Record of Racial and Religious Persecutions and Massacres*. Translated by Lois Perkins. Chicago: American Institute for Balkan Affairs, 1961.

Pattee, Richard. *The Case of Cardinal Aloysius Stepinac*. Milwaukee: Bruce Publishing Co., 1953.

Pavlowitch, Stevan K. *Yugoslavia*. Nations of the Modern World. New York: Praeger Publishers, 1971.

Paxton, Robert O. *Vichy France: Old Guard and New Order, 1940–1944*. New York: Alfred A. Knopf, 1972.

Peters, Richard A. "Nazi Germany and the Vatican, July 1933–January 1935." Ph.D. dissertation, University of Oklahoma, 1971.

Pierrard, Pierre. *Juifs et Catholiques Francais: de Drumont à Jules Isaac (1886–1945)* [Jews and French Catholics: From Drumont to Jules Isaac (1866–1945)]. Paris: Fayard, 1960.

Pillon, Caesare. "Pio XII e Tiso: Il 'Diletto Figlio' Deporta gli Ebrei" [Pius XII and Tiso: The "Beloved Son" Deports the Jews]. *Vie Nuove* 20, no. 6 (February 11, 1965): 33–43.

"Pius XII and the Third Reich." *Look*, May 17, 1966, pp. 36–38.

Poliakov, Leon. *Harvest of Hate: The Nazi Program For the Destruction of the Jews of Europe*. Syracuse: Syracuse University Press, 1954.

————. "The Vatican and the 'Jewish Question': The Record of the Hitler Period—and After." *Commentary* 10, no. 5 (November 1950): 439–449.

Rhodes, Anthony. *The Vatican in the Age of the Dictators, 1922–1945*. New York: Holt, Rinehart & Winston, 1975.

Ristic, Dragisa N. *Yugoslavia's Revolution of 1941*. Hoover Institution Publications. University Park: Pennsylvania State University Press, 1966.

Rothschild, Joseph. *East Central Europe Between the Two World Wars*. Seattle: University of Washington Press, 1974.

Rotkirchen, Livia. *The Destruction of Slovak Jewry: A Documentary History*. Jerusalem: Yad Vashem Martyrs' and Heroes' Memorial Authority, 1961.

————. "Vatican Policy and the 'Jewish Problem' in 'Independent' Slovakia (1939–1945)." *Yad Vashem Studies* 6 (1967): 27–53.

Safran, Alexandre. "L'Oeuvre de Sauvetage de la Population Juive Accomplie pendant l'Oppression Nazie en Roumanie" [The Work of Rescuing the Jewish Population Accomplished during the Nazi Oppression in Romania, 1939–1945]. In *Les Juifs en Europe: Première Conférence Européenne des Commissions Historiques et des Centres de Documentation Juifs*, [The Jews in Europe (1939–1945): Reports Presented at the First European Conference of Historical Commissions and Jewish Documentary Centers], pp. 208–213. Paris: Editions du Centre, 1949.

————. "The Rulers of Fascist Rumania Whom I Had to Deal With." *Yad Vashem Studies* 6 (1967): 175–180.

Secrétairie d'État de Sa Sainteté. *Actes et Documents du Saint Siège relatifs a la Seconde Guerre Mondiale* [Records and Documents of the Holy See Relating to the Second World War]. Edited by Pierre Blet, Robert A. Graham, Angelo Martini, and Burkhart Schneider. 9 vols. Vatican City: Libraria Editrice Vaticana, 1965–75.

    I. *Le Saint Siège et la Guerre en Europe, Mars 1939–Août 1940* [The Holy See and the War in Europe, March 1939–August 1940]. Rev. ed., 1970.

    II. *Lettres de Pie XII aux Evêques Allemands, 1939–1944* [Letters of Pius XII to the German Bishops, 1939–1944]. 2d ed., 1967.

III. *Le Saint Siège et la Situation Religieuse en Pologne et dans les Pays Baltes, 1939–1945* [The Holy See and the Religious Situation in Poland and the Baltic Countries, 1939–1945]. 2 vols., 1967.

IV. *Le Saint Siège et la Guerre en Europe, Juin 1940–Juin 1941* [The Holy See and the War in Europe, June 1940–June 1941]. 1967.

V. *Le Saint Siège et la Guerre Mondiale, Juillet 1941–Octobre 1942* [The Holy See and the World War, July 1941–October 1942]. 1969.

VI. *Le Saint Siège et les Victimes de la Guerre, Mars 1939–Décembre 1940* [The Holy See and the Victims of the War, March 1939–December 1940]. 1972.

VII. *Le Saint Siège et La Guerre Mondiale, Novembre 1942–Décembre 1943* [The Holy See and the World War, November 1942–December 1943]. 1973.

VIII. *Le Saint Siège et les Victimes de la Guerre, Janvier 1941–Décembre 1942* [The Holy See and the Victims of the War, January 1941–December 1942]. 1974.

IX. *Le Saint Siège et les Victimes de la Guerre, Janvier–Décembre 1943* [The Holy See and the Victims of the War, January–December 1943]. 1975.

Seton-Watson, Hugh. *Eastern Europe Between the Wars, 1918–1941.* 3d ed., rev. New York: Harper & Row, Harper Torchbooks, 1967.

Seton-Watson, Robert. *A History of the Czechs and Slovaks.* 1934. Hamden, Conn.: Archon Books, 1965.

Snoek, Johan M. *The Grey Book: A Collection of Protests against the Anti-Semitism and the Persecution of the Jews Issued by Non–Roman Catholic Churches and Church Leaders during Hitler's Rule.* Introduction by Uriel Tal. Assen, Netherlands: Van Gorcum & Comp., 1969.

Spinka, Matthew. "Modern Ecclesiastical Development." In Robert J. Kerner, ed., *Yugoslavia*, pp. 244–260. United Nations Series. Berkeley: University of California Press, 1949.

Spotts, Frederic. *The Churches and Politics in Germany.* Middletown, Conn.: Wesleyan University Press, 1973.

Staffa, Dino. *Le Delegazioni Apostoliche* [The Apostolic Delegations]. Rome: Desclee et Cie, 1958.

Steckel, Charles W. *Destruction and Survival.* Los Angeles: Delmar Publishing Co., 1973.

Steiner, Eugen. *The Slovak Dilemma.* Cambridge: At the University Press, 1973.

Tagliacozzo, Michael. *La Comunità di Roma sotto l'Incubo della Svastica: Le Grande Razzia del 16 Ottobre 1943.* [The Community of Rome under the Nightmare of the Swastika: The Great Raid of October 16, 1943]. Milan: n.p., 1963.

Talmon, Jacob L. "European History as the Seedbed of the Holocaust." *Jewish Quarterly* 21, nos. 1–2 (Winter 1973): 3–22.

Tardini, Domenico Cardinal. *Memories of Pius XII.* Translated by Rosemary Goldie. Westminister: Newman Press, 1961.

Thomson, S. Harrison. *Czechoslovakia in European History.* Princeton: Princeton University Press, 1953.

Trials of War Criminals before the Nuremberg Military Tribunals under Control Council Law No. 10. 15 vols. Washington: United States Government Printing Office, 1949–53.

Valeri, Valerio. *Le Relazioni Internazionali della Santa Sede dopo il Secundo Conflitto Mondiale.* [International Relations of the Holy See after the Second World War]. Rome: Centro Italiano di Studi per la Riconciliazione Internazionale, 1956.

Vallat, Xavier. "Affaires Juives." In Hoover Institute of War, Revolution and

Peace, *La Vie de France sous l'Occupation (1940–1944)* [Life in France under the Occupation (1940—1944)], pp. 659–677. 3 vols. Paris: Crete, 1957.

"Le Vatican Vu par Vichy" [The Vatican as Seen by Vichy]. *Le Monde Juif* 1, no. 2 (October 1946): 2–4.

Vischer, Lukas. "The Holy See, the Vatican State, and the Churches' Common Witness: A Neglected Ecumenical Problem." *Journal of Ecumenical Studies* 11, no. 4 (Fall 1974): 617–635.

von Oppen, Beate Ruhm. "Nazis and Christians." *World Politics* 21, no. 3 (April 1969): 392–424.

von Papen, Franz. *Memoirs.* Translated by Brian Connell. London: Andre Deutsch, 1952.

von Weizsäcker, Ernst. *Memoirs.* Translated by John Andrews. London: Victor Gollancz, 1951.

Warner, Geoffrey. *Pierre Laval and the Eclipse of France.* New York: Macmillan Co., 1969.

Warszawski, Giuseppe. "Una Prima Tappa della Lotta contro Pio XII nella Polonia durante la Seconda Guerra Mondiale" [The First Stage of the Battle against Pius XII in Poland during the Second War]. *La Civiltà Cattolica* 116, no. 2 (1965): 435–446.

————. "Una Tappa Imprevista nella Lotta contro Pio XII in Polonia durante la Seconda Guerra Mondiale" [An Unexpected Stage in the Battle against Pius XII in Poland during the Second World War]. *La Civiltà Cattolica* 116, no. 3 (1965): 313–324.

————. "I Veri Autori dell'Azione Antipapale in Polania durante la Seconda Guerra Mondiale" [The True Authors of the Antipapal Action in Poland during the Second World War]. *La Civiltà Cattolica* 116, no. 3 (1965): 540–551.

Weber, Eugen. "Romania." In Hans Rogger and Eugen Weber, eds., *The European Right: A Historical Profile,* pp. 501–574. Berkeley: University of California Press, 1965.

Werth, Alexander. *France, 1940–1955.* London: Robert Hale, 1956.

World Jewish Congress: The British Section. *Outline of Activities, 1936–1946.* London: British Section of the World Jewish Congress, 1948.

————. *Unity in Dispersion: A History of the World Jewish Congress.* 2d rev. ed. New York: Institute of Jewish Affairs of the World Jewish Congress, 1948.

World Jewish Congress Archives, Files for 1942, 1943, 1944, New York City.

Wuestenberg, Bruno. "Luigi Kardinal Maglione Staatssekretär Pius XII. 1939–1944" [Luigi Cardinal Maglione, Secretary of State of Pius XII, 1939–1944]. In Wilhelm Sandfuchs, ed., *Die Aussenminister der Päpste* [The Foreign Ministers of the Popes], pp. 124–130. Munich: Günter Olzog Verlag, 1962.

Yad Vashem Archives. Yad Vashem Martyrs' and Heroes' Remembrance Authority, Jerusalem.

Collection on Croatia.

Collection on Czechoslovakia (0-7).

Collection on France (0-9).

Collection on Romania (0-11).

Archives of William Filderman, Chairman, Union of Jewish Communities in Romania (P-6).

Archives of Abraham Silberschein of the Committee for the Relief of the Warstricken Jewish Population, World Jewish Congress, Geneva (M-20).

Archives of Ignacy Schwartzbart, Member of the Polish National Council (M-3).

Archives of Mark Yarblum, Underground Leader in France (P-7).

Testimonies Department (0-3).

Testimony of Father Marie Benoît (B-19).

Ysart, Federico. *España y los Judios en la Segunda Guerra Mundial* [Spain and the Jews in the Second World War]. Barcelona: Dopesa, 1973.

Yzermans, Vincent A., ed. and trans. *The Universal Advocate: Public Addresses of His Holiness Pope Pius XII*. St. Cloud, Minn.: offset, 1954.

Zahn, Gordon C. *German Catholics and Hitler's Wars*. New York: Sheed & Ward, 1962.

NOTES

CHAPTER ONE

1. Jacob L. Talmon, "European History as the Seedbed of the Holocaust," *Jewish Quarterly* 21, nos. 1 and 2 (Winter 1973): 4.

2. Judah L. Graubart, "The Vatican and the Jews: Cynicism and Indifference," *Judaism* 24, no. 2 (Spring 1975): 168.

3. Secretariat of State of His Holiness, *Actes et Documents du Saint Siège relatifs a la Seconde Guerre Mondiale,* [Records and Documents of the Holy See Relating to the Second World War], ed. Pierre Blet, Robert Graham, Angelo Martini, and Burkhart Schneider (Vatican City: Libreria Editrice Vaticana, 1965–75), 9 vols.

4. Louis Gottschalk, *Understanding History: A Primer of Historical Method* (New York: Alfred A. Knopf, 1950), pp. 93–94.

5. See Appendix A for a list of the countries with which the Vatican maintained diplomatic relations as of January 1, 1940.

6. Taped interview with Father Graham at his residence in Rome, June 1, 1976.

7. All translations from Italian, French, and Latin have been done by the researcher and checked by the Reverend Donald C. Smith, Assistant Professor in the Department of Modern Languages, Seton Hall University, unless otherwise indicated as previously published translations. Translations from the German are generally from published works. Exceptions were translated by Smith.

8. See below, chap. 2, for a discussion of the rationale and goals of Vatican diplomacy.

CHAPTER TWO

1. *Annuario Pontificio per l'Anno 1940* [Pontifical Yearbook for the Year 1940] (Vatican City: Tipografia Poliglotta Vaticana, 1940), pp. 766–775; see also Appendix A.

2. Igino Cardinale, *Le Saint-Siège et la Diplomatie: Apercu Historique, Juridique et Pratique de la Diplomatie Pontificale* [The Holy See and Diplomacy: An Historical, Juridical, and Practical Survey of Pontifical Diplomacy] (Paris: Desclee & Cie, Editeurs, 1962), p. 93.

3. Robert A. Graham, *Vatican Diplomacy: A Study of Church and State on the International Plane* (Princeton: Princeton University Press, 1959), p. 25.

4. Cardinale, *Le Saint-Siège*, pp. 45–46; see also Lukas Vischer, "The Holy See, the Vatican State, and the Churches' Common Witness: A Neglected Ecumenical Problem," *Journal of Ecumenical Studies* 11, no. 4 (Fall 1974): 625.

5. Sidney Z. Ehler and John B. Morrall, eds. and trans., *Church and State through the Centuries: A Collection of Historic Documents with Commentaries* (Westminster: Newman Press, 1954), p. 392.

6. Cardinale, *Le Saint-Siège,* p. 40.

7. Paolo Brezzi, *La Diplomazia Pontificia* [Pontifical Diplomacy], (Milan: Istituo per gli Studi di Politica Internazionale, 1942), p. 8.

8. Cardinale, *Le Saint Siège,* p. 41.

9. Ibid., p. 63.

10. Ibid., pp. 63–64.

11. Graham, pp. 11–12.

12. Valerio Valeri, *Le Relazioni Internazionali della Santa Sede dopo il Secundo Conflitto Mondiale* [International Relations of the Holy See After the Second World War], Speech given in Rome on February 23, 1956, under the auspices of the Italian Study Center for International Reconciliation (Rome: Banco di Roma, n.d.), pp. 23–24.

13. Cardinale, *Le Saint-Siège,* p. 18.

14. Ibid., pp. 18–19.

15. Ibid., p. 20.

16. Discourse by Monsignor Giovanni Battista Montini, on the occasion of the 250th anniversary of the Pontificia Accademia Ecclesiastica (the academy for the training of papal diplomats), Rome, April 25, 1951, in Cardinale, *Le Saint-Siège,* pp. 190–191; see also Graham, p. 32.

17. Montini, in Cardinale *Le Saint-Siège,* p. 194.

18. *Codex Iuris Canonici* [Code of Canon Law] (Vatican City: Typis Polyglottis Vaticanis, 1956), Canon 267, p. 72.

19. Ibid., Canon 265, p. 72.

20. Valeri, p. 23.

21. Montini, in Cardinale, *Le Saint Siège,* p. 197.

22. Hyginus [Igino] Cardinale, *The Holy See and the International Order* (Gerrards Cross: Colin Smythe, 1976), p. 38.

23. "Christ-like" is a term often used in Catholic circles to summarize those qualities of a person which are the most noble and altruistic.

24. *Sollicitudo Omnium Ecclesiarum* [The Care of All the Churches], the Apostolic Letter of Pope Paul VI on the Duties of Papal Representatives, June 24, 1969, in Cardinale, *The Holy See,* p. 314.

25. Cardinale, *The Holy See,* pp. 156–157, 400.

26. Ibid., p. 157.

27. Cardinale, *Le Saint Siège,* pp. 96–99.

28. Dino Staffa, *Le Delegazioni Apostoliche* [Apostolic Delegations] (Rome: Desclee et Cie, 1958), p. 190.

29. *Annuario Pontificio per l'Anno 1940* [Pontifical Yearbook for the Year 1940], pp. 766–775.

30. See below, p. 149.

31. Graham, pp. 127–128.

32. Bruno Wuestenberg, "Luigi Kardinal Maglione Staatssekretär Pius XII, 1939–1944" [Luigi Cardinal Maglione, Secretary of State of Pius XII, 1939–1944], in Wilhelm Sandfuchs, ed., *Die Aussenminister der Päpste* [The Foreign Ministers of the Popes] (Munich: G. Olzog, 1962), pp. 124–130; see also obituary in *L'Osservatore Romano,* August 23, 1944, p. 1.

33. *America,* September 2, 1944, p. 525; see also *New York Times,* March 12, 1939, p. 40.

34. Francois Charles-Roux, *Huit Ans au Vatican, 1932–1940* [Eight Years at the Vatican, 1932–1940] (Paris: Flammarion, 1947), p. 315.

35. Dino Alfieri, *Dictators Face to Face,* trans. David Moore (London: Elek Books, 1954), p. 5.

36. Raffaele Guariglia, *La Diplomatie Difficile: Memoires 1922–1946* [Difficult Diplomacy: Memoirs 1922–1946], trans. from Italian to French by Louis Bonalumi (Paris: Librairie Plon, 1955), p. 186.

37. Malcolm Muggeridge, ed., *Ciano's Diary 1939–1943,* (London: William Heinemann, 1947), p. 50.

38. Wuestenberg, p. 127.

39. Graham, p. 142.

40. Peter Nichols, *The Politics of the Vatican* (New York: Frederick A. Praeger, 1968), p. 105.

CHAPTER THREE

1. ADSS, VI, SSVG, 12.
2. Ibid., 62–67.
3. Ibid., 69.
4. Ibid., 98.
5. Ibid., 99.
6. Ibid., 102.
7. Ibid., 172.
8. Ibid., 253.
9. Ibid., 249.
10. Ibid., 252.
11. Ibid., 318–319.
12. Ibid., 325.
13. Ibid., 313.
14. Ibid., 314–315.
15. Ibid., 453, 460.
16. ADSS, VIII, SSVG, 90–92.
17. Ibid., 92–94.
18. Ibid., 116–119.
19. ADSS, VI, SSVG, 404–405.
20. ADSS, VIII, SSVG, 351.
21. Ibid., 383.
22. Ibid., 537.
23. Ibid., 600.
24. Ibid., 398 ("Come Ella certamente sarà stata informata . . . molti emigranti sono partiti e—mi rincresce il dirlo—, a quanto mi si riferisce, una buona parte di essi, e per la condotta scorretta e per esigenze accampate, non avrebbe corrisposto alle premure che la Santa Sede ha svolte in loro favore").
25. Ibid., n. 2., 351.
26. Ibid., 351.
27. Ibid., 351–352, n. 2 ("Le Saint Siège a appris avec peine la nouvelle de cette mesure, qui l'empêchera de venir en aide à bien des malheureux, et il souhaite que le voeu formulé par Votre Excellence touchant la révocation de cette mesure se réalise le plus tôt possible . . .").

CHAPTER FOUR

1. The census of 1930 indicated 728,115 Jews. See Jos. Rothschild, *East Central Europe Between the Two World Wars* (Seattle: University of Washington Press, 1974), p. 284.

2. Ibid., p. 289; other authors describe the situation in similar terms; see E. Weber, "Romania," in Hans Rogger and Eugen Weber, eds., *The European Right: A Historical Profile* (Berkeley: University of California Press, 1965), pp. 529–530; Nicholas M. Nagy-Talavera, *The Green Shirts and the Others: A History of Fascism in Hungary and Rumania* (Stanford: Hoover Institution Press, 1970), pp. 46–47.

3. Rothschild, p. 289.

4. See Ian M. Matley, *Romania: A Profile* (New York: Praeger Publishers, 1970), pp. 117–121, and Hugh Seton-Watson, *Eastern Europe Between the Wars, 1918–1941,* 3d ed. (New York: Harper Torchbooks, 1967), pp. 213–216.

5. *Enciclopedia Cattolica* (1953), 10:1291.

6. *Acta Apostolicae Sedis: Commentarium Officiale* [Acts of the Apostolic See: Official Commentary], XXI:9, 441, 449.

7. *L'Osservatore Romano,* January 11, 1952, p. 1.

8. ADSS, VI, SSVG, 44; see also Federico Ysart, *España y los Judios en la Segunda Guerra Mundial* [Spain and the Jews during the Second World War] (Barcelona: Dopesa, 1973), pp. 124–129, who indicates that the negotiations continued for several months during 1940.

9. FO 371/24903; see also YV, 0–11, Collection on Romania.

10. Raul Hilberg, *The Destruction of the European Jews* (Chicago: Quadrangle Books, 1967), p. 487.

11. ADSS, VIII, SSVG, 73.

12. ADSS, VI, SSVG, 502.

13. Ibid., 444.

14. Ibid., 476.

15. Ibid., 502.

16. ADSS, VIII, SSVG, 107–108.

17. Ibid., 109.

18. Ibid., 107.

19. Ibid., 147–148.

20. Hilberg, p. 491.

21. ADSS, VIII, SSVG, 161, n. 1.

22. Ibid., 162.

23. Ibid., 187, n. 2.

24. Ibid., n. 3.

25. Ibid., 235, n. 3, ("les élèves chrétiens sont admis, indifféremment de leur origine éthnique, dans les . . . écoles confessionnelles primaries et secondaires des cultes chrétiens. Les élèves chrétiens, dont un des parents est juif, sont admis même dans les écoles particulières non-confessionelles. En conséquence, les juifs qui ont passé à la religion catholique jouissent, en matière religieuse, de tous les droits reconnus par le Concordat et, notamment, le droit à l'instruction religieuse, le droit à l'assistance spirituelle de la part des prêtres catholiques ainsi que le droit d'être admis dans toutes les écoles primaires et secondaires confessionelles catholiques . . .").

26. Nagy-Talavera, pp. 330–334.

27. ADSS, VIII, SSVG, 245.

28. Angelo Martini, "La Santa Sede e gli Ebrei della Romania durante la Seconda Guerra Mondiale" [The Holy See and the Jews of Romania During the Second World War, *La Civiltà Cattolica* 112, no. 3 (1961): 451. ADSS contains no reference to this meeting.

29. "Chronicle of Jewish Events," August 1942, 5, British Section of the World Jewish Congress, IJA.

30. Alexander Safran, "L'Oeuvre de Sauvetage de la Population Juive Accomplie pendent l'Oppression Nazie en Roumanie" [The Work of Rescuing the Jewish Population Accomplished in Romania during the Nazi Oppression], in *Les Juifs en Europe (1939–1945): Rapports Presentés à la Première Conférence Européenne des Commissions Historiques et des Centres de Documentation Juifs* [The Jews in Europe (1939–1945): Reports Presented at the First European Conference of Historical Commissions and Jewish Documentation Centers] (Paris: Editions du Centre, 1949), pp. 210–211; see also YV, 0–11, Collection on Romania, Testimony of Israel Levanon.

31. ADSS, VIII, SSVG, 374.

32. Ibid., 371–372 ("Car englober sans distinction ces familles catholiques dans les obligations, les restrictions, les conditions de vie de leurs anciens co-religionnaires, serait les exposer à ne plus pouvoir vivre leur vie religieuse, à ne plus pouvoir donner à leurs enfants l'éducation religieuse à laquelle ils sont obligés et ils ont droit. On ne demande pas ici des privilèges, ni une protection spéciale, mais seulement qu'on leur fasse une condition covenable à la vie morale, spirituelle des chrétiens").

33. ADSS, VII, SSVG, 374.

34. Ibid., 189–190.

35. Ibid., 393.

36. Ibid., 393–394.

37. Ibid., 395 ("È chiaro che, i motivi di carattere umano non si possano negare, ma è pur vero che la Provvidenza si serve anche dei mezzi naturali per arrivare alla salute").

38. Hilberg, p. 494.

39. ADSS, VIII, SSVG, 510–511.

40. Ibid., 530.

41. Ibid., 545–546 ("Quando il governo rumeno nella sua alta saggezza e condiscendenza, ha fatto ragione alle nostre insistenze per la ricognizione dei diritti della Chiesa, specialmente per ciò che riguarda l'educazione e l'assistenza religiosa dei novelli battezzati, gli ebrei si sono sentiti efficacemente sostenuti e confortati, e questo ha giovato molto al movimento delle conversioni. È vero che tutto non si è potuto ottenere, ma il fatto di potersi chiamare cattolico, è una grande raccomandazione").

42. Hilberg, p. 494.

43. "Chronicle of Jewish Events," August 1942, 5, British Section of the World Jewish Congress, IJA.

44. ADSS, VIII, SSVG, 557.

45. Ibid., 587.

46. Ibid., 466.

47. A copy of the memorandum in French may be found in the files of the IJA. The translation used here is that published in Saul Friedländer, *Piux XII and the Third Reich: A Documentation*, trans. Charles Fullman (New York: Alfred A. Knopf, 1966), pp. 108–109; see below, Appendix B.

48. ADSS, VIII, SSVG, 586–587.

49. Ibid., 587 ("Presso il Governo rumeno non ho mancato di far sentire la mia voce in nome della carità che abbraccia tutte le genti, e, a dire il vero, il Governo in varie circostanze mi ha ascoltato, anche in vista del Concordato, nel quale trovano un valido appoggio gli ebrei battezzati per ciò che riguarda la parte religiosa. Non sempre, però, le autorità locali sanno o vogliono interpretare nel vero spirito le disposizioni emanate dal Governo, che, per se stesso, mentre tende ad eliminare gli abusi di un passato doloroso, non sarebbe così duro nelle misure adattate.

Data, peraltro, la delicatezza di tale problema, mi conviene andare sempre cauto perché si potrebbe guastare, invece di essere utili a tanti miseri che debbo spesso ascoltare, confortare ed assistere. Essi credono che Mons. Nunzio possa tutto, su tale punto. Si fa quello che si puó, anche per far comprendere come in questi momenti, la Chiesa cattolica è l'unica che può intervenire in nome di Dio a favore di tanti miseri; fatto che da tutti è riconosciuto").

50. Ibid., VIII, SSVG, 608–609.

51. Ibid., 615.

52. Ibid., 630, n. 2.

53. Ibid., 630.

54. Martini, 456; see also above pp. 26–27.

55. ADSS, VIII, SSVG, 637, n. 2.

56. Ibid., 637.

57. Ibid., 630–631, n. 3.

58. Ibid.

59. Hilberg, p. 503.

60. Matatias Carp, *Cartea Neagra: Suferintele Evreilor din Romania* [Black Book: Suffering of the Jews of Rumania], 3 vols. (Bucharest: Societatea Nationala de Editura, 1947), 3:237.

61. YV, M20/103, "Reports on the Situation of the Jews in Romania, 1942–1943," 7.

62. Hilberg, p. 503.

63. Safran, pp. 212–213.

64. Aide-Memoire, IJA.

65. ADSS, VIII, SSVG, 702 ("le barbare disposizioni prese contro i non ariani").

66. ADSS, IX, SSVG, 81 ("per temperare alcune misure così in contrasto con gl'insegnamenti della morale cristiana").

67. ADSS, VIII, SSVG, 659 ("Faccio di nuovo premure all' Ecc. V. Rev. affinché voglia interporre ancora una volta presso cotesto Governo i Suoi buoni uffici al fine di ottenere almeno un'attenuazione dei temuti provedimenti. V.E. faccia risaltare la situazione particolarmente triste che sarebbe creata, nel caso, a quei cittadini di razza ebraica che ormai avessero abbracciato la religione cattolica e ne fossero validi sostenitori").

68. Ibid., 723, n. 1.

69. *L'Osservatore Romano*, October 19, 1942.

70. ADSS, VIII, SSVG, 723, emphasis added ("Dès que le Gouvernement Royal Roumain a cru devoir examiner sous ses différents aspects la question juive en Roumanie et lui donner une solution dans l'intérêt du pays, le Saint-Siège, en dehors de toute autre considération, ne s'est préoccupé que de deux choses: du respect à assurer à toute personne innocente, abandonnée et

sans appui et du respect et de la tutelle envers le libre exercice de la Religion catholique, fondé sur le Droit divin et garanti par l'article premier du Concordat.

A cet effet, lorsque les premières dispositions de lois apparurent, le Saint-Siège a cru de son devoir d'examiner ces dispositions, non quant à leurs effets civils, mais en ce qui concerne, le baptême et le passage des juifs à la foi catholique . . .").

71. Martini, p. 457; not published in ADSS.

72. ADSS, VIII, SSVG, 751–752.

73. Ibid., 752 ("Mi pare quindi che, in seguito alla risposta ottenuta, la questione degli ebrei, sia per la parte dei battezzati, sia in tutto il suo complesso, si sia potuto metterla su una via meno minacciosa").

74. YV, Archives of A. Silberschein, M 20/103, "Reports on the Situation of Jews in Romania, 1942–1943," #14.

75. YV, Archives of A. Silberschein, M 20/104, "Situation of Jews in Transnistria, 1942–1943," #5.

76. See below, Appendix C.

77. ADSS, VIII, SSVG, 762–763; for original, see below, p. 219.

78. Ibid., 763; for original, see below, p. 219.

79. ADSS, SSVG, IX, 81.

80. Ibid., 127–128.

81. Ibid., 142, n. 2.

82. Ibid., 142.

83. See above, p. 35.

84. ADSS, IX, SSVG, 127–128.

85. Ibid., ("per l'assistenza e protezione della S. Sede a favore dei suoi correligionari, pregandomi di trasmettere al S. Padre l'espressione di gratitudine di tutta la sua comunità, che in questi difficili tempi aveva avuto nella nunziatura un efficace sostegno").

86. Ibid., 163.

87. Hilberg, p. 499.

88. ADSS, IX, SSVG, 335.

89. YV, M 20/103, Archives of A. Silberschein, "Reports on the Situation of Jews in Romania, 1942–1943," #17.

90. ADSS, IX, SSVG, 332, n. 5 ("forse la sua azione in favore dei suoi connazionali ebrei sarebbe più efficace se egli usasse col Governo un linguaggio meno forte e aggressivo").

91. YV, Collection on Romania, 0–11/12.

92. ADSS, IX, SSVG, 128.

93. Ibid., 243–244.

94. YV, Archives of A. Silberschein, M 20/69.

95. CDJC, X-4, "Report on the Situation of the Jews in Romania, June 1943."

96. Report received from Riegner and Lichtheim, Geneva, January 19, 1943, IJA.

97. ADSS, IX, SSVG, 163.

98. Ibid., 129.

99. ADSS, VIII, SSVG, 764; IX, SSVG, 560.

100. ADSS, IX, SSVG, 163, 330.

101. Ibid., 239.

102. Ibid., 282–285; see also *Ecclesia: Revista Mensile a Cura dell'Ufficio*

Informazioni [Church: A Monthly Review Edited by the Information Office], 2, no. 7 (July 1943): 51–54.

103. ADSS, IX, SSVG, 283 ("È un'opera, anche questa, alla quale il Governo rumeno, dedica le sue sollecitudini facendo quello che è possibile perché abbiano il necessario per la vita, per gli abiti, per la salute. L'opera è ridotta, modesta, ma non manca di avere tutte le cure che esigono la loro condizione e circostanze del momento. Sono passato in tutte le stanze, nei laboratori, interessandomi dei bisogni dei concentrati, che ho poi adunati rivolgendo loro parole di circostanza, accentuando che ero là in mezzo ad essi per incarico del Santo Padre che non li dimenticava nel Suo interessamento paterno, desideroso di far sentire anche a loro la Sua carità. Ho visto sul volto di tutti un raggio di vera gioia e di grande soddisfazione").

104. Ibid., 284–285.

105. YV, Archives of A. Silberschein, "Reports on the Situation of Jews in Romania, 1942–1943," June 1943, #17.

106. ADSS, SSVG, IX, 285, n. 9.

107. Chaim Barlas, הצלה בימי שואה [Rescue during the Holocaust] (Tel Aviv: Hakibbutz Hameuchad Publishing House, 1975), p. 351.

108. YV, M 20/103, Archives of A. Silberschein, "Reports on the Situation of the Jews in Romania, 1942–1943," June 1943, #17.

109. ADSS, IX, SSVG, 331–332.

110. Memorandum of conversation between London delegate of the International Committee of the Red Cross and officials of the British Section of the World Jewish Congress, April 1, 1943, IJA.

111. Memorandum from International Red Cross Committee, Geneva, to its London delegate, June 29, 1943, IJA.

112. ADSS, IX, SSVG, 361–362.

113. Ibid., 390–391.

114. Ibid., 410–411.

115. Ibid., 436.

116. Igino Giordani, *Vita contra Morte: La Santa Sede per le Vittime della Seconda Guerra Mondiale* [Life Against Death: The Holy See on Behalf of the Victims of the Second World War] (Rome: Arnolde Mondadori, 1956), p. 324.

117. September 6, 1943, Cassulo to Antonescu, ADSS, IX, SSVG, 475; September 20, 1943, Antonescu to Cassulo, ibid., 490, n. 2; September 23, 1943, Cassulo to Antonescu, ibid.

118. ADSS, IX, SSVG, 594.

119. See above, p. 42.

120. ADSS, IX, SSVG, 474.

121. Ibid., 474–475, n. 3.

122. Ibid.

123. YV, M 20/103, Archives of A. Silberschein, "Reports on the Situation of the Jews in Romania, 1942–1943," #18, January 13, 1943.

124. Ibid., #19, July 16, 1943.

125. Martini, pp. 460–461; not in ADSS.

126. Letter from Alex L. Easterman, Political Secretary of the British Section, World Jewish Congress, to Donald Hall of the British Foreign Office; FO 371/36669.

127. "A Scheme for the Romanian Jews," November 1943, IJA.

128. Cable, February 18, 1944, from Leon Kubowitzki, World Jewish Con-

gress, New York City, to Nahum Goldmann, World Jewish Congress, London; WJC.

129. Alexandre Safran, "The Rulers of Fascist Rumania Whom I Had to Deal With," *Yad Vashem Studies* 6 (1967): 179–180.

130. YV, P 6/95, Filderman Archives, February 5, 1944, 59.

131. February 28, 1944, Martini, p. 461; not in ADSS.

132. Barlas, pp. 352–353.

133. Theodore Lavi, "The Paradoxical Background of the Rescue of Rumanian Jewry during the Period of the Holocaust," Lecture given at an International Symposium at the University of Haifa, no date, 11-12, YV, 0-11, Collection on Romania.

134. See above, p. 28.

135. See above, p. 29.

136. See above, p. 32.

137. See above, pp. 34–35.

138. See above, p. 35; p. 38.

139. See above, p. 42.

140. Pinchas E. Lapide, *Three Popes and the Jews* (New York: Hawthorn Books, 1967), p. 169.

CHAPTER FIVE

1. For the history of this period, see Robert Aron, *Histoire de Vichy, 1940–1944* [History of Vichy, 1940–1944] (Montreal: Le Cercle du Livre de France, 1955).

2. Raul Hilberg, *The Destruction of the European Jews* (Chicago: Quadrangle Books, 1967), p. 392.

3. Nora Levin, *The Holocaust: The Destruction of European Jewry, 1933–1945* (New York: Thomas Y. Crowell, 1968), pp. 427–428; see also Xavier Vallat, "Affaires Juives" [Jewish Affairs], in Hoover Institute of War, Revolution and Peace, *La Vie de France sous l'Occupation (1940–1944)* [Life in France under the Occupation (1940–1944)], 3 vols. (Paris: Crété, 1957), 2:672.

4. Hilberg, p. 393.

5. Giuseppe de Marchi, *Le Nunciature Apostoliche dal 1800 al 1956* [Apostolic Nunciatures from 1800 to 1956] (Rome: Edizioni di Storia e Letteratura, 1957), pp. 130–131; see also *L'Osservatore Romano*, July 22–23, 1963, p. 2.

6. Jacques Duquesne, *Les Catholiques Francais sous l'Occupation* [French Catholics under the Occupation] (Paris: Editions Bernard Grasset, 1966), p. 104.

7. Alexander Werth, *France, 1940–1955* (London: Robert Hale, 1956), pp. 57–61; see also Paul Farmer, *Vichy: Political Dilemma* (New York: Columbia University Press, 1955), pp. 255–256.

8. Vallat, pp. 660–661; see also Lucy S. Dawidowicz, *The War Against the Jews, 1933–1945* (New York: Holt, Rinehart & Winston, 1975), p. 361, and Robert O. Paxton, *Vichy France: Old Guard and New Order, 1940–1944* (New York: Alfred A. Knopf, 1972), p. 174.

9. Dawidowicz, p. 362.

10. ADSS, IV, SSGE, 173 ("fuori di dubbio purtroppo gli ebrei hanno contribuito quanto hanno potute allo scoppo della guerra").

11. Ibid.

12. Ibid.

13. Dawidowicz, p. 362.

14. Vallat, pp. 660–661.

15. Dawidowicz, p. 361; see also Paxton, p. 178.

16. Pierre Pierrard, *Juifs et Catholiques Francais: de Drumont à Jules Isaac (1886–1945)* [Jews and French Catholics: From Drumont to Jules Isaac (1886–1945)] (Paris: Fayard, 1960), p. 295.

17. CDJC, XLII–110; see also *Le Monde Juif* 1, no. 2 (October 1946): 2–4, and Leon Poliakov, "The Vatican and the 'Jewish Question': The Record of the Hitler Period—and After," *Commentary* 10, no. 5 (November 1950): 444–445.

18. Marc Jarblum and Nina Gardinkel, "La Responsibilité de Pétain dans les Persecutions des Juifs en France" [The Responsibility of Petain in the Persecution of the Jews in France], YV, P-7/19, Archives of Marc Jarblum (Underground Leader, France).

19. *Le Monde Juif* 1, no. 2 (October 1946): 2.

20. Ibid., 3.

21. Ibid.

22. Ibid., 4.

23. Ibid. ("1. Qu'il ne soit ajouté à la loi sur les Juifs aucune disposition touchant au mariage. Là, nous irions au-devant de difficultés d'ordre religieux. On s'est fort emu, au Vatican, de ce que la Roumanie a adopté, sur ce point capital, des regles de droit inspirées ou imitées de la législation fasciste. 2. Qu'il soit tenu compte, dans l'application de la loi, des préceptes de la justice et de la charité. Mes interlocuteurs m'ont paru viser surtout la liquidation des affaires où des Juifs possedent des intérêts").

24. ADSS, VIII, SSVG, 295–296, Report of Valeri to Maglione, September 30, 1941; see also CDJC, CCXIV-85. Valeri had sent an earlier report, September 25, 1941, concerning other matters discussed by Pétain on the same occasion, namely the problems confronting the Vichy government. See ADSS, V, SSGM, 248–249.

25. ADSS, VIII, SSVG, 296 ("che la S. Sede aveva già manifestato le sue idee sul razismo ch'è alla base di tutte le disposizioni prese nei riguardi degli ebrei e che, perciò, il sig. Bérard non poteva essersi espresso in maniera così semplistica").

26. Ibid.

27. Ibid., 297.

28. Ibid., 334.

29. Ibid., 296.

30. The note is not published in ADSS.

31. ADSS, VIII, SSVG, 296; for an account of the other matters discussed by Pétain and Valeri, see ADSS, V, SSGM, 257–258.

32. CDJC, CIX-104, October 1, 1941.

33. CDJC, XLII-110 ("de renseignements pris aux sources les plus autorisées il résulte que rien dans la législation élaborée pour protéger la France de l'influence juive n'est en opposition avec la doctrine de l'Eglise"). See also *Le Monde Juif* 1, no. 2 (October 1946): 4.

34. ADSS, VIII, SSVG, 385; see also Hilberg, p. 404.

35. ADSS, V, SSGM, 331.

36. Hilberg, p. 406.

37. ADSS, VIII, SSVG, 610 ("Questa misura ed il modo brutale con il quale,

per disposizione delle autorità di occupazione venne eseguita, ha prodotto grande impressiona sulla popolazione parigine, già fortemente indisposta per un ordine in forza del quale tutti i non ariani sono obbligati a portare sul braccio la stella di David. Sopratutto quello che aveva maggiormente colpito gli animi era stata la decisione di separare i bambini che avessero appena superato i due anni di età dai loro genitori").

38. Ibid.
39. CDJC, CIX-114; see also Pinchas E. Lapide, *Three Popes and the Jews* (New York: Hawthorn Books, 1967), p. 191.
40. ADSS, VIII, SSVG, 610.
41. Ibid., 614.
42. Ibid.
43. Ibid., 295–297; see above, p. 53.
44. ADSS, V, SSGM, 331–332; see above, p. 54.
45. ADSS, VIII, SSVG, 615 ("Non ho mancato nemmeno a diverse riprese di far rilevare, specie a diplomatici del Sud America che non è vero che la Santa Sede si sia rinchiusa nel silenzio dinnanzi ad una persecuzione così inumana poiché più volte il Santo Padre vi ha fatto chiarissima allusione per condannarla mentre d'altronde il pericolo di nuovi rigori e di una estensione dei draconiani provvedimenti ad altre parti d'Europa, come per esempio all'Italia ed all'Ungheria, possono indurLo ad una prudente attesa e ad una illuminata riserva").
46. Ibid., 616.
47. Saul Friedländer, *Pius XII and the Third Reich: A Documentation*, trans. Charles Fullman (New York: Alfred A. Knopf, 1966), p. 111.
48. ADSS, VIII, SSVG, 620–621.
49. Ibid., 610; see above, p. 55.
50. CDJC, CDIV–62.
51. ADSS, VIII, SSVG, 621.
52. Ibid., 624; a few months earlier there had been reports circulating that Laval had been seeking papal approval for his anti-Jewish policies, but this was denied in a cable from the British minister at the Vatican to the Foreign Office on April 27, 1942, FO 371/31940; see also Geofrey Warner, *Pierre Laval and the Eclipse of France* (New York: Macmillan, 1969), pp. 304–307, 374–376, for a description of Laval's attitude toward the Jews.
53. ADSS, VIII, SSVG, 624 ("Gli feci presente, naturalmente, che coloro che nocquero alla Francia non si trovano nei campi di concentramento e che, d'altronde, tra essi vi è anche un buon numero di rifugiati politici e di cattolici. Ma compresi che tutte le argomentazioni erano inutili e che il massimo a cui si possa ormai riuscire è di salvare qualche unità come ho già cercato di fare ed ottenuto").
54. Ibid.
55. Ibid., 625–627.
56. For the text of the letter, see CDJC, CIX-115; see also Friedländer, pp. 115–116.
57. ADSS, VIII, SSVG, 625–627.
58. Ibid., 627 ("une espèce de Maison Mère en pologne").
59. NG 4578; see also CDJC, CXXVIa-12 and Friedländer, p. 112.
60. NG 4578; see also CDJC, CCXIII-111.
61. ADSS, VIII, SSVG, 48 ("Les rapports de Valeri montrent qu'en différentes occasions, au cours des semaines suivantes, il avait discuté la question

juive avec des personnages officiels de Vichy pour essayer de faire changer la politique, ou au moins pour obtenir quelques modifications aux ordres de déportation").

62. CDJC, CCXVIII-82 ("son indignation au sujet de l'attitude du gouvernement Laval et de la police de Vichy, tous deux complices des Nazis dans les traitments inhumains qu'ils infligèrent aux juifs"); see also Paul Duclos, *Le Vatican et la Seconde Guerre Mondiale: Action Doctrinal et Diplomatique en faveur de la Paix* [The Vatican and the Second World War: Doctrinal and Diplomatic Action in Favor of Peace] (Paris: Editions A. Pedone, 1955), p. 189. Duclos maintains that Valeri made known the Vatican's disapproval directly to Petain, but gives no source for his information.

63. FO 371/32680.

64. FO 371/36650.

65. NG 4578; see also CDJC, CXXVIa-12 and Friedländer, pp. 113–114.

66. ADSS, VIII, SSVG, 638–640.

67. CDJC, CIX-118.

68. CDJC, CIX-113.

69. ADSS, VIII, SSVG, 635, 658.

70. Vallat, p. 676.

71. ADSS, VIII, SSVG, 638–640.

72. Ibid., 640–641.

73. Ibid., 688.

74. NG 4577; see also CDJC, LXXVIa-11 and Friedländer, pp. 145–146.

75. ADSS, VIII, SSVG, 688 ("Purtroppo la risposta fu, come sempre, negative, nel senso che non può essere accolto un interessamento che riguarda regioni fuori del Reich. Qualcuno però mi ha suggerito di consigliare agli interessati di insistere, per il tramite di qualche distinta personalità, presso le autorità locali di Vichy, le quali, come responsabili della deportazione, sono anche tenute a non inasprirne le conseguenze").

76. ADSS, III, SSRP, pt. 1, 17–18, pt. 2, 517–524.

77. ADSS, VIII, SSVG, 632–633.

78. Ibid., 633 ("ces pauvres enfants juifs, qu'on a separés de leurs parents, au cours de scènes déchirantes, parents que, sans l'ombre d'un doute, ils ne reverront jamais").

79. Ibid. (". . . il importe absolument d'agir vite: c'est une question de jours et presque d'heures").

80. Ibid., 646.

81. Ibid., 633, n. 3.

82. Ibid., 660 ("Bambini ebrei rimasti Francia sono stati riuniti centri speciali et consegnati varie associazioni israelite. Anche altre organizzazioni cooperano assistenza").

83. Ibid., 656.

84. ADSS, V, SSGM, 702–703.

85. ADSS, VIII, SSVG, 647.

86. Ibid., 676.

87. Ibid., 690.

88. Ibid., 736.

89. FO 371/36656, telegram from Osborne to the British Foreign Office, March 22, 1943.

90. Cable from Gerhart Riegner, World Jewish Congress, Geneva, to Samuel S. Silverman, World Jewish Congress, London, March 18, 1943, IJA.

91. CDJC, CDIX-64.

92. ADSS, IX, SSVG, 398.

93. Ibid., 415.

94. Ibid., 440.

95. Ibid., 499.

96. Ibid., n. 3 ("Sono dolente di dover far sapere, come per il passato, che purtroppo non esiste qui nessuna possibilità di fare qualche passo allorché si tratta di persone non ariane trasferite al campo di Drancy, e, di là, generalmente, portate in Germania. Queste autorità mi hanno sempre risposto, fino a ieri sera stessa, che esse ignorano completamente dove e come si trovino dette persone senza essere mai riuscite a sapere qualche cosa anche di lontanamente preciso").

97. Hilberg, p. 417.

98. CDJC, XXVII-40.

99. CDJC, CDIV-67 ("les déportations de ceux des juifs contre lesquels on n'a d'autre grief à formuler que leur appartenance à une race déterminée").

100. Cable from Gerhart Riegner to World Jewish Congress Offices, London and New York, July 27, 1943, IJA.

101. Hilberg, p. 418.

102. Riegner cable, July 27, 1943, IJA.

103. Letter from the Reverend Edward H. Gaffney, Vice-Chancellor, to Dr. James Waterman Wise, September 9, 1943, WJC.

104. ADSS, IX, SSVG, 393–397.

105. YV, B/19-4, Father Marie Benoît, "Resumé de Mon Activité en faveur des Juifs Persecutés, 1940–1944."

106. YV, 0-9, Collection on France, Letter of Joseph Fisher, August 8, 1943.

107. YV, B/19-4, Benoît.

108. CDJC, I-65, "Exposé de Monsieur Donati."

109. ADSS, IX, SSVG, 396–397.

110. CDJC, I-65.

111. FO 371/36665.

112. FO 371 36666.

113. FO 371/36667.

114. *Foreign Relations of the United States: Diplomatic Papers, 1943*, 6 vols. (Washington: United States Government Printing Office, 1963), 1:346, 348–349.

115. Ibid., 350–352.

116. CDJC, I-65.

117. CDJC, CCXVIII-78, "Recit de Monsieur Donati" (". . . le Saint-Siège et ses hauts dignitaires, ne se décidèrent jamais à la moindre iniative et ne firent rien pour alléger la situation des israélites").

118. ADSS, IX, SSVG, 396.

119. Ibid., 417.

120. Ibid., 442.

121. Ibid.

122. YV, B/19-4.

123. Memorandum by Ben Rubenstein of the World Jewish Congress

concerning his conversation with the Duke of Alba, the Spanish ambassador in London, May 26, 1943, IJA.

124. ADSS, IX, SSVG, 636–637.

125. "Report of Conversation with Monsignor Carboni," January 12, 1944, IJA.

126. ADSS, IX, SSVG, 637–638.

127. Ibid., 638 ("La conseguenza di tutto questo è che i poveri ebrei sono in pericolo imminente di essere massacrati").

128. Ibid.

129. Ibid., 638, n.7; see also CDJC, X-6, "Note pour M.G. Kullmann," International Committee of the Red Cross."

130. See above, pp. 51-52.

131. See above, p. 53.

132. See above, pp. 54-55.

133. See above, p. 55.

134. See above, p. 57.

135. See above, pp. 57–58.

136. Milton Dank, *The French Against the French* (Philadelphia: Lippincott, 1974), p. 136.

137. ADSS, IX, SSVG, 558.

138. See above, pp. 60–61.

139. See above, p. 62.

140. Leon Bérard, "Ambassade du Vatican," in *La Vie de France sous l'Occupation*, Hoover Institute, p. 696.

141. See above, p. 55.

142. See above, p. 59.

143. ADSS, IX, SSVG, 160.

144. See above, p. 53.

145. ADSS, VIII, SSVG, 615 ("ad una prudente attesa e ad una illuminata riserva").

146. See above, p. 11.

CHAPTER SIX

1. Eugen Steiner, *The Slovak Dilemma* (Cambridge: At the University Press, 1973), pp. 17–18; for a more detailed history, see S. Harrison Thomson, *Czechoslovakia in European History* (Princeton: Princeton University Press, 1953), pp. 276–325.

2. Robert W. Seton-Watson, *A History of the Czechs and Slovaks* (Hamden, Conn.: Archon Books, 1965), p. 332.

3. Giuseppe de Marchi, *Le Nunziature Apostoliche del 1800 al 1956* [Apostolic Nunciatures from 1800 to 1956] (Rome: Edizioni di Storia e Letteratura, 1957), p. 84.

4. *Acta Apostolicae Sedis: Commentarium Officiale* [Acts of the Apostolic See: Official Commentary], March 1, 1928, XX:3, 65–66; see also Angelo Mercati, ed., *Raccolta di Concordati su Materie Ecclesiastiche fra la Santa Sede e le Autorità Civile* [Collection of Concordats on Ecclesiastical Matters Between the Holy See and Civil Authorities], 2 vols. (Vatican City: Tipografia Poliglotta Vaticana, 1954), pp. 67–68, and Seton-Watson, pp. 330–332.

5. Seton-Watson, pp. 375–380; see also Steiner, pp. 34–37.

6. Before the territorial adjustments of 1938, the Jewish population of the Slovak region had been as high as 4 percent. This was the figure used by the government in its anti-Jewish measures requiring quotas; see Joseph A. Mikus, *Slovakia: A Political History, 1918–1950,* trans. from the French by the author and Kathryn D. Wyatt (Milwaukee: Marquette University Press, 1963), pp. 96–97.

7. Ibid., pp. 96, 102; see also Lucy S. Dawidowicz, *The War Against the Jews, 1933–1945* (New York: Holt, Rinehart, & Winston, 1975), pp. 377–378.

8. Yeshayahu Jelinek, "The Vatican, the Catholic Church, the Catholics, and the Persecution of the Jews during World War II: The Case of Slovakia," in Bela Vago and George L. Mosse, eds., *Jews and Non-Jews in Eastern Europe, 1918–1945* (New York: John Wiley, 1974), p. 222; see also Yeshayahu Jelinek, *The Parish Republic: Hlinka's Slovak People's Party 1939–1945,* East European Monographs, no. 14 (New York: Columbia University Press, 1976), pp. 51–68.

9. Jelinek, "The Vatican," p. 222.

10. De Marchi, p. 233.

11. Mikus, p. 127.

12. ADSS, III, SSSRP, pt. 1, 17–18; pt. 2, 523–524.

13. Livia Rotkirchen, *The Destruction of Slovak Jewry: A Documentary History* (Jerusalem: Yad Vashem Martyrs' and Heroes' Memorial Authority, 1961), p. xxx.

14. Ibid.

15. ADSS, IV, SSGE, 362 ("I polacchi, i belgi e altri continuano ad aver contatti con la S. Sede; ma sin dal marzo 1939 nessun contatto è stato realizzato con i cechi. Il delegato slovacco presso la Santa Sede è completamente nelle mani del governo nazista. . . . Benché io riconosca di dover rispettare la politica di neutralità della Santa Sede, tuttavia mi sembra che contatti non-ufficiali, almeno per il momento, siano altamente desiderabili").

16. Ibid., 425–426.

17. FO 371/34322; Benes submitted a memorandum to the Vatican on May 10, 1943, asking for the establishment of diplomatic relations.

18. *L'Osservatore Romano,* June 15, 1940, p. 1.

19. Ibid., February 11, 1966, p. 1. Burzio's obituary contained no record of his years of service in Slovakia.

20. ADSS, IV, SSGE, 115–117.

21. Ibid., 146.

22. Ibid., 151–152.

23. Raul Hilberg, *The Destruction of the European Jews* (Chicago: Quadrangle Books, 1967), p. 459.

24. Livia Rotkirchen, "Vatican Policy and the 'Jewish Problem' in 'Independent' Slovakia (1939–1945)," *Yad Vashem Studies* 6 (1967), p. 34.

25. *L'Osservatore Romano,* August 1, 1940, p. 1.

26. ADSS, VI, SSVG, 408–410.

27. Ibid., 409.

28. Ibid., 410, n. 3.

29. ADSS, VIII, SSVG, 163.

30. Ibid., 279–285.

31. Hilberg, p. 460.

32. ADSS, VIII, SSVG, 280–282.

33. Ibid., 282 ("loro progressiva e totale eliminazione dalla vita politica, economica e sociale della nazione").

34. Ibid., 280–281.
35. Ibid., 283–284.
36. Ibid., 284 ("Non mi restava, nel mio colloquio col Dr. Tiso, che lamentare la cosa, esprimere il mio rincrescimento che in alcuni punti di detto codice i diritti della Chiesa e dei cattolici fossero misconosciuti e far voti che il signor Presidente della Repubblica si sarebbe valso opportunamente delle facoltà a lui concesse per riparare o attenuare le ingiustizie più patenti").
37. Ibid., 284–285.
38. Ibid., 308–312.
39. Ibid., 312.
40. Ibid., 345–347; see the full text in Appendix D; see also Fiorello Cavalli, "La Santa Sede contro le Deportazioni degli Ebrei dalla Slovacchia durante la Seconda Guerra Mondiale" [The Holy See Against the Deportations of the Jews of Slovakia during the Second World War], La Civiltà Cattolica, 112, no. 3 (1961): 3–18.
41. ADSS, VIII, SSVG, 345; for original, see p. 223.
42. Ibid., 345–346.
43. Ibid., 346; for original, see p. 224.
44. ADSS, IX, SSVG, 319–320, May 28, 1943.
45. ADSS, V, SSGM, 273–274.
46. Ibid., 273.
47. Ibid., 301–302.
48. ADSS, VIII, SSVG, 327–328.
49. Hilberg, p. 192.
50. ADSS, VIII, SSVG, 328.
51. Ibid., n. 3.
52. Ibid., 456 ("le autorità slovacche sono affatto estranee alle atrocità commesse contro gli ebrei nella Russia occupata. . . . Secondo notizie fornite da cappellano militare slovacco, i massacri sono stati compiuti dai reparti della milizia S.S. per ordine delle autorità governative tedesche. Tutti gli ebrei di un dato luogo erano concentrati lontano dall'abitato e trucidati a colpi di mitragliatrice").
53. Hilberg, pp. 463–465.
54. ADSS, VIII, SSVG, 453.
55. Ibid.
56. Ibid. ("Deportazione 80,000 persone in Polonia alla mercé dei tedeschi equivale condannarne gran parte morte sicura").
57. NG 5921, Testimony of Hans Gmelin, Counselor of the German Embassy in Bratislava. For the date of February 1942, see Saul Friedländer, Pius XII and the Third Reich: A Documentation, trans. Charles Fullman (New York: Alfred A. Knopf, 1966), p. 104; see also Hilberg, pp. 469–470, who indicates that the notes were given to Tuka after the deportations had begun.
58. ADSS, VIII, SSVG, 455.
59. Ibid., 466.
60. This memoir, given to the nuncio by the Jewish officials, is discussed at several places in this volume. It is mentioned in ADSS but not published there. For the full text, see Appendix B; see also Friedländer, pp. 104–110.
61. Copies of cables in files of IJA.
62. Copy of letter in files of IJA.
63. ADSS, VIII, SSVG, 457–459.

64. Ibid., 458–459 ("Heiligster Vater! . . . Die Judenschaft der ganzen Slowakei, 90.000 Seelen, wendet sich an Eure Heiligkeit um Hilfe und Rettung . . . Wir sind zum Untergang verurteilt. Wie wir es sicher wissen, sollen wir nach Polen [Lublin] hinaustransportiert werden. Man hat uns schon alles wegenommen [Vermögen, Wäsche, Kleider, Geschäfte, Häuser, Geld, Gold, Bankeinlagen, und sämtliches Hausgerät] und jetzt will man uns slowakische Bürger nach Polen verbannen und einen jeden ohne jede Barschaft und materielle Mittel dem sicheren Untergang und dem Hungertod preisgeben. . . . Niemand kann uns helfen. Wir setzen unsere ganze Hoffnung und Vertrauen an Eure Heiligkeit als die sicherste Zuflucht aller Verfolgten. . . . Weil der hiesige Herr Nuntius jetzt verreist ist und wir wissen nicht, wann er zurückkommt, so wenden wir uns an Eure Heiligkeit durch den Herrn Nuntius in Budapest, den wir am leichtesten erreichen. . . . Wollen gütigst Eure Heiligkeit auf den Präsidenten der Slowakei einwirken, dass er sich im Namen der Menschlichkeit und Nächstenliebe unser und unser Kinder annimmt und unsere Verbannung nicht zulässt").

65. Ibid., 470 ("almeno per alleviare di quanto è possibile la triste sorte di quei disgraziati, fra i quali molte donne e fanciulli, destinati in gran parte a morte sicura").

66. Ibid., 459–460.

67. Ibid., 460 ("La Segreteria di Stato ama sperare che tale notizia non sia corrispondente al vero, non potendosi ritenere che in un Paese che intende ispirarsi ai principi cattolici, abbiano ad essere adottati provvedimenti così grave e di conseguenze così penose per tante famiglie").

68. Ibid., 470, n. 3.

69. Ibid., 476.

70. Ibid., 475.

71. Ibid., 484.

72. Rotkirchen, "Vatican Policy," 39–40.

73. ADSS, VIII, SSVG, 489.

74. Ibid., 476.

75. Ibid., 478 (". . . Governo non ha desistito inumano proposito et presentemente è in corso concentramento diecimila uomini et altrettante donne come primo contingente. Successivamente si farà altro trasporto fino totale deportazione").

76. Ibid., 479.

77. FO 371/32680.

78. ADSS, VIII, SSVG, 480.

79. FO 371/32680.

80. ADSS, VIII, SSVG, 486–489; for full text, see below, Appendix E.

81. ADSS, VIII, SSVG, 486; for original, see below, p. 231.

82. Ibid., 487–488.

83. Ibid., 488.

84. Ibid., 489; for original, see below, p. 231.

85. Ibid., 489; for original, see below, p. 232.

86. Ibid., 501–502.

87. Jelinek, "The Vatican," p. 230.

88. Mikus, p. 97.

89. Hilberg, pp. 467–468.

90. ADSS, VIII, SSVG, 504.

VATICAN DIPLOMACY DURING THE HOLOCAUST

91. Ibid., 489.
92. Ibid., 504.
93. Ibid., 511.
94. Hilberg, p. 467.
95. ADSS, VIII, SSVG, 501.
96. Ibid., 509–510.
97. Ibid., 515–519.
98. Ibid., 517–518.
99. Ibid., 518 ("La tragedia della nazione ebraica sta nel fatto di non aver riconosciuto il Redentore e di avergli preparato una morte terribile e infamante sulla croce").
100. Ibid., 519 ("Anche da noi l'influenza degli ebrei è stata perniciosa. In poco tempo si sono impadroniti di quasi tutta la vita economica e finanziaria del Paese ai danni del nostro popolo. Non soltanto economicamente, ma anche nel campo culturale e morale, essi hanno danneggiato il nostro popolo. La Chiesa non può quindi essere contraria, se il potere statale con provvedimenti legali impedisce la dannosa influenza ebrea").
101. Ibid., 519.
102. Ibid., 487.
103. Ibid., 488.
104. YV 03/1200, Testimony of Chief Rabbi Samuel Reich; see also Jelinek, "The Vatican," p. 230.
105. ADSS, VIII, SSVG, 525–525.
106. Jirmejahu Oskar Neumann, *Im Schatten des Todes: Ein Tatsachenbericht vom Schicksalskampf des Slovakischen Judentums* [In the Shadow of Death: An Actual Report of the Fateful Struggle of the Slovak Jews] (Tel Aviv: Edition "Olamenu," 1956), p. 205.
107. Louis Mandel, *The Tragedy of Slovak Jewry in Slovakia* (New York: American Committee of Jews from Czechoslovakia, n.d.), p. 17.
108. ADSS, VIII, SSVG, 541.
109. Ibid., 561.
110. Ibid., 541–544; for full text, see below, Appendix F.
111. Ibid., 542–543; for original, see below, pp. 236–237.
112. Ibid., 543–544.
113. Rotkirchen, "Vatican Policy," p. 41; see also Rotkirchen, *Destruction of Slovak Jewry*, p. xxxii, and Nora Levin, *The Holocaust: The Destruction of European Jewry 1933–1945* (New York: Thomas Y. Crowell, 1968), p. 533.
114. ADSS, VIII, SSVG, 597–598.
115. Rotkirchen, "Vatican Policy," p. 42.
116. Jelinek, "The Vatican," p. 236; see also Rotkirchen, *Destruction of Slovak Jewry*, p. xxxii.
117. World Jewish Congress: British Section, *Outline of Activities 1936–1946* (London: British Section of the World Jewish Congress, 1948), p. 11.
118. ADSS, VIII, SSVG, 608 ("di viaggi disastrosi e persino di eccidi in massa di ebrei").
119. Ibid., 664–665.
120. Message from Gerhart Riegner, World Jewish Congress, Geneva, August 17, 1942, IJA.
121. *Foreign Relations of the United States: Diplomatic Papers 1942*, 7 vols. (Washington: United States Government Printing Office, 1961), 3:775.

122. ADSS, VIII, SSVG, 665.
123. Ibid., 665–666 ("Vi sono in queste ultime settimane due fatti gravi da notare: i bombardamenti delle città polacche da parte dei russi e i massacri sistematici degli ebrei. . . . I massacri degli ebrei hanno raggiunto proporzioni e forme esecrande spaventose. Incredibili eccidi sono operati ogni giorno; pare che per la metà di ottobre si vogliono vuotare interi ghetti di centinaia di migliaia di infelici languenti . . .").
124. Ibid., 679.
125. IJA; Cable from British Section of World Jewish Congress to New York Office, September 30, 1942.
126. IJA; Benes to Alexis L. Easterman, November 11, 1942.
127. Ibid.
128. ADSS, VIII, SSVG, 541; see above, p. 86.
129. Ibid., 664–665; see above, p. 88.
130. ADSS, IX, SSVG, 175–176.
131. Ibid., 176, n. 4.
132. Ibid., 246.
133. Jelinek, p. 239.
134. Cavalli, pp. 13–14; see also *L'Osservatore Romano,* June 6, 1943, p. 2.
135. Jelinek, p. 239.
136. Rotkirchen, "Vatican Policy," p. 44.
137. ADSS, IX, SSVG, 141–142.
138. Ibid., 170.
139. Ibid., 175–178.
140. Ibid., 175–176.
141. Ibid., 177–178, n. 6.
142. Ibid., 178–179.
143. Ibid., 179 ("la Santa Sede ha fatto e sta facendo tutto quello che è in suo potere a favore degli ebrei, in tutte le regioni in cui essi sono oggetto di misure odioso; e particolarmente, per quanto riguarda il caso attuale, a favore degli ebrei slovacchi").
144. Ibid., 179–180.
145. Ibid., 181 ("Deportazione degli ultimi 20.000 ebrei rimasti in [Slovacchia?] è molto probabile, ma non sembra imminente né è possibile ottenere informazioni sicure presso autorità governative che sono assai riservate et rispondono evasivamente").
146. Ibid., 185–186; see also Chaim Barlas, הצלה בימי שואה[Rescue During the Holocaust] (Tel Aviv: Hakibbutz Hameuchad Publishing House, 1975), p. 349.
147. ADSS, IX, SSVG, 272.
148. Ibid., 184.
149. Ibid., ("La S. Sede non ha mai approvato il progetto di far della Palestina una home ebraica. . . . Ma, pur troppo. l'Inghilterra non molla. . . . E la questione dei Luoghi Santi? . . . La Palestina è ormai più sacra per i cattolici che . . . per gli ebrei").
150. Ibid., 233.
151. Ibid., ("1. La questione ebraica è questione di umanità. Le persecuzioni cui sono sottoposti gli ebrei in Germania e nei paesi occupati o . . . sottomessi sono una offesa alla giustizia, alla carità, alla umanità. Lo stesso brutale trattamento viene esteso anche agli ebrei battezzati. Quindi la Chiesa Cattolica ha pienamente ragione di intervenire sia in nome del diritto divino sia in nome del diritto naturale.

2. In Slovacchia è capo dello Stato un sacerdote. Quindi lo scandalo è maggiore e maggiore è anche il pericolo che la responsabilità possa esser riversata sulla stessa Chiesa Cattolica. Per questi motivi sembrerebbe opportuno che la S. Sede elevasse ancora una volta la sua protesta, ripetendo—in forma anche più chiara—quanto già fu esposto l'anno scorso, in una nota diplomatica a S.E. Sidor.

3. Siccome, specialmente in quest'ultimo periodo, i capi degli ebrei si sono rivolti alla S. Sede per implorarne l'aiuto, non sarebbe fuor di luogo far poi discretamente conoscere al pubblico questa nota diplomatica della S. Sede (il fatto dell' invio, il contenuto del documento, più che il testo) Ciò per far vedere al mondo che la S. Sede adempie il suo dovere di carità più che per attirarsi la simpatia degli ebrei qualora fossero tra i vincitori (dato che gli ebrei—a quanto può prevedersi—non saranno mai troppo . . . amici della S. Sede e della Chiesa Cattolica).

Ma ciò renderà più meritoria l'opera caritatevole").

152. Ibid., 271–272.

153. Ibid., 302.

154. Ibid., ("È vero che un tempo la Palestina fu abitata dagli ebrei; ma come potrebbe storicamente adottarsi il criterio di riportare i popoli in quei territori dove furono fino a 19 secoli fa?

. . . non sembra difficile, qualora si voglia costituire una "home ebraica," trovare altri territori che meglio si prestino allo scopo, mentre la Palestina, sotto il predominio ebraico, farebbe sorgere nuovi e gravi problemi internazionali, non contenterebbe i cattolici di tutto il mondo, provocherebbe il giusto lamento della Santa Sede e male corrisponderebbe alle caritatevoli sollecitudini che la Santa Sede medesima ha avuto e continua ad avere per i non ariani").

155. Ibid., 303.

156. Ibid., 469.

157. Ibid., 245–251; see Appendix G, pp. 240–243.

158. Ibid., 248.

159. Ibid., 249.

160. Ibid., 249–250.

161. Ibid., 250–251.

162. Ibid., 311.

163. YV, *The Attorney General of the Government of Israel v. Adolf, the Son of Adolf Karl Eichmann,* Session 84, July 3, 1961, VI.

164. Caesare Pillon, "Pio XII e Tiso: Il 'Diletto Figlio' Deporta gli Ebrei," *Vie Nuove* 20, no. 6 (February 11, 1965): 33–43.

165. ADSS, IX, SSVG, 275–277.

166. Ibid., 276–277 ("La Santa Sede, pertanto, verrebbe meno al suo mandato divino se non deplorasse quelle disposizioni e quelle misure che colpiscono gravemente degli uomini nei loro naturali diritti, per il semplice fatto di appartenere ad una determinata stirpe . . .

Il dolore della Santa Sede è anche più vivo considerando che siffatte misure sono attuate in una nazione di profonde tradizioni cattoliche e da un governo che di tali tradizioni si sichiara seguace e custode").

167. Ibid., 319–320.

168. ADSS, VII, SSGM, 376.

169. Ibid., 725.

170. ADSS, IX, SSVG, 327.

171. Ibid., 329.

172. Ibid., n. 2.

173. YV, 0-7, Collection on Czechoslovakia, #25, Wenia Pomeraniec, Menachem Bader, and Zeev Shind to Israel Mereminski, Delegate of the Labor Federation and Head of the Jewish Labor Movement in the United States, July 25, 1943.

174. ADSS, IX, SSVG, 329, n. 2.

175. Hilberg, pp. 471–472.

176. Memo of January 15, 1944, World Jewish Congress, New York City.

177. IJA; "Report of Conversation with Msgr. Carboni, Apostolic Delegation, Washington, January 12, 1944," by Nahum Goldmann.

178. IJA; Cicognani to Perlzweig, February 11, 1944.

179. IJA; Cicognani to Goldmann, February 15, 1944.

180. WJC; Memorandum of Dr. Perlzweig, February 18, 1944.

181. Copy of Letter, WJC.

182. Pillon, pp. 42–43.

183. Hilberg, pp. 472–473.

184. See above, pp. 74-75.

185. See above, pp. 75-76.

186. ADSS, VIII, SSVG, 346 ("d'origine ebraica").

187. See above, pp. 81–82.

188. See above, p. 84.

189. See above, p. 87.

190. See above, pp. 90–91.

191. See above, pp. 94-95.

192. See above, p. 95.

193. Dawidowicz, p. 378; Rolf Hochhuth, *The Deputy,* trans. Richard and Clara Winston (New York: Grove Press, 1964).

194. Jelinek, "The Vatican," p. 237.

195. *L'Osservatore Romano,* July 3, 1942, p. 1.

196. ADSS, V, SSGM, 274.

CHAPTER SEVEN

1. Anthony Rhodes, *The Vatican in the Age of the Dictators 1922–1945* (New York: Holt, Rinehart & Winston, 1975), p. 174.

2. Lucy S. Dawidowicz, *The War Against the Jews 1933–1945* (New York: Holt, Rinehart & Winston, 1975), p. 374.

3. Rhodes, p. 174.

4. Bavaria: *Acta Apostolicae Sedis: Commentarium Officiale* (AAS) [Acts of the Holy See: Official Commentary], 1925, XVII:2, 41–54; Prussia: AAS, 1929, XXI:11, 521–535; Baden: AAS, 1933, XXV:7, 176–194; see also Angelo Mercati, ed., *Racolta di Concordati su Materie Ecclesiastiche tra la Santa Sede e le Autorità Civile* [Collection of Concordats on Ecclesiastical Matters Between the Holy See and the Civil Authorities], 2 vols. (Vatican City: Tipografia Poliglotta Vaticana, 1954), pp. 133–159.

5. AAS, 1933, XXV:14, 389–413; see also Mercati, pp. 184–202; the German negotiator was Franz von Papen, the vice-chancellor. For his comments, see Franz von Papen, *Memoirs,* trans. Brian Connell (London: Andre Deutsch, 1952), pp. 278–282.

6. Rhodes, p. 174.

7. June 2, 1945; the Pope said: "In the spring of 1933 the German Government asked the Holy See to conclude a concordat with the Reich; the proposal had the approval of the episcopate and of at least the greater number of German Catholics. In fact, they thought that neither the concordats up to then negotiated with some individual German states nor the Weimar Constitution gave adequate guarantee or assurance of respect for their convictions, for their faith, rights or liberty of action. In such conditions the guarantee could not be secured except through a settlement having the solemn form of a concordat with the central government of the Reich. It should be added that, since it was the Government that made the proposal, the responsibility for all regrettable consequences would have fallen on the Holy See if it had refused the proposed concordat." "Patronal Address to the College of Cardinals," in *The Universal Advocate: Public Addresses of His Holiness Pope Pius XII*, ed. and trans. by Vincent A. Yzermans, 3 vols. (St. Cloud, Minn.: offset, 1954), 2:22.

8. AAS, 1933, XXV:14, 402, Article 23 of the Concordat.

9. Ibid., 407, Article 32 of the Concordat.

10. Ibid., 396–399, Articles 14 and 16 of the Concordat.

11. Frederic Spotts, *The Churches and Politics in Germany* (Middletown, Conn.: Wesleyan University Press, 1973), pp. 209–210; see also Richard A. Peters, "Nazi Germany and the Vatican, July 1933–January 1935" (Ph.D. diss., University of Oklahoma, 1971); George O. Kent, "Pope Pius XII and Germany: Some Aspects of German-Vatican Relations, 1933–1943," *American Historical Review* 70, no. 1 (October 1964): 59–78.

12. Giuseppe de Marchi, *Le Nunziature Apostoliche dal 1800 al 1956* [Apostolic Nunciatures from 1800 to 1956] (Rome: Edizioni di Storia e Letterature, 1957), p. 133.

13. Spotts, p. 33; see also *L'Osservatore Romano*, April 3, 1946, p. 1.

14. AAS, 1946, XXXVIII:4, 103–104.

15. "Pius XII and the Third Reich," *Look*, May 17, 1966, p. 40.

16. Harold C. Deutsch, *The Conspiracy Against Hitler in the Twilight War* (Minneapolis: University of Minnesota Press, 1968), p. 112.

17. Beate Ruhm von Oppen, "Nazis and Christians," *World Politics* 21, no. 3 (April 1969): p. 406.

18. ADSS, II, LPEA, 48–49.

19. Ibid.

20. Rhodes, p. 246.

21. ADSS, II, LPEA, 49.

22. Ernst von Weizsäcker, *Memoirs*, trans. John Andrews (London: Victor Gollancz, 1951), p. 269.

23. Ibid.

24. ADSS, II, LPEA, xiii, 36–37.

25. Monsignor Carlo Colli was counsellor of the nunciature in Berlin; he had been sent by Orsenigo to Warsaw at the beginning of the war to recover the archives there and had been proposed as a candidate for the position of apostolic visitor in Poland; ADSS, I, SSGE, 386, 390; see also below, pp. 108–109.

26. ADSS, IX, SSVG, 93–94 ("Ernester scheint mir noch die Auswirkung der immer wieder zutage tretenden Stellungnahme des H.H. Nuntius in kirchlichen Fragen. Seine wie instinctive Stellungnahme gegen glaubenstreu

Elemente, die mit der Gestapo in Conflict kommen, hat ihn wohl bei den Katholiken in Deutschland jeder Sympathie und jeden Vertrauens beraubt. Nunmehr kommt seine Stellung in der Frage der Fürsorge für die deportierten Polen hinzu. . . . Hierauf entgegnete heftig der Nuntius, prudenza sei nicht genügend, die Geistlichen müssten wissen, dass die Reichsregierung die Polen nicht als Glieder eines besiegten Volkes, sondern als Staatsfeinde betrachte. . . . Ich befürchte grosse Schädigung der kirchlichen Interessen durch solche Auffassungen und Äusserungen des Vertreters Eurer Heiligkeit.

Wäre es nicht möglich, Msgre Colli durch einen Mann von Kopf und Herz zu ersetzen und ihn, hier eingeführt, mit der Wahrnehmung der Geschäfte zu betrauen, während der H.H. Nuntius einen längeren Urlaub anträte. Dieser Gedanke kommt mir immer wieder, auch deswegen, weil ich mich frage, ob es gut ist, dass die erhabene Person Eurer Heiligkeit zur Zeit (Judenfrage bzw.-verfolgung usw.) durch einen Botschafter bei der Reichsregierung vertreten sei.").

27. ADSS, VIII, SSVG, 534.
28. ADSS, II, LPEA, 23–24.
29. ADSS, I, SSGE, 308–309.
30. ADSS, III, SSSRP, 1, 110–111.
31. Ibid., 100.
32. Ibid., 5.
33. ADSS, IV, SSGE, 73–74; see also L. Papeleux, "La Diplomatie Vaticane et la Belgique (Juin 1940–Octobre 1942)" [Vatican Diplomacy and Belgium (June 1940–October 1942)], *La Vie Wallone* 47, no. 344 (Fall 1973): 215–224.
34. ADSS, IV, SSGE, 81–82.
35. Edmond F. Leclef, ed., *Le Cardinal van Roey et l'Occupation Allemande en Belgique* [Cardinal von Roey and the German Occupation in Belgium] (Brussels: A Goemaere Editeur, 1945), p. 36.
36. ADSS, III, SSSRP, 1, 435–436.
37. Ibid., 2, 523 ("È, poi, per la Santa Sede medesima norma e prassi costante di diritto, di prudenza e di riguardo, determinata da altissimi principi morali e giuridici, di non procedere, quali che possano essere le richieste di accordi o prerogative da parte degli Stati, a innovazioni nella vita religiosa di un Paese, comunque occupato o annesso in seguito ad operazioni militari, se non quando, terminate le ostilità, il nuovo stato di cose sia formalmente riconosciuto nei trattati di pace o dai competenti organismi internazionali eventualmente esistenti.

A tale prassi la Santa Sede si attenne anche in occasione dell'ultima guerra mondiale").
38. NG 4576; CDJC, CXXVIa-10; see also Weizsäcker, p. 269; Adolph Hitler, *Conversazioni Segrete* [Secret Conversations], arranged and edited by Martin Borman, trans. into Italian by Augusto Donaudy (Naples: Richter & Co., 1954), entry of July 4, 1942, p. 589; and Saul Friedländer, *Pius XII and the Third Reich: A Documentation*, trans. from the French and German by Charles Fullman (New York: Alfred A. Knopf, 1966), pp. 160–164.
39. ADSS, III, SSSRP, 2, 596–598.
40. ADSS, VI, SSVG, 90–91.
41. Ibid., 179.
42. Ibid., 188–189.
43. Ibid., 161–162.

44. Ibid., 164.
45. Ibid., 167–169.
46. Ibid., 168.
47. ADSS, III, SSSRP, 1, 103.
48. Ibid., 110–111.
49. Ibid., 228.
50. For the reasons behind Ribbentrop's visit, see William M. Harrigan, "Pius XII's Efforts to Effect a Détente in German-Vatican Relations, 1939–1940," *Catholic Historical Review* 49, no. 2 (July 1963): 187–190.
51. ADSS, I, SSGE, 383–393.
52. Ibid., 390.
53. ADSS, VI, SSVG, 241 ("Il sistema del trasporto forzoso delle persone meno grate da una regione all'altra, imposto con nessun riguardo né all'età né ai disagi del viaggio in un clima inclementissimo, né al diritto di tutelare le proprie masserizie, già praticato fra le varie regioni polacche, viene ora esteso anche alle regioni della vecchia Germania, donde si costringono i Giudei (uomini, donne, vecchi, fanciulli) a partire in treni speciali per riversarli poi in lontane regioni polacche, nei dintorni di Lublin").
54. Raul Hilberg, *The Destruction of the European Jews* (Chicago: Quadrangle Books, 1967), pp. 122–125.
55. *L'Osservatore Romano*, November 29, 1939, p. 1.
56. Ibid., February 5–6, 1940, p. 6; see also articles of December 23, 1939, p. 6, which detailed Jewish population figures for each country, and January 7, 1940, p. 4, which reported the obligatory labor service.
57. Hilberg, p. 138; several thousand other Jews from Vienna, Prague, and other places were included in this transport; see also *L'Osservatore Romano*, February 17, 1940, p. 4, which announced the deportation of 900 Jews from Stettin to Lublin.
58. Nora Levin, *The Holocaust: The Destruction of European Jewry, 1933–1945* (New York: Thomas Y. Crowell, 1968), p. 472.
59. Hilberg, pp. 260–261.
60. ADSS, VI, SSVG, 356–359, 368.
61. Ibid., 375–376.
62. Ibid., 112–116, 121, 218.
63. See above, chap. 3.
64. ADSS, VI, SSVG, 133.
65. Ibid., 331.
66. Ibid., 429–430.
67. Ibid., 481–482.
68. Hilberg, pp. 261–266.
69. ADSS, V, SSGM, 68.
70. Hilberg, p. 121.
71. ADSS, VIII, SSVG, 276 ("penosa umiliazione per i giudei").
72. Ibid., 275–276.
73. Ibid., 286–287.
74. ADSS, V, SSGM, 300; see also Hilberg, pp. 299–300.
75. Friedländer, pp. 100–101.
76. ADSS, VIII, SSVG, 418 ("Le penose condizioni in cui si compie questo trasferimento, e quelle non meno gravose di alloggio e lavoro, e di vita in genere, prescritte agli ebrei trasferiti in Polonia, rendono il trasferimento assai pericoloso per la vita dei sunnominati").

77. Ibid., 422.
78. Ibid., 508.
79. Ibid., 398–400; see also above, chap. 3.
80. Ibid., 512–513.
81. Hilberg, pp. 298–299.
82. ADSS, VIII, SSVG, 422.
83. Ibid., 552 ("La situazione dei non ariani dall' inizio del 1942 è sempre più peggiorata, nel senso che non si accordano più permessi di uscita").
84. Ibid., 569–570; see also ibid., 737–738, where the nuncio warned that merely mentioning people by name rendered their situation all the more precarious.
85. ADSS, III, SSSRP, 2, 615–616.
86. ADSS, VIII, SSVG, 570, n. 3.
87. Ibid., 607–608 (". . . devo a malincuore confessare che purtroppo qui nessuno è in grado di poter ottenere sicure informazioni circa i non ariani, anzi è persino sconsigliabile l'interessarsene, poiché pare che qui si esige con la deportazione di far perdere le traccie dei deportati; qui infatti è già pericoloso fermarsi lungo la via a confabulare con una persona non ariana, munito del distintivo della stella . . .
Come è facile comprendere, questa soppressione di notizie lascia adito alle più macabre supposizioni sulla sorte dei non ariani. Sgraziatamente corrono anche voci, difficili a controllarsi, di viaggi disastosi e persino di eccidi in massa di ebrei. Ogni intervento anche a favore soltanto dei non ariani cattolici fu finora respinto con la solita risposta che l'acqua battesimale non muta il sangue giudaico e che il Reich germanico si difende dalla razza non ariana, non dalla confessione religiosa dei giudei battezzati").
88. See above, pp. 59–60.
89. ADSS, VIII, SSVG, 687 ("La deportazione antisemita, di fronte al Corpo Diplomatico, vien qui considerata come un avvenimento di politica interna. Purtroppo l'impotenza a cui vien ridotta anche la Santa Sede verra da taluni qui male interpretata e commentata come fosse trascuratezza da parte della Chiesa stessa. Ora pero cominciano a persuadersi, che la responsabilità di queste incomprensibili misure antisemite va cercata completamente altrove, e che qualsiasi intervento della Santa Sede, quale fu anche ripetutamente tentato, viene sistematicamente o respinto o deviato").
90. Ibid., 708–709.
91. Ibid., 709 ("Questa atroce misura colpirà non poche buone famiglie, lascierà sul lastrico delle buone donne cattoliche sposate religiosamente con non ariani convertiti o sposate secondo le norme del Diritto Canonico a non ariani acattolici, metterà teneri fanciulli dinnanzi a dilemmi strazianti per il loro tenero cuore di figli e seminerà la miseria e la disperazione là, ove erano tranquilli, agiati focolari domestici").
92. Ibid.
93. Friedländer, p. 146.
94. ADSS, VIII, SSVG, 709.
95. See above, p. 120.
96. Guenter Lewy, *The Catholic Church and Nazi Germany* (New York: McGraw-Hill, 1964), p. 289.
97. ADSS, VIII, SSVG, 738–742; for full text, see below, Appendix H.
98. Ibid., 740; for original, see below, p. 253.
99. Ibid., 740–741.

100. Ibid.

101. Ibid., 742.

102. Ibid., 466; see above, chap. 6; for full text of this memorandum, see below, Appendix B.

103. See above, chap. 6, passim.

104. Leclef, pp. 232–234.

105. ADSS, VIII, SSVG, 352–353; ADSS, III SSSP, 2, 539.

106. ADSS, VIII, SSVG, 534 ("La lotta antiebraica è implacabile e va sempre più aggravandosi, con deportazioni ed esecuzioni anche in massa.

La strage degli ebrei in Ucraina è ormai al completo. In Polonia e in Germania la si vuole portare ugualmente al completo, col sistema delle uccisioni in massa").

See also Carlo Falconi, The Silence of Pius XII, trans. Bernard Wall (Boston: Little, Brown, 1970), p. 139.

107. Office of the United States Chief of Counsel, PS 2170, Triangle Report, 2135, May 6, 1945, YV; see Saul Friedländer, Kurt Gerstein: The Ambiguity of Good, trans. Charles Fullman (New York: Alfred A. Knopf, 1969), pp. 128–129.

108. Rolf Hochhuth, The Deputy, trans. Richard and Clara Winston, preface by Albert Schweitzer (New York: Grove Press, 1964), pp. 22–28, 292–293.

109. ADSS, VIII, SSVG, 497.

110. Ibid., 755.

111. Ibid.

112. See below, p. 138.

113. The text of the declaration may be found in Foreign Relations of the United States: Diplomatic Papers, 1942, (FRUS), 7 vols. (Washington: United States Government Printing Office, 1961), 1:68.

114. Ibid.

115. ADSS, VIII, SSVG, 758.

116. FRUS, 1942, I, 70–71; see also Henry L. Feingold, The Politics of Rescue: The Roosevelt Administration and the Holocaust, 1938–1945 (New Brunswick: Rutgers University Press, 1970), p. 186.

117. ADSS, IX, SSVG, 71.

118. The Pope said: "Mankind owes that vow [to form a large group of men to bring other men back to the law of God and to service of neighbor] to the countless dead who lie buried on the field of battle: The sacrifice of their lives in the fulfillment of their duty is a holocaust offered for a new and better social order. Mankind owes that vow to the innumerable sorrowing host of mothers, widows and orphans who have seen the light, the solace and the support of their lives wrenched from them. Mankind owes that vow to those numberless exiles whom the hurricane of war has torn from their native land and scattered in the land of the stranger; . . . Mankind owes that vow to the hundreds of thousands of persons who, without any fault on their part, sometimes only because of nationality or race, have been consigned to death or to a slow decline. Mankind owes that vow to the many thousands of noncombatants, women, children, sick and aged, from whom aerial warfare . . . has without discrimination or through inadequate precautions, taken life, goods, health, home, charitable refuge, or house of prayer. Mankind owes that vow to the flood of tears and bitterness, to the accumulation of sorrow and suffering, emanating from the murderous ruin of the dreadful conflict and crying to Heaven to send down the Holy Spirit to liberate the world from the inundation of violence and terror." Yzermans,

1:156, emphasis added; the Christmas address runs from 144–157; see also ADSS, VII, SSGM, 161–167.

119. FO 371/37538; see also ADSS, IX, SSVG, 71, n. 1.

120. Ibid.

121. *Foreign Relations of the United States: Diplomatic Papers, 1943*, 6 vols. (Washington: United States Government Printing Office, 1963), 2:912.

122. ADSS, IX, SSVG, 74, n. 2.

123. Ibid., 85, n. 3.

124. Ibid., 165, n. 2.

125. Ibid., 74–75, n. 2.

126. Ibid., 295–296.

127. Lewy, p. 289.

128. ADSS, IX, SSVG, 165 ("Realmente il 28 febbraio ed i 1° marzo p.p. furono due giorni particolarmente feroci per la deportazione degli ebrei da Berlino per . . . ignote destinazioni. Vi furono inclusi anche ebrei battezzati e coniugate con ariani, distruggendo così le famiglie").

129. See above, p. 115.

130. ADSS, IX, SSVG, 165.

131. Hilberg, pp. 53, 268–277.

132. ADSS, IX, SSVG, 241 ("la quale significa morte quasi certa").

133. Ibid., 240; Gerhard Lehfeldt, otherwise not known.

134. Ibid., 242.

135. ADSS, III, SSSRP, 2, 742–752.

136. Ibid., 652–653, 660–661.

137. Ibid., 753–754.

138. ADSS, VII, SSGM, 268–270; see also Weizsäcker's report, NG 4572, and CDJC, CXXVIa, 9.

139. Weizsäcker, p. 283.

140. ADSS, VII, SSGM, 304–305.

141. Ibid., 315–317.

142. Ibid., 392–396.

143. ADSS, III, SSSRP, 2, 653.

144. ADSS, IX, SSVG, 87–90.

145. Ibid., 82–83 ("ob nicht der Heilige Stuhl in dieser Sache etwas tun könne, einen Appell zu Gunsten der Unglücklichen erlassen?").

146. Ibid., 93–94; see above, p. 105.

147. Ibid., 143.

148. Ibid., 170.

149. ADSS, II, LPEA, 318–327; for the English translation of this letter, originally written in German, see Friedländer, pp. 135–143.

150. Friedländer, p. 139.

151. Ibid., pp. 141–142.

152. ADSS, VIII, SSVG, 78–79, 90–94, 116–119, 271–273, 340–342, 375–377, 397–398, 400, 427–429, 537.

153. ADSS, IX, SSVG, 229–230.

154. Ibid.

155. Ibid., 268 ("Quantunque tale notizia fosse già qui pervenuta da varie parti, tuttavia l'autorevole conferma di Vostra Eminenza non poteva non addolorare vivamente l'Augusto Pontefice per i gravi inconvenienti morali e materiali cui la minacciata deportazione darebbe luogo.

Ill Santo Padre ben comprende l'angustia dell'Eminenza Vostra al riguardo e quindi il filiale ricorso del Suo cuore alla medesima Santità Sua.

È noto a Vostra Eminenza come la Santa Sede abbia fatto e stia facendo quanto le è possibile per alleviare il triste stato degli ebrei in vari paesi e come si siano talora ottenuti non pochi frutti, particolarmente nel campo caritativo.

Per quanto concerne il problema delle deportazioni, la Santa Sede non ha finora mancato di usare di tutti i mezzi in suo potere, perché in vari Stati venisse risparmiata a tanti infelici una così dura sorte.

Non ho bisogno di aggiungere che essa continuerà a interessarsi con ogni premura, soprattutto quando si tratti di ebrei cattolici oppure congiunti in matrimonio con cattolici").

156. Hilberg, p. 276.

157. ADSS, IX, SSVG, 262.

158. Ibid., n. 1 ("Santa Sede ha fatto e continuerà fare tutto il possibile a favore ebrei").

159. Levin, p. 499.

160. ADSS, IX, SSVG, 491.

161. Levin, pp. 488–492.

162. ADSS, IX, SSVG, 491–492.

163. Ibid., 470.

164. *Documentation Catholique* 60, no. 1406 (August 18, 1963): 1074.

165. For Hitler's impression of the nuncio, see his *Conversazioni Segrete,* pp. 590–591.

166. John S. Conway, *The Nazi Persecution of the Churches, 1933–1945* (New York: Basic Books, 1968), pp. 306–307.

167. ADSS, IX, SSVG, 640–641.

168. See above, p. 60; p. 114.

169. See above, p. 117.

170. See above, p. 114.

171. See above, p. 115; p. 120.

172. Falconi, p. 139.

CHAPTER EIGHT

1. These territorial changes directly affected the entire diocesan system in Poland, separating dioceses from their metropolitan sees and splitting some dioceses in two. See Carlo Falconi, *The Silence of Pius XII,* trans. Bernard Wall (Boston: Little, Brown, 1970), p. 111.

2. "Dumping ground" is a term used by Lucy S. Dawidowicz in *The War Against the Jews, 1933–1945* (New York: Holt, Rinehart & Winston, 1975), p. 114.

3. Raul Hilberg, *The Destruction of the European Jews* (Chicago: Quadrangle Books, 1967), p. 126.

4. *Acta Apostolicae Sedis: Commentarium Officiale* [Acts of the Holy See: Official Commentary], 1925, XVII:8, 273–287; see also Angelo Mercati, ed., *Raccolta di Concordati su Materie Ecclesiastiche tra la Santa Sede e le Autorità Civile* [Collection of Concordats on Ecclesiastical Matters Between the Holy See and the Civil Authorities], 2 vols. (Vatican City: Tipografia Poliglotta Vaticana, 1954), pp. 30–40.

5. Giuseppe de Marchi, *Le Nunziature Apostoliche dal 1800 al 1956* [Apostolic

Nunciatures from 1800 to 1956] (Rome: Edizioni di Storia e Letteratura, 1957), p. 210; see also *L'Osservatore Romano,* February 2, 1947, p. 2.

6. ADSS, I, SSGE, 293, 308–309. One author maintains that the Poles were quite disillusioned by the unseemly haste with which Cortesi fled both Warsaw and Poland itself. See Falconi, p. 133.

7. ADSS, VI, SSVG, 147–148.

8. ADSS, VII, SSGM, 293, n. 4.

9. ADSS, VI, SSVG, 150, n. 3.

10. ADSS, IX, SSVG, 346–347.

11. ADSS, IV, SSGE, 69, 77–81.

12. ADSS, V, SSGM, 607.

13. Ibid., 628.

14. Ibid., 628–631.

15. Ibid., 629.

16. ADSS, VII, SSGM, 292–295.

17. Ibid., 317–318, 448.

18. See above, p. 108.

19. ADSS, III, SSSRP, 110–111.

20. Ibid., 228.

21. See above, p. 107; see also Falconi, pp. 136–139.

22. ADSS, III, SSSRP, 103; see also above, p. 108.

23. ADSS, III, SSSRP, 199–200.

24. Ibid., 207.

25. Ibid., 226–227.

26. Ibid., 335; see also François Charles-Roux, *Huit Ans au Vatican, 1932– 1940* [Eight Years at the Vatican, 1932–1940] (Paris: Flamarion, 1947), p. 353.

27. ADSS, III, SSSRP, 239.

28. Another problem for the Polish hierarchy was that its leader, the primate of Poland, Cardinal August Hlond, had fled the country at the time of the Nazi invasion. His hasty departure disappointed Polish Catholics and embarrassed the Vatican. See Falconi, pp. 142–143; see also ADSS, III, SSSRP, passim.

29. Falconi, p. 134.

30. ADSS, III, SSSRP, 83–86, 88–89, 90, 96–99.

31. Ibid., 165–166.

32. Ibid., 166.

33. Ibid., 131.

34. Ibid., 117–118.

35. Ibid., 168–173.

36. Ibid., 138.

37. ADSS, VI, SSVG, 215–216.

38. ADSS, III, SSSRP, 180.

39. Ibid., 234–235.

40. ADSS, VI, SSVG, 400, n. 3.

41. ADSS, III, SSSRP, 240.

42. Ibid., 295–296.

43. Hilberg, p. 190.

44. ADSS, VIII, SSVG, 328; see also above, pp. 78–79.

45. Ibid., 466; the text of the memorandum is not published in ADSS. A copy of the "aide-memoir," along with the letter of Lichtheim and Riegner to Bernardini, is in the files of IJA; for English translation, see Saul Friedländer,

Pius XII and the Third Reich: A Documentation, trans. from the French and German by Charles Fullman (New York: Alfred A. Knopf, 1966), pp. 105–110; see also below, Appendix B.

46. Friedländer, p. 108; see also below, p. 213.

47. Riegner to Arieh Tartakower, World Jewish Congress, New York City, IJA.

48. ADSS, VIII, SSVG, 534; see also above, p. 117.

49. Ibid., 669–670, n. 4 ("La eliminazione degli ebrei, con le uccisioni in massa, è quasi totalitaria, senza riguardo ai bambini nemmeno se lattanti. Del resto per loro—che sono tutti contrassegnati con un bracciale bianco—la vita civile è impossibile. Non possono andare in un mercato, entrare in un negozio, salire in tramvai o in carrozzella, assistere ad uno spettacolo, frequentare una case non di ebrei. Prima di essere deportati od uccisi, sono condannati a lavorare forzatamente in lavori materiali, anche se sono della classe colta. I pochi ebrei rimasti appaiono sereni, quasi ostentando orgoglio. Si dice che oltre due millioni di ebrei siano stati uccisi. . . . Si consente ai polacchi di rifugiarsi nelle case del ghetto, che giornalmente si vanno spopolando per gli eccidi sistematici degli ebrei"); see also Falconi, pp. 150–151, who reports that Scavizzi claimed to have seen the Pope twice when his hospital train came to Rome. He not only told the Pope about what he had witnessed of Nazi cruelties but also acted as a courier for Vatican documents to bishops in the area and from them to the Vatican.

50. ADSS, III, SSSRP, 625 ("Depuis, au moins un an, il n'y a pas de jour où ne soient commis les plus horribles crimes, assassinats, vols et rapines, confiscations et concussions. Les Juifs en sont les premières victimes. Le nombre des Juifs tués dans notre petit pays a certainement dépassé deux cent mille. A mesure que l'armée avancait vers l'est, le nombre des victimes grandissait").

51. Ibid., 625–628.

52. Ibid., 695–696.

53. August 17, 1942, Files of IJA.

54. Cable to Stephen Wise, World Jewish Congress (WJC), New York City, IJA.

55. Cable to Alexis Easterman, British Section, WJC, from Irving Miller and Maurice Perlzweig, WJC, New York City, October 1, 1942, IJA.

56. Memorandum, "Concerning the Persecution of the Jews of Europe," Geneva, October 1942, Files of IJA.

57. Copy of letter in files of IJA.

58. Cable to Stephen Wise, Maurice Perlzweig, and Irving Miller, WJC, New York City, from Noah Barou and Alexis Easterman, WJC, London, Files of IJA.

59. *Foreign Relations of the United States: Diplomatic Papers, 1942,* 7 vols. (Washington: United States Government Printing Office, 1961), 3:775–776.

60. ADSS, VIII, SSVG, 679.

61. Ibid., 670.

62. Ibid., 755 ("Les Allemands suppriment en Pologne le total des populations juives. Ce sont d'abord les vieillards, les infirmes, les femmes et les enfants qui sont emmenés, ce qui est une preuve qu'il ne s'agit pas de déportation pour les travaux, et ce qui confirme les informations, selon lesquelles les déportés sont mis à mort par differents procédés, dans des lieux spécialement préparés à cette fin. Les hommes jeunes et valides sont souvent

forcés à des travaux afin de les faire mourir de surmenage et de sousalimentation.

Quant au nombre de Juifs de Pologne exterminés par les Allemands, on estime qu'il a dépassé un million'').

63. Ibid., 756–757 (''la Santa Sede fa quel che può'').

64. ADSS, III, SSSRP, 633–636; see also Jean Chevalier, *La Politique du Vatican* [The Politics of the Vatican] (Paris: Planete et S.G.P.P., 1969), pp. 117–156.

65. ADSS, III, SSSRP, 713–717.

66. Ibid., 738.

67. Ibid., 631.

68. ADSS, VII, SSGM, 179–180.

69. Ibid., 215–216.

70. Ibid., 237–238.

71. Ibid., 238 (''Le Gouvernement Polonais est profondément persuadé qu'une condamnation explicite de ceux qui sèment l'injustice et la mort sera non seulement un soutien pour les Polonais dans leur malheur, mais qu'elle rappelerait aussi à la raison les masses allemandes en provoquant une réflexion salutaire, et contribuerait à mettre un frein aux crimes que commettent en Pologne les pouvoirs d'occupation'').

72. Ibid., 235–236.

73. See Angelo Martini, ''Silenzi e Parole di Pio XII per la Polonia durante la Seconda Guerra Mondiale [The Silence and the Words of Pius XII for Poland during the Second World War], *La Civiltà Cattolica (CC)*, 113, no. 2 (1962): 237–249; see also articles by Giuseppe Warszawski, who argues that it was German propagandists who stirred up resentment in Poland against the Pope: ''Una Prima Tappa della Lotta contro Pio XII nella Polonia durante la Seconda Guerra Mondiale'' [A First Step in the Battle against Pius XII in Poland during the Second World War], *CC* 116, no. 2 (1965): 435–446; ''Una Tappa Imprevista nella Lotta contro Pio XII in Polonia durante la Seconda Guerra Mondiale'' [An Unforeseen Step in the Battle against Pius XII in Poland during the Second World War], *CC* 116, no. 3 (1965): 313–324; ''I Veri Autori dell'Azione Antipapale in Polonia durante la Seconda Guerra Mondiale'' [The True Authors of the Antipapal Activity in Poland during the Second World War], *CC* 116, no. 3 (1965): 540–551.

74. ADSS, VII, SSGM, 287–288 (April 2, 1943).

75. ADSS, III, SSSRP, 777–778 (April 8, 1943).

76. Ibid., 779–780.

77. See above, p. 131.

78. ADSS, III, SSSRP, 798–801.

79. Ibid., 801–802; the Pope's words about Poland were these: ''In confiding to you these bitter experiences which make Our Heart bleed, We do not forget a single one of the suffering peoples—not a single one. We remember every one of them with paternal compassion, even if at the present moment We wish to direct your compassion in a special manner to the Polish people, which surrounded by powerful nations, is subjected to the blows of fate and to the changing tides of the gigantic tragedy of war. Our oft-repeated declarations and manifestations do not leave room for any doubt as to the principles by which a Christian conscience must judge such happenings. Whoever knows the history of Christian Europe realizes how much Poland's saints and heroes,

her scientists and thinkers, have contributed to the spiritual inheritance of Europe and the world; how much Poland's simple people, imbued with faith in the silent heroism of their sufferings, have contributed, for centuries, to the development and preservation of Christian Europe. We beseech the Queen of Heaven that this people, so cruelly tried, . . . may have reserved for them a future in keeping with their legitimate aspirations and the magnitude of their sufferings, in a Europe renewed on Christian foundations and within a body of nations free from the errors and waywardness of past and present times." This English translation is from *Catholic Mind* 41, no. 969 (September 1943): 3–4.

80. ADSS, VII, SSGM, 454–455.

81. ADSS, IX, SSVG, 182.

82. Ibid., n. 2 ("Santa Sede si è adoperata e continua adoperarsi a favore ebrei").

83. Ibid., 206–207.

84. Ibid., 207, n. 3 ("Santa Sede continua occuparsi favore ebrei").

85. Ibid., 216–217 ("Circa i passi fatti dalla Santa Sede riguardo alla deportazione degli ebrei e la risposta da inviare al qui unito telegramma di S.E. Mons. Cicognani.

Per evitare la deportazione in massa degli ebrei, che si verifica attualmente in vari paesi d'Europa, la Santa Sede ha interessato il Nunzio d'Italia, l'Incaricato di affari in Slovacchia e l'Incaricato della S. Sede in Croazia . . .

Poché l'interessamento della Santa Sede ha avuto, quantunque solo relativamente, qualche efficacia, non sarebbe opportuno farne un accenno, sia pure vago, nel telegramma di risposta all'ultimo telgramma di S. E. Mgr. Cicognani?

Un accenno aperto non sembrerebbe conveniente, non solo perché non si sa mai che cosa può avvenire da un momento all'altro . . . , ma anche per impedire che la Germania, venendo a conoscenza delle dichiarazioni della S. Sede, renda ancor più gravi le misure antiebraiche nei territori da essa occupati e faccia nuove e più forti insistenze presso i Governi aderenti all' Asse.

Si potrebbe, pertanto, rispondere a Mgr. Cicognani come segue nel qui unito progetto di telegramma").

86. Ibid., 274 ("Ebrei. Stiuazione orrenda. In Polonia stavano, prima della guerra, circa 4.500.000 di ebrei; si calcola ora che non ne rimangano (con tutto che ne vennero dagli altri paesi occupati dai tedeschi) neppure 100.000.

A Varsavia era stato creato un ghetto che ne conteneva circa 650.000: ora ce ne saranno 20–25.000.

Naturalmente parecchi ebrei sono sfuggiti al controllo; ma non è da dubitare che la maggior parte sia stata soppressa. Dopo mesi e mesi di trasporti di migliaia e migliaia di persone, queste non hanno fatto sapere più nulla: cosa che non si spiega altrimenti che con la morte, atteso sopratutto il carattere intrapprendente degli ebrei, che in qualche modo, se vive, si fa vivo.

Speciali campi di morte vicino a Lublino (Treblinka) e presso Brest Litowski. Si racconta che vengono chiusi a parecchie centinaia alla volta in cameroni, dove finirebbe sotto l'azione di gas. Trasportati in carri bestiame, ermeticamete chiusi, con pavimento di calce viva.

Nel ghetto di Varsavia erano state inchiuse anche chiese, che qualche tempo dopo dovettero essere sgombrate in due ore di tempo.

Ora queste chiese servono a magazzini, ecc.").

87. Ibid., 374.
88. NG 4943.
89. ADSS, IX, SSVG, 243; the contents of this report are not in ADSS or in the Silberschein Archives at Yad Vashem.
90. Silberschein to Bernardini, April 6, 1943; YV, M20/69, Silberschein Archives.
91. FO 371/36653.
92. IJA, "Précis for week of June 13–June 19, 1943."
93. FO 371/36663.
94. IJA, "Précis for week, June 27–July 3, 1943."
95. IJA, "Précis for weeks of July 1943."
96. Letter of Dr. Ignacy Schwartzbart, IJA files.
97. ADSS, IX, SSVG, 403–406.
98. Ibid.
99. Ibid., 493.
100. Ibid., 499–500.
101. Ibid., 500.
102. Ibid., 488, n. 1.
103. Ibid., 488.
104. Ibid., 503.
105. Ibid., 559–560.
106. Ibid., 618.
107. Ibid., 618, n. 3.
108. Falconi, pp. 201–202.
109. See above, p. 140.

CHAPTER NINE

1. For a brief history, see Stevan K. Pavlowitch, *Yugoslavia,* Nations of the Modern World Series (New York: Praeger Publishers, 1971), pp. 53–104.
2. Carlo Falconi, *The Silence of Pius XII,* trans. Bernard Wall (Boston: Little, Brown, 1970), pp. 266–268.
3. Angelo Mercati, ed., *Raccolta di Concordati su Materie Ecclesiastiche fra la Santa Sede e le Autorità Civile* [Collection of Concordats on Ecclesiastical Matters Between the Holy See and Civil Governments], 2 vols. (Vatican City: Tipografia Poliglotta Vaticana, 1954), pp. 202–216.
4. Matthew Spinka, "Modern Ecclesiastical Development," in Robert J. Kerner, ed., *Yugoslavia,* United Nations Series (Berkeley: University of California Press, 1949), pp. 256–258.
5. Giuseppe de Marchi, *Le Nunziature Apostoliche dal 1800 al 1956* [Apostolic Nunciatures from 1800 to 1956] (Rome: Edizioni di Storia e Letteratura, 1957), pp. 159–160.
6. Dragisa N. Ristic, *Yugoslavia's Revolution of 1941,* Hoover Institution Publications (University Park: Pennsylvania State University Press, 1966), pp. 79–112.
7. Nora Levin, *The Holocaust: The Destruction of European Jewry, 1933–1945* (New York: Thomas Y. Crowell, 1968), pp. 508–510; for a more detailed treatment, see Jacob B. Hoptner, *Yugoslavia in Crisis, 1934–1941,* East Central European Studies (New York: Columbia University Press, 1963).
8. Falconi, p. 274; according to Lucy S. Dawidowicz, *The War Against the*

Jews, 1933–1945 (New York: Holt, Rinehart & Winston, 1975), p. 392, the number of Jews was 30,000.

9. *Ustase* is derived from *ustati,* which means "to leap to one's feet," "to rise up."

10. Falconi, pp. 271–274.

11. Raul Hilberg, *The Destruction of the European Jews* (Chicago: Quadrangle Books, 1967), pp. 454–455.

12. See above, p. 72.

13. ADSS, IV, SSGE, 491–496, 498–503.

14. Ibid., 500 ("il populo croato desidera ispirare tutta la sua condotta e la sua legislazione al cattolicismo").

15. Ibid., 500–501.

16. Ibid., 537.

17. Ibid., 529–530.

18. Ibid., 547–548.

19. ADSS, V, SSGM, 90–91, 106; see also Falconi, pp. 322–325.

20. Ibid., 106.

21. Ibid., 401–402; see also Falconi, pp. 326–327.

22. ADSS, V, SSGM, 743.

23. Karlheinz Deschner, *Mitt Gott und den Faschisten: Der Vatikan in Bunde mit Mussolini, Franco, Hitler und Pavelić* [With God and the Fascists: The Vatican in League with Mussolini, Franco, Hitler and Pavelić] (Stüttgart: Hans E. Günther Verlag, 1965), pp. 254–255.

24. Falconi, p. 328.

25. Edmond Paris, *Genocide in Satellite Croatia, 1941–1945: A Record of Racial and Religious Persecutions and Massacres,* trans. Lois Perkins (Chicago: American Institute for Balkan Affairs, 1961), p. 220.

26. ADSS, VIII, SSVG, 261.

27. Ibid. ("Questo distintivo mal tollerato e l'odio dei croati verso di loro, nonché gli svantaggi economici a cui sono soggetti, determina spesso nell' animo degli ebrei il desiderio di passare alla Chiesa cattolica. Non si escludono con questo *a priori* i motivi soprannaturali ed il lavoro silenzioso della grazia divina. Il nostro clero agevola la loro conversione, pensando che almeno i loro figli saranno educati nelle scuole cattoliche e quindi saranno più sinceramente cristiani").

28. Ibid., 250–252.

29. Ibid., 250 (". . . senza mezzi, senza indumenti, perché costrette a partire portando solo quanto può contenere un sacco da montagna, è forzato a vivere all'aperto in zone rocciose, prive di vegetazione, a tipo carsico, con clima torrido, senza acqua sufficiente, prive di ogni risorsa agricola, senza tetto nel senso letterale della parola").

30. Ibid., 251.

31. Ibid., 261–262.

32. Ibid., 262 (di raccomandare a chi di dovere moderazione per quanto concerne il trattamento degli Ebrei residenti in territorio croato").

33. Ibid., 263.

34. Anthony Rhodes, *The Vatican in the Age of the Dictators, 1922–1945* (New York: Holt, Rinehart & Winston, 1973), p. 42.

35. ADSS, VIII, SSVG, 274.

36. Ibid., 318.

37. Ibid., 319.
38. Ibid., 368–370.
39. Ibid., 369; the full text of the letter is published in Richard Pattee, *The Case of Cardinal Aloysius Stepinac* (Milwaukee: Bruce Publishing Co., 1953), pp. 305–306.
40. ADSS, VIII, SSVG, 443 ("di ottenere un trattamento umano per i cittadini di discendenza ebraica"); see also Falconi, pp. 306–307.
41. ADSS, VIII, SSVG, 389–390.
42. Ibid., 505.
43. Ibid., 601 ("si erano chiuse in un silenzio inspiegabile").
44. Ibid., 409.
45. Ibid., 416–417.
46. Ibid., 409, n. 2.
47. Ibid., 749.
48. YV, M/2 538, Schwartzbart Archives, "Newsletter," World Jewish Congress, Dept. of European Jewish Affairs, September 8, 1942, 6.
49. ADSS, VIII, SSVG, 514.
50. Hilberg, pp. 455–456.
51. ADSS, VIII, SSVG, 601–602 ("Il governo tedesco ha imposto che entro lo spazio di sei mesi tutti gli ebrei residenti nello Stato croato debbono essere trasferiti in Germania, dove, secondo quanto mi ha riferito lo stesso Kvaternik, sono stati uccisi negli ultimi tempi due milioni di ebrei. Pare che la stessa sorte attenderà gli ebrei croati specialmente se vecchi ed incapaci al lavoro.

Essendosi questa notizia propagata nell'ambiente ebraico, io sono continuamente sollecitato a fare qualche passo per la loro salvezza. Anche il caporabbino di Zagrabia spesso viene a visitarmi ed a raccontarmi nuove sventure.

Io mi raccomando al capo della polizia, il quale, dietro mio suggerimento, ritarda, per quanto gli è possibile, l' esecuzione di questo ordine. Anzi egli sarebbe lieto se la S. Sede potesse interporsi per il ritiro di quest'ordine, o per lo meno per proporre che tutti gli ebrei croati fossero concentrati in un'isola o in una zona della Croazia, ove potessero vivere in pace").
52. Ibid., 602.
53. Ibid., 602, n. 3.
54. Ibid.
55. Ibid., 629.
56. YV, M 20/106, Collection on Croatia, Hugo Kon and Miroslav Freiberger to Charles Barlas, Istanbul, October 14, 1942.
57. ADSS, VIII, SSVG, 683–684.
58. ADSS, IX, SSVG, 139.
59. ADSS, VIII, SSVG, 611 ("Maintenant dans un moment où les restes des restes de notre communauté se trouvent dans la situation la plus critique,— dans un moment où l'on veut décider de leurs vies—nos yeux sont fixés sur Votre Sainteté. Nous prions Votre Sainteté dans le nom de quelques milliers de femmes et d'enfants abandonnés, dont les soutiens se trouvent dans les champs de concentration, dans le nom des veuves et des orphelins, dans le nom des vieux et des faibles, de leur aider afin qu'ils puissent rester dans leurs domiciles et y passer leurs jours s'il le faut dans des circonstances les plus humbles").
60. Ibid., 611–612 (". . . la Santa Sede, sempre desiderosa di porger soc-

corso e sollievo ai sofferenti, non abbia mancato di interessarsi in più occasioni in favore delle persone raccomandate").

61. Ibid., 668–669.

62. Ibid. ("Purtroppo non abbiamo potuto ottenere di mutare il corso degli eventi. Nondimeno molte eccezioni da noi proposte nella deportazione degli ebrei sono state concesse e le famiglie, a base di matrimoni misti tra ebrei anche non battezzati e cattolici, sono state senza eccezione risparmiate").

63. See above, p. 153.

64. See above, p. 154.

65. ADSS, VIII, SSVG, 445, 475–576.

66. See above, pp. 150–151.

67. ADSS, VIII, SSVG, 622–623.

68. Hilberg, p. 456.

69. ADSS, VIII, SSVG, 622–623 ("Comme les tristes experiences avec leurs frères en Croatie, où un grand nombre de Juifs a été exterminé d'une façon si inhumaine, sont dans la mémoire de tous, la nouvelle de cette récente déportation a jeté tous les Juifs dans la plus grande angoisse. Il y en a qui, pour échapper à une longue agonie dans les camps de concentrations et à des sévices de toutes sortes, se sont donné la mort").

70. ADSS, VIII, SSVG, 623.

71. Ibid., 643.

72. YV, JM 2895/2.

73. ADSS, VIII, SSVG, 712.

74. Ibid., n. 1.

75. Ibid., 709–710.

76. Ibid., 709 ("di alleviare le tristi condizioni degli ebrei croati").

77. Ibid., 710 ("ha vivamente con me deplorato gli eccessi commessi in Croazia contro gli ebrei, però mi ha apertamente cetto che egli non può mutare sostanzialmente i provvedimenti adottati contro quegli infelici e che o presto o tardi tutti debbono essere trasportati in Germania").

78. Ibid., 675.

79. "Note regarding the Germany Policy of Deliberate Annihilation of European Jewry," Geneva, October 22, 1942, IJA.

80. ADSS, VIII, SSVG, 735 ("Nelle mie visite al Poglavnik e nei miei contatti con le altre autorità civili, specie col capo della polizia, ho sempre insistito per un benevolo trattamento verso gli ebrei. Le risposte sono state sempre le stesse: "Gli ebrei devono lasciare la Croazia; non è nelle intenzioni del Governo di trattarli duramente." Il Poglavnik ha anche impartito ordini in questo senso.

Siccome questo Governo non ha la forza di farsi ubbidire, è facile, anzi è certo che le autorità dipendenti invece di ubbidire agli ordini superiori, tante volte si abbandonano agli eccessi deplorati").

81. ADSS, IX, SSVG, 124.

82. Ibid.

83. Ibid., n. 2.

84. Hilberg, p. 457.

85. ADSS, IX, SSVG, 183.

86. Telegram from Osborne to the Foreign Office, March 22, 1943, FO 371/36656.

87. ADSS, IX, SSVG, 171.

88. "Précis—Week of March 13–20, 1943," IJA.

89. Richard Law of the Foreign Office to Alexis L. Easterman, WJC, London, March 24, 1943, IJA; see also FO 371/36655 and "Précis—Week of March 29–April 3, 1943," IJA.
90. ADSS, IX, SSVG, 171, n. 3.
91. Ibid., 195.
92. Ibid., 254–256; see also below, p. 177.
93. Ibid., 256.
94. Ibid., 214 ("passi possibili ed opportuni per impedire tale grave misure").
95. Ibid., 215–216.
96. Ibid., 187–188.
97. Ibid. ("Non poche volte ho dovuto occuparmi degli ebrei croati presso il Capo dello Stato, presso vari ministeri e presso il Capo della Polizia. In ogni allarme gli ebrei affollano la mia abitazione.

Ripetute volte, a voce ed anche in iscritto, ho insistito presso il Poglavnik, affinché innanzi tutto non siano molestate le famigle sorte da matrimoni misti ed in genere tutti gli ebrei battezzati. Il Poglavnik mi ha sempre promesso di rispettare gli ebrei divenuti cattolici o sposati con cattolici.

In questi ultimi giorni vi è stato un altro allarme nell'ambiente ebraico a causa di un manifesto della Polizia, che invitava quegl'infelici a presentarsi presso gli uffici di pubblica sicurezza. Mosso dal desiderio di salvare almeno gli ebrei cattolici, ho scritto una lettera al Poglavnik, pregandolo di non molestare gli ebrei cattolici. Gli ricordai inoltre che io, fondandomi sulle sue promesse, avevo già dato in questo senso assicurazioni alla S. Sede. Non desideravo trovarmi in contradizione coi fatti.

Intanto sono venuto a sapere che il Poglavnik un giorno, alla presenza di alcune autorità affermò chiaramente al ministro del Reich che egli non intendeva perseguitare gli ebrei battezzati, avendo già dato assicurazioni in questo senso al rappresentante della S. Sede presso l'episcopato. Ma per mezzo di un ufficiale, buon cattolico addetto all'ambasciata tedesca, sono ora informato che il ministro del Reich protestante e fanatico nazista, dopo l'affissione del manifesto riguardante gli ebrei, abbia esclamato: "La S. Sede comincia a diventare troppo potente in Croazia; voglio vedere se questa volta vince essa o io." Prego il Signore che conceda al Poglavnik la forza di resistere").
98. Rhodes, p. 332.
99. ADSS, IX, SSVG, 217.
100. Ibid., 218.
101. Hilberg, p. 457.
102. Dawidowicz, p. 392.
103. ADSS, IX, SSVG, 214; see above, p. 158.
104. Ibid., 287.
105. Ibid.; Marcone's letter has not been published; Stepinac's may be seen in Pattee, pp. 312–313.
106. Given the record of Artukovic's cruelties against the Jews, it is difficult to believe that he ever "defended" the Jews. Attempts are still being made to extradite him from the United States as a war criminal. See Charles W. Steckel, *Destruction and Survival* (Los Angeles: Delmar Publishing Co., 1973), p. 52.
107. ADSS, IX, SSVG, 287.
108. Ibid., 312–313 (". . . sono oltremodo dolente significarLe che, eccetto

almeno per ora, i matrimoni misti, tutti gli ebrei, compresi quelli che sono stati già da anni battezzati, sono stati catturati e trasportati in Germania . . .

La scena della cattura di questi infelici è stata veramente commovente: Durante la notte, mentre tranquillamente si dormiva, agenti di Polizia, si sono presentati nelle abitazioni di questi e, senza alcun riguardo all'età, alla condizione sociale, al battesimo, li hanno catturati. Qualcuno dei più vecchi e morto per il terrore").

109. Ibid., 324 ("che sola in tristissimi tempi si prende cura anche di questi infelici figli d'Israele").

110. Ibid., n. 2.

111. Ibid., 321–322.

112. Ibid., 327–328.

113. Ibid., 328, n. 2.

114. Ibid., 337.

115. Ibid., n. 4.

116. Steckel, p. 20.

117. "Current Affairs—Italy," November 1943, British Section of the World Jewish Congress, YV, M 2/469, Schwartzbart Archives.

118. ADSS, IX, SSVG, 488–489.

119. Ibid., 599.

120. See above, p. 148.

121. ADSS, VII, SSGM, 337, 404.

122. Jürgen Holtkamp, "Werde Katholisch—Oder Stirb" [Become Catholic or Die], *Stern*, October 17, 1965, pp. 80–86.

123. See above, p. 150.

124. See above, p. 153.

125. See above, p. 154.

126. See above, p. 157.

127. See above, p. 156.

128. See above, pp. 158–159.

129. See above, p. 150.

130. See above, p. 159.

131. See above, p. 161.

132. See above, p. 160.

133. See above, pp. 158–159.

134. See above, p. 153.

CHAPTER TEN

1. Ivone Kirkpatrick, *Mussolini: A Study in Power* (New York: Hawthorn Books, 1964), p. 355.

2. Federico Chabod, *A History of Italian Fascism*, trans. Muriel Grindrod (New York: Howard Fertig, 1975), p. 81.

3. Lucy S. Dawidowicz, *The War Against the Jews, 1933–1945* (New York: Holt, Rinehart & Winston, 1975), p. 369.

4. For the background and rationale behind these negotiations, see Anthony Rhodes, *The Vatican in the Age of the Dictators (1922–1945)* (New York: Holt, Rinehart & Winston, 1973), pp. 23–52.

5. Hyginus E. Cardinale, *The Holy See and the International Order* (Gerrards Cross: Colin Smythe, 1976), pp. 103–104.

6. *Acta Apostolicae Sedis: Commentarium Officiale* [Acts of the Apostolic See: Official Commentary], 1929, XXI:6, 209–295. An English translation of the concordat appears in Cardinale, pp. 319–340. Article XXXIV would become the most controversial: "The Italian State wishing to reinvest the institution of marriage, which is the basis of the family, with the dignity conformable to the Catholic traditions of its people, recognizes the sacrament of matrimony performed according to canon law as fully effective in civil law" (Cardinale, p. 338).

7. Daniel A. Binchy, *Church and State in Fascist Italy* (London: Oxford University Press, 1941), p. 275.

8. *Ciano's Hidden Diary, 1937–1938*, trans. Andreas Mayor, intro. by Malcolm Muggeridge (New York: E. P. Dutton & Co., 1953), entry of July 30, 1938, p. 141.

9. *L'Osservatore Romano*, October 4–5, 1954, p. 2.

10. Rhodes, p. 42.

11. Raul Hilberg, *The Destruction of the European Jews* (Chicago: Quadrangle Books, 1967), pp. 423–424.

12. ADSS, VI, SSVG, 59, n. 9.

13. Hilberg, p. 423.

14. ADSS, VI, SSVG, 59–60.

15. Ibid., 71–72.

16. Ibid., 79–80.

17. The Law of June 19, 1939; Hilberg, p. 423.

18. ADSS, VI, SSVG, 85–86.

19. Ibid., 97.

20. Ibid., 89–90.

21. Hilberg, p. 421.

22. ADSS, VI, SSVG, 88.

23. Dawidowicz, p. 369.

24. ADSS, VI, SSVG, 70.

25. ADSS, IV, SSGE, 540 (June 10, 1941).

26. ADSS, VI, SSVG, 120.

27. Ibid., 122.

28. Ibid., 127–129.

29. Ibid., 128–129.

30. Ibid., 208.

31. Ibid., 247–248.

32. Ibid., 316–317.

33. Ibid., 323.

34. Ibid., 366–367.

35. Ibid., 371–372.

36. Ibid., 521.

37. ADSS, VIII, SSVG, 180–181.

38. Ibid., 198–199.

39. Ibid., 199.

40. Ibid., 200.

41. Ibid., 340.

42. Ibid., 483, n. 1.

43. Ibid., 662–663.

44. Ibid., 193–195.

45. Ibid., 195.
46. See above, chap. 3.
47. ADSS, VIII, SSVG, 120–121.
48. Ibid., 219–220.
49. Ibid., 220, n. 6.
50. Ibid.
51. Ibid., 232–233.
52. Ibid., 233, n. 2.
53. *Encyclopaedia Judaica*, 9:1135.
54. *Ecclesia: Revista Mensile a Cura dell'Ufficio Informazioni* [Ecclesia: Monthly Review published by the (Vatican) Information Office], December 1942, I:2, 34; II:2, 40–45.
55. ADSS, VIII, SSVG, 178–179, 217–218, 505–507.
56. Tarsia is located in southwestern Italy, in the province of Cosenza, 26 miles south of Naples.
57. ADSS, VIII, SSVG, 217, n. 1.
58. Ibid., 265.
59. Ibid., 506, n. 1.
60. Ibid., 481–482.
61. Ibid., 642.
62. Ibid., 490.
63. Pinchas E. Lapide, *Three Popes and the Jews* (New York: Hawthorn Books, 1967), pp. 129–130. Lapide claims that the refugees were "fed, clad and looked after at Vatican expense . . ." (p. 129).
64. FO 371/3665.
65. ADSS, VIII, SSVG, 386–387, 407, 416–417, 433.
66. Ibid., 556–557.
67. Ibid., 557.
68. Ibid., 560–561.
69. ADSS, VII, SSGM, 82.
70. ADSS, IX, SSVG, 109–113; for full text, see below, Appendix I.
71. Ibid., 109–110; for original, see below, pp. 259–260.
72. Ibid., 131, n. 1.
73. Ibid., 131.
74. Ibid., 131, n. 2.
75. Ibid., 171 ("Cio significa loro condanna a morte").
76. Ibid., n. 3.
77. "Précis—Week of March 13–20, 1943," IJA.
78. Ibid.
79. "Précis—Week of March 29–April 3, 1943," IJA.
80. ADSS, IX, SSVG, 197–198.
81. Ibid., 245.
82. Ibid., n. 2.
83. Ibid., 338, n. 1.
84. Ibid., 338.
85. Ibid., n. 3.
86. FO, 371/36663; see also YV, M 2/408, Schwartzbart Archives.
87. FO, 371/36663.
88. ADSS, IX, SSVG, 368.
89. Ibid., 368–369, n. 2.

90. "Précis for Weeks of July 1943," IJA.

91. ADSS, IX, SSVG, 406–408; for full text, see below, Appendix J.

92. Ibid., 407.

93. Ibid., 413.

94. Ibid., n. 2.

95. Ibid., 417–418.

96. Ibid.

97. Ibid., 437.

98. Ibid., 437–438, n. 2.

99. Ibid., 427.

100. Ibid., 254–256.

101. Ibid., 255 ("separazione, non persecuzione").

102. Ibid., 255.

103. Ibid., 321.

104. Ibid., 374–375.

105. Ibid., 431–432; see also Renzo De Felice, *Storia degli Ebrei Italiani sotto il Fascismo* [History of Italian Jews under Fascism] (Turin: Einaudi, 1972), pp. 615–616, which contains a more positive description of the work of the Delasem narrated by Father Benoît.

106. ADSS, IX, SSVG, 423–424.

107. Ibid., 433–434.

108. Ibid., 458–462.

109. Ibid., 480–481.

110. Ibid., 482–483.

111. Ibid., 496.

112. Ibid., 491.

113. Robert Leiber, "Pio XII e gli Ebrei di Roma, 1943–1944" [Pius XII and the Jews of Rome, 1943–1944], *La Civiltà Cattolica* 112, no. 1 (1961): 450.

114. ADSS, IX, SSVG, 494.

115. Ibid., 501.

116. NG 5027; see also Owen Chadwick, "Weizsäcker, the Vatican and the Jews of Rome," *Journal of Ecclesiastical History* 28, no. 2 (April 1977): 190.

117. Michael Tagliacozzo, *La Communità di Roma sotto l'incubo della Svastica: Le Grande Razzia del 16 Ottobre 1943* [The Community of Rome under the Nightmare of the Swastika: The Great Raid of October 16, 1943] (Milan: n.p., 1963), p. 19.

118. According to another source, the raid actually began the previous evening about 11:00 P.M. See ADSS, IX, SSVG, 505, n. 1; for a lengthy study of the events of this day, see Robert Katz, *Black Sabbath* (New York: Macmillan, 1969).

119. Robert A. Graham, "La Strana Condotta di E. von Weizsäcker Ambasciatore del Reich in Vaticano" [The Strange Conduct of E. von Weizsäcker, Ambassador of the Reich to the Vatican], *La Civiltà Cattolica* 121, no. 2 (1970): 455–471; see also Chadwick, pp. 179–199.

120. Graham, p. 467.

121. ADSS, IX, SSVG, 505–506 ("Avendo saputo chi i tedeschi hanno fatto stamane una retata di ebrei, ho pregato l'Ambasiciatore di Germania di venire da me e gli ho chiesto di voler intervenire a favore di quei poveretti. Gli ho parlato come meglio ho potuto in nome dell' umanità, della carità cristiana.

L'Ambasiciatore, che già sapeva degli arresti, ma dubitava si trattasse specificamente di ebrei, mi ha detto con sincero e commosso accento: "Io mi attendo sempre che mi si domandi: Perché mai Voi rimanete in cotesto vostro ufficio?"

Ho esclamato: No, signor Ambasiciatore, io non Le rivolgo e non Le rivolgerò simile domanda. Le dico semplicemente: Eccellenza, che ha un cuore tenero e buono, veda di salvare tanti innocenti. È doloroso per il Santo Padre, doloroso oltre ogni dire che proprio a Roma, sotto gli occhi del Padre Comune siano fatte soffrire tante persone unicamente perché appartengono ad una stirpe determinata . . .

L'Ambasicatore, dopo alcuni istanti di riflessione, mi ha domandato: "Che farebbe la Santa Sede se le cose avessero a continuare?"

Ho risposto: La Santa Sede non vorrebbe essere messa nella necessità di dire la sua parola di disapprovazione.

L'Ambasiciatore ha osservato: Sono più di quattro anni che seguo ed ammiro l'attitudine della Santa Sede. Essa è riuscita a guidare la barca in mezzo a scogli d'ogni genere e grandezza senza urti e, se pure ha avuto maggior fiducia negli alleati, ha saputo mantenere un perfetto equilibrio. Mi chiedo se, proprio ora che la barca è per giungere in porto, conviene metter tutto in pericolo. Io penso alle conseguenze, che provocherebbe un passo della Santa Sede. . . . Le note direttive vengono da altissimo luogo. . . . "Vostra Eminenza mi lascia libero di non 'faire etat' di questa conversazione ufficiale?"

Ho osservato che io l'avevo pregato d'intervenire facendo appello ai suoi sentimenti d'umanità. Mi rimettevo al suo giudizio di fare o non fare menzione della nostra conversazione, che era stata tanto amichevole.

Volevo ricordargli che la Santa Sede è stata, come egli stesso ha rilevato, tanto prudente per non dare al popolo germanico l'impressione di aver fatto o voler fare contro la Germania la minima cosa durante una guerra terribile.

Dovevo però pur dirgli che la Santa Sede non deve essere messa nella necessità di protestare: qualora la Santa Sede fosse obbligata a farlo, si affiderebbe, per le conseguenze, alla divina Provvidenza.

"Intanto, ripeto: V.E. mi ha detto che cercherà di fare qualche cosa per i poveri ebrei. Ne La ringrazio. Mi rimetto, quanto al resto, al suo giudizio. Se crede più opportuno di non far menzione di questa nostra conversazione, così sia").

122. Leonidas E. Hill III, "The Vatican Embassy of Ernst von Weizsäcker, 1943–1945," *Journal of Modern History* 39, no. 2 (June 1967): 149.

123. Graham, p. 468.

124. Bishop Alois Hudal, rector of the German College in Rome, sent a letter of protest to General Stahel. Weizsäcker sent a copy of the letter along with his telegram to Berlin, but apparently there were some alterations in the text. The original sources for the Hudal letter are NG5027 and ADSS, IX, SSVG, 509–510. For translation and comments, see Saul Friedländer, *Pius XII and the Third Reich*, trans. Charles Fullman (New York: Alfred A. Knopf, 1966), pp. 205–206; for the background of the origin of this letter, see Chadwick, pp. 191–194.

125. Note the similarity to Maglione's words, "under the eyes of the Common Father," above, p. 180.

126. NG 5027; translation from Friedländer, pp. 206–207.

127. See Ernst von Weizsäcker, *Memoirs*, trans. John Andrews (London:

Victor Gallancz, 1951), p. 289, where he refers to his efforts for the protection of Rome and papal interests.

128. Graham, pp. 468–471.
129. ADSS, IX, SSVG, 511; for full text of his notes, see below, Appendix K.
130. Ibid., 513.
131. Ibid., 517.
132. Ibid., 521.
133. Ibid., 540, n. 1.
134. Ibid., 512.
135. Ibid.
136. De Felice, p. 464.
137. ADSS, IX, SSVG, 519.
138. Ibid., 525.
139. Ibid., 530.
140. Ibid., 525–526 ("Vengo in modo speciale supplicato di ottenere che la Santa Sede faccia qualche stringente ufficio perché sia almeno fatto conoscere dove siano finiti tanti e tante ebrei anche cristiani, uomini e donne, giovani e vecchi, adolescenti e bambini barbaramente quasi bestie da macello trasportati la scorsa settimana dal Collegio Militare alla Lungara.

Un passo di questo genere compiuto dalla Santa Sede, anche se pur troppo non ottenesse il desiderato effetto varrà senza dubbio ad accrescere la venerazione e la gratitudine verso l'Augusta Persona del Santo Padre, sempre vindice dei conculcati diritti").

141. Ibid., 537.
142. Ibid., 527–528.
143. Ibid., 532.
144. Ibid., 536–537.
145. Ibid., 587.
146. Ibid., 632.
147. Ibid., 529.
148. *L'Osservatore Romano*, October 25–26, 1943, p. 1.
149. Tagliacozzo, pp. 34–35.
150. NG 5027; translation from Friedländer, pp. 207–208.
151. Polish Ministry for Foreign Affairs to Ignacy Schwartzbart, November 15, 1943; YV M/2, Schwartzbart Archives.
152. ADSS, IX, SSVG, 538–539.
153. Ibid., 549–550 ("La nobiltà d'animo dell'Eccellenza Vostra mi incoraggia a chiederLe, se non Le è possibile far sì che sia accolta l'aspirazione di molti parenti od amici dei non ariani, recentemente arrestati in Roma, i quali desidererebbero avere notizie dei propri cari, e far giungere loro, eventualmente, qualche aiuto materiale.

Numerose suppliche, infatti, sono giunte e continuano a giungere alla Santa Sede a questo scopo, così che un passo, in tal senso, di Vostra Eccellenza presso le superiori autorità darebbe modo alla stessa S. Sede di recare sollievo a tante famiglie").

154. Ibid., 559.
155. Alberto Giovanetti, *Roma Città Aperta* [Rome, Open City] (Milan: Editrice Ancora, 1962), p. 179.
156. Tagliacozzo, p. 29.

157. ADSS, IX, SSVG, 517.

158. One author claims that "The Pope sent by hand a letter to the bishops instructing them to lift the enclosure from convents and monasteries so that they could become refuges for the Jews." See Joseph L. Lichten, "Pius XII and the Jews," *Catholic Mind* 57, no. 1142 (March–April 1959): 161.

159. The names of the religious houses, the number of Jews involved, and the financial data are given in DeFelice, pp. 467–468, 610–614.

160. ADSS, IX, SSVG, 518.

161. Ibid., 518.

162. Ibid., 533.

163. Ibid., 570.

164. Ibid., 589–590.

165. Ibid., 524.

166. Ibid., 547–548.

167. Ibid., 548–549.

168. See above, pp. 64–65.

169. ADSS, IX, SSVG, 544.

170. Ibid., 549.

171. Polish Ministry for Foreign Affairs to Ignacy Schwartzbart, November 15, 1943, giving excerpts from a cable of the Polish Embassy, October 25, 1943, YV, M/2, Schwartzbart Archives.

172. ADSS, IX, SSVG, 568–569.

173. Hilberg, p. 427.

174. ADSS, IX, SSVG, 578.

175. Ibid., 585.

176. Hilberg, p. 431.

177. ADSS, IX, SSVG, 591.

178. Ibid., n. 3.

179. Ibid., 591–592, n. 3; Koester reported this conversation to Berlin but said it was a friend of his, not he himself, who had the conversation with the cardinal. The diplomat, in his dispatch, described Piazza as concerned and critical about how the Jews were being treated in Venice, yet at the same time quite pro-German in some of his sentiments; for the text of his dispatch, see Friedländer, pp. 209–210.

180. ADSS, IX, SSVG, 606–607.

181. Ibid., 607.

182. Ibid., 610–611.

183. Ibid., 611.

184. FO 371/37286; see also "News Digest," December 10, 1943, WJC.

185. Memorandum entitled "Relief for Jewish Children in Italy," January 15, 1944, WJC.

186. Cable to Irving Miller, WJC, New York City from Noah Barou and Alexis L. Easterman, January 10, 1944, IJA.

187. "Memo of Conversation with Monsignor Carboni," January 12, 1944, IJA.

188. Memorandum entitled "Relief for Jewish Children in Italy," January 15, 1944, WJC.

189. The appeal to the British Section of the World Jewish Congress early in January.

190. IJA.

191. See above, pp. 167–169.
192. See above, pp. 167-168.
193. See above, p. 178.
194. See above, p. 110; p. 172.
195. See above, pp. 18–21.
196. ADSS, IX, SSVG, 111; see below, p. 257.
197. See above, pp. 174–175.
198. See above, pp. 180–181.
199. See above, p. 183.
200. See above, p. 185.
201. See above, p. 185.
202. See above, pp. 188–190.
203. See above, p. 189.
204. See above, p. 189.
205. See above, p. 182.

CHAPTER ELEVEN

1. For the purposes of this chapter, the chargé d'affaires in Slovakia and the apostolic visitor in Croatia will be counted among, and considered "nuncios."
2. See above, chap. 2.
3. See above, chap. 3.
4. See above, p. 110; p. 172.
5. See above, pp. 30–31; p. 150.
6. Leon Poliakov, *Harvest of Hate: The Nazi Program for the Destruction of the Jews of Europe* (Syracuse: Syracuse University Press, 1954), p. 295.
7. See above, p. 50; p. 74.
8. See above, p. 28.
9. See above, p. 79; pp. 82–83.
10. See above, p. 153.
11. See above, pp. 54–55.
12. See above, pp. 114–115.
13. See above, pp. 35–36.
14. See above, p. 79; pp. 81–82.
15. See above, p. 57.
16. See above, p. 115.
17. See above, p. 159.
18. See above, pp. 180–186.
19. See above, pp. 14–15.
20. See above, pp. 167–170.
21. See above, p. 52.
22. See above, pp. 37–38.
23. See above, pp. 59–60; p. 114.
24. See above, pp. 81–82.
25. See above, p. 150; p. 156.
26. See above, pp. 180–181.
27. See above, p. 28.
28. See above, pp. 78–79.
29. See above, p. 114.
30. See above, p. 116.
31. See above, p. 117.

32. See above, p. 136.
33. See above, p. 136.
34. See above, p. 137.
35. See above, pp. 212–215.
36. See above, p. 138.
37. See above, pp. 118–119; 138.
38. See above, p. 119, p. 138.
39. See above, p. 142.
40. The nuncio in Prague left in 1925 because the government participated in ceremonies honoring John Hus. It was a temporary rupture but was interpreted as an effective Vatican protest. See *New Catholic Encyclopedia,* 4:596.
41. See above, p. 92.
42. See above, p. 20.
43. See above, pp. 92–93.
44. See above, p. 93.
45. See above, p. 92.
46. See above, p. 94.
47. Ibid., 506 ("per non dare al popolo germanico l'impressione di aver fatto o voler fare contro la Germania la minima cosa durante una guerra terrible").
48. See above, p. 105.
49. See above, pp. 123–134.
50. ADSS, IX, SSVG, 291–292.
51. Ibid., 406.
52. Ibid., 119.
53. Ibid., 271.

APPENDIX A

1. ADSS, I, SSGE, 523–526.
2. Ibid., 529–533.
3. Ibid., 526–528.

APPENDIX B

Source: This translation is taken from Saul Friedländer, *Pius XII and the Third Reich: A Documentation,* trans. from the French and German by Charles Fullman (New York: Alfred A. Knopf, 1966), pp. 104–110; the memorandum in its French original is in the files of IJA.

APPENDIX C

Source: ADSS, VIII, SSVG, 762–764.

APPENDIX D

Source: ADSS, VIII, SSVG, 345–347.

APPENDIX E

Source: ADSS, VIII, SSVG, 486–489.

APPENDIX F

Source: ADSS, VIII, SSVG, 541–544.

APPENDIX G

Source: ADSS, IX, SSVG, 245–251.

APPENDIX H

Source: ADSS, VIII, SSVG, 738–742.

APPENDIX I

Source: ADSS, IX, SSVG, 109–113.

APPENDIX J

Source: ADSS, IX, SSVG, 407–408.

APPENDIX K

Source: ADSS, IX, SSVG, 511.

INDEX